Mexico's Cinema

Mexico's Cinema

A Century of Film and Filmmakers

Edited by
Joanne Hershfield and
David R. Maciel

A Scholarly Resources, Inc. Imprint
Wilmington, Delaware

© 1999 by Scholarly Resources
All rights reserved
First published 1999
Printed and bound in the United States of America

Scholarly Resources
104 Greenhill Avenue
Wilmington, DE 19805-1897
www.scholarly.com

Source of illustrations: All photographs except those in
Chapter 12 are courtesy of the Cineteca Nacional, Mexico City

Library of Congress Cataloging-in-Publication Data

Mexico's cinema : a century of film and filmmakers / edited by Joanne
  Hershfield and David R. Maciel.
      p.   cm.—(Latin American silhouettes)
   Includes bibliographical references and index.
   ISBN 0–8420–2681–9 (cloth : alk. paper).—ISBN 0–8420–2682–7
(paper : alk. paper)
   1. Motion pictures—Mexico—History.   I. Hershfield, Joanne,
1950–   . II. Maciel, David R. III. Series.
PN1993.5.M4M465 1999
791.43'0972—dc21   99-24763
                                                                   CIP

♾ The paper used in this publication meets the minimum requirements of
the American National Standard for permanence of paper for printed library
materials, Z39.48, 1984.

To all those mujeres insumisas *of contemporary Mexican cinema, creative filmmakers, and dear friends*

About the Editors

JOANNE HERSHFIELD teaches media studies and production at the University of North Carolina at Chapel Hill. In addition to her recent book, *Mexican Cinema, Mexican Woman, 1940–1950* (1996), she has published essays in *Wide Angle, Spectator, The Canadian Journal of Film Studies,* and *Cinema Journal* as well as a number of anthologies. Her forthcoming book is *Imagining Another: The Invention of Dolores del Río.*

DAVID R. MACIEL is professor of history and chairperson of the Department of Chicano/Chicana Studies at California State University, Dominguez Hills. He has held academic appointments at the University of New Mexico, the University of Arizona, and Arizona State University. In addition, he has been a visiting professor at the Universidad Nacional Autónoma de México, the University of California at San Diego, the Universidad de Guadalajara, and the University of California, Irvine. He has served as a media consultant on the film *Break of Dawn* and on numerous documentaries and shorts in the United States and Mexico. His extensive publications on Mexican and Chicano themes include *El Norte: The U.S.-Mexican Border in Contemporary Cinema* (1990); *Chicanas/Chicanos at the Crossroads; El bandeolero, el pocho y la raza; Imagenes cinematográficas del Chicano; Ignacio Ramírez: Ideologo del liberalismo social en México;* and *Culture across Borders: Mexican Immigration and Popular Culture.* Dr. Maciel and Dr. Hershfield are currently completing a cultural history of the cinema of Mexico.

Acknowledgments

A s with most collective projects, this book owes much to many
people. Foremost are the contributors who submitted original,
innovative, and thoughtful essays. As a group, these authors exemplify a deep sense of professionalism and a strong commitment to the
project. Just as important for the completion of this study were various key institutions and personnel. The staff of the Filmoteca of the
Universidad Nacional Autónoma de México were gems of generosity
and assistance to the editors of this anthology. Various department directors provided special screenings, made copies of needed films in
video, reproduced stills, and offered invaluable suggestions. The
overall director, Iván Trujillo, has been a dear friend and ardent sup-
porter of this book since its origin.

The Instituto Mexicano de Cinematografía (IMCINE) has been
equally supportive in arranging special showings, assisting with interviews, and, through its generosity, providing both publicity and research materials as well as stills. Staff directors Enrique Ortega and
Marina Stavenhagen opened many doors and made film research that
much more enjoyable.

Ignacio Durán, the former general director of IMCINE, proffered
beyond all expectations an unqualified and rare level of kindness and
support for our film research. He made time for lengthy interviews
and placed all of IMCINE's films and source materials at our dis-
posal. The film studies program of the Universidad de Guadalajara,
especially its research faculty, made available to the editors its considerable depository materials.

Of critical importance for the completion of this anthology was
the paramount assistance rendered to the editors by the staff of
Scholarly Resources, particularly its vice president, Richard Hopper.
And in no small measure, special thanks go to William Beezley, who

has been the intellectual *padrino* of this project since it was first conceived at a memorable reunion in Santa Fe, New Mexico.

The staff of the Department of Chicano/Chicana Studies at California State University, Dominguez Hills, also merits special mention: Virginia Rodríguez, administrative assistant, and Alfonso González, student assistant, worked diligently on all phases of the preparation of the final manuscript. Claudia Serrano, Virginia Rodríguez, and Gabriela Díaz translated chapters from our Mexican contributors. Certainly, this book would not have been completed without their creative assistance. Thanks also go to Bill Balthrop, chair of the Department of Communication Studies at the University of North Carolina at Chapel Hill, and to that department's helpful administrative staff. The editors also extend their gratitude to the University Research Council at UNC-Chapel Hill for a grant that assisted the publication of this anthology.

Film scholars and close friends Gustavo García, Eduardo de la Vega, Patricia Torres, and Carlos Monsiváis have been a continuous source of information and have provided insights not found elsewhere. Their suggestions and perspectives certainly improved the final project. In the same vein, Alejandro Pelayo has gone beyond the usual, both as a colleague and as a special friend. He shared his extensive documentation of contemporary Mexican cinema, his two excellent documentary series, and, above all, offered an authoritative insider's knowledge of the film community.

As magical and unique as Mexican cinema is, its filmmakers are even more so. Few communities have been as open or have aided a research project more than have the Mexican filmmakers in this case. Their contributions are present in every part of this anthology. It is their art and craft that this volume addresses, critically examines, and honors.

Contents

Introduction

The Mexican people have a lengthy and glorious cinematic legacy. Throughout the Spanish-speaking world, Mexico has had the most advanced film industry in terms of economic resources, technical production, number of films produced, major filmmakers, and international distribution. From the late silent era to the present, it has produced more films than any other Spanish-language cinema. Classics such as *María Candelaria*, *Flor Silvestre*, and *Los Olvidados* have received an impressive number of awards at international festivals, and recent films have been honored at more than seventy-two prestigious festivals including those at Berlin, Cannes, Havana, Moscow, Toronto, and Venice. Not just in historical terms, but in cultural and social ones, Mexican cinema is one of the country's national treasures and most enduring cultural and artistic practices. It has been instrumental in constructing, defining, and representing national identity. The sociocultural evolution of twentieth-century Mexico is nowhere better represented than in its films, which have vividly captured and reflected its society and national character as well as its exciting past and complex present. The cinematic lens has recorded the continuing and often tumultuous transformation of Mexico from the late Porfirio Díaz period at the turn of the century through each subsequent decade. The rural and urban scenes, changing modes, dress, and gender roles, along with political, class, and even religious conflicts have been addressed by Mexican films, in addition to major national issues such as the 1910 revolution, immigration to the United States, poverty, machismo, the arrogance of power by the elite, prostitution, violence, and other social ills. For anyone interested in Mexico, the cinema is a marvelous source that reveals its traditions, folklore, musical heritage, regional diversity, archetypes, ethnic makeup, symbols, myths, and national character.

Throughout its past, Mexican cinema has been fortunate to have had among its cinematographers such creative talents as Jorge Stahl, Gabriel Figueroa (whom Diego Rivera once dubbed the country's greatest muralist), and Alex Phillips. Even more impressive is the extraordinary cadre of its directors. From the 1920s to the present day the list of acclaimed directors parallels few, if any, national cinemas. Those of the Golden Age, such as Fernando de Fuentes, Julio Bracho, Emilio Fernández, and Luis Buñuel (who directed in Mexico for twenty years), and more recent ones such as Paul Leduc, Arturo Ripstein, Marcela Fernández Violante, Alfonso Arau, and María Navaro have garnered critical and popular esteem.

No Spanish-speaking cinema except Mexico's can claim to have had a Golden Age that produced such a glamorous star system. Pedro Infante, Sara García, María Félix, Jorge Negrete, Dolores del Río, Pedro Armendáriz, Marga López, Mario Moreno "Cantinflas," Arturo de Córdova, and Germán Váldez "Tin Tan" became household names throughout Latin America, Spain, and the United States and are as revered today in Mexico as when their legends were created. In the heyday of its Golden Age, Mexican cinema dominated international Spanish-language foreign markets as well as domestic ones, providing important revenues for the film industry and the country. In addition the industry created critical avenues of employment for a significant sector of workers. The Estudios Churubusco and the Estudios América are still among the most advanced and productive studios in all of the Americas.

The cinema in Mexico has profited immensely from an intimate relationship with its writers. Many of the country's greatest literary figures have served as screenwriters; others successfully worked alongside filmmakers in the adaptation of major plays, novels, short stories, and traditional legends to the silver screen. In fact, throughout its history, Mexican cinema has found ample inspiration for its story material in its own culture, principally in its literature. Beginning with the novelists of the Revolution and continuing to the present with such writers as Laura Esquivel of *Como Agua por Chocolate* fame, literature has played an integral part in the magic and success of the cinema of Mexico.

A unique element in this cinema is its relationship with the state and other national institutions. The intimate and complex connection between the film industry and the state has pervaded the entire history of cinema in Mexico. Realizing the social importance of cinema during the Golden Age, the state instituted close control over the content and the exhibition of both domestic and foreign films while it often subsidized and promoted national cinema. Additionally, it founded and still supports one of the two leading film schools in

Mexico, the Centro de Capacitación Cinematográfica. Today, this center is recognized among the ten best in the world.

There are certainly more published studies on the country's cinema in Mexico than elsewhere, as would be expected. As a body of work, film analysis and scholarship in Mexico have been characterized by overviews, individual studies of directors and stars, and published interviews with filmmakers. Serious scholarship began in the 1960s with the publication of three fundamental studies: two by Emilio García Riera—his edited multivolume *Historia documental del cine mexicano* (1978) and *Historia del cine mexicano* (1985)—and the third by Jorge Ayala Blanco, *La aventura del cine mexicano*, which was the first critical attempt at analysis and interpretation.

These two scholars and film critics have dominated cinema studies to the present; in fact, their perspectives characterize the two opposing schools of film criticism in Mexico today. On the one hand, the followers of García Riera tend to favor state-produced cinema, are more closely affiliated with official institutions, and thus receive more governmental support. García Riera and his collaborators have founded important film review journals, promoted research, published valuable bibliographies, and worked under the Cineteca Nacional, the Filmoteca of the Universidad Nacional Autónoma de México (UNAM), and, most recently, at the Universidad de Guadalajara.

On the other hand, Professor Jorge Ayala Blanco and his students have worked out of the Centro de Estudios Cinematográficos of the UNAM and the Universidad Autónoma Metropolitana. In their writings, they emphasize independent cinema, particularly those works done at the UNAM and other universities. They tend to be more critical of films produced by the state or sponsored by the private sector. Generally their studies are more analytical and creative, but they also border on the polemic and at times seem overly negative. Unfortunately, their followers continue the rivalry to a degree so partisan that it has become detrimental to film analysis in Mexico. Outside of these two schools, few important cinematic studies have been published in Mexico. In fact, until recently, surprisingly few scholars, journalists, or popular writers have shown any interest in the study of the nation's cinema. Fortunately, a small group of independent film scholars and critics has emerged on the scene. For the most part, this recent trend is supported by universities and certain established commercial presses.

English-language scholarship is, however, inadequate. There is only one general survey, *Mexican Cinema: Reflections of a Society, 1896–1988* (1989) by Carl J. Mora; two monographs, Charles Ramírez Berg's *Cinema of Solitude: A Critical Study of Mexican*

Film, 1967–1983 (1992) and Joanne Hershfield's *Mexican Cinema, Mexican Woman, 1940–1950* (1996), the latter an analysis of the representation of women in the Golden Age; and one anthology, *Mexican Cinema*, edited by Paulo Antonio Paranaguá. The remaining scholarship is dispersed in academic and popular journal articles and book chapters.

This anthology addresses the lack of critical writing on Mexican cinema in English and includes new English-language writings by scholars in the United States as well as seminal Mexican scholarship in translation. The essays offered here thus represent a wide variety of theoretical and methodological approaches including cultural history, reception studies, textual analysis, political economy, and cultural studies. A number of them examine particular historical and cultural aspects of Mexican film, such as Carlos Monsiváis's consideration of the popularity of two of Mexico's most beloved comics, Tin Tan and Cantinflas. The authors of other contributions focus on diverse themes and issues that are central to contemporary film scholarship: the representation of race and gender, female authorship, and the place of national cinema in an era of transnational distribution and exhibition practices. Together, these essays offer the reader a thorough and critical look at the entire one hundred years of Mexican film from the origins of cinema at the beginning of the twentieth century to the 1990s.

D. R. M.
J. H.

I
The Silent Cinema

As soon as the new technology of the cinema reached Mexico City in 1896, Mexicans began shooting their own local versions of the Lumière brothers' *realités*. These early filmmakers used the new French apparatus to exhibit their one-reelers in theaters to upper-class audiences or in hastily erected tents to the peasants who lived in isolated villages spread out around the countryside. Historians have remarked on the itinerant nature of these first film entrepreneurs, who traveled across the nation to bring this new cinema of attractions to the people.

Hollywood and Europe offered a continuous supply of new product to other enterprising Mexican businessmen, who quickly bought up foreign films and set themselves up as distributors and exhibitors with whatever inventory they could afford. They screened their offerings before and after live vaudeville acts. In 1905 two of the most successful filmmakers/exhibitors/distributors, Salvador Toscano Barragan and Enrique Rosas, showed more than two hundred local and foreign films in Mexico City alone. By 1906 theaters devoted to film projection were being constructed in the capital and other major cities, and by 1907 the tents had all but disappeared. In 1911 there were over forty venues devoted exclusively to film just in Mexico City.

In these early years, Mexico controlled its own market, both aesthetically and economically. The first films celebrated the nation by documenting its landscapes, its indigenous cultures, and the political pomp and circumstance of President Porfirio Díaz's extended regime (1876–1910). Although the nonfiction genre dominated cinema during this first decade, a significant number of fiction films was also produced. When feature filmmaking came to a virtual standstill during the Revolution, documentaries about strategic encounters

1

between revolutionary factions and the *federales* proved popular and kept the fledgling film industry alive.

The end of the Revolutionary War marked the beginning of a studio system and the revitalization of feature-film production. In 1917 the actress, Mimi Derba, and the producer, Enrique Rosas, produced five films through their newly established Azteca Films. While most fiction was inspired by European models, Derba and Rosas released in 1919 the film that was to go down in history as the first feature-length, "specifically Mexican" narrative based on a famous public incident, *El Automóvil Gris*. Manuel de la Bandera opened Producciones Quetzal that same year; and, in 1919, Germán Camus commenced production in his studio with *Hasta Despues de la Muerte*. Three years later the Estudios Chapultepec opened its doors.

Despite these auspicious beginnings, Mexican filmmakers could not compete with a booming U.S. film industry that was already looking to expand its global reach. For the United States, international trade in Hollywood cinema was important not only for the revenue it brought in for the rental of films but also for the ways in which it enlarged the market for other mass-produced products. Private investors also realized the opportunities of a rapidly growing cinema audience across the border and began investing in Mexican distribution and exhibition. In an attempt to shift this balance and stabilize its growing domestic film industry, the Mexican government finally implemented protectionist legislation. In 1929 the Bureau of Public Amusements issued a circular requiring foreign distributors to purchase at least one Mexican film per year to show in their own domestic market. However, the government made no effort to put this quota into effect. In that same year, a governmental decree demanded that exhibitors show two reels of film per week devoted to national subjects, but the decree was difficult to enforce due to an inadequate supply of local product. Simultaneously, the domestic industry was also heavily taxed. Mexican producers were strapped with stamp taxes, production taxes, duties on imported materials, censorship fees, a tax on gross box office receipts, and an absentee tax on all monies sent abroad. By 1928, 90 percent of all films exhibited throughout Mexico as well as in the rest of Latin America were produced in the United States.

Despite the lack of money, equipment, and studios, the interference of the 1910 revolution, and Hollywood's dominance, Mexican filmmakers managed to produce an impressive number of silent fiction films: Salvador Toscano Barragan released *Don Juan Tenorio* in 1898; the Alva brothers produced *El Grito de Dolores* (1908), *El Suplico de Cuauhtémoc* (1910), and *La Banda del Automóvil Gris* (1919, with Enrique Rosas); Mimi Derba's Azteca Films released *En*

Defensa Propia (1917); and Miguel Contreras Torres produced and directed a total of eight films between 1919 and 1927. In all, over one hundred silent features and documentaries were released between 1898 and 1930. (Unfortunately, most of this work has been destroyed through accident or negligence.)

In the first essay in this section, cultural critic Gustavo García, relying on archival resources, recounts the cultural and aesthetic history of Mexican silent cinema in an attempt to rescue what has been lost from film history. He traces both the development of an industry as well as the construction of a national cinematic aesthetic, situating both within the context of the political transformations engendered by the Revolution. Film historian Federico Dávalos Orozco discusses the principal early directors, cinematic trends, and the transition period between the end of the silent era and the onset of sound. Orozco documents the struggles and successes of early filmmakers in their efforts to create a national film industry.

1

In Quest of a National Cinema
The Silent Era

Gustavo A. García

On August 14, 1896, in the Plateros Pharmacy in Mexico City, the first public exhibition took place in Mexico of the *cinematographe* apparatus invented by the brothers Louis Jean and Auguste Lumière and introduced in France in 1895. Before presenting the invention to the public, the Lumières' representatives, Bon Bernard & Vayre, showed the films and the cinematic apparatus to President Porfirio Díaz, his family, and important government officials at his residence, Chapultepec Castle. The dictator, for his part, "appeared pleased." It was said that he jumped for joy in the presence of this new toy.

The success of the Cinematograph was immediate and made obsolete its predecessor and weaker competitor, the Kinetoscope, invented by Thomas Alva Edison, whose apparatus was a minor amusement in the *carpas* (traveling tent shows held around Mexico at the turn of the century) and theaters. Spectators lined up to pay up to one peso to see the Lumière brothers' shorts, or *vistas: Arrival of a Train, The Groundskeeper, The Gardener and the Boy, The Bathers, The Child's Lunch, The Magic Hat*, and *The Card Players*. The center of Mexico City, the traditional meeting place of idle society, thus quickly became full of places dedicated to the exhibition of Cinematographs, Kinetoscopes, and other similar inventions such as the Pasionoscopo, the Cicloscosmorama, and the Aristógrafo (an attempt at 3-D cinema made possible by the use of eyeglasses invented in 1898 by Adrian Lavie, which were electrically driven to quickly cover and uncover the eyes while one watched the movie).

On August 25, 1896, Bon Bernard & Vayre showed the first scenes filmed in Mexico, including, of course, General Díaz and his family in *General Díaz Strolling through Chapultepec Park*—the beginning of a collaboration between the general and the cinema that would show him in a carriage returning from Chapultepec with his officials, wandering about the main plaza (Zócalo), prancing around on horseback, and saluting, standing, or sitting, alone or in a crowd. The image of the country that they wanted to be filmed was so premeditated and consciously chosen that on August 30, in the newspaper *Gil Blas*, the filmmakers invited the upper class to stroll along the Paseo de la Reforma between three and four o'clock in the afternoon so that they could film some *vistas* when the light was favorable.

In the meantime, the purchase of projectors, movies, cameras, and equipment for developing film expanded rapidly. Ignacio Aguirre bought all of Bon Bernard & Vayre's equipment and traveled around the center of the country demonstrating the invention. A twenty-one-year-old student, Salvador Toscano Barragan, sacrificed his savings in order to import a projector and the fantastic short films of Georges Melies: *A Trip to the Moon* and *The Kingdom of the Fairies*. Toscano filmed a few actors from the Teatro Principal and, in 1898, a short version of *Don Juan Tenorio*. Although it was only a documentary project, it became not only the first Mexican movie with a real narrative but also the first example of local *film d'art*—unintentionally anticipating the style that would later be initiated in France with *L'Assassinat du Duc de Guise* in 1908. Aguirre, Toscano, and a number of other cinematographers (Carlos Mongrand, Enrique Rosas, the Stahl brothers, and Guillermo Becerril), using the railroad network, traveled around Mexico setting up temporary silent cinemas and competing against each other. Itinerant "illuminators" appeared at ranches and small towns with ethereal images of Don Porfirio, Mephistopheles, or Czar Nicholas under their arms.

Guillermo Becerril helped define the situation by opening his own *carpas* in Mexico City, starting with three in 1899. By the end of that year the capital had twenty-two movie houses. The competition caused the admission prices to drop from twenty-five to ten centavos; in 1900 the fee went down to five centavos in the theaters, while in the *carpas* it was two or three centavos. The inexpensive admission fees and the proliferation of *carpas* in the outskirts of the city economically abolished the elitist nature of the show. However, going to the movies was still an adventure, not so much for what could be seen on the screen but for the frequent risk of fires provoked by the incorrect use of projectors or obvious sabotage by a competitor.

The achievement of the fledgling exhibition industry precipitated its own decline: all of the movie houses in the country depended on material sent by Pathé Frères or Edison or purchased through the medium of agents or on trips abroad. The films were then continually replayed in all of the exhibition venues, whether in the elegant National Theater in Mexico City or the run-down *carpas* in the remote Candelaria de los Patos. By 1900, twenty of the twenty-two movie houses were closed. The competition and the limited selection of titles were aggravated by the hostility of the Church and other Catholic groups, who were incensed by films of North American boxing matches or performances "for men only" that provoked scandals in the towns where they were advertised. In order to reclaim social approval, exhibitors tried every trick: they asked for recommendations from priests before the film's arrival, they preceded the performance with small celebrations, or they donated a portion of the day's receipts to a worthy cause (the construction of a school, aid to needy families). The Mexican cinematographic culture was founded under these circumstances.

In 1903, Enrique Rosas filmed the 60-meter *Aventuras del Sexteto*. Three years later, he produced the first important Mexican documentary (significant because of its length and its attention to detail): the visit by Díaz to Mérida that followed his departure from Mexico City and his return from Veracruz, as well as his farewell from the Yucatán. By 1906 official film distribution networks had been established: the North American-owned Mexican National Phonograph Company and the French-owned Pathé Frères, which competed not with the Americans but with the Mexican distributor, Jorge A. Alcalde, who sold the Pathé films at a lower price. Most important, the main office gave exclusive distribution rights to the branches. These distributors made possible the establishment of permanent venues that might be either simple rooms or complex amusement centers such as the Salon Rojo (on the corner of Plateros and Bolívar), which attracted viewers not so much for the movies but for the distorting mirrors on the lower floor, the variety shows between performances (marionettes, dancers, musicians), and, most of all, the escalators that conveyed them at an amazing speed, staggering and distrustful, to the upper floors. In 1906 the Sala Pathé was inaugurated, the sixteenth movie theater in Mexico City. That same year, Enrique Rosas, manager of the Riva Palacio, imported from Cuba a Cinematograph synchronized with a phonograph, thus offering a rudimentary sound cinema in which each scene had its appropriate music. To the annoyance of many *aficionados* of the theater, the Romualda sisters and Genara Moriones turned their theater, El Principal, one of the greatest traditional stages, into a movie house. However, the public outrage soon subsided.

In that same year, *El San Lunes del Valedor*, a short comedy about a drunk who seeks to woo the daughter of a fishwife, appeared. In 1908, *El Grito de Dolores*, the fourth Mexican movie with a plot, performed and directed by Felipe de Jesús Haro, was filmed by the Alva brothers in a rudimentary studio built by the American Amusement Company. The film reproduced the aesthetics of the commemorative theatrical works that were presented every year on September 15 (Independence Day). These theater pieces developed as a succession of portraits of the insurgent uprising, the *grito* (or cry of liberty) of the humble priest Hidalgo, and the skirmishes between the insurgents and "the police of San Miguel el Grande."

In 1910 the attention of the movie makers was concentrated on the preparation and realization of the spectacular commemoration of the Centennial of Mexico's Independence. During this time, some of the most impressive building projects of the regime were started (the mental institution of Castañeda, the Normal School for Teachers, the Column of Independence, the National University, the Grand Drainage Canal, the placing of the first stone of the Legislative Palace). There were also many parades, official receptions, and popular holidays. Everything was recorded by the cameras of the Alva brothers, Salvador Toscano, and Rosas, who had already demonstrated their capacity to represent different events simultaneously. This style became the base for the great tradition of the Mexican documentary, which showed itself as a pioneer and a model superior to the English one (overwhelmed with false and deceptive documentaries). To commemorate the Centennial, the Cinematographers' Union produced *El Suplico de Cuauhtémoc*, which it promoted as being "performed by Mexican actors and filmed in the actual place of the events."

The outbreak of the Revolution did not take the filmmakers, who were already well trained in the art of ubiquitousness, completely by surprise. Toscano filmed Francisco Madero's visit to Pachuca and the public meeting of the Anti-Reelection Club in Puebla. On November 18 the Serdán family rose up in arms in Puebla, and the next day Toscano filmed their house, riddled with bullets, and the corpse of Aquiles Serdán.

The Revolution directly affected the cinema, and it became the emblematic instrument of the armed movement. Suddenly, the fictional cinema of the Porfiriato was left behind, whether it was epic histories or comedies (*El San Lunes del Valedor* or *Aventuras de Tip-Top en Chapultepec*), in order to leave the field to the documentarians. As the struggle within the country spread, the filmmakers recorded whatever occurred—treaties, battles, conquests, rebellions, troops, trains, walks around the main squares of the conquered towns, all that was done by every roving gang. The Sonoran filmmaker, Jesús H. Abitia, demonstrated his loyalty to Madero by providing lodging for the candidate during his electoral tour throughout

Scene from the film La Revolución de Veracruz, *directed by Enrique Rosas and based on the actual events of the Revolution of 1910.*

the North. Then, to lessen hostilities, he united with the Division of the Northeast as the official cinematographer, following his childhood friend, Alvaro Obregón. Each faction and almost every general had a more or less permanent cinematographer, although only Abitia identified himself fully with a particular group, as he personally suffered Obregón's ups-and-downs.

The railroad facilitated the quick movement of both troops and filmmakers who, in turn, showed within a few days images of the Revolution that the newspapers frequently either did not report or distorted through partisanship. If the cinema of the Porfiriato presented a biased and idealized view of the country, then that of the Revolution was the closest to a complete record of reality, due to an objectivity that other filmmakers searched for in vain. These documentary filmmakers, compelled by the competition to "sell the news," filmed everything—what the competition was unable to film, what no one else had yet filmed—and went where only the troops and bullets had gone.

This was the great epoch of documentary film. The tendency of Rosas to present the events chronologically—as with Díaz's trip to the Yucatán—was preserved, and it resulted in long, methodical films with ambitions of objectivity—films such as Rosas's *La Revolución de Veracruz*, about the reactionary rebellion of Feliz Díaz, whose life is pardoned by Madero; and *La Revolución en Chihuahua* (or *Revolución Orozquista*), filmed by the Alva brothers, about various actions of Pascual Orozco, an anti-Madero leader, and his persecutor, Victoriano Huerta, the Minister of War, who defeats him in a battle at Bachimba between May 22 and 23, 1912, the battle that ended the film.

These movies had as much, if not more, success than the comedies of Max Linder, North American adventure films, or the grand Italian epics. The informative, newspaper-like style of the Mexican cinema was influenced by the newsreel, Revista Nacional. This newsreel was introduced in 1912 by the distributors Navascues and Camus but did not continue past its first publication. Subsequently, Germán Camus became the great promoter of the national film culture. He imported into Mexico several Italian divas, the French series of Judex and Fantomas, German Expressionism (*The Golem, The Blue Angel*), and Ernst Lubitsch's German films with Pola Negri and Emil Jannings (*A Night in Arabia, Anne Boleyn*). However, in the midst of total warfare, without opportunities for artistic expression, the cinema only allowed for the Alva brothers to make the short comedy, *El Aniversario de la Muerte de la Suegra de Enhart*, a film about the misadventures of the popular clown, Vicente Enhart, and his sidekick, Alegria. When they go to leave flowers at the tomb of Enhart's mother-in-law, the drunk men fall into a grave, are arrested, and immediately released so that they can arrive at the theater in time to give their performance.

In 1911 the municipal government of Mexico City appointed inspectors to regulate the chaotic performances at cinemas that were overcrowded, lacked age restrictions, and were unsanitary, unsafe, and full of fleas. The inspectors had the power not only to penalize the management for these irregularities but also to scrutinize the morality of the films: any police officer could interrupt any showing when he believed that it violated public decency. Instead of controling who entered the movie theaters, the inspectors controled the content of the films. In 1912 they shut down the Sala Pathé and mistreated and jailed the manager and an actress whose dances and cheerful expressions between performances were considered too daring.

The downfall and death of Madero on February 22, 1913, and the ascent to power of General Victoriano Huerta increased the work of the Office of Censorship. In Mexico City an advance screening of films for inspectors became mandatory. The inspector now was looking not only for eroticism but also for any unfavorable references to the new regime. To surmount this obstacle, the documentary film abandoned its efforts toward impartiality: on the screen, the battles between the followers of Huerta and the revolutionaries became propagandistic anthems in honor of the ruling power. In February 1914, *Sangre Hermana*, a full-length feature film, premiered with great success. According to the publicity, viewers could see "our brave army in combat against the followers of [Emiliano] Zapata, towns consumed by fire, and the horrific punishment of those found guilty." In May, *La Batalla de San Pedro de las Colonias*, filmed by Pathé Frères cameramen, was screened. The plot deals with a "tremendous encounter between the federal forces commanded by the heroic generals."

And all the action was in Mexico: people came from all over the world to film. North Americans and the English followed politicians and revolutionaries throughout the northern part of the country (it is believed that Francisco "Pancho" Villa's permanent cameraman was North American and that Venustiano Carranza's was an Englishman, while Obregón counted on Abitia), and the French covered the central part of the country, only returning to Europe upon the outbreak of World War I. The strident indignation of the public in response to *La Invasión Norteamericana* (most probably filmed by the Alva brothers or Toscano) sanctioned the addition of a clause to the cinematographic regulations by the municipal government of Mexico City that prohibited movies that could provoke scandals. Curiously, the box-office hit of that period was *El General Díaz en París*.

In the southeast, Salvador Alvarado, from Sinaloa, arrived in the Yucatán and found the peasantry enslaved by the upper class. The owners of large agricultural estates had turned the area into a separate aristocratic world related more closely to Havana or New Orleans than with the rest of Mexico. Some cinematographic activity was developing there, sustained by two spirited filmmakers, Carlos Martínez de Arredondo and Manuel Cirerol Sansores. Martínez de Arredondo specialized in historical melodramas of ambitious dimension and nationalistic orientation, although the influence on his plots of the Porfiriano drama, *En la Hacienda*, is well known. *En Tiempos Mayas* (1914) relates the efforts of a Mayan warrior to gain favor with a princess. *La Voz de Su Raza* (1914) portrays the confrontation between a peasant and a landowner for the love of a young Mayan woman. And *1810 o Los Libertadores de México* tells the story of a romance that took place during the War of Independence between Carmen and Nicolas, characters representing the Mexican nation. Cirerol Sansores, an associate of Martínez de Arredondo on his early films, specialized in producing documentaries for the revolutionary government.

Taking advantage of a new stability after 1916, the first film production companies were created and with them, the first movie stars. The European cinema had attracted a public weary of the recent violence who saw in the melodramas and the Italian historical epics dominated by forbidden passions or heroic gestures an avenue of escape to the memory of a harmonious world. The Mexican actress, Emma

Padilla, exploited her notable resemblance to the Italian diva, Pina Menichelli, in *La Luz* (1915, J. Jamet), which was brazenly plagiarized from the Italian film *Il Fuoco* (1915, Piero Fosco), starring Menichelli in the role of Gabriele d'Annunzio. Padilla was introduced into the prematurely nostalgic sensibility of the Porfirianos, who were trapped by the Revolution and who viewed as the erotic ideal the prostitutes of French naturalism, nationalized with *Santa* by Federico Gamboa, or *femmes fatales* like Menichelli, or the celebrated Bella Otero, whom Juan José Tablada had described as "Archangel, wolf, princess, light, succubus, star." The same model would be given a Mexican nature with *Salamandra* (1919) by Efrén Rebolledo, at that time an exiled diplomat. (Tablada, not content with his mockery of Madero, had worked under Huerta and, like Gamboa and Leopoldo Beristain, had escaped, fleeing with the Zapatistas snapping at his heels.)

In 1917, Mimi Derba founded Azteca Films with director and filmmaker Enrique Rosas. In its first and only year of existence, Azteca Films sponsored five feature-length movies that were primarily a channel for Derba's screenplays. She also went on to become the first female film director in Mexico with *La Tigresa*, which she neither acted in nor wrote. (In those same years, the sisters Adriana and Dolores Elhers also made documentaries.) When the company dissolved, several of its members reunited two years later to film *La Banda del Automóvil Gris* (directed by Enrique Rosas, Joaquín Coss, and Juan Canal de Homes), a retelling of the atrocities of a gang disguised in uniforms of the Constitutionalist Army, with search warrants stolen from police headquarters, who storm various mansions in the capital in 1915, kidnap, and murder. The actual events provoked a political scandal due to connections discovered between the gang and judicial officials. However, the film limited itself to enumerating the crimes, the investigation, the capture of the gang, and the execution of the criminals (using documentary footage filmed by Rosas in 1916, useful for the dark moral ending).

Unexpectedly, the government emerged as a film producer on behalf of the Secretary of War and the Navy beginning with *Patria Nueva* (1917), an exaltation of the patriotic goals of the still powerful military regime; and continuing with *Juan Soldado* (1919, Enrique Castilla), *El Precio de la Gloria*, and *Honor Militar*, directed by Lieutenant Colonel Fernando Orozco y Berra in 1919. Between the militants and Mimi Derba, the end of the second decade of the century, and the first of the Revolution, there loomed the promise of a splendid future for Mexican cinema.

It had emerged as the escapist medium par excellence. The era of the documentary's glory was past and now the atmosphere was full of optimistic messages: women powdered and made up like the European marchionesses of the eighteenth century (*La Soñadora*, 1917, Eduardo Arozamena); nationalist reaffirmationists such as *Cuauhtémoc* (1918, Manuel de la Bandera), *Partida Ganada* (1920, Enrique Castilla), and *De Raza Azteca* (1922, Fernando Martorel); literary adaptations that gave hope equally to the Mexicanist or Latin Americanist vocation of cinematic cults such as *Tabare* (1917, Luis Lezama), *María* (1918, Rafael Bermúdez Zataráin), *Santa* (1918) and *La Llaga* (1918), both directed by Luis G. Peredo and adapted from novels by Federico Gamboa, *El Zarco* (1920, José M. Ramos), *La Parcela* (1921, Ernesto Vohllrath), and, of course, *En la Hacienda*, also directed by Vohllrath in 1921. This grand drama by Federico Carlos Kegel, a follower of Porfirio Díaz, was to the relations between peasants and landowners as Gamboa's *Santa* was to the image of unmarried female sexuality. Through a combination of both positions,

Elena Sánchez Valenzuela as Santa *in the first of the most remade of Mexican films. Directed by Luis G. Peredo, the film traces the tragic story of loss of innocence, morality, and sin at the turn of the century.*

the melodramas of *De Raza Azteca* and *Fulgaración de Raza* were created. Both take place in Xochimilco, at that time representative of a province that was nearly a virgin jungle, where there arises the impossible love of the poor Indian, Diego, for the rich girl, Catalina, in the film by Miguel Contreras Torres; and the perverse sexuality of the evil native girl, Lupita (Ligia d'Golconda), the cause of the troubles of the good peasant, Juan, in the film by Martorel.

Although the revolutionary process and the 1917 Constitution had stirred up, legitimated, and activated anticlerical positions, always latent in the old *porfirista* liberals and in the new syndicalist and socialist scholars from the university, something must have occurred in the Mexican cinema so that it could secretly fall into the hands of indisputably reactionary artists. This shift transpired even though the power was now in the hands of politicians, militants, and intellectuals very determined to demonstrate the benefits of the progress they stood for (or dreamed of, in any case the same).

The Virgin of Guadalupe becomes a film character in *Tepeyac* (1917, José M. Ramos and Carlos E. González) and in the documentary *La Virgin de Guadalupe* (1918, George D. Wright) and *El Milagro de la Virgin* (1925, written by Blanche T. Earle). However, there were other stars: Pancho Villa was filmed by Charles Rosher and Raoul Walsh in 1915 for *The Life of Villa*, in which the Revolution served as a stage mounted by Villa especially for the filmmakers. In 1920 the Spaniard, Francisco Elias, traveled to the hacienda of retired General Canutillo to propose the filming of a fiction film with him as the star. According to some accounts the movie was never made, yet Elias's journal stated that one was filmed with the title of *Epopeya*, but the negative and the copy were burned by direct orders of Obregón. In 1923 the Alva brothers put together a good part of their material about Villa, including his bullet-ridden corpse inside his automobile in *Vida, Hechos y Hazañas*, where the enemy of the regime, already dead, was an object of minimal homage; the same treatment was accorded to Zapata with the documentary by Rosas, *Emiliano Zapata*, which premiered the same week that the commander died.

Around 1924 the production of feature-length narrative films declined to an alarming level (one film per year) that was only occasionally surpassed. The Mexican cinema was no longer a promising art form: the dominant discourse was the plagiarization of successful North American adventure films, overloaded with morality. *El Puño de Hierro* (1927, Gabriel García Moreno) warns against the harmfulness of drug addiction, represented by Chinamen who have an opium den, distinguished by Chinese lettering chalked over walls that escape the tapestry of Saltillo serapes; and *El Tren Fantasma* (1927, also by García Moreno), about the wrongdoings of a railroad worker put in his place by an honest inspector.

The regime generated in its filmmakers the search for a superhero, the new Mexican (the urban version featured leading man Carlos Villatoro)—son of the Revolution, conqueror of all obstacles, pride of the race—found in such films as *El Indio Yaqui* (1926, Guillermo Calles) and *El Coloso de Mármol*. Unexpectedly understood as a didactic appeal more than as a spectacle, the Mexican cinema ended the 1920s in a harsh mood. As evidenced by the drug addiction in *El Puño de Hierro*, advertisements supported the prenuptial examinations of *Los Hijos del Destino* (1930) and opposed the alcoholism in *Vicio* (1930). As if that were not enough, those still faithful to Porfirio Díaz showed their partisanship through Gustavo Sáenz de Sicilia, who filmed *La Boda de Rosario* (1929), starring Carlos Rincón Gallardo, Marquis of Guadalupe.

The success of sound cinema following the premiere of *The Jazz Singer* (1927, Alan Crosland) imposed upon Hollywood the problem of language. The silent cinema had created its own visual language that transcended borders. So that they would not lose the Spanish-speaking public, the North American studios quickly contracted Spanish and Latin American artists to make Spanish versions of their English films, producing such curiosities as the Spanish version of *Dracula* by Tod Browning, starring Lupita Tovar as Mina, Carlos Villar as Dracula, and Eduardo Arozamena as the valiant Dr. Van Helsing.

The arrival of the first sound movies in Mexico was a heavy blow to the already weak production industry. Contreras Torres filmed the short, *El Águila y el Nópal*, using phonograph records for sound. Salvador Pruneda made *Abismos* with Magda Haller; however, it never premiered. Angel E. Alvarez directed *Alas de Gloria* with the aviators Pablo L. Sidar and Carlos Rovirosa, which was seen only in Puebla. In 1930, Rafael J. Sevilla used fifty thousand feet of new celluloid given to him by Warner Brothers, where he had been the technical adviser, for the filming of *Más Fuerte que el Deber*, which was later exhibited with great success.

Thus, the silent cinema of Mexico came to an end. How difficult is it to consider what immediately happened to the cinema. New stars emerged—Pardavé, Antonio R. Fausto, and Carlos Orellana would have their best years, but Roberto Soto Panzón would see his decline. Then, Mimi Derba resurfaced with a version of *Santa* (1931, Antonio Moreno). The followers of José Vasconcelos, Juan Bustillo Oro and Mauricio Magdaleno, would have various opportunities to demonstrate their rancor against the revolutionary regime, primarily in the 1940s, while the Cristeros filtered their messages too late on behalf of René Capistrán Garza, screenwriter of *La Virgen que Forjó una Patria* (1943, Julio Bracho).

Almost the entire production of silent cinema has disappeared in fires, through negligence, or through necessity—entire sections of silent films were sold by impoverished filmmakers to paint manufacturers, who used the nitrate from the silver emulsion. Jesús H. Abitia, without the protection of Obregón, saw his films reduced to ashes in 1928 in an "accidental" fire. Perhaps the spirit of the significance of the silent movies for the Mexican culture of that period is best exemplified in the parody written by Guz Aguilar in 1920 to be recited by Manuel Tamez—a script that grieved for the transformation of the Alarcón Theater into a movie house.

2

The Birth of the Film Industry and the Emergence of Sound*

Federico Dávalos Orozco

During the 1920s the rise in production of silent features that began in 1917 could not sustain itself, and by mid-decade, production declined. More than twenty full-length films were completed in 1921. This figure was reduced to only four in 1923. A brief recovery occurred in 1925 but did not last for the rest of the decade.

There were three important trends in the Mexican cinema of the 1920s. First, certain silent productions were inspired by the vaudeville and theatrical traditions that were in vogue. In fact, from then on, theater became a permanent influence upon the cinema in Mexico. Second, a small but significant number of productions were completed by and in the various states of Mexico. Over half of all the films of the 1920s were inspired by Mexican themes, and many were adaptations of classic literary works. Within this "Mexicanista school" consistent with nationalistic trends following the Revolution, writers and journalists such as Rafael Bermúdez Zataraín and Carlos Noriega Hope clamored for a cinema that would reflect their country's history, traditions, and landscape. They argued that only the originality of *lo mexicano* on the silver screen would distinguish and bring appeal to Mexican cinema abroad.

This cinematic nationalism highlighted only superficial aspects of Mexico and did not reveal its regional diversities or include a critical view of its historical legacy. Nevertheless, the films were able to extol an abstract patriotism, the indigenous presence, and regional folklore. However, the vigorous nationalistic crusades fostered by the Ministry of Education under philosopher José Vasconcelos during the presidency of Alvaro Obregón (1920–1924) were poorly represented in cinema. In this early period, postrevolutionary governments did

*This chapter is based largely on the author's *Albores del cine mexicano* (México: Editorial Clío Libros y Videos S.A. de C.V., 1996).

not elaborate a set of official policies. At best, the state conceived the cinema as a useful pedagogical tool for mass education.

Third, the role of Hollywood increased in Mexico in the 1920s. While in the early years of Mexican cinema all facets of filmmaking were usually handled by one dominant person or company, by the 1920s the various aspects were divided and shared, especially that of the role of producers, who by then had to confront the challenge of U.S. films. Hollywood implemented an aggressive policy of cinematic expansion abroad, which involved the setting up of distribution chains and financial support for exhibitors who promoted American films. The foreign press was cultivated and pressured to write favorably about American cinema. In addition, Mexican exhibitors started to favor the established and consistent production by Hollywood over Mexican inconsistency.

The efforts to establish a bona fide movie industry in Mexico were fruitless prior to 1931, due to the enormous competition of foreign films and the difficult circumstances of production in the country. The introduction of sound functioned as a catalyst, and by the end of the 1920s the need to make Spanish-language sound films for Latin American audiences was evident. A worldwide public was attracted by the novelty of being able to watch movies for the first time with dialogue spoken in their own tongue. The first Mexican experiments with sound, however, revealed the early technical and financial inferiorities of Spanish speaking-countries vis-à-vis the Spanish-language cinema made in the United States.

In 1929 five sound films were produced in Mexico: *Dios y la Ley*, produced, directed, and written by Guillermo Calles, who was also the star; *El Indio Yaqui*, filmed in California by Calles during the months of August and September and probably the first sound feature movie produced in Mexico; *El Águila y el Nópal*, directed and produced by Miguel Contreras Torres, originally a short silent film (according to Roberto Panzón Soto) that was made in Hollywood and later transformed into a full-length film; and *La Boda de Rosario*, by Gustavo Sáenz de Sicilia, which originally premiered as a silent feature. Later, there was an unsuccessful attempt to provide sound for this production.

The Spanish-language film industry in Hollywood was fundamental not only for the growth of Mexican movies but also for the rest of Latin American cinema and for that of Spain. In Hollywood, prospective filmmakers acquired the training that enabled them to direct a host of people in the various branches of production. Latin America's cinematographers favored the repatriation of those persons already trained in Hollywood into their respective national cinemas.

Scene of jealousy and betrayal from the second Santa, *starring Lupita Tovar, Carlos Orellana, and Juan José Martínez Casado and directed by Antonio Moreno.*

In Mexico, this advantage was seized by those theatrical managers who had the audacity to risk large sums of money on the production of films with Hollywood-trained personnel and Hollywood equipment. When the National Production Company of Films began *Santa* in November 1931, it employed technical and artistic devices that had been perfected in Hollywood. An international cast was then secured by the Spanish director and actor, Antonio Moreno— Canadian cinematographer Alex Phillips; Mexican stars such as Lupita Tovar, who played Santa, Carlos Orellana, who played Hipolito, and Donald Reed (Ernesto Gullien was his real name), who played Marcelino; Cuban actors René Cardona and Juan José Martínez Casado as El Jarameño; and Mexican soundmen Roberto and José Rodríguez, who, by using their own system of recording, were able to overcome the technical difficulties of their predecessors. However, the production of *Santa* was still deficient in overall quality, and the direction of the actors was clumsy.

Even though director Moreno introduced U.S. technical aspects of production to Mexico, *Santa*'s format had more to do with the production of silent films of Spain. The setting of *Santa* was moved from the time of the Porfiriato to the 1930s. The movie follows the life of the protagonist from her upbringing in a sort of idyllic paradise—the town of Chimalistac, San Angel—to Hell, which is represented by the modern city and the brothel. Santa, the prostitute, although she loses her virtue, does not lose her spiritual purity, which she demonstrates by becoming a martyr to circumstances and to the morality of the period. (In all Mexican films thereafter, this standard portrayal of the prostitute is continued. In addition, the misogynist attitude toward the Santa archetype predominates throughout the history of Mexican melodrama.) The melodramatic plot of *Santa* ensured its commercial success. The film originally premiered on March 30, 1932, and lasted for three weeks at the Palacio Theater. Newspaper reporters considered *Santa* the inaugural film of a national cinema because of its box-office results.

Seducing the Public

Santa, and the sound films previously mentioned, demonstrate that in Mexico it was indeed possible to produce successful feature films with sound. Moreover, the directors of the silent film period accepted the challenge that Miguel Contreras Torres had issued: the transition to sound. Only he was able to achieve it with clear success. Certain pioneers never had the opportunity to direct sound movies because they were unable to function in the new era. Their initial attempts were of very poor quality, and soon thereafter they gave up working in film productions.

Once sound films were proven to be productive, theatrical managers, directors, and screenwriters began the search for capital that would permit them to finance such films for a growing market. Thus, commercial productions dominated an uncertain film industry. The organization of the industry and its methods of production and exhibition followed the standards established earlier by Hollywood. Mexican production grew rapidly. The number of sound films climbed to six in 1932; from 1933 to 1936 more than twenty such films were completed annually. The overwhelming success of *Allá en el Rancho Grande* in 1936 by Fernando de Fuentes permitted the industry to make thirty-eight feature films in 1937. It was inevitable that the financial benefits of Mexican films were secured in the theaters, mostly through their second screening.

In analyzing the national film production from 1932 to 1936, a wide variety of styles and themes are noted. They range from the sentimental vignette to personal cinematic expressions that had as their goal not only the creation of solid artistic works but also the attainment of economic success. The majority of directors were looking for the means to open doors to the existing market for films in Mexico and Latin America. The decade of the 1930s was a period of experimentation for some Argentinian and Spanish productions and also for Hollywood's Spanish-speaking films. Generally speaking, there existed an atmosphere of freedom that permitted such experimentation, given the absence of dramatic and thematic conventions in an industry characterized by its cautious economic fortunes and its insecurity with exhibition and distribution formulas.

Filmmakers such as Arcady Boytler, Juan Bustillo Oro, Fernando de Fuentes, Gabriel Soria, and Chano Urueta considered films essentially as art and approached them as such in their early works. The artistic value of these works seemed to be in direct opposition to the needs of the film industry and the public, who considered movies predominantly as popular entertainment. This situation explains the reason why certain directors became good artisans. The Mexican film industry needed successful films like Hollywood's, and consequently those were the films that were categorized as artistic. In this early period, few directors achieved genuine success, and even fewer transcended the characterization of artisans.

The Early Directors

Miguel Contreras Torres

The most prolific director of the "Mexicanista school" was Contreras Torres, a native of Michoacán and former revolutionary officer, who enjoyed a particularly long-lasting filmmaking career. He debuted as the star of José Manuel Ramos's *El Zarco* (1920). From the outset, Contreras Torres showed great ability as a publicist and theater manager. In spite of his nationalistic tendencies, he was compared as an actor to the Hollywood Western star, William S. Hart. His supposed mimetic acting was derided by certain critics as deficient—an assertion that mattered little to Contreras Torres.

Early in his career, Contreras Torres served in his films as producer, screenwriter, director, and lead actor. After producing *De Raza Azteca* in 1922, he continued with two films that dealt with regional themes: *El Caporal* (1921), which focuses on the struggles of the rugged frontier life of the Mexican north; and its sequel, *El Sueño del Caporal* (1922). In *El Hombre sin Patria* (1922), he addressed for the first time in Mexican cinema the challenges of emigration to the United States. This was also the first Mexican film to be shot on location in the United States.

As a filmmaker, Contreras Torres addressed a multitude of Mexican themes. *Almas Tropicales* (1923), codirected by Manuel R. Ojeda, deals with a young man's love. He and his sweetheart ultimately triumph in spite of the opposition and tactics of the villain and the charms of a sensual rival. The film ends with a dramatic camera shot of the couple embracing with a striking sunset in the background. In *Aguiluchos Mexicanos* (1924), codirected by Gustavo Sáenz de Sicilia, Contreras Torres successfully employed footage of early aviation and incorporated it into a melodrama of a mother's resignation and fear for the career of her son, a pilot. In *Oro, Sangre y Sol* (1923), based on the life of famed Spanish bull-fighter Rodolfo Gaona, Contreras Torres employed a traditional plot

Publicity stills of scenes from the historical epic Juárez y Maximiliano, *directed by Miguel Contreras Torres.*

to detail daily events in the bullfighting experience for a general audience. In addition, Contreras Torres continued to film abroad with *El Relicario* (1926), shot in Mexico, Spain, and Hollywood; and *El León de Sierra Morena* (1927–28), shot in Spain. In 1929 he returned to Mexico and produced, directed, and wrote two early nationalistic films: *Soñadores de la Gloria* and *El Águila y el Nópal.* In 1931 he filmed his last silent production, *Zitán.*

In 1933 the première that grossed the most money of that decade was the super production, *Juárez y Maximiliano*, directed by Contreras Torres. The film debuted in the Principal Theater on June 20, and remained there for six weeks.

Medea de Novara starred as Carlota and Enrique Herrera as Maximiliano, with a secondary role given to the figure of Benito Juárez. Contreras Torres dealt with similar themes of royalty in *La Paloma* in 1937, *La Emperatriz Loca* in 1939, and *Caballeria del Imperio* in 1942. He continued to produce and direct films until the 1960s. Contreras Torres was the one early director who was able successfully to make the transition from silent films to sound.

Arcady Boytler

Born in 1893, Boytler was a Russian immigrant with a theatrical background. He had performed both as an actor and director of comedies in his homeland prior to the Bolshevik revolution of 1917, and in Germany between 1920 and 1923. He directed *El Buscador de Fortunas* in Chile in 1927 as well as various shorts for the Mexican film industry in the United States during 1929. In 1932 he began his film career in Mexico after a brief appearance in *¡Que Viva México!*

Throughout his works he developed dramatic characters. In *Celos* (1935), Vilma Vidal is the victim of the sick jealousy of her husband, Fernando Soler, who literally goes mad and is put in an asylum. In *La Mujer del Puerto* (1933), the protagonists are barely redeemed by the

Photo from the set of La Mujer del Puerto.

exalted lyricism. This film, with a script by Guz Aguilar, based on
short stories by Leo Tolstoy and Guy de Maupassant, allowed for

Andrea Palma is the definitive fallen woman in La Mujer del
Puerto, *directed by Arcady Boytler.*

the Mexican film debut of Andrea Palma, who played a prostitute
driven to a violent and dramatic suicide after unknowingly commit-
ting incest.

Boytler also directed musical shorts and comedies: *El Especta-
dor Impertinente* (1932), an experimental and creative short; and
Aguila o Sol (1937) and its sequel, *Así es Mi Tierra* (1937), starring
Cantinflas and Manuel Medel. In 1944, Boytler retired from film-
making. Later, he became the manager of his two movie theaters
(Arcadia and Cinelandia) until his death in 1965.

Fernando de Fuentes

Born in Veracruz in 1894, de Fuentes was educated in Mexico and the United States. His initiation into the film industry came with his management of the Olympia movie theater. The most important Mexican filmmaker of the 1930s, he began his film work with the production of *Santa* as Ramon Peón's assistant, who was, in turn, the

Star Lupe Vélez, the Mexican Spitfire, in the title role as La Zandunga, *directed by Fernando de Fuentes.*

director's assistant. Later he was director of dialogue for *Una Vida por Otra* by John H. Auer (1932). The following year, he would begin his lifelong preoccupation: an exploration of diverse creative possibilities for Mexican cinema.

His best work is his Revolution trilogy: *El Prisionero Número Trece* (1933), *El Compadre Mendoza* (1933), and *Vámonos con Pancho Villa* (1935). In these films, de Fuentes, as a distant observer of the Mexican Revolution, questions the meaning of war. He also attempts to revive and analyze the atmosphere and extreme situations of the period that led many of his characters into corruption, treason, and a meaningless death in either a futile pursuit of glory or an effort to satisfy the ambitions of a general. De Fuentes's narrative technique resembled the efficient narrative of American cinema, and he masterfully exploited the lack of stereotypes and the dramatic conventions of newly emerging sound film in order to develop stories with a moral lesson. In *El Prisionero Número Trece* he presents an official whose dishonesty leads to the execution of his own son. The military considered the movie to be offensive to the armed forces and thus censored it by changing the ending into one more palatable. Continuing his revolutionary theme, in *Vámonos con Pancho Villa*, he explores in a critical manner the various facets of the personality of the famous chief of the Division of the North and icon of the Revolution.

Of the trilogy, *El Compadre Mendoza* is undeniably the masterpiece. It is based on a story by Mauricio Magdaleno with a script by Juan Bustillo Oro and de Fuentes himself. In the context of an allegory based on Emiliano Zapata's murder, the film shows, on the one hand, the destruction of a complacent man, Rosalío Mendoza (played by Alfredo de Diestro), an opportunist who sacrifices friendship for immediate gain. On the other hand, the movie highlights platonic, innocent, and sincere love between Dolores, the wife (Carmen Guerrero), and the general, Felipe Nieto (Antonio R. Fausto), through a sensitive and tender narrative.

De Fuentes also explored in his films other Mexican themes, ambiances, and styles: the provincial and traditionalist melodrama in *La Calandria* (1933), the adaptation of the Western into a nineteenth-century epic in *El Tigre de Yautepec* (1933), the horror genre in a Carmelite convent in *El Fantasma del Convento* (1934), the family drama about a questionable and authoritarian mother in *La Familia Dressel* (1935), and the dangers of extramarital affairs in *Las Mujeres Mandan* (1936). *Cruz Diablo*, a swashbuckling adventure story, was set in the Colonial period. It starred Jorge Negrete, who would later become one of the icons of Mexican cinema. Imitations by other filmmakers followed, such as *Martín Garatuza* by Gabriel Soria in 1935 and *Monja, Casada, Virgen y Mártir* by Juan Bustillo Oro in 1935, both adaptations of popular historical novels by Vicente Riva Palacio.

De Fuentes's promising film career did not always achieve economic success, and he was often not fully understood by his contemporaries. After the box-office success of *Allá en el Rancho Grande* (1936), de Fuentes transformed himself from a filmmaker into an entrepreneur. Until his death in 1958 he was, without doubt, the single most important Mexican film director prior to the Golden Age.

Juan Bustillo Oro

Born in Mexico City in 1904, Bustillo Oro graduated from law school and later pursued a career as an author, journalist, and screenwriter. His studies made him a follower of José Vasconcelos. He shared equal enthusiasm for working in film as in theater. Both genres reflected his sensitivity and knowledge of elite and popular culture. The influences of popular skits, *zarzuela*, and *genero chico* theater nourished his appreciation for artistic film. The blending of such influences impacted some of his most interesting works, but it is also responsible for overly melodramatic films with excessive dialogue. While young, he wrote for several theaters and for the Teatro de Ahora, which he cofounded with Mauricio Magdaleno. His first work as a film director was in the silent film, *Yo y Tu Padre* (1927). Later, he turned down the opportunity to direct the film adaptation of his own work, *Tiburón*, which was later directed by Ramon Peña in 1933. He also declined to shoot the novel of Magdaleno's *El Compadre Mendoza* (1933), which was to be Fernando de Fuentes's masterpiece.

Bustillo Oro's first work in a sound film was *Dos Monjes* (1934). In this pretentious and gaudy production, clearly influenced by German Expressionism, Bustillo Oro plays with shots, costumes, lighting, music, and aesthetic formality by employing the camera in often abusive ways. However, the slow pace and melodramatic tone resulted in a simple and scant storyline, which a critic called a sample of romantic insanity. These elements worked against the movie, which tells the story of a love triangle whose web is woven by two opposing perspectives: those of two monks played by Victor Urrucha and Carlos Villatoro. Each version gives a different view of the events, represented by a change in the protagonist's wardrobe, from black to white and vice versa, and by the monks' distorted visions of reality, which are achieved through out-of-focus shots, scenes full of sinuous lines and twisted objects, and abrupt movements of the camera. The public's disapproval was evident.

In 1935, Bustillo Oro repeated that Expressionist experience, with results that were less than laudable, in the Gothic tale, *El Misterio del Rostro Pálido*, a tribute to Gaston Leroux's *Phantom of the Opera*. He sought to provoke anguish by contrasting the climate of horror with the luminous and white aspects of the Art Deco sets and costumes. Subsequently he filmed a New Spain theme: *Monja, Casada, Virgen y Mártir* (1935), based on the novel by Vicente Riva Palacio. This film was able to sustain itself at the box office for four weeks, which at the time was a major accomplishment, and its success made the director realize the need to go down more familiar paths.

Madre Querida (1935), directed and produced by Juan Orol, inaugurated the genre of melodrama that exalted maternity and the relationship of mother and son. This film premiered on May 10, 1935, with great success, evoking numerous imitations, such as *Los Desheredados* (1935) by Guillermo Baqueriza, *Maternostra* (1936) by Gabriel Soria, *Madres del Mundo* (1936) by Rolando Aguilar, and *Honrarás a Tus Padres* (1936) by Juan Orol.

Like Fernando de Fuentes and Arcady Boytler, Bustillo Oro combined his particular conception of film as a medium of personal and artistic expression with the urgent need to create box-office hits. His popularity culminated with the invention of dramatic and generic prototypes such as "Porfirian nostalgia" and family dramas. He was also responsible, in 1940, for the cinematic portrayal that would finally establish Cantinflas as a comedy star in *Ahí Está el Detalle*.

José "Che" Bohr

Actor, director, singer, and composer, José Bohr was born in 1901 in Germany and raised in Chile and Argentina. During the mid-1920s he lived in the United States where in 1926 he worked on some of his first short musical films in Spanish for Lee de Forest, the inventor of optical sound. He starred in numerous films with Spanish dialogue, especially as a singer, before arriving in the Mexican cinema world in the 1930s. While Bohr was the principal in all of his films—producer, director, scriptwriter, star, singer, and composer of the music—important to his work was the Chilean pianist Eva Liminana, who, under the pseudonym of Duquesa Olga, often participated as producer and scriptwriter. The characteristically improvisational nature of Bohr's films was blended with dialogue full of logic and coherence, always in the service of the exhibitionist nature and delusions of grandeur of their creator.

Fascinated by the thriller genre, Bohr produced Mexican films that are disconcerting, horrifying, chaotic, extravagant, baroque, and confusing. They were made, however, with an enviable joy—always with a paradoxical tone, self-conscious and fun, and filmed with great imagination and an acute cinematographer's sense. Bohr's presence on the screen was simultaneously delightful and oppressive. His love of costumes and his interpretations of songs with comic and romantic themes, usually written by himself, served to lighten the burden of his plain and ungraceful appearance.

His first Mexican film was a drama that pretended to be ideologically socialist, *La Sangre Manda* (1933). In *¿Quien Mató a Eva?* (1934), he plays a millionaire playboy who, out of boredom, acts like a gangster and dresses like the notorious Chicago mobsters. The story is about a bank employee who robs a bank, then alters his fea-

tures through the help of a plastic surgeon, and finally ends up riddled with bullets at the exit of a movie theater—just like the infamous gangster John Dillinger. *Tu Hijo* (1934) is a drama with great
moments in cinematic intuition. In *Así Es la Mujer* (1936), Bohr
made a grand effort in what seems to be a musical comedy in the
kaleidoscopic style of the Hollywood producer and choreographer,
Busby Berkeley.

In *Marihuana (El Monstruo Verde)* (1936), Bohr goes from being
a lawman in pursuit of a gang called "El Monstruo Verde" to its
leader. Following some unforeseen events, he disguises himself as
"Gringo Daniel" but fools nobody and winds up dead, the victim of
an airplane accident. Subsequently, Bohr was compelled to make
films that were less personal and more conventional with less than
positive results. In 1939 he made his last Mexican film.

Guillermo Calles

One major proponent of a nationalist cinema was Guillermo Calles,
dubbed "El Indio." Calles was born in the city of Chihuahua in
1893. From a young age, he appeared in Hollywood Westerns, usually typecast as a Native American. Occasionally, he even directed
for the emerging Hollywood film industry. In his Mexican films, the
theme of *indigenismo* prevailed, and he was always the leading
actor. In *De Raza Azteca* (1921), a film co-directed with Miguel
Contreras Torres, Calles plays the role of a charro from Xochimilco
who performs outstanding feats of horsemanship.

Calles's second movie, *El Indio Yaqui*, was filmed in the state of
Sonora as well as in the Hollywood studio. The director attempted to
defend the Native American and Mexican characters who were the
traditional villains in the Hollywood Westerns of the time. In this
production, a young Yaqui maiden tragically commits suicide after
being raped by an evil American. A Yaqui Indian, a lifelong friend of
the deceased, pursues the villain and avenges her dishonor and death.
Another of his films, *Raza de Bronce* (1927), shot in Mexicali, Baja
California, "presented one of the most noble heroic gestures in the
history of our Native American people in the modern age." Another
review stated that it depicted some of the most glorious episodes of
the Mexican Revolution.

Calles, as a pioneer of sound films, had a brief career in the new
medium. His first sound feature, *Dios y la Ley* (1929), takes place on
the Isthmus of Tehuantepec and tells the tragic story of the unrelin-
quished love of a Native American for a white woman. Ultimately,
the protagonist faces the inevitable and gives up his love to his rival:

"She is yours. God has so ordained. She is of your race." The sound-track of *Dios y la Ley* featured traditional music and songs. Calles continued to direct films until 1939. Throughout his filmmaking years, he faced great adversity. After this period, he worked as a supporting actor until his death in 1958.

The Official Aesthetics

After 1930, nationalist exhaltation was experienced through re-creations of the Revolution or through ethnographic films that resulted in the superficial nationalism of *ranchera* musical comedies and folk dramas. Beginning in the mid-1930s, the Mexican state was interested in employing the great influence of cinema to create not merely propaganda films but also those with social content for a mass audience. *Redes*, by Fred Zinnemann and Emilio Gómez Muriel, a project sponsored by the Ministry of Public Education, and *Janitzio* (Carlos Navarro), a risky, privately funded project (both

Tito Guizar and Esther Fernandez as the idyllic couple in Allá en el Rancho Grande, *the first blockbuster of Mexican cinema, directed by Fernando de Fuentes.*

Movie poster of Vámonos con Pancho Villa.

made in 1934) were inspired by Russian director Sergei Eisenstein's aesthetics and his glorified views of indigenous life. The first film was made with the aid of the natives of Alvarado, Veracruz. It narrates the efforts conducted by a group of fishermen to avoid exploitation by a greedy cacique. Showcased in the film were the debuts of composer Silvestre Revueltas and the photography of Paul Strand. There were many elements of Eisenstein's style, such as allusions to the collective hero and the montage and narrative style of *Potemkin*. The second film was based upon a story about the Purepecha (indigenous people of the state of Michoacán) and starred Emilio Fernández, who subsequently shot two related versions of the same story: *María Candelaria* (1943) and *Maclovia* (1948).

Rebelión (1934) by Manuel G. Gómez, *Vámonos con Pancho Villa* (1935) by Fernando de Fuentes, and *Judas* by Manuel R. Ojeda were films fully inspired by the Revolution. *Rebelión* was based on the research of Manuel Gamio, former director of the Coordination of Anthropology. *Vámonos con Pancho Villa* was the first production of CLASA Films, one of the most important independent production companies; it secured strong official support: Alberto J. Pani, former Minister of the Treasury, was one of the producers, and the federal army collaborated on the battle scenes. Escalating production costs came close to bankrupting the company. *Judas* had clear agrarian sentiments. Through pressure from the dominant National Revolutionary Party, the film remained in theaters only two weeks.

Two short films, *Humanidad* (1934) by Adolfo Best Maugard, made for the public good, as well as one produced by the National Irrigation Commission, *Irrigación en México* (1935) by Ignacio Miranda, were highly praised by Diego Rivera and Luis Cardoza y Aragón as clear examples of an ideal Mexican cinema—the first for its utilitarianism, as opposed to the superficiality of commercial cinema, and the second for its artistic beauty. However, such attempts at nationalistic inspiration were box-office failures in spite of their cinematic relevance: these projects suffered because of their emphasis on political content over artistic craft.

Paradoxically, the vigor of revolutionary nationalism with all of its populist and authoritarian contradictions generated a reactionary response with characteristics of Catholicism and anti-United States thoughts. This response idealized the *ancien régime*: the Porfiriato and the patriarchal hacienda structure. *Allá en el Rancho Grande* has as its principal characteristic a peculiar vision of *lo mexicano*: its nationalism, even though deformed to a certain degree and adapted to the necessities of the market; and an absolute identification with the rural societies of Latin America. The combination of both elements made the film one of the greatest box-office hits of all time. With the release of *Allá en el Rancho Grande*, a period of cinematic experimentation concluded and the conditions were set for the emergence of the Golden Age.

II
The Golden Age

The mass appeal and popularity of cinema during its first few decades ensured its future, and, by the end of the silent era, it had begun the process of consolidation into a viable industry. By the late 1930s, Mexican cinema had already become a major form of mass entertainment, and the stage was set for the marvelous flowering that was to appear a decade later. The coming of sound, along with the introduction of dialogue and novel themes, brought about the advent of the greatest era in the cinema of Mexico known as the Golden Age. Early sound films exemplified the unique characteristics of a truly national cinema. Television had not yet come into its own, and the major form of mass media and entertainment in the Mexico of the 1940s was cinema. Even in the smallest, most remote villages, films were shown and enjoyed by all.

Many factors made this glorious moment possible. First and foremost were the filmmakers themselves. It was during this period that many Mexican filmmakers returned to their homeland after working in Hollywood, where they learned important cinematic skills and improved existing ones. Other important directors such as Arcady Boytler, Jesús Contreras Torres, and Fernando de Fuentes had already made their mark in Mexico.

In all areas and phases of the filmmaking process, talented and creative individuals participated. Actors from cinema, theater, vaudeville, and stand-up comedy blessed Mexican films with their exceptional artistry. And in every genre of cinema—action, comedy, musical, drama, horror, melodrama, and mystery—these actors excelled. In comedy, Mario Moreno "Cantinflas," Joaquin Pardavé, Adalberto Martínez "Resortes," Germán Valdés "Tin Tan," and others proved themselves to be masters of every situation and skit. In drama, Pedro Armendáriz, Roberto Cañedo, Arturo de Córdoba,

Dolores del Río, María Félix, Marga López, Carlos López Moctezuma, Andrea Palma, and David Silva created memorable characters and gave unforgettable performances.

Entirely new genres were created that met with great success. The *ranchera*, which combined a rural setting with popular music and song, romance, comedic archetypes, and a happy ending, introduced two of the greatest stars of the Golden Age, Pedro Infante and Jorge Negrete. Although both Infante and Negrete acted in other types of roles, they were always identified with the *ranchera*. Many other actors and singers, such as Miguel Acevedes Mejía, Antonio Aguilar, Luis Aguilar, Sofía Alvarez, Lola Beltrán, José Alfredo Jiménez, Rosita Quintana, and Lucha Villa, made the *ranchera* into one of the most popular and enduring genres of Mexican cinema.

Movie still of the film Pueblerina, *directed by Emilio "El Indio" Fernández and starring Roberto Cañedo and Columbia Domínguez.*

A second and equally popular new genre was the *rumbera*, or *cabaretera*. These narratives showcased the beauty and dancing talent of new stars such as Meche Barba, Rosa Carmina, María Antonieta Pons, Ninón Sevilla, and Tongolele. In melodrama, familiar themes and issues resonated with audiences. Film melodrama of the period clearly reflected the society, mores, and mentalities of the 1940s and 1950s. Although the dialogue addressed existing gender relationships and morals, these films also explored social conflicts of the times.

In addition, the Golden Age signaled the emergence of a new generation of producers who were perhaps the single most important group responsible for the flowering of the cinema in the 1940s and 1950s. They were not only resourceful businesspeople who realized the profit side, but they also were involved intimately in the filmmaking process. They sought out the entertaining, popular, and even intelligent stories that audiences were clamoring for. They knew who their audience was and favored films that were family-oriented—that is, movies that could be enjoyed and appreciated by every member of the family. Their films contained no nudity or objectionable language, and violence was kept within accepted norms. Sexual situations were either hinted at or left to the imagination, and no cultural taboos were brought to the screen. In putting the various elements to work for a successful film (script, director, cast, and technicians), the producers of the Golden Age went beyond giving the people what they wanted. Their films reflected the desires, social structures, morality, and popular culture of the period. These producers not only met with great success in building up the film industry to become one of the ten most important economic enterprises of the country, but they also captured important distribution markets throughout Latin America, Spain, and the United States. At the height of the Golden Age, in the United States alone there were three hundred movie theaters in the Southwest, Midwest, and East that exclusively showed Mexican cinema.

No less important for the rise and development of the Golden Age was a special generation of directors that included Julio Bracho, Emilio "El Indio" Fernández, Roberto Gavaldón, Alejandro Galindo, Alberto Gout, Matilde Landeta, Gilberto Martínez Solares, and Ismael Rodríguez, all of whom enriched the existing film genres and introduced new ones. They drew performances from their actors that remain today as classics. Above all, they placed Mexican cinema on the world stage.

An unexpected and indisputable catalyst in the development of the Golden Age was the advent of World War II. Hollywood directed its efforts and priorities to the war, using its cinema as a vehicle to foster nationalism and anti-Axis sentiment. Audiences in the Spanish-speaking world were not attracted by Hollywood war films, and thus one of the repercussions was that, for the first time, Mexican cinema did not have to compete with Hollywood for foreign market shares. And just as important to the success of the Golden Age was the financial infusion of money and resources that Hollywood and the United States gave to Mexican cinema. Authorities north of the border realized that having an ally in the Spanish-language cinema and media was critical to their cause. As a result, U.S. aid to renovate and modernize the film studios was instrumental in the growth of the industry during the war years.

The essays in this section look closely at the directors, stars, themes, and social contexts of the films of the Golden Age. Patricia Torres San Martín introduces non-Mexican audiences to the works of Adela Sequeyro and Matilde Landeta, two seminal women directors of that period. While the films of these two pioneers are very different in terms of aesthetics and style, they place the women in the foreground of film and cultural narratives.

Two essays by Mexico's preeminent cultural critic, Carlos Monsiváis, look at two beloved film comedians, Cantinflas and Tin Tan. According to Monsiváis, the careers of these two stars both reflected the desires and beliefs of their audiences and mirrored the rise and fall of Mexican cinema in the 1940s and 1950s.

Joanne Hershfield questions the representation of race and ethnicity in classical cinema. Her essay examines how directors, caught up in the social and political fervor to portray national identity, relied upon various ideologies that defined the nation after the Revolution—*mestizaje*, *hispanismo*, and *indigenismo*—and that were ultimately grounded in racism.

Rafael Hernández Rodríguez analyzes two important genres of the Golden Age, the melodrama and the urban social comedy of Alejandro Galindo, Luis Buñuel, and Ismael Rodríguez. He argues that many of these directors' films may be seen as sophisticated social commentaries that connected powerfully with their audiences.

In his essay, historian Seth Fein offers a novel perspective on the political economy of the Mexican film industry during the Golden Age and its important ties and interdependence with Hollywood. His exhaustive research documents a critical and little-known key aspect of Mexican cinema in the late 1940s and throughout the 1950s.

Finally, Eduardo de la Vega Alfaro directly addresses the multitude of factors that together culminated in the eventual demise of the greatest period of the cinema. Although the decline of the Golden Age signaled the onset of the institutionalization of the crisis for Mexico's cinema in periods to follow, the films of the Golden Age endure. Their charm and grace continue to be enjoyed by succeeding generations. The legendary stature of the filmmakers of the Golden Age has transcended time and space.

3

Adela Sequeyro and Matilde Landeta
Two Pioneer Women Directors

Patricia Torres de San Martín

After the Revolution of 1910, the concept of Mexico as a "nation" as well as the discourse of *mexicanidad* were redesigned and promoted by intellectual, artistic, and educational movements committed to the task of making Mexico modern. According to educators and artists of the postrevolutionary moment, what the Mexican people needed, above all, was a better understanding of their historical and cultural legacy. In response, a new identity was fostered that looked neither exclusively to the "indigenous" past nor solely to the "noble heritage" of Spanish blood. This new identity was legitimated through different cultural manifestations, cinema being one of the most important.

During the 1930s, the Mexican cinema discovered its own generic formula, the melodramatic *ranchera (comedia ranchera)*, which transformed the nation's cinema project into a real film industry. *Allá en el Rancho Grande* (1936, Fernando de Fuentes) was the genre's birth certificate. Inspired by the huge success of this film, more than twenty-eight imitations of *Allá en el Rancho Grande* followed and a new idyllic universe was created: the feudal farm, a happy rural Arcadia, which not only ignored the 1910 Revolution and agrarian reform but also worked to oppose the 1930s epilogue to the Revolution.

Two Feminist Visions

By the 1940s, the cinema of the Golden Age had became one of the best vehicles for emphasizing national discourses that stressed modernity and unity. The postrevolutionary rhetoric, the mestizo melancholy, and the memories of a utopian past that had never

37

existed were now replaced by an exaltation of a new Mexican identity. However, prior to the 1940s, when the cinematic infrastructure
was formally institutionalized, there had been a brief period
(1929–1934) in which Mexican filmmaking was open ground for
creative experimentation and for individual and collective adventure—ground that allowed for the participation of two important
early women filmmakers, Adela Sequeyro Haro (1901–1992) and
Matilde Soto Landeta (b. 1913). Both women came from upper-
class families, were educated in exclusive universities, and were
self-taught in the craft of filmmaking. They produced their films
within the historical context of postrevolutionary Mexico, a period
characterized by the construction of a new national project wherein
"order and progress" meant modernity.[1]

Adela Sequeyro was born in the port city of Veracruz on March
11, 1901, to a well-established family headed by Federico Sequeyro
Arreola and Virginia Haro y Gutiérrez-Zamora. The Revolution that
began in 1910 devastated their fortune and compelled the family to
move to the town of Cuautitlán, on the outskirts of Mexico City.
Sequeyro studied at the French-English School in the capital and, at
an unusually early age, began a career in journalism. In the 1920s she
appeared occasionally in films, using the name "Perlita." In 1923 she
starred in *El Hijo de la Loca* by José S. Ortiz, followed by leading
roles in at least five other silent features: *Atavismo* (1923) and *Un
Drama en la Aristocracia* (1924), both directed by Gustavo Sáenz de
Sicilia; *No Matarás* (1924, Ortiz); *Los Compañeros del Silencio*
(1925, Basilio Zubiaur); and *El Sendero Gris* (1927, Jesús Cárdenas).
After the introduction of sound, Sequeyro appeared in *El Prisionero
Número Trece* (1933), as an extra in José Bohr's *La Sangre Manda*
(1933), and in a small part in *Mujeres sin Alma* (1934), directed by
Ramón Peón and Juan Orol. Finally, in 1937, she made her debut as a
director with the narrative, *La Mujer de Nadie*. In addition to her film
career, Sequeyro was a cinema journalist for *El Demócrata* in 1923
and *El Universal Gráfico* from 1929 to 1953.[2]

Matilde Landeta was born in Mexico City on September 20,
1913. Her mother, Matilde Landeta Dávalos, was originally from San
Luis Potosí; her father, Gregorio Soto Conde, was from Spain. She
completed her initial schooling in Mexico City and then studied at
the Colegio de Gran Cocteau in the state of Texas. Landeta entered
the film industry by chance: one day in 1933 she accompanied her
brother to a screen test at the El Nacional studios and decided to stay
and observe the day's filming. There, she found her calling. Starting
as a script girl, she worked on more than seventy films. Later, from
1938 to 1943, she was an assistant director, collaborating with several of the most important Mexican directors of the time, such as

Roberto Gavaldón, Emilio "El Indio" Fernández, and Julio Bracho. Finally, in 1948, she was able to direct her first film, *Lola Casanova*.

Both Sequeyro and Landeta overcame social and cultural limitations within a context of conflict. For these women filmmakers, it was not easy to succeed in an industry dominated by a hierarchical and patriarchal system. Their experiences not only bring to light the subordination of women in the film industry but also point to the ways in which gender limited social and economic options in Mexico. However, it is important to understand that despite those constraints, the cinematic projects of Sequeyro and Landeta developed as part of the process of the development of social modernity in Mexico.

First of all, both women were able to produce narrative films despite the labor regulations of the film industry. When Sequeyro was prevented from joining the industry's labor union because she was a woman, she founded a film cooperative to make her work possible.[3] Additionally, both women had to fight against not only bureaucracy but also the daily aggravations of producing films within adverse industrial and economic contexts. For example, during the filming of *La Mujer de Nadie*, Sequeyro was forced to rebuild her sets every day because of existing traditions of using temporary sets. Landeta lost some already developed rushes through careless laboratory procedures. Often at the end of the week the administrative staff were not given their salaries, so Landeta had to pay her crew with her own money. Further, her own script originals were stolen just before she started filming. Sequeyro wrote *La Mujer de Nadie* in 1935, but her producer asked Chano Urueta to direct it. There were some disagreements with Sequeyro, and the project was canceled. (Later, Urueta plagiarized *La Mujer de Nadie* to make *Una Mujer en Venta*.) It was not until 1937 that Sequeyro was able to make her own film from the original script. In addition to production obstacles, when Landeta and Sequeyro finally made their debuts as directors, their films had to survive the worst possible conditions of exhibition and distribution.

Their films broke with the traditional rules of Mexican filming as well as with the Mexican social system. Landeta and Sequeyro exercised their creative powers through their own distinctive narrative and stylistic practices, which evolved out of the conventional melodramatic structures of the nation's cinema. This symbolic and expressive power is what distinguishes their work from that of their contemporaries. The metaphors and discourses of Landeta's and Sequeyro's films were created from their own lives within social and historical aspects linked to questions of gender. As women, both filmmakers had to transform everyday practices into processes

Movie poster of La Mujer de Nadie.

of reconstruction and reinterpretation in a context of taboos, sanctions, and cultural proscriptions. According to Pierre Bourdieu, "the social division of society" is a perception that emerges from the symbolic and real organization of social life. These perceptions and references construct personal visions of the world as well as of daily social life.[4]

National and Gendered Transgressions

In 1935, Sequeyro made her debut as producer, screenwriter, and codirector (with Ramón Peón) with the release of *Más Allá de la Muerte*, a love story about an abandoned wife, Yolanda (played by Sequeyro), her macho husband (Enrique Arenas), and her lover (Mario Tenorio), who dies tragically at the end of the film. Yolanda (probably Sequeyro's alter ego) is nothing like the conventional Mexican cinematic woman—the rejected lover or the prostitute. She is a well-educated woman, interested in the arts, who gets involved in an extramarital affair in order to find love and satisfaction.

The considerable narrative and stylistic virtues of Sequeyro's first two films, *Más Allá de la Muerte* and *La Mujer de Nadie*, were not coincidental. It was during the silent period that Sequeyro learned the secrets of directing, and she probably derived her taste for melodrama from the same source. Both films were made from the director's own scripts and based on her own creative ideas and experiences. She wrote *Más Allá de la Muerte* because she wanted to film a story about the bullfights that would offer the female perspective on both a national sport and on human betrayal. She codirected the movie with the Cuban filmmaker, Ramon Peón; however, it is clear that a feminist point of view dominates the narrative. Peón found in Adela not only an intelligent and sensitive codirector but also a filmmaker who was able to craft a movie outside of conventional discourse and with a sophisticated stylistic sense. This style is expressed all through the narrative structure, which is given an intimate feminist perspective.

Más Allá de la Muerte, read by some journalists as a "woman's poem of love," begins with a shot of a flower vase and then pans over to the protagonist, Yolanda. From the beginning, flowers become a leitmotif that, at several times during the film, is linked with Yolanda's feelings. Thus, before any details about Yolanda and her husband's personal life are revealed, we are already involved in a display of passion. When Yolanda falls in love with Eduardo, the bullfighter, she throws a handful of violets into the bullring. Indeed, there are several images of nature that represent the movement and depth of her emotions. For example, in a beautiful shot of Yolanda in her garden, she pricks her finger on a rose thorn and drops blood onto every flower petal. The bloodied flower is symbolic of both the crisis in her marriage and the final tragedy, Eduardo's death. In contrast to other conventional Mexican melodramas about extramarital relations (such as *Sagrario* or *La Prima Basilio*), Sequeyro offered a different point of view. She wanted to analyze the personal and deeply felt female motivations behind an affair. Therefore, from the moment she decides to file for divorce, Yolanda is no longer preoccupied with her social and cultural status, but with her own feelings. Ultimately, she decides that neither the husband nor the lover is enough to satisfy her life's desires.

In 1935, encouraged by ideas of collective production and with the support of a group of film technicians and the Banco de Crédito Popular, Sequeyro founded the filmmaking cooperative Exito, which produced *Más Allá de la Muerte*. Unfortunately, she was made bankrupt by its failure at the box office. Two years later, with her husband, Mario Tenorio, she founded another cooperative, Carola, in order to produce her second film, *La Mujer de Nadie*, which garnered qualified praise from some critics but was ignored by most others.

With *La Mujer de Nadie*, Sequeyro became an *auteur* and finally was allowed to reveal her creative ability as a filmmaker. It premiered on October 27 at Mexico City's Belmori Theater. In Sequeyro's own judgment, *La Mujer de Nadie* was daring for its time because it involved a "woman doing traditional men's work."[5] In an obvious progression from *Más Allá de la Muerte*, the film also celebrated woman's capacity for loving. The protagonist, played with great intensity by Sequeyro at the height of her beauty, projects feelings of equal intensity toward the three gallant bohemian artists who court her.

La Mujer de Nadie is the story of a young woman, Ana María, who escapes from an abusive stepfather and is rescued by three artists (a poet, a musician, and a painter) who all fall in love with her. This melodramatic comedy displays not only Sequeyro's vision about love but also a new kind of female character: the muse/mother who is a strong and erotic woman. With this transgressive female character, Sequeyro again inverted the classical representation of gender and reversed traditional gender roles. Ana María, the central character, is not dependent on any male desire. For example, she expresses her love to the painter; and, breaking tradition, she is the one who takes the initiative. After playing the role of muse, in another departure from tradition, she decides to abandon the artists and remain free. The setting in which the three artists and Ana María move is an imaginary nineteenth-century country where the familiar social patterns of Mexican audiences do not exist; thus, the narrative evolves within a truly fictional world. Within this symbolic strategy employed by Sequeyro, there is no representation of the nation or national identity. She imbues the rural context with an international (European) dimension, rather than a national one. Deliberately, Sequeyro transforms the dominant Mexican cinematic stereotypes that identify a romantic and idyllic rural society. The three artists

and Ana María eat bread, fruit, and soup rather than tortillas and fri-
joles. They talk about painting, music, and poetry rather than revolution or agrarian reform. And the topic of the family is not mentioned
at all.

There is no doubt that *La Mujer de Nadie* expresses a specifically
female erotic universe in strikingly modern filmic language. From the
first shots, Sequeyro anticipates her aesthetic concerns: a very slow
traveling shot from left to right introduces the male gaze and the female character's response to it. Later, as the three men are choosing
Ana María's bed, we see a wonderful view of her body's shadow projected behind a piece of cloth. The three men's faces are emphasized
in three successive close-ups, which represent different male erotic
fantasies. This suggestive gaze from the director's point of view will
be intentionally employed throughout the most important sequences
of the film and represent Sequeyro's pleasure in employing the camera as an extension of her own passionate vision. The film is therefore
a kind of visual seduction from the female perspective.

The symbolic discourse of the film is based upon two important
elements: nature and fire, both represented at the beginning and the
end and both tied to female expectations. The love of nature is discovered by Ana María when she finds in the three artists the possibility of a new life. In one scene, as Ana María and the three men
enjoy an idyllic evening walk, a fire breaks out. Here, fire symbolizes the joyous moment of passion. In contrast, fire is also the
metaphor of Ana María's death in the final scene: the three artists
throw a painting, a poem, and a musical composition into the fire as
Ana María walks off into the night. Unmistakably, from a retrospec-
tive point of view, *La Mujer de Nadie* anticipated a feminist film
discourse, and it has earned a place in the gallery of Mexican film
classics of the 1930s.

According to Carlos del Paso, in his review published in *Revista
de Revistas* (October 29, 1937), "this film may not be one of the best
films ever made, but on the other hand some of its achievements are
without precedent in national film culture: concise, well-placed dialogue, for example, which avoids bloated clichés. This film successfully navigates the jagged reefs of sentimental comedy with scenes of
good-humored mischief and without posing the least offense to
morality. With only four characters and three sets, this work comes
alive." Another critic, María Celia del Villar, writing in *El Universal
Gráfico* (October 30, 1937), used Sequeyro's film to argue her case
for women's rights as creative artists: "Due to her unflagging effort
and artistic enthusiasm, Adela Sequeyro has achieved great success
in all aspects of her chosen form of expression—as a screenwriter, as
an artistic director, and as a national screen star."

Despite economic difficulties, Sequeyro managed to direct another feature film, *Diablillos de Arrabal*, which, however, bears no resemblance to its predecessors.[6] *Diablillos de Arrabal* was clearly a thematic concession and a departure from the topics and aesthetics that had motivated Sequeyro. The film was inspired by the famous American series, *Our Gang*, released during the early 1930s by Hal Roach. Sequeyro's film narrates the adventures of two rival youth gangs who end up joining forces to defend their neighborhood from the ravages of a group of outside criminals. Sequeyro later said that she agreed on this theme as a concession to her husband and that she herself would have preferred to keep costs down by doing another film with fewer sets and a very small cast. Unfortunately, *Diablillos de Arrabal* failed at the box office. The director had to forfeit her rights to the film and was left virtually destitute.

From the 1940s to the 1960s, Sequeyro endeavored to return to the cinema by writing a number of scripts that were never filmed. Compelled to give up her filmmaking career, she returned to journalism, which she undertook through the 1950s by writing interviews, columns on local color and customs, and even bullfight reviews under the pseudonym, Perlita. The following decades buried her in ill-deserved oblivion until filmmaker Marcela Fernández Violante located her and interviewed her for a project on Mexican women film pioneers that appeared in print in 1987. Thanks to director Fernández Violante, who used various means to bring the long-forgotten contributions of pioneers such as Sequeyro and Matilde Landeta back into the public eye, Sequeyro had the satisfaction of renewed recognition late in life. She lived out her declining years in very modest conditions, under the care of her only child, Sandra, and died in Mexico City on December 24, 1992, at the age of 91.[7]

Unlike Sequeyro, Matilde Landeta has had the good fortune of receiving recognition for her life's work, thanks in large measure to her strong desire and active decision to continue her involvement with Mexican cinema up to the present.[8] Her films and other contributions have garnered extensive commentary in published interviews, documentaries, and various tributes. Landeta also reconsiders national cinematic constructions, but through a different lens than Sequeyro. In regard to Landeta's visual and narrative style, her films epitomize her desire to feminize her stories while at the same time maintaining the conventions of Mexican cinema. She works with the conventional melodramatic structure and employs allegory to construct her symbolic discourses. Her heroines, Lola Casanova and the revolutionary *coronela*, Angustias Ferrara, are quite different from Emilio Fernández's female archetypes (played by María Félix and Dolores del Río) and from Sequeyro's mythical female characters.

Landeta's women have given a new dimension to Mexican female stereotypes: they are real, strong, authentic. Lola Casanova thwarts her own sacrifice at the hands of Indians and instead becomes an active member of the community. Angustias Ferrara punishes male abusiveness and goes on to lead men in battle. These representations broke the rules in more than one sense: the female figures replace the traditional male heroes while, at the same time, the major discourses of the films represent and vocalize the social reality and subjectivity of female experience.

Like her characters, Landeta has worked within a system of gender inequity, but her representations of women are more than merely a reaction against the usual male protagonist. She looks for her own way of portraying Mexican women. In addition, her characters re-

The coronela *of the Revolution,* La Negra Angustías, *starring María Elena Márquez in the title role.*

sponded to the national project of remaking Mexican identity. With *Trotacalles* (1951), Landeta is again concerned with nation-building, which inspired both *Lola Casanova* and *La Negra Angustías*, but her third film looks at the project within an urban context of the 1950s. While it is true that *Trotacalles* reduces desire to its lowest denominator (commerce), Landeta makes it clear that for the protagonist, Azalea, being a prostitute is a question of survival. At the same time, the film demands that prostitutes change their lives without considering the ambiguity of this demand. However, Landeta's critical gaze equally condemns other women who sell themselves for money (as mistresses) or for marriage. Despite the ideological implications of some of her arguments, Landeta's female characters must be considered for the ways in which they affirm women as real, active subjects.

Landeta uses the camera to construct a context for subjects and places, rather than to produce a "personal vision." Her first two features, *Lola Casanova* and *La Negra Angustías*, are based on novels by Francisco Rojas. *Lola Casanova* can be read as an anthropological film that is contextualized within the contemporary ideal of the nation.[9] In spite of the spirit of paternalism toward the Indian that is stressed throughout the film, it is the first step in director Landeta's quest toward striking out against the representation of female subordination. Lola Casanova (played by Mercedes Barba) is the portrait of an active, urban woman who gives up her position in Mexico City in order to support Indian rights and who subsequently becomes emotionally involved with an Indian man.

La Negra Angustías takes place during the Mexican Revolution. Angustias (played by María Elena Márquez) is a *soldadera* who did not intend to join the Revolution but was forced to do so in order to escape male oppression. When she does join the military forces, she begins to exert feminist policies in the revolutionary army. For example, La Negra Angustias orders castration as the punishment for a cacique who abuses women and supports prostitutes. She falls in love with a white upper-class man and almost gives up her "revolutionary" position when he rejects her. Overcoming feelings of despair, however, she does an about-face and decides to carry on with her revolutionary principles and goals. The Angustias character is ambiguous and contradictory, a kind of sexless person, an incarnation of the radical feminist position drawn from populist discourse. However, in this revolutionary melodrama, the social position of the Angustias character breaks away from the typical female cinematic representation: she is not merely a moral.

In most of the Mexican revolutionary films, the female image is placed within the context of national discourse. In this film, Angustias is thrust into a public place rather than a private one, the home. She does not represent the purity of woman but, rather, her own race and dignity. She does not belong to any formal family structure because she is an orphan. Given her race and class, her education takes place in the practical, rural conditions of life. Her world offers the possibility of being different, a *soldadera*. Yet Angustias is not the typical *soldadera* who marches behind or beside her man as his lover, nurse, or cook. Angustias becomes the *coronela*, or colonel, and the men serve under or beside her. In charge, she gives the orders and commands the respect of her army.

Trotacalles, a prostitute melodrama, is another film about gender. However, in terms of narrative structure, this film differed from Landeta's previous two features because of its formal attributes and creative discoveries within the world of the urban prostitutes of Mexico City. The main character (Elda Peralta) is again the redeeming subject, in opposition to the other principal characters. In parallel stories of two sisters, the prostitute and the married woman, *Trotacalle*s is a subtle and corrosive criticism of the dominant patriarchal society. This film, in the opinion of critic Jorge Ayala Blanco, "is more than a curious example of historic interest. It is an antecedent of future filmmaking, and it introduces a clear feminist perspective in cinema."[10]

After more than forty years, Landeta returned to the craft of filmmaking with the 1992 feature, *Nocturno a Rosarío*. This costume drama is based on the life and times of the well-known romantic poet Manuel Acuña, who committed suicide in 1873 at the young age of twenty-four. Landeta re-creates the life of the poet (played by the Spanish actor, Simon Guevara) through the eyes of three women: the aristocratic Rosarío de la Peña (Ofelia Medina), the poetess Laura Méndez (Evangelina Sosa), and the laundress Soledad (Patricia Reyes Spíndola). Though the period reconstruction of the film is beautiful, the camera placement lacks imagination and creativity. The narrative structure aims for the correct historical and reverential look, but the story and its characters never are able to achieve any depth.

Divergence and convergence define the relations between Sequeyro's and Landeta's films. Their productions are dissimilar in narrative and aesthetic dimensions, but both of their discourses involve a subjective searching for a new cinematic identity. In all of their films, symbolic constructions are developed through female characters as social and active subjects. Their feminist proposals transgress and contradict, in different ways, the dominant image of woman from a very personal gaze. Sequeyro's lyricism looked toward the visual pleasure of the female's erotic world, while Landeta's allegory seeks a new feminine historical dimension.

Notes

1. Alan Touraine, *Critica de la modernidad* (México: FCE, 1995), 345–46.

2. Eduardo de la Vega Alfaro and Patricia Torres San Martín, *Adela Sequeyro* (México: Universidad de Guadalajara-Universidad de Veracruz, 1997), 13–34.

3. In January 1935, President Lázaro Cárdenas signed a new agreement with the film industry, giving impetus for the creation of a cooperative.

4. Pierre Bourdieu, "La dominación masculina," *La Ventana* (Guadalajara) No. 3 (1996): 8–95.

5. See Vega Alfaro and Torres San Martín, *Sequeyro*, 13–34.

6. This film was lost until 1992. In spite of its restoration, it is still not complete.

7. Since 1993, Sequeyro's films have been screened in several international and national film forums.

8. Landeta is still working at the Cinematography Labor Union.

9. Roger Bartra, *La jaula de la melancolía: Identidad y metamorfosis del mexicano* (México: Ed. Grijalvo, 1987).

10. Jorge Ayala Blanco, "Feminisimus, Matilde Landeta: Nosotros te amamos," *Siempre* (México), July 23, 1975, Suplemento cultural.

4

Cantinflas and Tin Tan
Mexico's Greatest Comedians

Carlos Monsiváis

Mexico City, Tuesday, April 20, 1993: the apotheosis. The funeral lasts three days and is divided between Félix Cuevas's Gayosso agency, the ANDA, and the Palacio de las Bellas Artes. A quarter of a million people march in front of the coffin and form lines along Alameda Street, oblivious to the rain. The press, radio, and television offer the deceased an unusual amount of space and time. There are also displays of mourning in Spain and in Latin America. President Carlos Salinas de Gortari intones: "He is gone; however, he will continue to live in the memory and in the hearts of all Mexicans." Declarations vary from the exaltations of newspaper headlines: "Mexico weeps," "The sky also wept," to the beatific proclamation of the Archdiocese of Mexico: "His death should be considered a triumphal birth of eternal life." There are unexpected praises such as the one from Carlos Fuentes: "Through Cantinflas, the people of Latin America began to laugh at their politicians because they spoke like him, a man who was almost an opposition party . . . laughter has left this country and now we're all crying, but we should not suffer because now he rests. And up there, he's making those who went before us laugh." There is an announcement of the arrival of the remains at the Rotonda de los Hombres Ilustres (which, as it is told to us, he did not want). The *cantinflomanía* is reactivated with special shows. The police, firefighters, shoeshiners, people in mourning—the procession is extraordinary and ends at the Spanish Cemetery.

People march in an orderly fashion. Banners can be seen: "Good-bye. . . . Chato," and prayers: "May God keep him in his glory." There is no lack of children and adults dressed up as Cantinflas. The president of Peru, Alberto Fujimori, says: "A great loss: he knew how to criticize without bitterness and create humor

without acidity." Gabriel García Márquez is emphatic: "I, like no
one else, enjoyed Cantinflas's movies. In my life, I have never seen
a greater tribute, more felt and more deserved." The phrases accu-
mulate: "He is now in Heaven with Pedro, and on Earth he's with
us!" Pedro is, needless to say, *Pedro* [Armendáriz], an actor who at
his death in 1957 caused the largest outpouring of sentimentality
given by any country or by Mexico City to any one person. So, in
conversations the comparisons are made: "What's the burial of the
century? Who attracted more people?" The difference, according to
some, lies in the emotional level, sharper and overflowing for
Pedrito, more discreet with Mario—with Don Mario, as he is already being called, in a new mark of respect to a national symbol.

"Mario, you left. Cantinflas, you remain to tell my grandchildren
about everything you filmed." Faintings, a multitude of people with
flowers in their hands, people of the trades he sometimes represented
(postal workers, shoeshiners, priests, merchants, newspaper hawkers,
janitors, diplomats, movie extras, police officers). "Number 777, present." Tens of thousands of photographic and video cameras, a flood of
tape recorders. Secretary of Protection and Transport René
Monterrubio López maintains that "Don Mario continues to be not
only an honorary member, but also a very distinguished member of
the Police Force of the Federal District. With his 777 character, he did
a great favor to police officers. Without a doubt, he contributed to giving dignity to the police, and we will continue with his example."

The cremation lasts three hours. People wait. He dictated his own
epitaph: "It seems like he's gone, but it's not true."

The Tents

Mario Moreno Reyes is born on August 12, 1911, in Mexico City in
the Santa María la Redonda neighborhood, the son of Pedro Moreno
Esquivel and Soledad Reyes. In 1930 he works in the *carpa* (small
tents of traveling circus-like groups) of Sotelo de Azcapozalco. In
1933 he acts in the Valentina *carpa*, and on October 15, 1936, he debuts in the Folies Bergère Theater. In the tents he is a boxer ("Chato
Moreno"), a gofer, a mailman, an apprentice to a bullfighter, and a
dancer of the Charleston: "And the things of life . . . ! Right . . . ?
What are we to do . . . ! I had to earn a living. Because those who
don't earn a living, lose it. And since it's better to win than to lose, I
became a comedian, and . . . That's the will of God . . . ! I wish that
I had not dedicated myself to something else . . . ! because if not, I
would have wanted to become a government representative, and . . .
well, . . . what for?"

Cantinflas is a notorious product of circumstances, as he likes to describe himself to those who live in the central areas of the capital in the 1930s and who make mischief their strategy of urban exploration. Balancing between a joke and pretentiousness (between the love of improvisation and amazement in the presence of virtuosity) is the technique that he uses to infiltrate and become rooted in the city that, though not entirely provincial, ceases to be fundamentally provincial. In the *carpas*, where the goodwill of the spectator takes charge of the continuity and the rhythm of the show, Cantinflas reveals the intelligence and the abilities of the marginalized urban populations. According to a legend that he agrees with, a young Mario Moreno, overwhelmed by stage fright, once, in the Ofelia *carpa*, forgets his original monologue. He begins to say what comes to mind in a complete emancipation of phrases and words, and what comes to mind is an incoherent brilliance. His assistants recite his attack on syntax, and Mario becomes aware of it: destiny has placed in his hands the distinctive characteristic, the style that is the manipulation of chaos. Weeks later, the name that will mark the invention is invented. Someone, taken in by the nonsense, screams: "Cuanto inflas!" [C'ntinflas] (You're annoying!) or "En la cantina inflas!" (You become egotistical in the barroom). The contraction catches on and becomes the proof of baptism that the character needs. It is no longer important to know if this really happened this way. When speaking of the origins of legends, what is probable is what is real.

According to Ricardo Pérez Escamilla, Cantinflas's image, without a doubt, originates in caricature—not only in his most obvious inspiration, *Aventuras de Chupamirto*, by Rodolfo Acosta, but in the unfinished aspect, the exaltation of the fleeting outline that is the character's substance. He not only comes from the *carpas*, but he is also the product of the common things that move from caricature to real life, from parody to sentimental profundity. And this image persists, regardless of whether Cantinflas changes his outfit or moves away from the image of the *pelado*.* The public, whether or not it follows the development of the character, remembers the original myth. There is only one Cantinflas, the immobile dancer of the neighborhoods. Other variations are appreciated but are basically not taken into account.

Let us consider "dialectical relationships" in the *carpa*. *Thesis*: the comical or musical interpretation; *antithesis*: the famous affec-

---

*"*Pelado*" was a term invented to describe a certain class of urban "bum" in Mexico in the 1920s. According to philosopher Samuel Ramos, "the *pelado* belongs to the lowest of social categories, and represents the human detritus of the big city." See Ramos, *Profile of Man and Culture*, trans. Peter C. Earle (Austin: University of Texas Press, 1962).

tions of the mother; *synthesis*: the applause that forgives or rewards. Here, the humor does not need constructed phrases, and improvisation is counterbalanced with corporal discipline, the mimicry that is an instant translation of what has not been pronounced, and a bravado that, to some, is irreverence. Cantinflas teams up with Estanislao Shilinsky, goes from the Ofelia to the Sotelo and Valentina *carpas*, and marries Valentina.

Recall the sequences of *Aguila o Sol*, the only visual testimony of the *carpa* days. Cantinflas and Manuel Medel converse:

> MEDEL: And what angers me the most is the way you treat the police. That's the reason why you always get taken away. When the officer arrived, instead of saying "Sir, this is a street fight," when he said, "Come with me," what did you say?
>
> CANTINFLAS: You're not my type. (Laughter)
>
> MEDEL: There's the problem, sir.
>
> CANTINFLAS: So if a man says "Come with me," only because I go with him. . . .
>
> MEDEL: If it's a figure of authority, one must go with him wherever, anywhere.
>
> CANTINFLAS: Wait, you as an authority. Let's make believe that you're an authority. Why do you have a need for that? (Laughter).

The "other classes" admit how funny an outcast can be when he cannot help himself. But this is a socializing inducement, and in the Cantinflas of the first phase—and the testimonies abound—the determining factor is the leap from marginality to the forefront. What is discovered in the laughter is that the language is also a treasure chest from which everyone takes what he can, and meanings will come later. Cantinflas does not assign, nor can he assign, sense to his nonsense or to what he says without speaking. In this sense, I venture into the hypothesis: the determining context of the first Cantinflas is the nation's reigning illiteracy: the 70 percent of the population in 1930 who could not read. Later, while moralizing, Cantinflas will dedicate a movie to this subject (*El Analfabeto*), but during the emergence of his character, illiteracy is the perfect context. Cantinflas is the illiterate who takes control of the language by whatever means he can.

The first spectators, still subjects of *peladaje* or already installed in the monotony of the living room, the kitchen, and the bedroom, admire the comedian's demeanor, the quickness with which he hits it off with strangers, the language that does not go anywhere but seems to be everywhere, the victory over his neighbors unarmed in the presence of his verbosity and subdued by his passion. In his struggle for articulation, Cantinflas surrenders to facial and verbal expressions (autobiographical flashes): the eyebrows interrogate, the arms rest at his sides, and the body moves to the autonomous quality of the words. A feat of nonsense, the verb (the infinite verbosity) of Cantinflas reveals a double tactic: joking can also be an audible trap, and the attacks of nonsense liberate us from the jail of language.

Cantinflas is the shrewd version of the *peladito* (who, lacking even a hide, owns nothing and takes nothing)—cynical, inoffensive, and tender, one of the historical representations of the urban pariah. The *peladito*, according to Cantinflas, is the creature who came from the *carpas* with a face stained with flour or white paint, dressed in rags, the pants below the waist and covered with patches, the belt replaced by an old tie, the peaked cap representing a hat, the ruffled underwear that shows at any provocation, the torn shirt, and *gabardine* across his left shoulder—at that time, the emblem of the porters in the markets. Thus, Cantinflas in the 1930s is a fugitive of sordidness and beggary, the generous rogue who is emancipated from everything: from verbal logic, from social constraints, from the simplest explanation of his presence in the world, from the respectability granted his walk that like a *danzón*. His is the reign of the popular class, whose sudden visibility is equal to a miraculous apparition. Brashness is the only variety of impunity within reach of the poor.

The Theater

If the entertainers of the *carpas* are persuasive enough, they move on from there to popular theater, and then, however they can, they go into cinema. Such is the career path of Leopoldo Chato Ortín, Cantinflas, Manuel Medel, Adalberto Martínez Resortes, and Jesús Martínez Palillo. In the Folies Bergère Theater, Cantinflas, wanting to take control of the situation, complies with a new imperative: the political joke, mislaid or eliminated in the *carpas* among a flood of gleeful obscenities. And due to the double effort of politics and the opinion of intellectuals, there appears the term *cantinflismo*—an interpretation from the outside that pretends to give something a fixed sense that it would usually not admit to.

The birth of *cantinflismo* can almost be given an exact date. In 1937, Luis N. Morones, director of the CROM political party, calls the leader of the CTM, Vicente Lombardo Toledano, a "traitor, coward, trembling weakling, and Niño Fidencio of Teziutlán." Lombardo answers with disdain: "If Morones has decided to show his dialectical prowess, let him argue with Cantinflas." Aroused by that which does not require a response, Cantinflas for the first time admits the direction of his humor and the meaning of his speech that makes no sense:

The first thing I did was think of going to see Lombardo to ask him what his purpose was . . . but then I thought. . . . Well, no! because thinking about it, right, he couldn't have chosen anyone better than me to solve the solution to the problem . . . because, like I said, naturally, if he can't solve anything and he talks so much, the same thing happens to me, and I never get anywhere. . . .

Ah!, but let me make one thing clear, I have moments of lucidity, and I speak very clearly. And now I will speak with clarity. . . . Friends! There are moments in life that are really momentary. . . . And it's not because one says it, but we must see it! What do we see? that's what we must see . . . because, what a coincidence, friends, that supposing that in the case— let's not say what it could be—but we must think about it and understand the psychology of life to make an analogy of the synthesis of humanity. Right? Well, that's the point!

Cantinflismo goes into action—now no longer the torrent of the *carpa*, but its articulated elaboration. During the Lázaro Cárdenas presidency, the Left is in power, and its passionately demagogic and redemptory language lends itself amazingly well to Cantinflas's transformation through the accumulation of words. To mock proletariat discourse from glorious senselessness is easy for someone who has been trained in nonsense. Cantinflas replies to the question, "What has been your most important theatrical interpretation?" (*Excelsior*, October 20, 1938):

Let's take things one at a time. You ask me what's been my most important interpretation? And I would have to respond that . . . ? What do I have to respond to you? Or do you respond to me? Well, what kind of game is this? OK, Let's do this again: You want me to tell you what has been, is, and will be, through the coming of the historical, materialistic, and dialectical time, the best of my proletariat interpretations. And I believe, up to a certain point, and if not, still, because you know that, even if, and still if, the best of all my interpretations has been the national and exact interpretations of the universe according to Article III. . . . What? Not that? . . . Well, what are you talking about?

The acoustic bravado engendered in the *carpa* finds its ideal, and, up to a certain point, unexpected, mirror: the revolutionary nationalism of Marxist influence. Cantinflas, himself a creature of word mania, suddenly sees his actions explained: it is satire, it is parody, it is a criticism of the government and of its leaders. Before the attack, Cantinflas accepts what is said about him: "But let it be clear that I have moments of lucidity, and I speak very clearly." Whatever his initial purpose, the struggle to take possession of the codes of language, the "theft" of words of those who fit the bill of he who hears without understanding, the mere rapture in the presence of the sounds—the analyses of Cantinflas describe his purpose as a critique of political jargon. Salvador Novo supports this trend to signification: "In condensing them (the leaders of the world and of Mexico), in the giving back to the healthy laughter of the people the demagogic state of their empty confusion, merit is sustained and glory is ensured for the self-contained son of the Spanish-speaking mocker of Mexico, who is Cantinflas."

(In *Nueva Grandeza Mexicana*): During his first years in Mexico, Victor Serge describes in April 1944 "the natural self-assurance of the poor synthetic devil to whom everything happens because nothing is worth anything. The only trait that he owes to the Mexican revolutions is a certain feeling of his dignity: he doesn't have any inferiority complexes, he's not humiliated like the comic characters of Chekhov" (Quoted in *Carnets*, 1965). At best, such a trait of spiritual sufficiency is typical of the popular comedians, who, more than rebellious, are deaf and blind to the furies of classicism and establish their resistance through joking.

Between 1936 and 1938, Cantinflas becomes the emblem of the metropolis, indispensable to magazine covers, collaborator, "animator of all Mexico," wandering essence of the people, promoter of a self-deprecating sense of humor: "I was always particular to journalism. I would sell about ten *Gráficos* without counting the ones that my buddies would steal." In the Folies Bergère Theater in Garibaldi Plaza, Cantinflas is required in a double bill. "It's as if Cantinflas were, more than anyone, the Mexican dictator of optimism. The city pays close attention to what he says when, from the stage of the theater, he flirts with politics as if he were the most experienced politician. He becomes a leader and a proletariat, with only a change of a hat or a phrase" (Miguel del Río, *Vea*, September 9, 1938). Such a formidable comic vein needs interpreters, and the interpreters modify the nature of the discovery. And the verb *cantinflear* becomes a synonym for incomprehensible speech as it will be authorized in the catalogs of the Academia de la Lengua.

The Movies

The step to the movies is hardly natural. After his disregarded debut in an inauspicious film, *No te Engañes Corazón* (1936, Miguel Contreras Torres), Cantinflas, in one of his first three appearances with Medel, makes *Así es Mi Tierra* (1936, Arcady Boytler), a rural comedy in which the *peladito* is completely out of place. He is not, nor can he be, a peasant who lives on a communal farm. Now it is his responsibility to watch the new urban sensibility, made up of shoves and hypocritical submissions of sentimentality and malice, of a dizziness in speech, and of a jive that substitutes for a lack of expression. That is why his first great opportunity, *Aguila o Sol* (1937, Arcady

Boytler), is, I believe, Cantinflas's movie *par excellence*—not the best, but the one that best expresses the essence of the character, described in its essentialness: a product of the people who can only be a product of the people, the *peladito* whose charm is all the autobiography that he is permitted. Impatiently, Cantinflas moves quickly through melodramatic situations and delights in that which is his: the convoluted monologue, the dancing, the confused look that is both mockery and perplexity. In 1939, Chano Urueta directs him in *El Signo de la Muerte* with a story by Salvador Novo and music by Silvestre Revueltas. The plot—an "Aztec" detective comedy—does not prevent Cantinflas from completely expressing himself: he plays to bewilderment, gives life to verbal inertia, and fully immerses himself in the transvestite act.

Publicity photo for the film El Bolero de Raquel, *directed by Miguel Delgado.*

There is still something missing for the absolute metamorphosis, however, and Cantinflas lives on the edge between self-criticism and the mocking that surrounds it. Success is considerable. In 1939, Cantinflas establishes Posa Films, producing shorts. Fernando Rivera directs him in *Siempre Listo en las Tinieblas* (1939), *Jengibre contra Dinamita* (1939), *Cantinflas Boxeador* (1940), and *Cantinflas Ruletero* (1940), while Carlos Toussaint is responsible for *Cantinflas y Su Prima*. At that moment, Cantinflas captures the enthusiasm of all classes and all ages. And in 1940, Juan Bustillo Oro directs him in

Ahí Está el Detalle, with Joaquín Pardavé, Sofía Alvárez, and Dolores Camarillo "Fraustita." If the *carpa* and the frivolous theater are the perfect sets for the legend of Mexico City, *Ahí Está el Detalle* deploys Cantinflas throughout the rest of Mexico and in Latin America. More than the storyline, a contrived adaptation of boulevard theater, I believe that the comedy of *Ahí Está el Detalle* rests in the "insolence" of Cantinflas (his presence in the world, his capacity to have a psychological rapport with anyone), who arranges crazy and circuitous speech, the improbable aspect that transfers the circus to the street and moves the character from one difficulty to another guided by an instinct for chaos—not the chaos of Laurel and Hardy or Buster Keaton, where objects collide on their way to the abyss, or the chaos of elementary forces pursuing comedians, but the other chaos, the one where words have no meaning, clothing is ragged, situations that are simple are not understood, and an incomprehensible speech is worth as much as the suspicion of adultery and criminal conjectures.

El Gendarme Desconocido (1941, Miguel M. Delgado), is the story of a police officer, Badge Number 777, who takes possession of a visible symbol of authority (not one from afar but that which is the most common), in order to subvert it. Through Cantinflas, delirium penetrates the group; it contaminates chiefs of police and judges. He infiltrates dance floors and police stations and is award-winning in his profusion of errors. Notwithstanding the deficiencies of the film's rhythm and of its plot, the energy of Cantinflas mobilizes the sphere of popular representations in his favor. From that moment on (and film history so demonstrates), Cantinflas is a mobile symbol of the lower classes, the *peladito* who can be anything under the condition that he refuses a change of status. Without freeing himself completely from his days in the *carpa* (he never really will), Cantinflas becomes a direct interlocutor with the camera.

In 1941, Alejandro Galindo directs him in *Ni Sangre ni Arena*, a movie about bullfighting where Cantinflas and Fernando Soto "Mantequilla" complement each other and the mimicry reaches new, classic heights. Around that time, a permanent team is formed composed of Miguel M. Delgado, director, and Jaime Salvador, scriptwriter, with the occasional help of Carlos León, a professional comedy writer who contributes to many of the scripts that Cantinflas stars in from the 1940s onward. In 1942, there are three movies: *Los Tres Mosqueteros*, *El Circo* (a direct or indirect tribute to Charlie Chaplin), and *Romeo y Julieta*. For the first time, newspaper critics respond to the very poor quality of these parodies. In an unusual reaction that would never be repeated, Cantinflas criticizes himself, though not without reprimanding the press: "*Romeo y Julieta* might have been a bad movie with great mistakes in the acting, but to us, it represented a great effort and many sacrifices. Nevertheless, false criticism, which believes it has something to gain, only concerned itself with mentioning the mistakes of the movie and never talked about its good points. It forgot about its awesome presentation." (Quoted in *Historia documental del cine mexicano* by Emilio García Riera, volume II, 1970).

In those years, this thesis is not disputed: Cantinflas is the creator of a child-like taste for comedy, the one who teaches children how to laugh at the stupidities of the adults. In regard to comedy, his more conventional traits are saved by the timing of both his body and his speech. The character—what is known about him, what is expected of him—makes forgivable any ineptitude in his films, whose sketches reveal elementary plots in which Cantinflas, man of the people, falls in love with a humble young girl while, behind his back, some malicious men make fun of his gullibility only to be struck by his unexpected astuteness. This same theme runs though the movies directed by Miguel M. Delgado: *Un Día con el Diablo* (1945), *Soy un Prófugo* (1946), *A Volar Joven* (1947), *El Supersabio* (1948), *El Mago* (1948), *Puerta Joven* (1949), *El Siete Machos* (1950), *El Bombero Atómico* (1950), *Si Yo Fuera Diputado* (1951), and *El Señor Fotógrafo* (1952).

Cantinflas squanders himself and is, without fail, the "primitive," with the delirious ingeniousness that always inexplicably conforms to the educational process of the country. And, in every movie, the story acquires a strange cohesiveness after getting lost on the way— the danced bravados, the answering back that does not stop, the creations sculpted in a vacuum, the exits that the public memorizes: "Accompany me/ Let him accompany? I don't have a guitar." The *peladito* slowly disappears. In *Si Yo Fuera Diputado*, the sermon appears, with the warnings that will plague the work of Cantinflas from then on. "You are not ready to know it, nor am I ready to tell you."

Image: The Proteus of One Shape

Thanks to the movies, the image of Cantinflas becomes essential to what is popular. Rufino Tamayo paints him as the *peladito* in the cosmos; and at regional fairs and in toy stores, hundreds of thousands of figures represent him in clay, wood, lead, and, later, in plastic. From the 1930s on, Cantinflas is a comical bullfighter, and his success is uneven. In the bullring, he is the clown, the *peladito* who ends up being an apology for the stupid cruelty of the "art of bullfighting." He boasts about one of his basic duties: ". . . but what creates a loss of control is blowing air, and I found out why the bull blows air. The bull blows (in the good sense of the word) because as it is logical to understand . . . , at the moment of executing the mentioned verb, he feels air, and since he is looking for the bulge (*bulto*), he must think, 'If I blow, and this is the point, I'll make him cold, and it'll be easier to grab him.' That's why, after he has fallen, he doesn't blow air anymore."

In the 1940s and 1950s the character reaches his highest point. The presidents of the country look for and celebrate him. The press flatters and praises him in order to better demean him. Theories are built around him about the humanism of mimicry, and he is favorably compared to Chaplin. The so-called guarantee of comedy is such that, as soon as he is introduced on stage, laughter instantly erupts, in gratitude for past and future laughter. And the movies—one or two per year—overwhelm the Spanish-speaking world, where the references to everyday life are understood as satire, and where even some notice the potential "surrealism" of serious reasoning. The name of Cantinflas can be seen on presidential ballots, and his fame grows as a philanthropist and as a man of the people for now and forever.

Moreover, reputation in Latin America is totalizing, as proved by an unexpected film buff, Cuba's Commander Fidel Castro, in an interview by Tomás Borge:

> BORGE: If you had to chose a literary author as your favorite author, who would it be?
>
> CASTRO: Cervantes.
>
> BORGE: You said it without a doubt?
>
> CASTRO: I don't have any doubts because at that time, literary techniques didn't exist and what Cervantes wrote, for its theme, its beauty and its content—*Don Quixote*—I've read about five or six times, at least. The same thing happens to me with Cantinflas's movies. I can watch them every two to three years, and they seem new to me. Because Cantinflas's movies have no plot, they're about a character who can't be any more likable, then I can see them again, and the way of speaking, the nonsense that he says, make me laugh. I can watch a Cantinflas movie more than once, and in three years, I can watch it again. Just like Chaplin's movies, but Chaplin's movies have content, that's the difference.

The phenomenon is unique: the apparent lack of communication is a technique of multiple germinations and localization so that "exotic" becomes international. And for the Chicanos, Cantinflas is a fundamental symbol.

Between 1944 and 1948 a group led by Mario Moreno, Jorge Negrete, and Gabriel Figueroa considers the formation of labor unions in the film industry as essential; not independent from the government—at that time inconceivable—but only heirs of the existing trade groups. The leading labor union, the Workers' Union of the Film Industry (STIC), reacted with anger and repudiated the efforts by the National Association of Actors (ANDA) and of the Workers' Union of Film Production (STPC). Figueroa describes the Cantinflas of those times:

> The worst part of the dispute (over the control of union representation) happened in front of President Avila Camacho, and it ended up becoming a spectacle. Because of a meeting called by the President himself, both sides of the controversy got together. What was euphemistically called the "presidential commendation," which in reality turned out to be a permanent bruise for the cinema, was going to be signed that day. It was a deceitful invention to calm things down in an underhanded way. It was conjured up by an army of lawyers. The consignment: to leave happy the STIC organization and, if possible, the STPC of the RM (Workers Union of Cinematographic Production of Mexico). The ceremony lasted three hours. Once the commendation was signed, Avila Camacho, who was a very solemn man, began to speak: "I will now ask both parties to work in harmony for the good of the Mexican cinema. And I want you to know that I care about both parties just the same." That's when things started to happen. Cantinflas jumped up and said: "I'm embarrassed about what's happening, I will find work outside of Mexico. I don't accept what has just been said here. Mr. President, how can you care the same for that bunch of crooks as you do for this group of honest workers?" And after saying this, he rapidly moved to the door. Avila Camacho snapped out of his surprise and screamed, "Mario, come here!" I managed to stop Cantinflas. I tried to explain that his outburst, in spite of its moral justification, could have disastrous consequences for the conflict we were trying to solve, and provoke problems for everyone. Mario looked at me, and he seemed to understand. We went to the President, who, more than ever, was the image of paternal kindness—chubby and smiling—and said: "Mario, I'm going to punish you for offending the President of Mexico." "Yes, sir," answered Mario. "Are you going to accept my punishment?" "Yes, sir," he repeated.
>
> The entire room was attentive to what was happening. Avila Camacho commanded like Solomon: "You will invite these men to lunch," and he motioned to the STIC group. Cantinflas, very serious, didn't say anything. "I'll pay," said the President, jokingly. Then, Cantinflas took in a breath and said: "I won't accept that either. I will not sit down and eat with these crooks." All hell broke loose. We left in the middle of this uncontrollable confusion. This incident was never published. (Alberto Isaac, *Conversaciones con Gabriel Figueroa*).

The Tears in the "Garment"

In 1953, with the scandal still resonating, Cantinflas inaugurates the Teatro de los Insurgentes with *Yo Colón*. In 1952 the owner of the theater, José María Dávila, asks Diego Rivera, the Communist painter, for a mural, and Diego places Cantinflas, already converted into the irrefutable incarnation of the "Mexican," in the middle of his sketch. Diego describes his project, which will represent the theater in Mexican history:

> In order to immediately establish the theme of the mural and the purpose of the building, I painted in the middle of the lower side a large head with a mask with two very feminine hands wearing delicate evening gloves made out of lace. I covered the rest with scenes of different plays that reflect the history of Mexico before the Conquest to the present time, meeting in the middle with a drawing of Cantinflas, the Mexican genius of popular farce, asking the rich for money, and giving it to the poor, like he does in reality.

He had barely finished sketching the outline, when someone finds the Virgin of Guadalupe in the mural. "Immediately," remembers Rivera, "all hell broke loose. It was considered blasphemy to connect something so low—like a comedy character—with something so sacred as the Virgin." Very probably, the intention of God was to equate Cantinflas with Juan Diego and make Cantinflas's rag the new site of the apparitions of the Virgin, but the protests keep him from doing so. The most important archbishop in Mexico, Luis María Martínez, is upset: "This new audacity by Diego Rivera offends the Catholic feelings of the Mexican people, and it constitutes an insult to religion because it attacks an image like the Virgin of Guadalupe, who is an object of the national cult."

In his excellent chronicle of the Teatro de los Insurgentes, Vicente Leñero describes the scandal: The Partido Acción Nacional (PAN) and several Catholic institutions protest. Dávila declares that all religious beliefs should be respected: "Diego was not looking to represent the Indian Juan Diego in Cantinflas. If Cantinflas is in the mural, it is because of his indisputable significance in the art of the modern Mexican theater." Cantinflas defends himself and asserts that if Diego offended the Virgin in his mural, he would not permit any of his movies to be shown in any theater: "No one can ever take my medallion of the Virgin or make fun of my reverence and love." Diego recalls:

> When Cantinflas saw my sketch, he was completely satisfied. He even posed with me in the scaffold next to the place where I had sketched the Virgin so that some photographers could take pictures. He was next to me showing his medallion with pride. . . . Because I had the support of Cantinflas, the press was on my side, saying that there was nothing contradictory between Cantinflas and the Virgin of Guadalupe. Cantinflas was an artist who symbolized the Mexican people, and the Virgin was the flag of his faith. A great number of people subscribed to this interpretation. But that wasn't enough to stop the agitation over my painting. In reality, it was

organized by a band of ruffians led by professional extortionists who
claimed to be strong supporters of the faith.

The protest continues; Dávila and Cantinflas panic, Diego gives in
and does not paint the Virgin, thus "giving friends and enemies, false
and true, an opportunity. Making this sudden change, I have to con-
fess, didn't make me happy." But Diego gets away with it in his own
way: among the holes of Cantinflas's rags, the outline of the Virgin
of Guadalupe remains sketched.

Colón's Egg: Which Came First,
the Admiration or the Applause?

On April 30, 1953, the Teatro de los Insurgentes was inaugurated in a
gala event with *Yo Colón*, with Cantinflas leading the cast of eighty
actors and demanding one thousand pesos per night (close to one
hundred dollars), a very high salary for those times. Cantinflas does
not welcome the directing of Seki Sano, a director of avant garde theater; he gives stage credit to Ernesto Finance, and as usual directs
himself. He employs two of his permanent writers, Alfredo Robledo
and Carlos León, for the sketches, not because he plans to follow
their scripts but because they can help him with his improvisations.
Cantinflas, product of the popular theater, switches jokes every night
depending on the news and on his whims.

The titles of the scenes indicate the comedy of *Yo Colón*: "1900:
Colón in the time of Porfirio Díaz"; "1953: Colón, a member of the
PRI, presides over the Spring Festival"; "Football will speak for my
race"; "Musical coeducation"; "For a society with classes . . . of
history"; "Open, pair of kings"; "Party in the court"; "Land! . . . for
filling pots"; "In the empire of monopolies"; "Offering to the gods
(or, for that matter, I'll ask for my handout)"; "The Indian throughout history"; "Christopher, get up and pull!"; "Tribute to the
Huehuenche race"; and so forth. Comedy taken directly from the
frivolous theater is always on the spur of the moment; and in a
world repressed politically and socially, a lot depends on the power
of allusions. In an example taken from a story by Leñero,
Cantinflas-Colón meets a North American who asks him, "How can
I get to Moneda (coin) Street?" Cantinflas replies: "Walk by Casas
Alemán Avenue (regent of the Federal District during the Alemán
presidency), then through a street called Miguel Alemán (then president of Mexico). Next, you need to continue through Amargura (bitterness) in order to get to Sonrisal (Alemán's nickname), where you
will find the Moneda (coin)." The North American refuses to go
through the Amargura (bitterness), and Cantinflas-Colón then says,

"Well, what can we say after having gone through it for six years?" Another time, Cantinflas-Colón finds in his nautical blueprints the map of the great Tenochtitlán and exclaims: "The great Tenochtitlán that Miguel Alemán dominated. . . . Oh, no! The domino is the one that follows: Ruis Corti . . . Cortinas. . . . But this is very old. We must find him in the chapter about the pharaohs."

Movie still of Germán Váldez "Tin Tan" and Yolanda Montes "Tongolele" from the film Calabacitas Tiernas, *directed by Gilberto Martínez Solares.*

Kitsch choreography and scenery, flags of America, twirlers, fencers, and Cantinflas in the middle, the triumphant *peladito* among people loyal to Porfirio Díaz, townspeople, cadets, school girls, football players, sailors. . . . The criticism is very flattering, with political reservations. Armando de María y Campo asks himself why the jokes against the government of the recently deceased Miguel Alemán are so different from the praises that Mario Moreno offered during Alemán's presidency. The businessman Dávila excuses himself ("the ironies spoken at the Teatro de los Insurgentes are completely foreign to my way of thinking"), and even Cantinflas—reacting to the negative campaign that follows him throughout the entire presentation of *Yo Colón*—is forced to reply:

> I'm happy to know that there are people like the aforementioned, who appreciate the individual effort that one does in unison. But then, there you have it, Mister Director, there's no lack of individuals who are not happy, who, without apparent reason, appear to be what they are not and even call themselves reporters, when I have seen them closely; and, frankly, they don't justify such a respectable profession. As I was telling you, sir, these individuals without their own individuality, who even fall back on anonymity, have attacked me in order to see what they can get out of it, and have only shown their morality and the interests that they pursue because I think that everything they say about me is not really necessary. What's needed more is to know everything that can be said about them, and frankly, I'm too busy discovering America and not in discovering individuals who only discover themselves, when the police don't discover them first—like in the case of the blackmailer who had distributed some flyers that didn't have an address, and in those who worry themselves with wondering if I was a proletariat or a boss (*Mañana* magazine, June 1953).

The decision to abandon the stage does not agree with him. He, like others of his generation, needs the conflictive dialogue with the public that compensates for the insulation or distancing of the movies.

Laughter Is the Comfort of Humanity

In his third film phase, beginning in the 1950s, Cantinflas slowly accepts, in his attitude and in his movies, what is said about him. Moreno now thoroughly believes himself to be Cantinflas. The comedy decreases, solemnity takes precedence, and messages abound. Miguel M. Delgado lets him do what he wants in *Caballero a la Medida* (1953), *Abajo el Telón* (1954), *El Bolero de Raquel* (1956), *Sube y Baja* (1958), *El Analfabeto* (1960), *El Extra* (1962), *Entrega Inmediata* (1963), *El Padrecito* (1964), *El Señor Doctor* (1965), *Su Excelencia* (1966), *Por Mi Pistolas* (1968), *Un Quijote sin Mancha* (1969), and *El Profe* (1970). In this parade of movies, all identical, only two directors interrupt Delgado's monopoly: *Ama a Tu Prójimo* (1958), a melodrama by Tulio Demicheli; and *Don Quijote Cabalga de Nuevo* (1971) by Roberto Gavaldón, another attempt to make Cantinflas the center of classical humanism. *El Padrecito* and *Su Excelencia* overflow with sermons; they are sad or melancholy like *Conserje en Condominio* (1973), *El Ministro y Yo* (1975), and in *El Patrullero 777* (1977), with the impossible return to the vehemence of *El Gendarme Desconocido*.

In 1955, Cantinflas considers himself ready for the international stardom that only Hollywood can offer. Mike Todd produces and

Michael Anderson directs *La Vuelta al Mundo en 80 Días* (Around the World in Eighty Days). David Niven is Phileas Fogg and Cantinflas is Passepartout, with an international cast, the most extensive to date: Marlene Dietrich, Frank Sinatra, Red Skelton, Robert Newton, Buster Keaton, José Greco, John Gielgud, George Raft, Shirley MacLaine, Fernandel, Charles Boyer, Martine Carol, Joe E. Brown, and Charles Coburn. Cantinflas reveals himself, infusing his role with all possible charm with a "showcase" of comedy characteristic of the "primitive" comics. Then, in 1960, Cantinflas stars in *Pepe*, directed by George Sidney, a film that amplifies the mistakes of *La Vuelta al Mundo* and underscores the colonial optic that frames the character. The criticism of the film in Mexico is inauspicious, but the public is still faithful to him.

In his last movie, *El Barrendero* (1981), Cantinflas looks tired, unsure of the distance that separates him from the strength of his origins. And the final years go by among interrupted plans, court battles, facial reconstructions, tributes (an honorary member of the Guatemalan police, honorary chief of the Colombian police, honorary doctor of the University of Michigan). The Mexican and Spanish governments announce celebrations for 1993. At his death, the myth is suddenly reestablished. Free at last in his labyrinth of crazy words, assured in the nonchalance of his gestures, shy and libidinous at the same time, orgiastic in his gait, and doctrinaire in his facial movements, Mario Moreno "Cantinflas" settles himself comfortably in a mural (very probably outlined by Diego Rivera) that we call in Mexico the national memory.

~

The secret of Tin Tan's lasting appeal lies in his effective combination of attitude and language: anarchy and liveliness, disorder and solemnity last just long enough before giving way to more chaos. During the debut of his first movies, Tin Tan was a glimmer of modernity during a time of transculturation and disorder; today, for those who consider him only as a television phenomenon, he represents humor without control, someone who "saves the honor" of a time when jokes proliferated like commemorative plaques, when respect was the death mask of society.

Tin Tan, the great comic actor whom a vulgar industry was forced to accept, was barely understood and exploited without measure. In 1943, the year of his debut, nothing foreshadowed such a radical apparition. Cantinflas, a prisoner in the jail of his own unique and magnificent discovery, dominated a film humor that was more verbal than visual; and the rest of the comics performed a series of variations and adaptations from the traditional frivolous theater (see,

for instance, *Los Millones de Chaflán* or *Lo que Palillo se Llevó*). Tin
Tan was a leap of faith, if you will; he was not an escapee from the
circus, nor the *pelado*, nor the swindler hidden behind the insignifi-
cance of his acts. He was simply a young man who walked, talked,
and charmed people as if he had his head in a jukebox filled with
boogie-woogie and boleros.

The Comedians

A few comments may be inserted here about the duties of the comedian. In Mexican cinema, the honored and consecrated comedians
stick to a few variables. Some of their obligations are:

- to belong to the masses and be able to express themselves in
  their language and in their movements (not to speak of facial
  expressions). The comedian should be likable and obedient, las-
  civious and subordinate, treacherous and honest. A comedian or
  a comic leading man of the upper classes is inconceivable.

- to avoid any class conflict and merely represent the limitations
  of the dispossessed—their shyness, their false arrogance, their
  mania for myths. The comedian should turn social resent-
  ments into a folklore of gratitude and use humor to appease
  rebellious or turbulent impulses.

- to show, even in conflicts of love, the "essence of comedy,"
  which, according to the industry, is the prolongation of sentimentality. Tears and laughter are, after all, the same, and the
  joke merely expands and moderates emotion. One laughs in
  order not to cry; one cries at a funeral because no one has
  thought of stopping the tears with a few good jokes.

- to maintain their original capital—that is, the personality that
  brought them to the screen. If the comedian transforms himself and loses his tics and his tried-and-true techniques, then
  the audience will be disappointed or cry fraud. His initial resources (his expressions, voice, and gestures) will tend to be
  the final resources in a world where the only things that count
  are comical verbosity and an appreciation for the most simple
  gag or the visual joke.

- to remain true to their origins regardless of what happens. The
  comedian may know unexpected success, live among the
  bourgeoisie, travel, and be famous, but after all is said and
  done, he will come back to his own kind, defeated or victorious, to the richness of poverty.

- to accept the humble use of their talents. Notable comedians (including the more talented) serve as a relief from melodrama, as a foil for the "perfect couple." (Even if it wanted to, the Mexican film industry could not produce a Groucho Marx or even a Bob Hope.) Humor, for the society of the 1940s, had a degraded function, and the cinema, as a magical instrument that contemporizes and changes its spectators, was attentive to melodrama, the only genre considered significant because it was there that the resources of industry and audience coincided.

- to serve as a vehicle for childish language that, through inversion, sanctions a culture of submission (the reproduction of Indian, peasant, and, most often, popular urban speech as the expressions of the adult-child).

- to resign themselves to the lack of evolution of their character. It is the creed of their trade that a comedian develops only *one* character throughout his career.

- to accept these "natural" limitations, the levels of Hollywood production and the Cantinflas myth. While a successful comedian may become an idol, he must remember that it is not his duty to represent the People (with a capital "P") but only variations of what is popular. Cantinflas monopolizes the emblemization of the People to such a degree that the members of the audience not only enjoy themselves for what they see and know of the ingenuity of their idol but also for the jokes they hear, for the ones they imagine, and for those that they will tell with delight on the next day. The weight of his legend is such that, in the memory of the audience, even the insignificant movies of Cantinflas grow to such a degree that they become part of the national sense of humor.

"What's the Matter with the Baisa?"

The *pachuco* is a unique individual/ who should never hustle/ and who should dominate the "honeys"/ so that they will suit him very fine: for dancing. Every sister who wants to be happy/ with a man with whom she will have her indiscretion,/ go to your pad and grab your suitcase/ and then hustle to support the poor wretch.

—Signature song of Tin Tan, lyrics by Marcelo Chávez.

Tin Tan (Germán Genero Ciprano Gómez Valdéz Castillo) is born on September 19, 1925, in Mexico City. The family moves in 1927 to

Ciudad Juárez, where his father works for the customs office and his mother is a housewife. Germán grows up in the barrio that will become the bastion of *pachuquismo*. (According to his brother Manuel, Germán's greatest influence is Los Angeles, but the barrios of Ciudad Juárez and El Paso are also very formative with their *vatos locos* (crazy boys), dressed in coattails and known for their rhythmic walk with their hands deep in their pockets and their shoulders slouched.) He does every kind of job and even works as a tourist guide.

> My first job was gluing labels on every record album of a radio station. In order to save saliva, I found a stray dog and taught him to stick out his tongue, and that's how I would wet the labels. Later, I was a gofer and a sweeper. But my first true opportunity was due to a broken microphone. This is how it was: I've always liked to make jokes, and at the radio station, I enjoyed imitating my buddies and my bosses. At that time (the late 1930s), Agustín Lara, whom I also imitated, was very popular. One blessed day, the microphone broke down. It was fixed and Mr. Meneses [his boss] ordered for it to be tested. The order was passed down to me. I then began to sing, imitating Lara. Mr. Meneses thought that it was an album of the great man from Veracruz. But no, it was me, joking around. By the following week I was working in a show entitled "Tin Tin Larará" with a script from Mr. Meneses. After that, I wanted to become a singer, but ended up becoming a radio announcer and an impersonator. I imitated everyone, and it seems I wasn't bad at it. Thanks to that skill I got my first stage name, "Topillo Tapas," and began to tour with it.

Soon, Germán Valdéz is a comedian (and a singer) in the Paco Miller company who worked in Mexico and in the southern United States. Another comedian who worked with Paco Miller was Donato, whose *patiño* (the straight man in the pie-throwing routines) was Marcelo Chávez. For more than twenty years, Chávez would be Tin Tan's buddy. "One day, not being really into it, we began to rehearse. That same night we went out on stage, and they really liked us. We were encouraged to continue together, write more songs and rehearse even more."

In the usual stories about Tin Tan there is usually one forgotten detail: his amazement in response to what was happening in Los Angeles. Between 1938 and 1942 in the Mexican-American barrios of Texas and California, the *pachuco* was the first great aesthetic result of migration, the dandy outside of mainstream fashion, the bearer of a concept of new elegance and extremes that, for the Anglos (and the parents of the *pachucos*) represents a huge provocation. The audacity of his clothing and his gestures helps the *pachuco* mark his new territory and, on the way, challenge discrimination (like his model, the "dude" of Harlem). The *pachuco* is tied eccentrically to the American way of life, and he is embraced by the Mexican culture because he confronts racism. The *pachuco* endures as much as he can. He is a symbol (involuntarily) of cultural resistance and ends up by being cornered and persecuted in a campaign of segregation that culminates in the Los Angeles Zoot-suit Riots.

By the time Tin Tan acquires his name, the *pachuco* had disappeared in the United States, and in Mexico it was now synonymous with the bum obsessed with a radical taste—the pretty-boy, the pimp of the *arrabal* (suburban slum), the good-time Charlie who represents the new masculinity of the barrios as it is portrayed by Víctor Parra in *El Suavecito* (1950, Fernando Méndez) and by Rodolfo Acosta in two movies by Emilio Fernández "El Indio," *Salón México* (1945) and *Victimas del Pecado* (1950). In *El Suavecito* the *pachuco's* father scorns his son and ousts him from the family and society: "That's not a man; he's a barber shop sample." And the traditional society (the only one that exists at this time) sees in such a

Movie still of the film El Rey del Barrio, *directed by Gilberto Martínez Solares.*

"reckless" wardrobe—knee-length coats, frock coattails, extremely wide lapels, a chain dangling dangerously to the floor, false suspenders, a feathered hat, flower-printed shirts whose cuffs almost cover the hands—an incendiary proclamation, and it is offended by these outfits that provoke the notion of decent attire.

Since the times of Porfirio Díaz, the Mexican who is "American-ized" has been an object of jest and scorn. According to popular culture, whoever renounces the "national condition" (dressing and behaving like one's parents and grandparents) becomes insignificant in a humorous way. Thus, Agustín Yáñez in his much-publicized novel, *Al filo del agua*, set in 1909, enumerates the townspeople's reaction to the *norteños*, the ones who went to North America and came back: "Poor town, poor country. They're the wisest, the most courageous, because of the words that they mix with the Christian language (Spanish), even if they still don't know how to read as when they left. Because of the gold teeth that they're always picking. And because they wear big shoes, felt hats, ballooned pants, and shirts with shiny cufflinks. They fix their hair, like dandies, shaved in the back, shaggy. . . . And what about their way of speaking? It seems that they've forgotten the language that their parents taught them." With marvelous impudence, Tin Tan, without pretending to be aware of it, does away with the rejection and the incomprehension. His dress and his manner decree for the first time popular modernity and anticipate its overflow of style.

The Guilty Conscience

In the Mexican capital during the 1940s, Tin Tan triumphantly becomes the archetype of the *pocho*, a category that was demonized at that time both linguistically and socially. A *pocho* is someone without a race who has forgotten his roots and who has exchanged the vitality of idiosyncrasy for the superficiality of Americanization. In his column of June 20, 1944, Salvador Novo reflects on one of his articles about "The Purity of Language": "It is certainly a good article. I was inspired by all that was occurring around Tin Tan, whom they accused of corrupting the language with his *pocho* speech that kids repeated. Of course, I had no room to develop the whole theory as I should have, but essentially—and intelligent readers, I'm sure, understood—it rests in making Cantinflas the representation of Mexican unconsciousness, and recognizing that when Tin Tan bothers us, it is because he incarnates the guilty conscience of our own voluntary or passive loss of a caste."

Tin Tan elaborates to perfection the linguistic collage of those Anglo-Saxon words imposed by the need to name whatever is new, a peasant Spanish that is filled with archaisms and sayings and expressions of the entire country. Tin Tan asks Marcelo: "And the *jale* that you got as a *guachador*? And do your *relativos* still *forgetean* you?" And one has to translate on the spot that *jale* is job and *guachador* is night watchman, and the *relativos* who *forgetean* are the relatives who forget. Nevertheless, Tin Tan is not an emblem of extermination, as he will be in later years; he only interprets the syncretism that will mark the second half of the century. Many theatrical grievances still await the *pocho* in movies, plays, radio shows, sermons, and threatening editorial comments by the columnists, but the continual migrations will end up normalizing them. There are so many *pochos* that the use of the pejorative collapses.

Tin Tan realized a monologue in opposition to convention. He is the *pachuco*, a word that in Mexico City alternates between friendly irony and insult. There is a considerable leap from the riots of Los Angeles to the dance halls of Mexico City; and the urban *pachucos*, who do not attack the "other," the North American, but rather the "other," the respectable man, bet everything on a personality that is fearless in dress and on the challenge of the conversion of the immigrant in an urban fantasy.

"Turirurá tundá tundá tundá." Even this is too much, a classicism that fakes a preoccupation with syntax and casts scorn at innovations in the name of linguistic purity. And if Cantinflas is accepted in the name of an incoherence proper to the common people, then Tin Tan is rejected for "attempting a crime" against immutable speech, the ideal property of the elite. Tin Tan is denounced by reporters and academics of "language" who lay siege to his precursory attitude. Somewhat by force, however, producers and scriptwriters incorporate the comedian, the *pachuco*, into their scenes of the urban barrios. They do not completely suppress the North American acculturation or his popular style, but they do dispel his linguistic experimentation.

The process of Tin Tan's career is not as linear as is believed. In fact, even though he was inspired by the *pachucos* of Los Angeles, his most recognizable influence is Cab Calloway, the singer and director of the famous Harlem orchestra of the New York of the 1930s. From Calloway, Tin Tan gets his gestures of optimistic ecstasy, his dress, his sense of movement on stage, and a syncopated malice that distorts, elevates, and magnifies the songs. In *Stormy Weather*, for instance, Calloway is revealed as the undeniable model for Tin Tan, with his circus-like humor, the labial exaggerations that "devour" and ironically re-create the songs, the "architectural" outfits that save him preambles and explanations ("Let the outfit describe me and I will immediately get into my role"). To this, Tin Tan adds his experience of the *carpas* and the music hall, his idea of cinematographic sequence-like sketches, his fertile improvisations, and his great self-confidence: besides the spectators, no one else is watching.

"Come Out Here, My Father,
See that I Am Braver than a Lion"

On November 5, 1943, Tin Tan debuts in the Iris Theater in Mexico City with a salary of 40 pesos. The star of the cast is Cantinflas. Tin Tan is moderately liked. It's not surprising. Only gradually will the impetus, the amusement, and the insults that are concentrated in his linguistic jumble be understood and, from there, be disseminated. His partner, the "carnal" Marcelo, is an old-fashioned comedian, the interlocutor who takes all the jokes and who yields to the jeering rituals some of his own physical characteristics (in his case, obesity and baldness, or in the complementary case of the midget José René Ruíz "Tun Tun," proximity to the floor). With a bit of a stretch, Marcelo is to Tin Tan what Margaret Dumont is to Groucho Marx: the ideal victim of jokes and comic situations, the recipient of the blows that had been directed at the comedian, the exemplar of respectability, frequently offended and offendable, his face swollen with surprise by gratuitous verbal or physical assault.

Tin Tan and Marcelo receive contracts from the Folies Bergère Theater, a fashionable nightclub called El Patio, and from XEW, a weekly radio show. Tin Tan acquires a small part in *Hotel de Verano*, a film by René Cardona: "For one number, I was paid 350 pesos; of course, it was very little, but since I was still very inexperienced in the movies, well, why not?" The cast in *Hotel de Verano* was a bit extravagant, combining crooners, singers, and comedians of theatrical farce: Ramón Armengod, Consuelo Guerrero de Luna, Jorge Reyes "El Che," Enrique Herrera, and Pedro Vargas.

Tin Tan's first movies are uneven. His success depends on the audience's understanding of the *pachuco* identity: the future that is rejected, the future as a *carpa*, the future as the laughter that is part of the acceptance of the transcultural model. The director of his first five movies, Humberto Gómez Landero, is monotonous, lacking any imagination and acting more like a script illustrator. Nevertheless, in *El Hijo Desobediente* (1945), *Hay Muertos que No Hacen Ruido* (1946), *Con la Música por Dentro* (1946), *El Niño Perdido* (1947), and *Músico, Poeta y Loco* (1947), Tin Tan's intensity makes an impression: he acts as if the spectators physically surround him. And through his humorous spontaneity, Tin Tan transfers the public onto the screen.

Tin Tan is not a humorist, although he resorts to the vaudeville humor of the United States in his offensive improvisations. He does not have a repertoire of tried-and-true jokes, nor has he timed the rhythm of his comical phrases. His allies are the ferocity of the gesture, the aggressiveness of the word, an enthusiasm for chaos, a sentimentality dissolved by irony, and a lack of respect for solemnity and its natural ally, the sense of propriety. With the juggling and the small catastrophes that always surround him, he makes fun of decorum. Unlike the Marx Brothers, he does not destroy everything around him out of hatred of institutions, nor does he call for universal ruin, like Buster Keaton. Nevertheless, the results are just as apocalyptic: when Tin Tan walks by, nothing is left standing, nothing escapes the all-encompassing destruction. From the Gómez Landero series of films, the character already possesses the characteristics that Tin Tan will polish to perfection: impudence, cynicism, frivolousness, multiple love affairs, and the incompetence that finds its equilibrium point through destructive efficiency.

"Shake It, Sister, Shake It!"

Urban speech emancipated from the social norms is as offensive as it is solicitous. Tin Tan does not leave any word unturned; he wrings them, stretches them, and finds their sonorous relationships. In the movies by Gómez Landero, the credit for the dialogue and plot go to Guz Aguila (Guzmán Aguilera). But Aguila, a great writer of the frivolous theater for two decades, is inadequate for Tin Tan's linguistic vitality. In a dialogue from *Músico, Poeta y Loco*, Tin Tan, an employee of a shop that sells glassware, says to a woman client: "Hey, you know my *chompeta* (ear) doesn't work too well. . . . And your *guaifo* (husband), how's he doing? (Looking at her coat) You use good rags. Look—that's cool, Sister, that's cool! . . . No, no, no *jainita* (honey)." And Marcelo responds: "I think you came down hard on that woman, and now your head is spinning." And in that way, Tin Tan continually jazzes up speech, improvises, weaves neologisms, and blasts away idiomatic rigidity.

In 1948, Tin Tan begins his collaboration with director Gilberto Martínez Solares and writer Juan García "El Peralvillo." In his interview in *Cuadernos de la Cineteca*, Martínez Solares speaks disdainfully: "Tin Tan was an extraordinary comedian. At first I didn't really trust him, nor did I have a great desire to work with him because he was a bit crass in the characters he played and in the places where he worked, no? Circus tents, theaters. . . . I wrote stories even but I've never been able to write street language, especially from the barrio. That was the specialty of my colleague, Juan García."

Calabacitas Tiernas, the film that inaugurates the work of the team of Tin Tan, Martínez Solares, and Juan García is, to this day, enjoyable for its energy despite the faults in the storyline. Tin Tan sings, dances, romances, pretends to be what he is not, doubts what he is, confronts himself in the mirror like Harpo Marx in *Duck Soup*. He moves on the edge between theater and film; he walks to the beat of the barrios, from *danzón* to swing. In *Calabacitas Tiernas*, the modern, urban comedian appears emancipated from a fundamental sentimentality that situates the logic of survival within the territory of the joke, while aware of being continually condemned to failure. Without the clothes of the *pachuco*, without the varnish of modernity that Anglo words confer, Tin Tan in *Calabacitas Tiernas* is as modern (in an irreverent sense) as the moment allows. He improvises, charms the camera, addresses the audience ("the master of one-thousand brains"), is not afraid of sentimental uncertainty, becomes bored with old-fashioned dignity, does not protect his honor, and does not respect proper speech. At the same time, it does not bother him if he offends the interlocutor.

"Hey, Marcelino, Play One for Me that Makes Me Cry from Here to the Next Song"

The inevitable environment of Tin Tan is the picaresque, which I quickly define as the gift for taking advantage of all circumstances except for the truly advantageous ones. He's a good-for-nothing who does not permit justice or injustice, does not take anything from anyone yet takes it from everyone. His character perfectly combines the extremes of adulation and lust, sentimentality and pillage, solidarity and plunder. And in this coming and going from heroism to antiheroism (from radical failure to fleeting victory), Tin Tan displays a modernity that is never known by those who are faithful to the circular resignation of the circus—Cantinflas, Palillo, Manolin and Shilinsky, Polo Ortín, El Chaflán, El Chicote, Mantequilla, and even Resortes (who is only modern when he dances).

    The Tin Tan who endures is the product of fifteen years of filming and recording, from 1945 to 1959. What follows is melancholy, the sadness that comes with seeing a great comic actor squandered, misunderstood, and abandoned by an industry that used him without ever recognizing his enormous genius. But from *El Hijo Desobediente* to *El Violetero* (1959), Tin Tan is the uncontrollable figure who marks a generation (in a way not understood until much later), transcends deplorable scripts, democratizes the relationship with the audience, redeems poorly written scenes with improvisations, and introduces a modern humor that will promote modern television comedians (Héctor Suárez, the Polivoces, Alejandro Suárez, and El Loco Váldez) and that will also influence, through its mythic projection, the most recent comedians (Andrés Bustamante, Ausencio Cruz, and Víctor Trujillo).

Tin Tan never completely abandons frivolous theater. He is, without doubt, a film comedian, full of quick reactions, with an aptitude for acrobatics, dance, and extreme facial mobility. But he is also a creature of the theatrical sketch, where he always returns every time he feels abandoned or lacking support.

TIN TAN: Marcelino, now you're going to have to work with UNESCO.

MARCELO: With UNESCO?

TIN TAN: Yes, with a broom (*una escoba*).

For years, Cantinflas's strategy of only making one movie per annum was praised; then, in the 1950s, Tin Tan overextended himself by filming every two to three months. Nevertheless, while almost none of Cantinflas's movies can be endured today (with the exception, I believe, of *Aguila o Sol, El Signo de la Muerte, Ahí Está el Detalle, El Gendarme Desconocido*, and *Ni Sangre ni Arena*), even the worst of Tin Tan's contain memorable sequences, songs, attitudes, and unexpected jokes. His ebullience allows Tin Tan to survive the limitations that the industry imposed on the character—the coarseness of the screenplays (when they exist), the idea that film is speed and

Movie still from the film Ahí Está el Detalle, *directed by Juan Bustillo Oro with the actors Mario Moreno "Cantinflas" and Joaquín Pardavé.*

distraction, and the charming ineptitude of the "young ladies" (one exception: Silvia Pinal in *El Rey del Barrio*). If the lack of critical interest does not matter, what is overwhelming is the partial incomprehension of the public, who celebrates him without realizing the modernness of his boldness—a boldness that is only partially sustained by the freedoms that are allowed him by Martínez Solares, who, according to Wolf Ruvinskis, upon seeing Tin Tan improvise, laughs and continues taping without stopping him; the great popular mode from Juan García "El Peralvillo"; the discretion and competence of Marcelo, Vitola, and Ruvinskis; and the repertoire of comic characters of the Mexican cinema.

And his achievements are not limited. In the Golden Age of Mexican cinema only one other comic actor breaks the barriers of inflexibility: Joaquin Pardavé, who preserves and transmits the great wisdom of the actors from the frivolous theater whose delayed and ceremonious diction takes on the role of an architecture of irony and whose voices are, almost literally, decorations of the epoch. In saying this, I am not forgetting the contributions of Resortes, Mantequilla, El Chaflán, El Chicote, Oscar Pulido, Amelia Wilhemy, and Delia Magaña, but none of them was able to satisfactorily transcend the inertia of their screenwriters and the haste of their directors. Pardavé achieves success through his skillful understanding of traditional sensibility and Tin Tan through his recklessness. As his compadre, Manuel, will do later, Tin Tan does not capitulate to the camera; he makes it his accomplice, his witness, his own.

"Your Kisses Were Re-created Here in My Mouth"

El Rey del Barrio (1949) is Tin Tan's best movie. In saying this, I am not forgetting *Sinbad el Mareado*, *El Revoltoso*, *El Ceniciento*, *Ay Amor . . . Como Me Has Puesto*, and *El Sultán Descalzo*. But in *El Rey del Barrio*, Tin Tan reaches his apogee. He is flexible, ironic, sentimental, and destructive; and his character, a product of the industry's shrewdness and of his own autobiographical contributions, is perfect, as defenseless as a catastrophe, with the eloquence of someone who has nothing to lose. Tin Tan is the most joyful emanation from the barrios, someone who is explained by the light of the devastation he spreads, and who, at the same time, is contemporary in attitude and as anachronistic as the neighborhoods that will soon be demolished, like the crooks in the pool halls and the corner stores, like the methods used to inject authenticity into the past and the rhythm of a party into the movie-going experience. And *El Rey del Barrio* has some of Tin Tan's best sequences: the humiliation of the detective Marcelo in the house they are painting, the fabulous duet with Vitola in the "Cirivirivi" that pursues the grotesque by apprehending the ridiculous, and the bolero "Contigo" that Tin Tan, drunk and in love, sings while he transmits the quality of a scene from *Romeo and Juliet.*

In his comic songs, *rancheros*, or boleros, Tin Tan is supremely effective. His style is naturally exaggerated, but he does not distort either the meaning of the joke or the virtues of romance. When dancing, Tin Tan is the *pachuco* who livens up jive while singing that he's the dandy from the barrios. And in the bolero, he celebrates, without pretensions or vocal excellence, the binding spirit, the crazed expressions of love that are the invasion of machismo by lyricism. And his style contributes to the transculturated relic that censorship condemned in his speech.

Tin Tan is the crooner and the bolero singer filled with the onomatopoeia of boogie-woogie, who sings with his whole mouth ("my mouth spreads all over the place"). If he cannot be solemn like Juan Arvizu or Emilio Tuero, or sensual like Frank Sinatra, Tin Tan does succeed in parodying those diverse styles, unifying them into his own ironically pretentious and openly reticent one, through the careful use of the vocal virtues that are ultimately never very important. As a singer, Tin Tan accomplishes the unthinkable: he is at the same time parodic and orthodox.

Chaos within Chaos

How is a Tin Tan movie put together? In most cases his films are poor distortions of classics or contemporary successes. The immediacy of a joke or pun is marked with their names: *La Marca del Zorrillo* (The Mark of the Fox), *Los Tres Mosqueteros y Medio* (The Three-and-one-half Musketeers), *El Ceniciento* (Cinderello), *Sinbad el Mareado* (Seasick Sinbad), *El Bello Durmiente* (Sleeping Beau), *El Vizconde de Montecristo* (The Viscount of Monte Cristo), *El Barba Azul* (Blue Beard), *Lo Que le Pasó a Sansón* (Look What Happened to Samson!), *Rebelde sin Casa* (Rebel without a Home), *El Gato sin Botas* (Puss without Boots), *El Fantasma de la Opereta* (The Phantom of the Operetta). Even *El Violetero* is a caricature of the 1943 classic, *María Candelaria*, a humorous homage for Tin Tan, who happily imitates El Indios's style of Castilian speech in Xochimilco (and, from there, immediately returns to Spanglish).

To the weakness of the plots and to the lack of responsibility of the producers (who are convinced that film is the art of the immediate return of investments), Tin Tan opposes his obsession for parody, his hatred of boredom. For him, improvisation is the only known method to avoid memorizing the script and being mired in monotony. The task of "nationalizing" the delirium is joined with the abundance of everyday life, and reality is something that happens before and after every sequence. In this kind of film, parody is something more than a transformation of grotesque or ridiculous situations. Parody is the continuous and wrecked invention of the world as it should be, where satire is the "master of ceremonies" for melodramatic situations, passionate love affairs, or incomprehensible plots. Nothing is serious except for death—and that always happens in other movies.

To a large extent, Tin Tan is a product of his own spirited energy, expressed in dances, jumps, irreverence, or frantic escapes from persecutors and from the lack of persecution. Tin Tan sings the mambo and the cha-cha-cha, twists, serenades, throws and destroys everything in sight, fails as if his life depended on it, and mobilizes everything around him. But over the years, he concentrated his energy on verbal humor. Lacking a competent team in his final movies, tired of the wear and tear, Tin Tan looks fed up, disenchanted, powerless in the face of routine (though always with magnificent moments: see *El Quelito*, for instance). His ranting is admired, he is celebrated, he is frequently hired, but he is not considered lasting. He is as he is. Thus, he is or was a *pachuco* curtailed by linguistic censorship. He is or was a product of popular theater of the barrios in the poor towns. He is or was a comedian who was not intimidated by the movies. With so much time passed, it is useless to quarrel with the stupidity of the Mexican movie industry, which also wasted in abominable melodramas the talents of Resortes and Mantequilla and drowned Pardavé, Pedro Armendáriz, Fernando and Andrés Soler, David Silva, Tito Junco, Roberto Cañedo, and other excellent actors.

The industry used and controlled Tin Tan, but to a lesser extent than the other actors. It was in part because of this that Tin Tan acted without being intimidated by what was sacred. He did what he wanted as often as he could and became, for future generations, the emblem of an urban vitality that still shines for us, when it is time to joke around.

~

At what point do the humanistic natures of Cantinflas and Tin Tan converge? The differences between the two are clear. Initially, Cantinflas represented the *lumpenproletariat* of Mexico City, while Tin Tan portrayed the *pachuco*, the man who has nothing but his abilities that extend from the use of language to expressive body language. By the early 1940s, Cantinflas is already a celebrated mythical figure in Mexico: he is the essence of poverty, of expressive cleverness, and of the choreography of the marginalized. Tin Tan's mythic status comes years later, after his death, thanks to the replay of his films on television. In life, he was the symbol of a carefree soul and the linguistic model of popular modernity. Cantinflas's popularity declines because of his seriousness and his tendency to sermonize. For Tin Tan, the fall from grace is a result of improper agents who insisted on casting him in whatever film was offered, regardless of the screenplay. Tin Tan was forced to rely on his improvisational talents to make the films work.

So much for the differences. The similarities between the two great comedians are considerable. Cantinflas and Tin Tan represent a certain type of humor—oral and expressive—of their public who, in turn, learned from the comedians dancing styles, cutting repartee, techniques of seduction, mischievous games or innocent mischief, jokes that transcend generations, and how to readily produce sentences—Cantinflas's "Ahí está el detalle" and Tin Tan's "Que mene, carnalita, que mene." Their social satire was launched with incredible accuracy and great insight into the sentimentalism of their audiences. Celebrated actors seemingly without anything in common, and legendary icons in different ways, Tin Tan and Cantinflas are still today the greatest reference points for a multigenerational audience who learned to laugh while watching them and who, in revering them, smile triumphantly as if they just saw them at yesterday's fiesta.

5

Race and Ethnicity
in the Classical Cinema

Joanne Hershfield

.De aquí que este último elemento, el pigmento, revista importancia tan
grande en el ánimo del mexicano. No puede renunciar a él. Lo siente como
una carga que al no poderse librar de ella limita su libertad, sus ambiciones,
sus vuelos. Lo identifica, lo fija, lo coloca, lo distingue, lo clasifica.

—*Alejandro Galindo*[1]

Mexican critic Roger Bartra has proposed that through the cinema and other forms of popular and mass culture, the subjects
of cultural practices—Mexican popular audiences—became the primary actors in the postrevolutionary reconstruction of the nation.[2]
The enigma of a politically useful and unifying notion of Mexican
identity was central to the refashioning of the nation during the
decades following the end of the military phase of the Revolution.
Historian Alan Knight describes as "strenuous" the "efforts at cultural engineering undertaken by Mexico's revolutionary regime" to
deal with this enigma.[3]

Like most national cinemas, Mexican cinema has portrayed various contradictory relations among the country's history, Mexico as
a national geographic and discursive space, and Mexican identity.
And, as with other national cinemas, representations of the nation
and national identity have been continually contested and transformed on the screens of Mexico, especially during moments of internal and external crises. The political and cultural revisioning of
national identity coincided with the development of the vibrant cinema industry. The notion of a mythic Mexico populated by mythical
Mexicans can be traced through film history from the silent *El
Automóvil Gris* (1919) through Golden Age films such as *Allá en el
Rancho Grande* (1936) and *María Candelaria* (1943). During the
Golden Age from (1935 to 1955), filmmakers, intent on transforming an industry long dominated by Hollywood and European models

into a uniquely Mexican cinema, made national identity a prominent theme of their output.

In their search to represent Mexico and *lo mexicano*, directors such as Fernando de Fuentes, Alejandro Galindo, Ismael Rodríguez, and Emilio Fernández referred to various nationalistic ideologies that defined the nation after the Revolution—*mestizaje, hispanismo*, and *indigenismo*—and that had a racialistic foundation. This strategy was intended to forge a national solidarity among a population divided by language, gender, and ethnicity as well as by regional affiliation. Looking at a number of films from the classical era of Mexican cinema, this essay will analyze the ways in which Mexican cinema represented racial and ethnic differences, two visible markers of national identity. At a more general level, the argument will be made that films, as cultural texts, evidence the ways in which race, ethnicity, and nation-building are inexorably interconnected.

Race has proven to be a central term in Mexico's postrevolutionary search for a common national identity. This search began in the nineteenth-century struggle for independence from Spain and France. Mexican intellectuals, expounding an alternative to the culture of colonialism, declared that their nation was united through a common culture that superseded any apparent racial, ethnic, or historical differences. The motive of writers such as Justo Sierra in the nineteenth century and José Vasconcelos in 1920 was to forge an identity that would either incorporate or erase diversity and at the same time construct an "authentic" Mexican culture in opposition to European influences. The ideology of *indigenismo* venerated Mexico's past and its pre-Columbian indigenous history, *hispanismo* glorified its Euro-Spanish heritage, while *mestizaje* celebrated the racial mix of the majority of the population.

As critics Michael Omi and Howard Winant have demonstrated, race is a sociohistorical construction of essential identities that is grounded in conceptions of cultural and biological difference. Social notions and categories of difference are not static but are "created, inhabited, transformed, and destroyed" as a function of historical processes.[4] Like gender, race is conceived of in terms of biological difference and used to classify and set apart groups of people based on empirically verifiable "evidence" such as skin color or facial characteristics. Since the nineteenth century, racial categorization in Europe, the United States, and Latin America has been informed by "eugenics," a pseudoscientific body of work influenced by the evolutionary writings of Charles Darwin and Mendelian genetics. Racists saw eugenics both as a descriptive science that proved that human races were biologically "unequal" and as a prescriptive practice of race improvement.

Despite shared assumptions, eugenics, as promoted and practiced in various social and national settings, was shaped by factors
specific to historical and social contexts. Like other Latin American
countries, Mexican eugenicists were well read in European views
that miscegenation was the leading cause of racial degeneration.
However, these eugenicists were faced with a profound ambiguity
when confronted with Anglo-European views on racial hybridization.[5] Like most Latin American countries, Mexico's population had
been racially mixed since the Spanish Conquest of the sixteenth century.[6] Race as a signifier of breeding or blood was subsequently
used to differentiate among criollos, Indians, and Mexicans of
"mixed" blood. Between 1810 and 1940, racial categories were continually modified to reflect changing notions about what constituted
"racial difference." Howard Cline reports that after the 1921 national
census, subsequent censuses "disregard this emotionally-loaded category in favor of providing social and economic data from which
anyone can attempt to work out his own system."[7] From 1921 to
1940, Mexico promoted a number of different and often conflicting
racial ideologies, and the division between Indians and non-Indians,
the country's most visible Other, shifted according to changing political objectives.[8]

Mexican philosopher Leopoldo Zea, writing in the early twentieth century, argued that individual, personal identity is historical in
that it derives from cultural identity. For Zea, the roots of a specifically Mexican cultural identity—an identity he defined as
mestizaje—were to be "found in the sexual union between the
Spanish conqueror [Hernán Cortés] and the Indian woman [Malinale
or "La Malinche"] who is part of a conquered people."[9] According
to Henry Schmidt, this evolutionary view of Mexican identity as a
Euro-American identity is rooted in "the European ideas of the New
World" and expounded in the writings of explorers such as
Columbus and Cortés.[10] Europe needed to incorporate aboriginal
peoples and cultures into an already existing conception of the
world as "proof of the fullness of God and Nature"—a conception
that was, however, open to change. Thus, during the early years of
Spanish rule, "Mexican identity followed a shifting cultural and political pattern whose signals marked the evolution of Mexico from
colony to state."[11]

By the end of the sixteenth century, Mexican national identity
was further modified in response to the emergence of a criollo consciousness that recognized a cultural, if not a racial, *mestizaje*.
According to Knight, the Spanish initially attempted to maintain
cultural and biological distinctions between Indians and Spanish
immigrants but were unsuccessful. Consequently, the term "Indian"

came to refer to a *fiscal* or class category rather than an ethnic one. By the time of Porfirio Díaz's rise to power in 1876, the majority of Mexicans were mestizo, and social and ethnic classifications were subsequently defined through a confluence of categories found in "language, dress, religion, social organization, culture, and consciousness."[12] Despite the sanctioning of *mestizaje* as the marker of Mexican identity, other ideologies rose to challenge its authority.

In 1925, as part of a project of postrevolutionary nation-building, José Vasconcelos, the Minister of Education in the administration of President Alvaro Obregón, published a long essay, *La raza cósmica*. On the surface, Vasconcelos appeared to hail the mestizo as the "quintessential" Mexican. He wrote of the coming of a new age wherein a fusion of races and classes in Latin America would culminate in the creation of a mestizo race, or what Vasconcelos called the "cosmic race."[13] However, while proclaiming to celebrate Mexicans' racial mixture, Vasconcelos's thesis promoted the notion that this new race would emerge as a result of a "cleansing" of indigenous blood through European intermarriage. Vasconcelos's ideology of "fusion" (shared by many of his contemporaries) was thus actually a thinly disguised conviction that Mexico's pre-Columbian roots should and would eventually be whitened into extinction. It was, in essence, a thesis of spiritual eugenics, or what Nancy Leys Stepan calls "constructive miscegenation."[14]

Mexican theories of eugenics were most prominent in the 1930s during a consolidation of postrevolutionary nationalism. The country was absorbed in the construction of a social and cultural nationalism that involved a redefining of national identity and the making of an essential "Mexicanness." Among other considerations, this new definition had to consider what to do with the country's marginalized subjects, the Indians.[15] One of the most far-reaching philosophies promoted during this era was *indigenismo*, Mexico's own particular brand of racial ideology. *Indigenismo* was a network of intellectual and political ideas that called for a unified national identity under the banner of a common Indian heritage. Proponents of *indigenismo* argued that the roots of modern Mexican identity—*lo mexicano*—lay in the cultural legacy of the pre-Columbian Indian cultures whose populations were devastated during the prolonged Spanish Conquest. Gonzalo Aguirre Beltrán argues that "indigenism, basing itself on the mestizo status of the country's population and on the arrogation of the indigenous past, rationalizes the fight which it believes it has to impose as a single way out to the Indian: Mexican nationality."[16] As Stepan points out, this notion of a unique Mexican identity actually denied the authenticity of the Indian in favor of "a new homogeneity, the Europeanized [whitened] mestizo."[17] During this decade, Vasconcelos's thesis of the "cosmic race" was implicitly promoted, and the mestizo was venerated as the ideal of national identity.

Although *indigenismo* purported to recognize the fundamental contribution of Indians to Mexican culture, its champions often failed to acknowledge linguistic, historical, and cultural differences or even variations in racial stock among the diverse groups that made up the indigenous populations. In point of fact, by the late 1930s, most Mexicans fell into the racial category of mestizo or mixed-race. In 1810 about 60 percent of the population was classified as Indian. One hundred years later, that figure had dropped to 7.6 percent.[18] By the 1920s, light-skinned criollos and mestizos comprised the economically and politically dominant classes while darker-skinned Indians "still occupied the lowest rung of society."[19] Racial categories fell along class and cultural lines, rather than bloodlines, for the most part. Because most Indians had become relatively Westernized by the postrevolutionary era, "tradition and culture tend in these instances to be the distinguishing marks, not blood and race."[20]

According to Knight, the call for a unified national identity under the banner of a common Indian heritage was mobilized because those in power firmly believed that Indians could only benefit from Mexico's growth if they became fully integrated into the society from which they had been previously excluded. Indians thus became the "object" of *indigenismo* rather than its producer.[21] Although many groups still viewed themselves as Indian, carried on local and regional traditions, and spoke indigenous languages, their needs were ignored in order to further the needs of "the nation."[22] Moreover, "mestizo culture regarded its Indian heritage as a source of shame and its European aspects as superior."[23]

Indigenismo

In 1934 two films introduced the "Indianist" genre, whose purpose was to legitimize the Indians' status in Mexico as poor but honorable: *Redes*, codirected by Fred Zinnemann, Paul Strand, Augustin Velásquez Chávez, and Emilio Gómez Muriel; and *Janitzio*, directed by Carlos Navarro and starring the young actor Emilio "El Indio" Fernández (he would later go on to direct more than twenty films, including a number of remakes of *Janitzio*), who was of Indian ancestry. *Janitzio* narrates the story of a young Indian girl, Erendia, who becomes the mistress of a white engineer in order to save her fiancé and who is subsequently stoned to death by the villagers for violating local sexual taboos.[24] The film updates Mexico's myth of origination: the La Malinche-Cortés union, the famous first interracial romance in Mexican myth and history. Despite the fact that La Malinche was a slave, she is remembered as the woman who betrayed her people. In *Janitzio*, an Indian woman is again punished for the sins of the white male.

Redes, Mexico's first sound film sponsored by the government's Secretaría de Educación Pública, was shot on location over seven months in a fishing village near Veracruz using local, nonprofessional actors.[25] It tells the story of a group of poor Indian fishermen who go on strike against a greedy criollo agent.[26] Clarifying what he believed was the purpose of the film for Mexican audiences, Zinnemann wrote that "it was hoped that films [such as *Redes*] might help to extend their awareness of each other as compatriots sharing the same human problems."[27] According to Mexican critic Carlos Monsiváis, despite the noble intentions of the government and the filmmakers, *Redes* glorifies the marginal status of the Indians and their stoic acceptance of poverty rather than interrogating its social causes. He writes that the film "exalted physical work as epic class consciousness and the beauty of community sentiments."[28]

Scholars point to the influence of Sergei Eisenstein's quasi-historical epic, *¡Que Viva México!* on both *Redes* and *Janitzio*.[29] In fact, Eisenstein's visit to Mexico in 1932 and his film are credited with having an impact on both the style and content of the Indianist cinema, as exemplified by Emilio Fernández. Despite the Soviet director's undeniable influence on directors such as Fernández, there is substantial evidence that Eisenstein's film and the Indianist genre as a whole were inspired by postrevolutionary Mexican theater (*tandas* and *carpas*) and art and the intellectual promotion of *indigenismo* during the 1920s and 1930s. Artists such as Diego Rivera and David Alfaro Siquieros were intent on creating a revolutionary Mexican art through an expression of *mexicanidad* grounded in the ideology of *indigenismo*. Their work and discourse repudiated European influences (although many of these artists were trained in France or Spain) and celebrated the Indian peasant, Mexican folklore, and Mexico's landscape, drawing inspiration from pre-Columbian art and contemporary Indian clothing and handicrafts. However, their paintings reinforce stereotypical representations of racial and ethnic divisions that marked Mexican society since the Spanish conquistadors first mated with Indian women in the fifteenth century. Indians in this "national art" were portrayed as pure and simple, like children who had to be led to social (and revolutionary) consciousness by the intellectual mestizo elite. The Indianist films of the Golden Age reproduced these stereotypes.

A decade after the release of *Redes* and *Janitzio*, Emilio Fernández, considered by many to be the father of Mexican cinema, revived the indigenist genre with *María Candelaria, Flor Silvestre* (1943), *La Perla* (1945), *Enamorada* (1946), *Maclovia* (1948), and *Río Escondido* (1948). Fernández maintained that his purpose as a filmmaker was to neutralize Hollywood's influence and to dramatize Mexico's past and present in order to portray what he believed was an authentic national identity.[30] He elevated the Indians to mythic stature, romanticized their lives, and, following the model of the earlier films, linked the meaning of *lo mexicano* visually and narratively to Mexico's indigenous roots. At the same time, Fernández used light-skinned, European-looking women such as Dolores del Río and María Félix, two of Mexican cinema's major stars, in roles as Indian women. In *María Candelaria*, a remake of *Janitzio*, del Río plays a young Indian woman who poses for a criollo painter who declares that his artistic mission is to "paint Mexico." In the body of María Candelaria he has found what he calls "an Indian of the pure Mexican race. . . . It was as if an old princess had come to judge the conquistadors."

Many of the shots in films such as *Salón México* (1948), *La Perla*, and *María Candelaria* link the past to the present through the depiction of Mexico's "eternal" Indianness. In the opening sequence of *María Candelaria*, images of pre-Columbian stone faces play against the same high cheekbones and proud facial expression of the live woman. Historian Julia Tuñon has suggested that Fernández's images establish Indians as "living remains, a sign containing an eternal essence that goes beyond history."[31]

Fernández's later film, *Río Escondido*, pursues a similar narrative of *indigenismo* and national identity. It tells the story of a young mestiza teacher, Rosaura (María Félix), who is assigned to a remote area in northern Mexico to educate the local Indians through the rhetoric of the Revolution. The film narrativizes the government's attempt to incorporate the uneducated, poverty-stricken rural Indians into modern Mexico by giving them a symbolic place in the story of the nation. In substituting the rhetoric of *indigenismo* for economic and social reform, however, neither the film nor the state offered indigenous people material sustenance or apologies for hundreds of years of subjugation. At the same time, Fernández portrays Indians as subservient and docile, and the film suggests that they have always been this way and will continue to be this way forever.

In all of Fernández's films, race and class appear to be synonymous: Indians are at the bottom of the socioeconomic ladder; at the next rung are the mestizos, who occupy positions of power denied to Indians. In the new postrevolutionary society, it seems that relations

*Pedro Armendáriz and María Elena Márquez and their infant son fleeing
for their lives in the film* La Perla, *directed by Emilio "El Indio"
Fernández.*

among men are still predicated on class and race. The narratives of
both *María Candelaria* and *Río Escondido* portray Mexican social relations that place Indians at the economic and political mercy of mestizos and criollos. Additionally, race and class also define moral
character: generally, if criollos are shown as superior but benevolent
and Indians are simple but honest, mestizos are the embodiment of
evil. In *María Candelaria*, for example, Don Damián (Miguel Inclán),
the violent and racist mestizo owner of the town's only general store,
controls the Indians' lives and livelihoods and serves as intercessor in
their relations with the state, as represented by white doctors.

As I discuss elsewhere, "while glorifying both an Indian past and
the Indian people, these films did not concern themselves with the
fact that these people were Mexico's most exploited group, perse-

cuted on the basis of race as well as class."[32] The call for unity under the banner of a common Indian heritage was thus no more than the promotion of an imagined alliance among diverse ethnic, religious, cultural, and regional groups.

Hispanismo

While *indigenismo* may have been the most visible racial discourse during the postrevolutionary reformation, during the 1920s another ideology emerged to challenge the assumption of the cohesiveness of national identity. An unlikely alliance of Catholic peasants and conservative landowners in the northwestern region of the country sought to define Mexican identity and culture in terms of Mexico's Catholic Euro-Spanish heritage. If *mestizaje* was privileged by the state and *indigenismo* by the left-wing intelligentsia, then *hispanismo* was brought into the discussion through an alliance of right-wing landowning groups who opposed postrevolutionary land and social reforms and the Catholic Church and of Catholic peasants who resented the new regime's anticlerical position and opposed its socialist programs.[33]

According to James Cockcroft, the postrevolutionary period "was one in which no major social class could assert total or clear-cut hegemony."[34] The wealthy northern industrial capitalists who seized power after the Revolution in the 1920s were immediately faced with opposition from factions on the left and the right: a peasant class that demanded the realization of reforms promised during the Revolution, and radical right-wing landowning groups aligned with the Church who opposed what they saw as the socialist-influenced demands of agrarian reform and the incorporation of Indians.[35] This alliance led to a series of armed resistance, the Cristero Rebellion (1926–1929), a bloody guerrilla war that cost eighty thousand peasant lives.[36]

Many historians view this conflict as primarily political, however. Jean Meyer argues that although the Church did disagree with the state about the kinds of agrarian reform that were necessary, "contrary to the official version of events, it had not sold itself to the big landowners." Instead, the Church was in battle with the government over "the spirit of the peasant."[37] In Meyer's estimation, the Cristero Rebellion was not politically motivated but inspired by spiritual and cultural concerns. The peasants of Jalisco did not take up arms only because of their opposition to land reforms but "because the Revolution was trying to take the priest away from them."[38] These peasants were fiercely Catholic, in the traditional sense of the practice, free from the syncretic influence of Indian paganism or U.S. Protestantism. The Cristeros combined their fervent Catholicism with fervent patriotism and fought under the red, white, and green flag of Independence with "the Virgin of Guadalupe on one side and the eagle devouring the serpent on the other."[39]

Despite the eventual defeat of the Cristeros, their champions carried their philosophies into Lázaro Cárdenas's presidency. Needing a people who could personify *hispanismo*, its proponents found them in Los Altos de Jalisco, the isolated northwestern mountain region of the state of Jalisco. The mythology of Los Altos created a horse-riding people who were devoutly Catholic and capitalistic, had never intermarried with Indians, and played Mariachi music. The political-cultural discourse of *hispanismo* was romanticized on the movie screens of Mexico with the introduction of the *comedia ranchera*, a romantic genre based on the farcical musical theater of the early 1900s that featured folkloric themes and popular music. The 1936 film directed by Fernando de Fuentes, *Allá en el Rancho Grande*, and shot by Gabriel Figueroa, who would later become Fernández's cinematographer, made the reputation of the *comedia ranchera* and distributed it across Latin America. Emilio García Riera has argued that the film gave foreign audiences a picture of Mexico that fit their imaginary visions.[40]

According to Charles Ramírez Berg, the *comedia ranchera* was concerned with "maintaining a well-ordered status quo" set in place during the prerevolutionary reign of Porfirio Díaz.[41] The ideology of the *comedia ranchera* narratives was a reaction against the agrarian reform policies of Cárdenas and a romanticization of the prerevolutionary Mexico of class and race differentiation and of male superiority. The genre made famous Maríachi music as well as two of the biggest stars in Mexican film history, Pedro Infante and Jorge Negrete, by elevating the singing cowboy, or *charro*, with his huge sombrero and his embroidered costume, to mythical proportions. According to Monsiváis, the *charro* is "a macho who expressed himself through chauvinism and haughtiness."[42]

As personified by Negrete in *¡Ay, Jalisco, No Te Rajes!*, the *charro* is a symbol of Hispanic masculinity, light-skinned, handsome, and respectful of the "inherent" divisions within Mexican society. Although only a ranchhand on the hacienda, his role is to be what Gustavo García defines as the "mediator," the protector of the peons against the powerful hacendado.[43] At the same time, the *charro* works to maintain the patriarchal feudal system that kept classes, races, and genders in their place. In *Allá en el Rancho Grande*, for example, the *charro*, José Francisco (Tito Guizar), is forced to defend the reputation of his fiancée, Eulalia, from the attentions of his childhood friend, Felipe, now the hacendado. But through various displays of virile masculinity, the two men eventually resolve their quarrel, José and Eulalia are reunited, everyone resumes their social place, and everything returns to normal. Monsiváis writes that "the film delighted Mexican moviegoers who knew that what they were watching wasn't Mexico, but maybe only what it could or should have been."[44]

Through the image of the *charro*, this singularly Mexican film genre glorified the machismo of the nation, drawing a link between the patriarchal hacendado, the state, and paternalism. The *comedia ranchera* may be read as a thinly disguised challenge, in the form of a musical love story, to Cárdenas's social and economic reforms: land reform, the nationalization of private industry, and the limited promotion of women's rights. How could such reactionary films as

Stars Pedro Armendáriz and Dolores del Río as the tragic lovers in María Candelaria, *directed by Emilio "El Indio" Fernández.*

Allá en el Rancho Grande, *Bajo el Cielo de México* (de Fuentes),
La Zandunga (de Fuentes, starring Lupe Vélez), *Nobleza Ranchera*
(Alfredo de Diestro, 1938), and *La Tierra del Mariachi* (Rául de
Anda) be released during the presidency of Cárdenas? García Riera
suggests that it was because Mexican and Latin American audiences adored characters with "humble origins, big peasant-style
skirts and hair bows, and virile field workers as mates." He links
the conditions of reception with the concerns of production—
"innovation and intelligence [were] poison at the box office"—and
Mexican producers "wanted no risks and sought maximum profits
at minimal effort."[45] In the words of John King, the films were produced because they "made a lot of money abroad."[46]

While the *comedia ranchera* genre persevered through the 1940s,
many of the films of that decade were more melodramatic and incorporated a more ambiguous social message into the basic structure of
the musical love story. Ramírez Berg writes that through these later
films "walks a charro hero who embodies the unsullied revolutionary
ideal, a man on the side of the people who cares about and fights for
justice, liberty, and civil and agrarian rights against the evil hacenda-
dos."[47] In a sense, the *charro* of the 1940s reversed the meanings of
the 1930s *comedia ranchera* by situating *hispanismo* as just another
revolutionary discourse.

Pedro Armendáriz exemplifies this new kind of *charro* hero in
Emilio Fernández's *Flor Silvestre*, starring Dolores del Río.[48] This
film is less conservative than earlier *comedias rancheras* as it explores the intricacy of the Revolution's complex political, class, and
regional loyalties. Armendáriz stars as an idealistic revolutionary
hero whose wealthy hacendado parents reject Esperanza (played by
del Río), the girl he loves, because she is from the peasant class.
Ramírez Berg writes that "the charro is politically reborn. . . . If he
was of the hacendado class . . . he left his class affiliations behind for
the greater glory of the Mexican nation."[49]

Cinematic Images of Afro-Mexican Identity

Although the institution of slavery never flourished on Mexican
shores, runaway slaves from other Latin and Central American
slave-holding nations did. By the early 1800s, 0.2 percent of the
Mexican population was classified as being part of an African
ethno-cultural group. José Iturriaga's analysis of national census
data from 1940 ascertains that "African and Afro-crosses . . .
formed as much as 5 percent" of the population.[50] Though the
question of antiblack racist attitudes has never been a central theme

of Mexican cinema, there are at least two films from the Golden Age that address the issue.[51]

La Negra Angustías (Matilde Landeta, 1949) is one of many films that took part in the cinema's ongoing debate about the Revolution. Landeta's film, adapted from a novel by Francisco Rojas Gonzáles, narrates the story of a young mulatta, the daughter of Antón, an Afro-Mexican Robin Hood. Growing up, Angustías (played by María Elena Márquez) is nurtured by stories of Antón's exploits and his hatred of dictator Porfirio Díaz. As a young woman, Angustías is shunned by her people for being a *marimacho*, a kind of tomboy, but also for her racial heritage. She is thus marked early by the troubling confluence of race and sex. The consequences of this

María Elena Márquez as a revolutionary officer in the film La Negra Angustías, *directed by Matilde Landeta.*

marking will lead her into revolutionary practice, but it will also precipitate her temporary undoing.

Angustías is forced to flee her village after she kills a man when he tries to rape her. She is captured and treated roughly by a roving band of desperados, finally escaping with the help of one of the bandits who befriends her. Motivated by her heritage as well as by her own experience of oppression at the hands of men, Angustías emerges into political consciousness and becomes a colonel in a small Zapatista army in the Mexican Revolution, stepping into her father's shoes and leading her men into victorious battles against Díaz's supporters on behalf of the peasants.

Women were actively involved in the revolutionary struggle as soldaderas, or female soldiers, working as cooks and nurses and even carrying weapons. As Elizabeth Salas has documented, women of various ages came from all regions of Mexico and joined up with the Revolution's armies for many different reasons.[52] While a number of these women became famous in legend, in songs, and in the movies—La Adelita, La Valentina, La Cucaracha, and Juana Gallo— the majority of cultural representations have focused on the soldadera's sexuality and on discourses about femininity, gender equality, and gender roles. Landeta's film is remarkable in that race lies at the heart of the narrative.

Despite her hatred of men (she orders a rapist castrated and calmly watches the procedure), Angustías falls in love with Manolo, an educated "mama's boy" who is teaching her to read and write. When he rejects her because she is a poor mulatta, Angustías falls apart. It is only the call of the Revolution that ultimately pulls her out of her depression. As a number of writers have noted, Landeta changed the novel's ending significantly.[53] Rojas Gonzáles has Angustías marry Manolo, give birth to a child, and yield up her identity as *la coronela*. In the film, conversely, Angustías abandons Manolo and rides off to lead her army toward a victorious Revolution. More central to this discussion, however, is that Landeta depicts the mulatta Angustías as the only strong female character in the film. As Carmen Huaco-Nuzam argues, "her colour encodes her difference"—a difference that supersedes gender and class. Landeta has used Angustías's blackness to accentuate the chasm that socially and economically divided white criollos from darker-skinned Indians, mestizos, and mulattos. In a film about the Revolution, this difference articulates the political discourse of that struggle which promised social and economic equality for all of Mexico's citizens. In Huaco-Nuzam's words, "Landeta anticipated the multiple concerns of modern feminism—the articulation of oppression across gender, race, and class."[54]

Angelitos Negros (Joselito Rodríguez, Jr., 1948) set questions of race, miscegenation, and racism in Mexico in a contemporary light. A wealthy young woman, Ana Luisa (Emilia Guiú), works as the director of an exclusive school for young women from the upper classes. She does not know that her black maid is really her mother. Mercé, the maid, who had been seduced by Ana Luisa's rich white father, raised the girl after the father died and never revealed the circumstances of her daughter's birth. Ana Luisa grows up believing that both her parents were white and that she is an orphan.

Movie poster of Angelitos Negros.

Angelitos Negros fit in with the structure of many early Mexican melodramas that were concerned with narrativizing social issues. According to Gustavo García, while "the melodramatic sensibility was slow to develop in Mexican cinema," by the end of the second decade of cinema "the most successful melodramas attempted to capture the lamentable conditions of class-based racist society."[55] Jesús Martín-Barbero suggests that in Latin America, melodrama has functioned as a "mediation" between existing and emergent cultures or, to put it another way, between tradition and modernity. According to Martín-Barbero and Monsiváis, these mediations have addressed the specific social and cultural needs of changing populations moving through the uneven and erratic boundaries of modernity and postmodernity.[56] Within dramas of family, romance, and sexual relations, these social melodramas explored contradictory questions raised by new political and familial structures.

Thus, in *Angelitos Negros*, Ana Luisa meets and falls in love with a famous singer, José Carlos Ruíz (Pedro Infante), who works with a group of close friends, black musicians and dancers. At the beginning of their romance, she goes to the nightclub to watch José Carlos perform and is shocked and dismayed when he comes onstage in blackface. Ana Luisa's racism reemerges throughout the narrative as an expression of unconscious self-hatred. She treats Mercé badly and refuses to shake hands with José Carlos's best friend. José Carlos reminds her that "black or white, we're all the same in God's eyes." Ana Luisa acknowledges her hatred of blacks but cannot explain the basis for her feelings.

When Mercé finds out that José Carlos and Ana Luisa plan to marry, she confesses the truth to her priest. He advises her that she is obligated to tell Ana Luisa, but she is unable to do so, knowing the pain it will cause her daughter. Ana Luisa and José Carlos marry without knowing the secret of her birth. They travel around Latin America while José Carlos performs in concert; and by the time they return to Mexico, Ana Luisa is pregnant. When a dark-skinned baby with Negroid features is born, the new mother rejects her. Ana Luisa also rejects José Carlos, believing that he had hidden his Afro parentage from her. Both the priest and Mercé beg José Carlos not to tell Ana Luisa the truth because she is too emotionally fragile, so the family lives a lie for four years. It is only on Mercé's deathbed that Ana Luisa's heritage is revealed. The daughter asks for forgiveness from her mother, but it is too late: the mother dies moments after Ana Luisa apologizes. It is not too late for her husband and daughter, however, and the film ends with the family embracing around Mercé's deathbed.

This conclusion to the problem of racial identity and racism in *Angelitos Negros* exemplifies how film melodrama is able to accommodate cultural uncertainties surrounding issues of race in ways that fit within the limits of proscribed social attitudes and beliefs. As I have argued, in the case of Mexican cinema, the overarching discourse of identity was *mestizaje*, or racial mixing. The ending of Rodríguez's film confirms the validity of this discourse. The myth of Mexico's *gran familia* is strengthened by the family Ruíz: the mulatta, Ana Luisa, and her child, whose blood has been "lightened" by the infusion of her father's criollo blood. The film thus recapitulates Vasconcelos's prophecy, his thesis of spiritual eugenics: eventually, all traces of nonwhite blood will be extinguished and Mexico will become a nation of the "cosmic race."

Conclusion

Mexican ideologies of nationalism have long been wedded to those of race, and those ideologies have been repeatedly explored and contested in Mexican cultural practices such as the cinema. Through an examination of a number of films from the Golden Age I have shown how cultural texts evidence the ways in which race, ethnicity, and nation-building are linked. I have also discussed how Mexican political and cultural discussions about national identity constructed a kind of melting pot model, not unlike that of the United States. This idea of a "natural" fusion of cultures and races recognized that Mexico was a nation of heterogeneous ancestry. On the other hand, discourses of *mestizaje, indigenismo*, and *hispanismo* (which were by no means always "official") challenged the melting pot theory and complicated the postrevolutionary ideal of a new nation whose people were unified through a common history.

I have demonstrated how cultural practices, such as the cinema, take part in the process of nation-building. The portrayal of national identity through popular media is not one of simple reproduction. As popular culture clarifies and embodies dominant discourses, it also challenges and reconstructs those discourses. According to Ramírez Berg, Mexico's classical cinema used skin color as a "marker of morality and social standing." He concludes that "light skin confers righteousness and high social station; dark skin usually signifies a lower-class villain or clown."[57] Skin color does matter in the representations of social characters in Mexican films, but I have argued that the complexity of racial ideologies in Mexico articulated a much more complicated set of cinematic racial and ethnic representations during the Golden Age of cinema.

Although cinema did not have the tools for resolving social complexity, it did provide a space wherein social subjects could take part in deciphering the puzzle of Mexican national identity. In a recent essay on film melodrama, Laura Mulvey clarifies a concept of "collective fantasy" which, for her, evidences "the presence of psychic symptoms within the social traces of unassimilated historical traumas."[58] These symptoms are played out, represented, and renarrativized in cultural practices such as cinema. And it is through their interaction with this cultural practice that Mexican audiences found a place in which to confront their social and personal ambivalence about race and national identity.

Notes

1. "Consequently, this final element, skin color, assumes a great importance in the spirit of the Mexican. He is not able to repudiate it. It is regretful that he cannot free himself of this restriction of his liberty, his ambitions, the fullness of his life. It identifies, it fixes, it distinguishes, it classifies." Alejando Galindo, *El cine mexicano: Un personal punto de vista* (Mexico City: Editores Asociados Mexicanos, S.A., 1985), 82–83.

2. Roger Bartra, *The Cage of Melancholy: Identity and Metamorphosis in the Mexican Character*, trans. Christopher J. Hall (New Brunswick, NJ: Rutgers University Press, 1992), 2–3.

3. Alan Knight, "Weapons and Arches in the Mexican Revolutionary Landscape," in *Everyday Forms of State Formation: Revolution and the Negotiation of Rule in Modern Mexico*, ed. Gilbert M. Joseph and Daniel Nugent (Durham, NC: Duke University Press, 1994), 59.

4. Michael Omi and Howard Winant, *Racial Formation in the United States*, 2d ed. (New York: Routledge, 1994), 55.

5. Nancy Leys Stepan, *The Hour of Eugenics: Race, Gender, and Nation in Latin America* (Ithaca, NY: Cornell University Press, 1991), 10.

6. Unlike the British colonialists of North America who did not intermarry with the native population, the Spanish did so in great numbers. By the time of the Revolution, most Mexicans could trace their ancestry to various combinations of European, Indian, and African blood.

7. Howard F. Cline, *Mexico: Revolution to Evolution, 1940–1960* (New York: Oxford University Press, 1963), 89.

8. Ibid., 92.

9. Leopoldo Zea, *The Latin-American Mind*, trans. James H. Abbott and Lowell Dunham (Norman: University of Oklahoma Press, 1963), 114.

10. Henry C. Schmidt, *The Roots of Lo Mexicano: Self and Society in Mexican Thought, 1900–1934* (College Station: Texas A & M University Press, 1978), 5.

11. Ibid., 8–9.

12. Alan Knight, "Racism, Revolution, and Indigenismo: Mexico, 1920–1940," in *The Idea of Race in Latin America, 1870–1940* (Austin: University of Texas Press, 1990), 72–73.

13. José Vasconcelos, *The Cosmic Race*, trans. Didier T. Joen (Los Angeles: California State University, 1979).

14. Stepan, *The Hour of Eugenics*, 147.

15. The 1930s also witnessed the founding of the Mexican Eugenics Society for the Improvement of Race, whose members included medical doctors and scientists. The debates among these professionals reflected popular and political arguments about the "integration" and physical "betterment" of the Indian population. See Stepan, *The Hour of Eugenics*, 55.

16. Gonzalo Aguirre Beltrán, "El indigenismo y su contribución a la idea de nacionalidad," *América Indígena* XXIX (México: Instituto Indigenista Interamericano, 1969), 404.

17. Stepan, *The Hour of Eugenics*, 150.

18. Quoted in Cline, *Mexico*, 89–90. In 1810 the remaining 40 percent of the population was divided into three major mestizo groups: Euro-Mestizo (17.9 percent), Afro-Mestizo (10.1 percent), and Indo-Mestizo (11.5 percent). A mere 0.3 percent was identified as "European," while 0.2 percent was classified as African. Cline cites a study done by José E. Iturriaga in 1940 which found that "pure" Indians made up 7.6 percent of the population, mixed ethnicities 91.4 percent, and whites 0.9 percent (90). Iturriaga's data were collected from the 1940 national census. Neither Iturriaga nor Cline addresses the question of "self-identification." In other words, it is possible that many individuals may have defined themselves as part of a particular socioethnic group regardless of the actual makeup of their bloodlines.

19. Ilene V. O'Malley, *The Myth of the Revolution: Hero Cults and the Institutionalization of the Mexican State, 1920–1940* (New York: Greenwood Press, 1986), 118.

20. Cline, *Mexico*, 91.

21. Knight, "Racism, Revolution, and Indigenismo," 77.

22. Ibid., 73.

23. O'Malley, *The Myth of the Revolution*, 118.

24. Janitzio is a small island located in the state of Michoacán near Patzcuarro. Julia Tuñon has noted that "the island is a perfect space for the representation" of the marginalization of Mexico's Indians. Julia Tuñon, "Emilio Fernández: A Look Behind the Bars," in *Mexican Cinema*, ed. Paulo Antonio Paranagua, trans. Ana M. López (London: British Film Institute, 1995), 180.

25. The American photographer, Paul Strand, shot the entire film using a silent, hand-cranked camera. *Redes* is most often cited for Strand's aesthetic compositions of Indians and their environment—compositions that were later to have a profound effect on the films of director Emilio Fernández and cinematographer Gabriel Figueroa.

26. The film was originally intended to be a documentary, an educational film aimed at Mexico's huge and diverse illiterate population, but it was transformed into a narrative when Strand and Zinnemann were brought in.

27. Fred Zinnemann, *An Autobiography: A Life in the Movies* (New York: Charles Scribner's Sons, 1992), 31.

28. Carlos Monsiváis, "Mythologies," in *Mexican Cinema*, 119.

29. While Eisenstein never completed his version of *¡Que Viva Mexico!*, a number of different films were made from footage that the director shot over two years in Mexico. For a discussion of *¡Que Viva Mexico!*, see my "Paradise Regained: Eisenstein's *¡Que Viva Mexico!* as Ethnography," in *Documenting the Documentary*, ed. Barry K. Grant and Jeanette Sloniowski (Wayne State University Press, forthcoming).

30. Julia Tuñon, *En su propio espejo. Entrevista con Emilio "El Indio" Fernández* (México: Universidad Autónoma Metropolitana-Ixtapalalpa, 1988).

31. Julia Tuñon, "Between the Nation and Utopia: The Image of Mexico in the Films of Emilio "El Indio" Fernández," *Studies in Latin American Popular Culture* 12 (1993): 167.

32. Joanne Hershfield, *Mexican Cinema, Mexican Woman, 1940–1950* (Tucson: University of Arizona Press, 1996), 57.

33. For various discussions of this relation see Marjorie Becker, *Setting the Virgin on Fire: Lázaro Cárdenas, Michoacán Peasants, and the Redemption of the Mexican Revolution* (Berkeley: University of California Press, 1995); Knight, "Weapons and Arches in the Mexican Revolutionary Landscape," 24–66; and Jean Meyer, *The Cristero Rebellion: The Mexican People Between Church and State, 1926–1929* (London: Cambridge University Press, 1976).

34. James D. Cockcroft, *Mexico: Class Formation, Capital Accumulation, and the State* (New York: Monthly Review Press, 1983), 116.

35. Article 27 of the 1917 Constitution had laid the ground for land redistribution and placed restrictions on the ownership of land, specifically by the Church and by foreigners. However, it was not until Lázaro Cárdenas assumed power in 1934 that land reform was implemented. In 1910, U.S. citizens owned more than 40 percent of Mexican agricultural land. See Judith Adler Hellman, *Mexico in Crisis*, 2d ed. (New York: Holmes & Meier, 1983), 26.

36. Becker, *Setting the Virgin on Fire*, 6.

37. Meyer, *The Cristero Rebellion*, 23.

38. Ibid., 187.

39. Ibid., 186.

40. Emilio García Riera, "The Impact of *Rancho Grande*," in *Mexican Cinema*, 131.

41. Charles Ramírez Berg, *Cinema of Solitude: A Critical Study of Mexican Films, 1967–1983* (Austin: University of Texas Press, 1992), 98.

42. Monsiváis, "Mythologies," 124.

43. Gustavo García, "Melodrama: The Passion Machine," in *Mexican Cinema*, 156.

44. Carlos Monsiváis, "Gabriel Figueroa: Establishing a Point of View," in *Artes de Mexico* 2, 2d ed. (Autumn 1992): 93.

45. García Riera, "The Impact of *Rancho Grande*," 130–31.

46. John King, *Magical Reels: A History of Cinema in Latin America* (London: Verso, 1991), 47.

47. Ramírez Berg, *Cinema of Solitude*, 99.

48. Ramírez Berg discusses the reappearance of the *charro* in the 1960s, as personified by Antonio Aguilar, who starred in rural melodramas "that mixed corridos with warmed-over revolutionary fervor," and in the 1970s, in satires that "greatly devalued" the *charro's* masculinity (100–106).

49. Ibid., 99.

50. Cline, *Mexico*, 89–90.

51. Mexican cinema's recent international success, *Como Agua para Chocolate* (1994), also addresses the question of mulattos in the nation's history.

52. For a critical discussion of *soldaderas* see O'Malley, *The Myth of the Revolution*; and Elizabeth Salas, *Soldaderas in the Mexican Military: Myth and History* (Austin: University of Texas Press, 1990).

53. See, for example, Carmen Huaco-Nuzam, "Matilde Landeta," *Screen* 28 no. 4 (Autumn 1987).

54. Ibid., 105.

55. García, "Melodrama," 153.

56. See Jesús Martín-Barbero, *Communication, Culture and Hegemony: From the Media to Mediations*, trans. Elizabeth Fox and Robert A. White (London: SAGE Publications, 1993), 119; also, Monsiváis, "Mythologies," 117–27. Monsiváis writes that "the public plagiarized the cinema as much as possible: its way of speaking and gesturing, humor, respect of institutions and its typical perception of duties and pleasures" (117).

57. Ramírez Berg, *Cinema of Solitude*, 27.

58. Laura Mulvey, " 'It will be a magnificent obsession': The Melodrama's Role in the Development of Contemporary Film Theory," in *Melodrama: Stage, Picture, Screen*, ed. Jacky Bratton, Jim Cook, and Christine Gledhill (London: BFI, 1994), 126.

6

Melodrama and Social Comedy in the Cinema of the Golden Age

Rafael Hernández Rodríguez

The Mexican Revolution, even though it was largely concerned with the injustices suffered by rural farmers and peasants, had started a process of transformation that would affect the city directly. During the first decades of this century, Mexico City became the privileged space where the contradictions of a country struggling for its modernization became evident. No one failed to recognize the contradictions of life in the big city and its repercussions on Mexican cinema, although not everyone interpreted them in the same way. For some, these contradictions were simply the price that Mexicans had to pay to join the modern world—suspiciously, the official version. For others, they revealed the incompetence of the new government's attempt to correct an unjust system. Yet, for many others, such contradictions were clearly the result of the intervention of foreign capitalist interests in the nation's economy.

The city thus became an ideal space for artists, intellectuals, and filmmakers to explore and question both the obsession with progress and the sacrifices that such an obsession could imply for a traditional society. Mexican movies found in melodrama the ideal vehicle for such explorations. This essay will focus on melodramas and city comedies produced during the 1940s and 1950s by some of the most interesting directors, especially Alejandro Galindo, Luis Buñuel, and Ismael Rodríguez, because I believe that even extremely conventional movies of the period often contained elements of social commentary. The works of these directors, although very different, converge in a similar social consciousness reflected in the use they made of popular language (which found in the movies, for the first time, a vehicle of self-exploration) as well as urban space—not merely the big city itself but also the spaces inhabited by the working class. This interest in the popular persisted because of its originality; but by the middle of the 1950s, when it had become a cliché, it disappeared.

Mexican melodramas and social comedies of the 1940s and 1950s grew to reflect the city and mimic its speech. Inasmuch as the country was changing, new ruling and middle classes were concentrated in the big city, where the working class was also struggling to adapt to a new, industrialized nation. In this nation, the capital became the point of junction of the two Mexicos, the geographic one and the one built on studio sets; movies were their shared vehicle of communication. Typically, most urban comedies and melodramas began and ended with panoramic shots of the city, showing its streets, avenues, parks, markets, and buildings, in order to physically locate the story as well as to demonstrate that Mexico City was just like any other big city in the world.

Most of the time this recourse constituted a tendentious way of softening the unjust reality of postrevolutionary society by making people believe that their problems were not theirs exclusively, but something shared with modern and industrialized nations. Sometimes it was also used to avoid censure, as in the case of Buñuel's *Los Olvidados* (1950), which opens with the observation that what the audience is about to see is a consequence of life in the big city, something very similar to what we could find in Paris, New York, or London, and by no means the result of social injustice in Mexican society. According to Buñuel, this introductory comment was not imposed by censors: "It was my idea so the movie could pass. Since I saw that it was a theme in Mexican cinema at the time, I thought of starting with such an observation."[1]

Melodrama, far from what we would assume at first glance, functioned as a purveyor of collective conventions and provided a sort of sentimental education of the tribe, with roots in the schematic rhetoric and theatricality of popular spectacles, not only in Mexico but also in most of the Western World. This didactic aspect of melodrama has been mentioned many times before, but I would like to complement it with an aspect not always acknowledged: the highly critical and occasionally subversive way that the public interacts with melodrama, as clearly seen in Mexican films of that era.

Many of the urban comedies and melodramas of the Golden Age provide examples of the way that these movies reflected and even worked as instruments of criticism against an unjust society, based on class division, which condemned portions of its population to a marginal and colonized existence. Just as important, they give testimony to the force of Mexican popular culture. From Galindo and Rodríguez to Buñuel, what distinguishes the cinema of this period is its manipulation of the conventions of urban comedies

The consequences of life in the big city: Los Olvidados, *directed by Luis Buñuel.*

and melodramas as well as the insistent use and mastery of popular language.

However, it is their connection and complicity with the audience, above all, that makes these movies truly examples of a Golden Age. The Mexican film industry developed and valued its dynamic relationship with its public. Melodramas and urban comedies in particular remained popular until the 1950s chiefly because while the former established a connection with the emotional needs or illusions of the moviegoers, the latter mirrored, either voluntarily or involuntarily, the changing society that was creating them.

Certainly it would not be fair to assume that people did not know that what they were watching was an exaggeration, and that therefore it was necessary to protect them. At the beginning of *Crepúsculo* (Julio Bracho, 1944), for example, there is a scene where Arturo de Córdova gives a book to his butler; that book is also titled *Crepúsculo*, and it is supposed to be the diary of a mentally ill person. The movie is retelling, or rather illustrating, the story of that ill person, who happens to be the famous doctor portrayed by de Córdova, who, in turn, happens to be the author of the book. When the surprised butler asks his bourgeois master if he thinks he .

will be able to understand it, his employer replies that he must do so—actually, that everybody must.

This scene is a very revealing one, because it is clearly working as a metaphor of the mechanism of melodrama: the butler is given a book that he probably will not understand, so someone else (the director) interprets it for him through images. This interpretation is nothing but the movie itself. Now, although the film might be seen as an interpretation (or illustration) of the text to the butler, and through him to the spectator, in this process the movie becomes something independent in itself. In other words, what starts as an interpretation becomes creation. This same technique would be used by Rodríguez a few years later in his Pepe el Toro movies, which are narrated through a book of stamps found in a garbage can by two street children, although Rodríguez simplifies the idea to the level of caricature.

This preoccupation with interpreting things for the public is one of the reasons behind the accusation of servility against melodrama. Most critics, however, do not take into consideration the way the viewer receives and interprets those stories. Rather, it seems that they disdain melodrama due to their paternalistic approach: these critics focus on the "ideologized" message but ignore the way that message is decoded. Ana M. López writes that such tendencies are proof of the inability of some critics "to see in the popularity of the melodrama anything but the alienation of a mass audience controlled by the dominant classes' capitalist interests."[2]

Viewers, then, are not necessarily passive. The most direct way that an audience has to interact with a movie is certainly by accepting or rejecting either it or its theme, but this is far from being the only way. In the Mexican case, more sophisticated ways of interaction were perfected along with the development of the industry. One of those moments is offered by Galindo in *Una Familia de Tantas* (1948), an intelligent fable of the clash between two of the most powerful symbols not only of Mexico but also of most Judeo-Christian societies: the fragile maiden, Maru (Martha Roth), and her father, the almighty patriarch, Rodrigo (Fernando Soler).

The story revolves around Maru's struggle for independence from her traditional family through an encounter and a sentimental involvement with an ambitious young man, Roberto (David Silva). He is well-spoken, lives with his understanding mother, and sells modern home appliances. Maru grows apart not only from her tyrannical father but also from her submissive mother. Unlike Maru, who finally succeeds in her rebellion against authority by marrying the man she loves, her older sister and brother are unable to liberate themselves from an unjust and particularly old-fashioned authority: both of them fail to form mature and independent relationships. The brother is forced to marry a girl he impregnated; the sister runs away from her parents' house, presumably with a man, after her father has beaten her. To add more symbolism to the fable, the movie ends on a hopeful note with a shot of Rodrigo's youngest children, also a boy and a girl, playing innocently in the patio, after Maru's mother has confronted the patriarch to defend their right to do so.

Unlike what we might have expected from a conventional Mexican movie, this film is always at odds with the rigid form of the melodrama and proposes instead a more sophisticated structure. It offers the spectator all the conventions of a melodramatic story—an unselfish mother, a girl in love, a cynical son, a loving and strict father—but purposely displaces these conventions to force the audience to attempt a different interpretation. For example, the mother will turn out to be strong and oppose the father in the end, while Maru will fight for her right to choose and marry the man she loves. Additionally, both Maru and her mother are sometimes melodramatic and sometimes ironic. While both melodrama and irony represent different aspects of life, neither one excludes the other.

It is true that we rarely see in Mexican films this practice of giving the audience all the pieces of the puzzle so that they can decide what to do with them. In *Una Familia de Tantas*, for example, the irresponsible son ends up marrying a girl who is expecting his child, the maid often criticizes openly the patriarch's decisions, and the charismatic and confident Roberto fascinates Rodrigo because of his devotion to his mother. Intelligent melodramas like this one frequently supply enough parts of the puzzle for the audience to attempt a less conventional interpretation of the story. Two of the most frequently used strategies in Mexican movies are exaggeration (sometimes genuine parody) and the assumption that melodrama implies an accomplice—the viewer—who decides what and what not to accept and how to interpret the message.

Exaggeration is more visible in movies such as *Un Rincón Cerca del Cielo* (Rogelio A. González, 1952), where the story is constructed with very typical, if not stereotypical, characters: the provincial young man who has to endure humiliation, hunger, and inequities to survive in the big city; the pious, humble, dark-haired girl who loves him; the ambitious and exuberant blonde who uses her beauty to seduce rich men, and who laughs at the traditional views of the couple and the audience. Added to these characters are stereotypical situations: the film repeatedly shows the frustrated attempts of a simple man to became an effective patriarch.

Although this film makes no direct reference to a corrupt system, the public knows that it lies at the bottom of such frustrations, no matter how much the characters try to convince them otherwise. Thus, when the good girl confesses her darker thoughts, she sounds almost cynical: "Sometimes I wish I had no dignity, so I could have money. But since one cannot be what one is not, first things come first." However, to sweeten that bitter and potentially dangerous comment, her boyfriend comes to the rescue: "Well, that's to have dignity." She has no choice but to swallow that with a sad smile, and so does the audience. We understand, however, that neither the girl nor the audience could possibly believe that life could be that simple. Such a judgment is only accepted in the make-believe world of movies.

For the provincial moviegoer, urban comedies offer the chance for him to become acquainted with the ways of the city; for the decent girl, melodrama offers an opportunity to experience the exciting, though socially condemned life of the prostitute; for a submissive wife, both comedy and melodrama reveal a glimpse into the world of jewelry, champagne, and nightlife that a more independent woman can enjoy—a world to which the wife is not even supposed to aspire. Traditional melodrama's focus on opposites frequently serves as an indirect way of showing, if not glorifying, what it claims to reject. Even in the most conventional melodramas such as *Un Rincón Cerca del Cielo*, we can find scenes containing elements of social commentary.

Un Rincón Cerca del Cielo tells the story of Pedro González (Pedro Infante), who leaves the provinces for the city to look for a better life, only to find that he has neither the ambition nor the lack of scruples to succeed. After all, he is, as he describes himself, "Mexican, thirty years old, Catholic, orphaned, with all my teeth, a loving heart, and the desire to have many, many children." In the city he meets Margarita (Marga López) and marries her. When Margarita gets pregnant, she is fired from her job; Pedro loses his job as well and, for the rest of the movie, is unable to keep one. He and his wife end up in the worst poverty, aggravated by the illness and death of their only child.

Although the movie is full of stereotypes and reactionary views, it contains a few potentially subversive scenes. Among them is one that offers some of the most enjoyable moments in the film: we see Pedro and Margarita kissing at the movies. A police officer tries to arrest them for offending public decency, but finally desists due to the intervention of the other members of the audience. The officer leaves with the warning that next time he will arrest them. Of course, once the cop has gone, Pedro and Margarita go back to kissing, while he tells her "Nobody loves each other the way we do, right?" But as if to make fun of this attitude, the director shows a view of the movie theater, which is full of couples kissing in what seems to be an open challenge to the authority represented by the policeman.

Similarly, this movie, which seems to sympathize with all the troubles that a young man has to endure to become a good provider, especially when he has to face a tough world, raises interesting questions about gender division in Mexican society while never giving them central importance. The movie is clearly not preoccupied with exploring the causes of machismo and female submission—presented as if it was exclusively Mexican. Instead, the audience is expected to accept the traditional view of those roles as the norm, even if only to ridicule them. The premise that the traditional male and female roles were changing in Mexico is fundamental to the story, yet those changes are not interpreted as either bad or good. It is this ambiguity that makes this film weak and, in the end, conventional.

Pedro fails every time he tries to behave like a man (which for him means being an authoritarian and a good provider), while Margarita often finds herself torn between the traditional role and a more modern view of female comportment. Her modern views, however, seem to disappear in front of her boyfriend. When Pedro and Margarita go out for the first time, he insists in paying for her lunch, which she cannot accept: "We both pay for our own lunch, or I won't accept another invitation." "Well, don't accept it again," Pedro replies, "but things must be done the way they should be done." Margarita yields only to find out that Pedro has not enough money, so she pays for both lunches and discreetly calls it a loan.

Later, when Pedro finds out that Margarita has paid for part of the wedding banquet and asks her why she has hurt his pride, she cries and begs for forgiveness. In an earlier scene, however, Pedro and Margarita have an argument about whether she should work or not after she gets married. A street vendor, overhearing the conversation, presents the point of view of the people or, it can be argued, of the audience. The vendor's interventions are both funny and ironic: First he agrees with Pedro that it is not right for a wife to work ("one has his pride") but changes his mind when he finds out that Pedro makes less than two hundred pesos per month. In that case, he advises: "Think about it, my friend, let her work." The image of the macho husband who cannot dare to take money from his wife is continuously ridiculed in the movie by Pedro's unsuccessful attempts to be a real provider for his family. In the end, he must depend on Margarita's salary.

Similarly, the film problematizes the oversimplified and divided view of the female figure as represented by the ambitious blonde, Sonia (Silvia Pinal), and the faithful and unselfish brunette, Margarita. Sonia is shown flirting with rich men and expressing her opinions about money and love in a cynical way, especially in front of Margarita. "I was born to enjoy life," says Sonia emphatically, while

Margarita replies: "We all are born to suffer." Sonia answers only by pointing to a group of poor children. The audience understands that Sonia has her feet firmly on the ground.

Regardless of the supposed moral intention of the movie, it is hard to sympathize completely with Margarita, whose opinions are ambiguous and who has some of the most predictable and terrible lines. In an early scene she complains that she is taken advantage of at work because she is a woman: "Sure, since I don't wear pants." And at the beginning of the film she gives the impression of being a less traditional woman—after all, she is independent, has no family, and supports herself. Yet after meeting Pedro, she quickly becomes the *noviecita santa* (innocent little girlfriend), who is religious and a

Star David Silva as a boxer by necessity in the title role of Un Campeón sin Corona, *directed by Alejandro Galindo.*

mother figure, who comforts her man and keeps his faith alive. As some critics have observed, in melodramas "the dominant moral weakens and fortifies."[3]

In contrast to this angel-like girl, the *femme fatale*, embodied by Sonia, seems more in touch with her circumstances and faithful to her actions. The daughter of Pedro's protector, Sonia is also the best friend of Margarita, who tries to persuade her to give up her ambition of becoming a rich woman at any cost. When Margarita tells her that a woman only needs love to be happy, Sonia replies that it is not true, that all she sees around her are fat, dirty women with too many filthy children and neither love nor a man to care for them; later, when the two heroines see some kids sleeping on the street, Sonia adds: "Their misery doesn't let me lie." What is intended as cynicism becomes incisive social commentary. Margarita disagrees, and Sonia dares her to see who will be happier in the end: "You with happiness and I with money."

Melodrama can be seen as a critical instrument of a society that has created it to show another image of that society through its desires, ghosts, taboos, limitations, and longings. Mexican melodrama thus can be understood as subversive and not necessarily the expression of immature people, as critics such as Michael Wood imply. Wood compares Mexican melodramas to those of the Spaniard, Luis Buñuel. For Wood, Buñuel's movies, which deal with supposedly sophisticated topics such as religious rebellion, desire and fetishism, or psychological analysis, are European, while those that deal with poverty, superstition, or vulgar passions are Mexican. For Wood, the Mexican characteristic of Buñuel's movies is clear especially when he deals with abused children, since "any visitor to Mexico has seen those handsome, unsmiling Indian faces."[4] Aside from the fact that this shows a very narrow Eurocentric—and, in the case of Spain, most likely inexplicable—perspective, Wood's opinion is wrong.

Buñuel is an interesting case because he emigrated to Mexico when he already had some prestige as an avant-garde artist, and because he is perhaps the only Spanish-speaking director who has been accepted into the circle of classic directors. But in opposition to the tendency to consider him a Lone Ranger figure galloping in the arid desert of the Mexican film industry, fighting the bourgeois ideology of tearful mothers, *charros* on their cardboard horses, and authoritarian but good-hearted patriarchs, I perceive him to be a dynamic part of the industry, as a matter of fact—so related to it that, as Víctor Fuentes mentions, he constantly returns to Mexican-style melodrama even in his more "personal" films.[5]

Most critics, when discussing the presence of melodrama in Buñuel's Mexican movies, are inclined to interpret it as something imposed by the conventions of the industry. But unfortunately, what they cannot grasp, according to Fuentes, is the other aspect of that relationship: the attraction of melodrama, never confessed but always evident in Buñuel's movies, as a way of recovering basic dramatic aspects of life and the tragedy of people through the powerful force of their passions and emotions. Melodrama, then, is not tragically immature and exclusively Mexican, as most critics would agree, but rather a universal way of expression.

These attitudes toward the relationship of Buñuel with melodrama and Mexican cinema are not new, but rather a commonplace among his critics and followers—from Elliot Rubinstein, who considers that it was precisely the "unredeemability" of this industry that caused Buñuel's "wickedest self to be projected,"[6] to Octavio Paz, who thinks that Buñuel's enterprise was a difficult task not only in Mexico but also in the contemporary world at large.[7] Curiously enough, Buñuel, despite his constant declarations against sentimentality, had no problem in accepting the labeling of some of his movies as melodramas. Responding to the question of whether *El Bruto* (1952) was a melodrama, he asks: "Melodrama? I don't care. When I made the movie I didn't tell myself: 'I'm going to make a melodrama.' "[8] So if it is a melodrama, it is because that was the ideal narrative structure for the movie.

By looking at Mexican cinema as a whole, it seems evident that what most critics cannot—or do not even attempt to—understand is that when Buñuel went to Mexico, he joined a vital and already established tradition of making movies, one that for the most part had a dynamic relationship with the public. The Mexican audience had long been an essential part of the making of a film culture, and both filmmakers and the public were at the same time creating and shaping the habit of watching and making movies. This cinema was already crossing national borders and becoming the most vital film industry not only of Latin America but also of all the Spanish-speaking world. According to the critic Ernesto Giménez Caballero, even in the 1930s it is not surprising that Mexican movies "pack Spanish theaters for weeks, or even months, and that our public goes to them with an excitement that is beyond a simple spectacle."[9]

The "sophistication" of Buñuel's movies is, at least in part, directly related to the process of Mexican cinema. Similarly, if in melodramas such as *La Mujer del Puerto* (1933), *Distinto Amanecer* (Julio Bracho, 1943), *El Esqueleto de la Señora Morales* (1959), or *Una Familia de Tantas* we find "sophisticated" elements such as the relationship of political power and corruption, repressed sexuality, irreverence, black humor, parody of the religiosity of some sectors of society, or even incest, it is because that was the way Galindo, Arcady Boytler, Rogelio González, or Julio Bracho decided to narrate their stories. Mexican society, like any other, could be incestuous, irreverent, or fetishist. In the same way, a Spanish director could be melodramatic. Not to recognize this reduces criticism to judgments based on stereotypes.

Fernando Soler as a tyrannical father in the title role of Una Familia de Tantas, *directed by Alejandro Galindo.*

What happens more often is that movies present different elements combined. And in that way, *Una Familia de Tantas* is perhaps one of the most accomplished films of the Golden Age. In this movie, Maru's dilemma is at the same time in open opposition to the old regime and the acceptance of her womanhood. In the scene that marks the transition between Maru-the-girl and Maru-the-woman, just before her fifteenth birthday party—the Mexican equivalent of Sweet Sixteen—Maru presses her new shoes against her chest while declaring: "I'm going to be a woman." The melodrama is there, but so are other elements for Maru: growing up, coming to terms with her sexuality, rebelling against authority, and an increasing sense of independence.

Far from being simplistic and conventional, classical Mexican cinema was capable of more sophisticated messages and techniques. One example is the constant use of feet to narrate a scene, almost an obsession in many of these movies and clearly present in Galindo's films. In *Una Familia de Tantas,* for example, her feet determine whether Maru is a woman or not while they are also the center of the most unspoken sexuality. Thus, in the party scene, once Maru has been accepted in society as a woman, she cannot let any man see her feet. Even after all the guests have left, when, exhausted, she takes off her shoes, the presence still in the house of her sister's boyfriend prompts her father to shout furiously: "How dare you take your shoes off! Don't you see that there are men present, and you're now a woman?"

This preoccupation with modesty can be seen as a moral lesson teaching that decency and virtue are the result of sacrifice. But as in many melodramas, a more perverse interpretation can be attempted. Since showing her feet is associated with the idea of Maru's being a sexually active woman, and since the men present were members of her own family, her father's comment is not merely an innocent admonition that young ladies should behave in this or that way. Instead, a latent struggle with desire and incest appears to be troubling Rodrigo. It is almost as if he asks his daughter not to show her feet to him, her brother, and her future brother-in-law, or they cannot be responsible for their actions.

Buñuel's films also present scenes of suggested incest and sexually charged feet (for example, *Viridiana*, 1961), although the director denies that he is a fetishist: "I am not a foot fetishist, but in many of my movies feet appear often."[10] In the opening of *El Gran Calavera* (1949), all we see are the intertwined legs of a group of men. By looking at their legs we immediately know the social status of those men, and where they are. Yet, according to Buñuel, the scene was not in the script but occurred to him while filming.[11] It is not hard to believe this, especially since the precedent had been set earlier in many Mexican movies. I prefer to think that Buñuel was aware of it and chose to establish contact with this aspect of the Mexican cinema.

Not to acknowledge this contact risks misinterpreting some of Buñuel's scenes by denying them the possibility of dialogue with other Mexican movies. Rubinstein, in commenting on *El Bruto*, writes that the audience—a New York audience—can find in it "tiny pieces of the jigsaw of the maestro's career." As evidence, he mentions the "unusually ugly shoes" of Katy Jurado, and then he wonders "what quaint allusion to his signature fetish is Buñuel insinuating?"[12] Perhaps none. Perhaps if Rubinstein had known Mexican movies and tried to understand Buñuel's films from that perspective, he could have offered a richer interpretation instead of trying to solve a puzzle with missing pieces. (It also would have helped if he had explained what he meant by "unusually ugly shoes.")

With similar misleading comments, Rubinstein refers to *La Ilusión Viaja en Tranvía* (1953). He sees one of its several memorable sequences—the slaughtered beasts hanging from the baggage racks of the streetcar—as a sign of Buñuel's iconoclastic sensibility. It is clear that for Rubinstein the interesting aspect of such a scene is its lack of realism, or rather its surrealism, which would have been less surprising if he had been more familiar with Mexican culture or with Buñuel's own views. "In Mexico," the director Tomás Pérez Turrent, referring to the incredible features that critics find in many of his scenes, "it's believable."[13]

Writing about *La Ilusión Viaja en Tranvía*, Gastón Lillo recognizes the importance of those moments traditionally accepted as the "redeemable ones" in Buñuel's Mexican movies, but he prefers to interpret them as instruments of a subversive manipulation of melodrama. I think we can agree with him, although that subversive force, I would add, is already implicit in the very nature of melodrama itself. In other words, if Buñuel is able to change and manipulate "all the situations that melodrama treats with sentimentality, with a moral intention based on a Manichaean dichotomy of good and evil, leading to an homage to virtue,"[14] it is because in its exaggeration, melodrama contains the seed of its own parody and deconstruction. To assume that an audience cannot distinguish between reality and the exaggeration of reality is, at best, a patronizing view of the people.

Most melodramas establish from the beginning an oversimplified view of life's problems that no one can take seriously. "I don't judge you because I love you," says Gloria Marín on the phone to a tormented Arturo de Córdova in *Crepúsculo*. This confession is at once intentionally dramatic and unintentionally comic; if it had been really that easy, there would have been no need for this movie, but that is not the case, and this is what the audience understands. Melodramas are an invitation to play an elaborate game where someone presents something as the real thing; and although everybody knows it is not, they pretend to accept it. Buñuel would be, in any case, the killjoy, the one who openly reveals that everything is just a trick. Galindo follows Buñuel closely, but it is clear that for him to play the game respectfully is part of the craft of a director. Both men, in any case, are aware of the intelligence of the audience.

There are certain aspects of Buñuel's movies that single out his genius—for example, the egg that an angry Pedro throws at the camera (and the viewer) in *Los Olvidados*, or the scene of dreamy love-making inside a bus on the top of a mountain in *Subida al Cielo* (1952). But even these movies can be seen as melodramas, although both films occasionally turn to a dreamlike atmosphere. This is in opposition to what José Agustín Mahieu supposes when he writes that in *Subida al Cielo*, Buñuel "separates himself from the preceding melodramatic themes to reach a dreamlike tone."[15]

Some of these elements are shared with other Mexican artists, movies, and cultural manifestations in general. *La Ilusión Viaja en Tranvía* provides a wonderful example of the constant dialogue between Buñuel's movies and popular culture in the *pastorela* (a popular Christmas play), where the streetcar drivers represent God and the Devil with a naiveté that is at once powerful and farcical. José de la Colina, in a conversation with Buñuel, mentions this *pastorela* and tells the director that it is not believable that "people in a poor Mexican neighborhood . . . represent God with such boldness." "Why not?" asks a surprised Buñuel. He explains that it is not boldness, since the people are not professional actors: "They tried to do something dignified, but it turns out to be comic."[16] Comments like this one show how conscious Buñuel was of the popular influence. He insists on making it clear that those things that might seem strange to a foreigner are really part of a concrete cultural reality. Even the *pastorela,* he adds, is "real": it is a *pastorela* published in Mexico in the nineteenth century.

Preoccupied with establishing the differences between Spain and Mexico, Michael Wood asks how much we see of Mexico in these films. He answers: "I want to say 'not much.' "[17] But in reality, Buñuel's contact with the Mexican popular culture is revealed in *La Ilusión Viaja en Tranvía* as well as in his other movies. It is possible that much of this popular presence is José Revueltas's or Mauricio Magdaleno's work, but there is no doubt that Buñuel himself was interested in it.

Although rarely mentioned, the collaboration of Mexican writers with Buñuel seems to me extremely important, since those writers, especially Revueltas, share with the director not only a clear preference for the popular and the social but also the same distrust of established power. Buñuel, in the words of Robert Stam that could apply to Revueltas as well, "consistently places in the foreground the realities of class, of physical hunger and its social causes."[18] Whatever the case, these interactions with the popular and the social are present in Mexican culture in general; and, in part, at least we could argue that Buñuel is taking that into consideration.

In melodramas and urban comedies of other directors, especially Galindo, preoccupation with the popular is also present, and perhaps more than anything else it is the language that serves as the direct link between the public and the film. Galindo's characters reflect in their dialogues the summary of urban speech. David Silva, and especially Fernando Soto "Mantequilla," take from the people their way of talking and teach it back to them. According to Jorge Ayala Blanco, most of the power of Galindo's movies resides in the director's ability to restrain his tenderness toward the characters of his films and in the economical way he uses popular language. Thanks to these virtues, continues Ayala Blanco, Mantequilla could personify the *peladito* (the poor devil who uses his ingenious and picaresque speech and sympathy to survive in the city) with "a dignity that Mario Moreno," or Cantinflas, "never foresaw."[19]

Language has, in the films of Buñuel as well as in those of Galindo and even in most of Rodríguez's movies, the function of disclosing and confronting identity. The identification with the popular accent in the speech of David Silva, Fernando Soto, Lilia Prado, Carlos Navarro, Pedro Infante, or Blanca Estela Pavón reveals to the audience their own voice. Movies, perhaps, achieved what no writer did: they captured the urban language of Mexico.

In *Un Campeón sin Corona* (1945), language and popular realism are instruments stretched by Galindo to explore a somehow more intricate problem, that of the inferiority complex of Mexicans, which is not seen in the movie as an isolated phenomenon but rather as a concrete problem related directly to the marginal and colonized condition of society, or even more as a result of the nation's geographic proximity to the United States. Language is cultural identity, proposes Galindo, and if on one hand we can see Mexican culture revealed by the speech of its people, on the other it is English that embodies the power and impenetrable center from which Mexicans have been cast out.

"Kid" Terranova (David Silva), the world boxing champion, is literally invincible in the ring until he has to fight the Chicano boxer, Joe Ronda (Victor Parra). Clearly impressed by the fact that Ronda speaks English, Terranova cannot conquer him—not because he is physically unable to do so but because he admits his rival's superiority due to his linguistic skill. Terranova's manager realizes this and tries to convince him that it is not true. His argument is that anybody can learn English: "Chinese is more difficult," he jokes, "and Chinese people do not boast about it." Ronda's manager has also noticed the boxer's problem and tries to take advantage of it. Whenever Terranova seems to be winning, he tells Ronda to speak English.

The whole conflict for Terranova is not, of course, any linguistic inability but rather the superiority of another culture to which he does not belong and what that other culture implies for him: girls, fine cigarettes, clothes, social status, etc. If language is the key that locks Mexicans out of the civilized and refined world, then in a genial twist, Galindo makes Regalito (Fernando Soto) invent one and speak to Terranova in terribly broken English, in an attempt to exorcise the boxer's ghosts. It is almost as if Regalito is trying to appropriate and tame that language.

Like Galindo, Buñuel also uses popular language to denounce an unjust system. In *Los Olvidados*, popular language is a clear identifier of the social marginality of the characters: Pedro, one of the forgotten ones, thinks himself to be superior and thus has the right to abuse El Ojitos, who is after all a *fuereño* (out-of-towner), which he realizes after he hears him talking. In *El Gran Calavera*, the division between classes is most clearly marked by language. When two women from the poor neighborhood, where a bourgeois family has moved after their phony bankruptcy, talk about the new neighbors, one says that she is sure they have seen better times. When her companion asks why, she answers: "Because they speak so funny." And later, once Remedios (Maruja Grifell) starts to accept the fact that

Stars Pedro Infante and Blanca Estela Pavón in the title roles of the single most popular film in Mexican cinema, Nosotros los Pobres, *directed by Ismael Rodríguez.*

now they are also poor, she starts to talk "like them," but in an exaggerated way.

This exaggeration is at the same time a tribute to the colorful way that the people speak and a parody of the patronizing way in which the bourgeoisie often accept the popular culture. So when Remedios later encounters the poor women and talks to them in a way that she believes is the way they speak, they look at each other with sarcasm. There is irony as well in the fact that the bourgeois woman has lost her identity along with her high-society speech without acquiring a new one—without genuinely mastering the popular way of talking.

Galindo, more than Buñuel, takes popular language as one of his most important concerns, whereas Rodríguez manipulates and tortures it with a baroque sensibility that reveals its own farcical aspect. Buñuel, nevertheless, is genuinely preoccupied with popular language to the point that Michael Wood considers it a problem for the universal understanding of the message that the director is trying to deliver: "The paradox then is that the message is clearly international while the faces and the voices and the words are clearly Mexican."[20] However, it seems that Buñuel was less preoccupied than Wood with oppositions such as Mexican/European, local/universal, or popular/high culture. To write the dialogue of *Los Olvidados*, he had no problem in requesting the collaboration of Pedro de Urdimalas, who was also responsible for the dialogue of *Nosotros los Pobres* (Ismael Rodríguez, 1947).

Before these movie directors, only certain poets, especially López Velarde, had re-created the Mexican idiom, that of one's province, in a way that was half real expression (the everyday language) and half nostalgia (the reminiscence of the speech of the poet's hometown). But precisely because of this, people considered it more authentic. Only through films, particularly in urban comedies and melodramas, does the city speak equally convincingly and self-consciously. It is not an accident that *Nosotros los Pobres*, whose power resides in popular language, is considered the most popular Mexican movie ever. This film exploits to extremes the language of the people, not only in their everyday speech but also in the ludicrous or poetic writings on streetcars and trucks,[21] or even the graffiti on the *vecindad's* walls.

Popular language and culture cannot be understood completely without understanding the space where they exist: the neighborhoods of lower-class housing, or *vecindades*. The *vecindad* finds perhaps its most emblematic function as a place of dialogue and exchange of ideas in *Ustedes los Ricos* (Ismael Rodríguez, 1948). In this movie— a sequel to *Nosotros los Pobres*, with a title so predictable that it is

silly and magical at the same time—the *vecindad* becomes what
Gustavo García describes as "the space of solidarity of the working
people, of the poor but honorable; it was the space one left to climb
the social ladder only to return, repentant, to one's roots and to the
warmth that could not be found among the bourgeoisie."[22] This space
is used by Rodríguez also as a sort of public forum where his characters interact with other aspects of Mexican life, such as the controversial mural of Diego Rivera painted on the walls of the Hotel del
Prado in Mexico City that included the phrase: "God does not exist."
As a response, some invisible hand had painted on the wall of Pepe
el Toro's vecindad: "He does exist!"

Paradoxically, the director who created the most stereotypical
popular characters and idealized the poor neighborhoods of Mexico
City also gave to the *vecindad* its most subversive function—that of
providing a space for the underprivileged classes to express and
question Mexican life and culture, even if it was only to reflect some
of the most reactionary and tendentious views. Only Buñuel, in *El
Ángel Exterminador* (1962), offers through an opposite process a better example of the potentially subversive social criticism of which inhabited spaces are capable. Robert Stam has offered the best
interpretation of this subversiveness in his analysis of the transformation suffered by the rich in this movie. According to Stam, "the noble
mansion becomes an overcrowded mini-slum, without running water,
with people sleeping on the floor in promiscuous cohabitation. . . .
The same aristocrats who spilled expensive food as an amusing theatrical device are now ravaged by hunger."[23]

Unlike Italian neorealism, where social elements become a real
issue through the testimonial aspects of documentary-like filming,
Mexican social films, usually tragicomedies, were mostly urban
movies that combined all the characters and all the elements expected in an urban environment—from gangsters under the bridge of
Nonoalco and *peladitos* in the *vecindad* to cabaret girls, corrupt
politicians, prostitutes with a heart of gold, and phony labor leaders
as well as the new class of bureaucrats. An extreme example of this
mix of characters is presented by Rodríguez in his movies about the
rich and the poor, where the characters are reduced to popular types:
"the physical one," "the romantic one," "the paralytic one," "the cynical one," "the marijuana-addicted one," and "the one who gets up
late." In all these movies, however, the city becomes the stage for a
Mexican human comedy.

As the center of Mexican life, the city revealed a more accurate
and complex picture of society. The early Cantinflas, perhaps more
than anybody else, embodies the contradictions of the new society,
which is not only as unjust as the one before the Revolution but also

has an official discourse attached to it. The new ruling class used an empty and haughty speech that was full of promises but completely estranged from the real needs of the people. This discourse is not only institutionalized, but glorified; it, however, does not communicate. In this context, the observations of Xavier Villaurrutia about the character created by Mario Moreno can help us to understand his nonsensical speech as a mockery of that official discourse, since *el peladito* is "representative of a social class whose tragedy resides in that its desire to express itself finds no vehicle, no appropriate language."[24]

The assertiveness of Cantinflas is evident in his use of language. Despite his inability to express what he wants to, he nevertheless communicates, although in a bizarre way. The classic example of this technique is the scene of a trial in *Ahí Esta el Detalle* (Juan Bustillo Oro, 1940). Because of his twisted way of expressing himself, Cantinflas is sentenced to death, only to be saved by the real criminal who turns himself in. This scene is highly subversive, I think, since after justice has been served, the judge, the defense, and the prosecutor start imitating Cantinflas, thus unmasking a disturbing system. In the middle of this burlesque, we hear Cantinflas saying: "Everything is clear now, if it's just a matter of speaking Christian to understand each other, isn't it?" The irony here is that nobody really understands anything and Cantinflas is not liberated because of his ability to speak clearly, or "Christian."

By the late 1950s, Mexican society was already in the process of becoming "modern." The new ruling class had agreed to follow the American model of progress, which required a dependency on that society. At the same time, this alliance was a guarantee of the faithful "partnership" between Mexico and the United States. Mexico City, though still visible in movies, was being presented more and more as a cosmopolitan urban space. Supermarkets, music stores, and motorcycles were displacing local markets, neighborhood stores, and bicycles. With the old city, much of the popular spirit that had made the work of Rodríguez and Galindo possible disappeared as well. It was at this time that melodramas started to take seriously their role as educators.

One of the movies that shows this change clearly is *¿A Donde Van Nuestros Hijos?* (Benito Alazraki, 1956). This film about the breaking up of a provincial family of bureaucrats who have just moved to Mexico City tries to sermonize the gospel of modernity. However, unlike the classical melodramas, this one lacks naiveté and freshness. Much of the dialogue, for example, is solemnly forced. Thus, in opposition to her tyrannical father, a daughter argues: "Look, Dad, one can't live like in the Middle Ages, see how

Americans have changed everything." The patriarch will say later, while reprimanding his children, that the young people "sometimes mistake love, true love, for a passing illusion." The problem with these lines is that there is no irony. Even when Alazraki tries to be universal, the dialogue of his characters sounds more like propaganda or wishful thinking. When the young man decides to leave the country with a scholarship, his father accuses him of selling his country for an all-expenses-paid trip. The son answers: "I don't think in terms of countries. I think of a better world."

The urban space itself had changed, and now we see a city with an impressive university, with neatly trimmed parks, and new automobiles—a city where Dolores del Río has exchanged Xochimilco's *chinampas* for an American-style supermarket. Times certainly were changing, and so was the concept of making movies. The audience, too, had changed its taste and abandoned the simple plots. "With the introduction of sophisticated U.S. and European movies, the Mexican middle class came to 'abhor machismo, the picturesque and naive,' " according to recent declarations by Carlos Monsiváis to the *Los Angeles Times*.[25] Whatever the case, no matter which changed first—the audience or the movies—what is undeniable is that by the end of the 1950s, Mexican cinema had already lost its connection with its once faithful audience.

Notes

1. Tomas Pérez Turrent and José de la Colina, *Buñuel por Buñuel* (Madrid, 1993), 53.

2. Ana M. López, "Tears and Desire: Women and Melodrama in the 'Old' Mexican Cinema," in *Mediating Two Worlds: Cinematic Encounters in the Americas*, ed. John King, Ana M. López, and Manuel Alvarado (London, 1993), 148.

3. Carlos Monsiváis, *Amor perdido* (México, 1984), 38.

4. Michael Wood, "Buñuel in Mexico," in *Mediating Two Worlds*, 46.

5. Víctor Fuentes, *Buñuel en México* (Zaragoza, 1993), 44.

6. Elliot Rubenstein, "Buñuel in Mexico," *Latin American Literature and Art Review* 20 (Spring 1977): 31.

7. See Octavio Paz, "El cine filosófico de Buñuel," in *Los signos en rotación y otros ensayos* (Madrid, 1993), 177–82.

8. Pérez Turrent and Colina, *Buñuel por Buñuel*, 71.

9. Cited in Aurelio de los Reyes, *Medio siglo de cine mexicano (1896–1947)* (México, 1988), 167.

10. Pérez Turrent and Colina, *Buñuel por Buñuel*, 48.

11. Ibid., 45.

12. Rubinstein, "Buñuel in Mexico," 31.

13. Pérez Turrent and Colina, *Buñuel por Buñuel*, 88.

14. Gastón Lillo, "Buñuel y los generos cinematográficos: Un acercamiento pragmatico a sus filmes mexicanos," *Sociocriticism* 6, nos. 1–2 (1985): 103

15. See José Agustín Mahieu, "El período mexicano de Luis Buñuel," *Cuadernos Hispanoamericanos* 358 (April 1980): 163.

16. Pérez Turrent and Colina, *Buñuel por Buñuel*, 88–89.

17. Wood, "Buñuel in Mexico," 48.

18. Robert Stam, "Hitchcock and Buñuel: Desire and the Law," *Studies in the Literary Imagination* 16, no. 1 (Spring 1983): 26.

19. Jorge Ayala Blanco, *La aventura del cine mexicano (1931–1967)* (México, 1993), 129.

20. Wood, "Buñuel in Mexico," 50.

21. See Jorge Luis Borges, "Las inscripciones de los carros," *Ficcionarío* (México, 1985), 19–23.

22. Gustavo García, *Mexican Cinema*, ed. Paulo António Paranagua (London, 1995), 157.

23. Stam, "Hitchcock and Buñuel," 25–26.

24. Cited in Reyes, *Medio siglo*, 175.

25. Chris Kraul and Shasta Darlington, "Mexican Cinema Is Fading Out," *Los Angeles Times*, January 8, 1996.

7

From Collaboration to Containment
Hollywood and the International Political Economy of Mexican Cinema after the Second World War[1]

Seth Fein

> The Mexican film cannot be compared with any other export products, be-
> cause it combines economic considerations, cultural and even political sig-
> nificance, that no other national product does . . . When we speak of having
> an influence, first in our Spanish-speaking markets and then in the other
> important world markets, we have spoken of something that provides the
> force and the central ingredient for that, it is the need for high quality!
> —*Santiago Reachi, President of Posa Films, 1955*[2]

The 1948 release of *Río Escondido* was a triumph of the Mexican
film industry. It represented the possibilities that seemed in reach
of Mexico's postwar film sector: sovereign control of an economically
viable, artistically vibrant, nationally dominant, and internationally
recognized film industry to produce Mexican stories, myths, and images. For many film scholars, *Río Escondido* exemplifies the "nationalist" idiom that symbolizes the apex of Golden Age cinema in the
late 1940s (especially associated with the work of director Emilio
Fernández "El Indio" and cinematographer Gabriel Figueroa). In this
view, what is most significant about *Río Escondido* is its national plot
and theme, expressed through Fernández's writing and direction and
Figueroa's award-winning cinematography.[3] The film's many conventions notwithstanding, such as its sentimentalized treatment of stereotypical Indians and the glorification of state authority, *Río Escondido*
is a decidedly Mexican film of very high technical quality.[4]

However, casting *Río Escondido* as nationalist is problematic, if
nationalism is taken to signify some variant of anti-imperialism.
While the movie is a "classic" example of *national* filmmaking, it is
not ideologically, industrially, or aesthetically opposed to Hollywood's hegemony. In fact, in all three areas, it exemplifies the
Mexican industry's historic connections to U.S. studios. Not only did

many Mexican artists such as Figueroa train in the U.S. industry, contributing to Mexican cinema's inherently international style, but also the film sector more broadly adapted various domestic and foreign influences to produce the nexus of narratives and images promoted internationally as *lo mexicano*. Moreover, that distinctive national style served the cultural project of the Mexican state, supporting ideologically an authoritarian regime (whose patronage was crucial to national film producers) committed to alliance with U.S. foreign policy and transnational capital. The stylistic and thematic "nationalism" of Mexican cinema buttressed that relationship in two ways: by creating an international symbol of cultural prestige, and by producing a cinematic idiom that concealed both the depth of the Mexican industry's transnationalization and the broader structures that linked the government's project (not to mention the nation's development) to its northern neighbor, upon whose political support it depended. This does not mean that Mexican film was simply an instrument of the state (or, even less, of U.S. foreign policy). Much like the radical murals sponsored by the government as it pursued reactionary policies in the immediate postrevolutionary epoch, "nationalist" films served to legitimize Mexico's ruling group as it lurched to the right, again, in the early post-World War II period.[5]

~

As *Río Escondido* begins, the scene is Mexico City. Rosaura Salazar (played by María Félix) arrives late at the National Palace for a ceremony launching the government's rural social modernization program, which sends teachers and doctors trained in the capital into the countryside. In the Zócalo, the narrator points out sites surrounding the central government's seat of power over panoramic views of the plaza, including shots of the Cathedral and the National Palace. As Rosaura ascends the staircase, the voice-over explains the building's significance as the historic center of the modern Mexican state. He combines his national civics lesson with an explanation of the rich ancient, colonial, national, and revolutionary history portrayed in Diego Rivera's famous murals adorning the building's courtyard walls. The sequence underlines how Golden Age film had superseded the central role played earlier by public painting in the state's sponsorship of popular culture and history as political instruction.

The president of the republic—played in a cameo by President Miguel Alemán—personally sends Rosaura to the town of Río Escondido to teach in a public school. Shot over the shoulder, seated at his desk (thus enhancing the president's aura as the people's patriarch), Alemán explains to the beautiful young teacher that it is her duty to fulfill the nation's destiny for a modern literate soci-

María Félix in a scene from Río Escondido, *the film that exemplifies Mexican cinema's "nationalist" idiom.*

ety. In the town, aided by an idealistic doctor, Felipe Navarro (Fernando Fernández), another member of the federal government's corps of young missionaries providing their "social service," she challenges the authority of the corrupt and violent local cacique (Carlos Moctezuma) by devotedly carrying forth the educational program. Unlike Cardenismo's anticlerical "socialist education" project of the 1930s, Rosaura's work neither attacks the Church nor promotes socially charged symbols of the Mexican Revolution as alternatives to Catholic iconography. Instead, in teaching her Indian students, she invokes the politically consensual icon of Mexican nationalism, the figure of the nineteenth-century Liberal Indian president, Benito Juárez, as a national symbol of progress and patriotism. She points to the legendary leader's portrait, which is hung prominently in the front of her classroom (where Lázaro Cárdenas's photograph frequently was displayed in the *escuela normal rural* during the mid-1930s). The postwar education project is not anti-clerical, as was the Cardenista program; rather, it attacks local bossism, which was popularly associated with the underside of the Revolution in the countryside—that is, the manipulation of local affairs for private gain by *políticos* who abused their power in defiance (rather than as clients) of a more progressive federal government committed to social reform.

If Cardenismo's populist mass-media project sought to mobilize (and incorporate) peasant and worker activism, Alemanismo's aimed to pacify proletarian and agrarian demands while expanding the state's corporatist controls. The constancy of cinematic practices (and producers), amid changing messages, mirrored the regime's broader maintenance of political practices (and politicians) even as its project and rhetoric metamorphosed from leftist to rightist populism. For example, while the previous decade's cinematic representation of *indigenismo*—exemplified by the socially realist *Janitzio* (1934) starring Emilio Fernández, the government-backed *Redes* (1934), or *La Noche de los Mayas* (1939), all of which dramatized local popular action initiated by provincial Indians against social injustices inflicted by middle-class white or mestizo interlopers—*Río Escondido* reproduced the post-World War II state's political culture, emphasizing state-directed, centralized, top-down mobilization and incorporation carried out by middle-class urbanites in the interest of social progress, economic modernization, and national integration.

Progressive reform replaced radical restructuring in the postwar state's discourse and Mexican cinema's images and narratives. *Río Escondido* supported that conservative agenda, which was tightly tied, despite short-term conflicts and medium-term differences, to transnational economic and political alliances with the United States. However, if shifting messages did not signify a changed relationship between cinema and official culture domestically, neither did it mark a radical break in the state's promotion of cinema as central to its international relations, not so much to convey specific messages through particular films but as a sign of cultural modernity and national accomplishment conveyed by the entire industry's output.

These ambitions notwithstanding, *Río Escondido's* production as well as ideology demonstrate the depth of transnationalization in the very sector presented by official and intellectual discourses (during the Golden Age and today) as the symbol of Mexican cultural nationalism in the 1940s. The film was the direct product of an industry shaped by wartime collaboration with the U.S. government and Hollywood. Made in 1947 at the studios of Azteca Films, along with CLASA Films, a chief recipient of wartime U.S. assistance provided by the Office of the Coordinator for Inter-American Affairs (OCIAA), *Río Escondido* combined the technical proficiency achieved by Fernández and Figueroa in their equally sentimental *indígena* classic, *María Candelaria* (1943), with the pro-Mexican nontheatrical wartime propaganda produced by the U.S. government. For example, in a scene reminiscent of *Mexico Builds a Democracy* (OCIAA, 1942)—as well as John Steinbeck and Herbert Kline's independently produced pseudodocumentary, *Forgotten Village* (1941)—Rosaura Salazar assists Navarro in inoculating Río Escondido's population to prevent the outbreak of an epidemic. In doing so, they win the confidence of the pueblo and its support for the government's mission. If *Río Escondido* expressed an ideologically nationalist perspective, it was an official version of Mexican nationalism; if its narrative structure and images were different than Hollywood's, they were a Mexicanized version of a visual discourse linked intertextually to U.S.-Mexican wartime propaganda.[6]

Forged during World War II, the persistence of this pseudonationalist discourse in the postwar period continued to conceal a regressive political economy and authoritarian state increasingly tied by official policies to its North American neighbor.[7] *Río Escondido*'s producer, Raúl de Anda, exemplified the inherent ironies of Golden Age Mexican cinema. During the war he made the U.S.-backed prowar propaganda features *Espionaje en el Golfo* (1942) and *Soy Puro Mexicano* (1942)[8]; after the war he continued to reproduce official rhetoric, but he also pleaded (as we will see) for state protection from the same U.S. film industry with which he had profitably collaborated a few years earlier. President Alemán's cameo, too, is an appropriate mark of the key role that motion pictures played in the state's domestic and international projects.[9] It was emblematic not only of the broad interaction of the Mexican state and film industry in the 1940s but also of the dilemmas produced by wartime collaboration with the United States. As Secretary of the Interior in the administration of his predecessor, Manuel Avila Camacho (1940–1946), Alemán had overseen the Mexican industry's wartime collaboration with the United States.[10] As President himself (1946–1952), Alemán authorized federal bureaucracies to defend national film production from Hollywood's domination. The state viewed Mexican cinema as a crucial mass-cultural dimension to national socialization and international relations. It utilized motion pictures as a means of political centralization and ideological dissemination. The postwar state expanded its propaganda relationship with leading domestic producers, subsidizing motion pictures that carried propaganda to the enlarged domestic film audience forged during the Second World War.[11]

Alemán's own work, first as facilitator of wartime collaboration and then as architect of moderate postwar protection, demonstrates the ambiguities and contradictions of the Mexican film industry's development and of U.S.-Mexican economic and cultural relations. Internationally collaborative policies that yielded growth also produced dependence; official ambitions for sovereign national mass media were at odds with the Mexican industry's links to Hollywood and the U.S. government. Rather than an example of Mexican cultural and economic nationalism, *Río Escondido* was the product of transnationalism. While the historiography of Mexican cinema often refers to the intentional postwar "crisis" of national production, the actual nature of that declension has been inadequately studied. A lack of empirical investigation has led to oversimple and underscrutinized generalizations that elide the complexity of the postwar situation and its connections to broader questions of Mexican and U.S. political economy and ideology. This essay, based in international, multiarchival research, aims to begin to delve into these dynamics.[12]

~

Río Escondido's release came during a period of tremendous quantitative and qualitative growth in the Mexican film sector. Movies represented the country's third largest industry by 1947, employing around 32,000 workers. Mexico had 72 producers of films who invested 66,000,000 pesos (approximately U.S.$13 million) in filming motion pictures in 1946 and 1947, four active studios with 40,000,000 pesos of invested capital, and national and international distributors. There were approximately 1,500 theaters throughout the nation, with about 200 in Mexico City alone.[13] Mexican films in the late 1940s would command over 40 percent of domestic screentime; and roughly 15 percent of motion pictures exhibited in Mexico were domestically produced, more than twice the average during the 1930s.[14]

In the 1940s and 1950s, Mexico, the leading producer of Spanish-language movies, had one of the most important film industries in the world. Besides María Félix and Fernando Fernández there were numerous stars immensely popular throughout the Spanish-speaking Americas, especially in the Latino United States. Exemplary films such as *Río Escondido* were regularly exhibited and won prizes during these years at such major international competitions as Venice, Locarno, and Cannes[15] (demonstrating classic characteristics attributed to postwar Second Cinema, that is, postwar art-house fare).[16] Nationally, the epoch remains a powerful contemporary force in popular culture and collective memory. *Río Escondido* might be one of the most internationally recognized Mexican films of the period, but what is more significant is that it was only one of many high-quality motion pictures, focusing on national subjects, produced and distributed by domestic companies during the so-called Golden Age of Mexican cinema, which climaxed in the late 1940s.

Films Exhibited in Mexico, 1930–1955

	1930	*1935*	*1940*	*1945*	*1950*	*1955*
United States	212	207	338	245	249	211
Mexico	4	24	37	67	105	77
Argentina	–	1	26	31	9	1
Others	58	55	48	20	103	70

Source: Compiled from data in María Luisa Amador and Jorge Ayala Blanco, *Cartelera cinematográfica*, Vols. 1–3 (Mexico City: Centro Universitario de Estudios Cinematográficos, UNAM, 1980, 1982, 1985).

Cooperation into Competition

Mexican commercial expansion during World War II reflected an odd combination of factors: it was both a product of import-substitution development and of U.S.-led modernization. The lapse in wartime European film production and international distribution, combined with Hollywood's reduced production of entertainment films, created a new demand for Mexican films not only domestically but also throughout the Western Hemisphere. Through the intervention of the OCIAA, the U.S. government multiplied the impact of wartime global economic and political conditions to advance the growth of the Mexican film industry. The OCIAA undertook the modernization of Mexican film studios in order to develop a more authentic source of wartime propaganda for Latin American audiences. In addition, the United States allowed raw film stock—a commodity whose production it controlled in the Western Hemisphere and distributed through wartime quotas—to flow to Mexico and not to Argentina, the other major Latin American film producer, whose neutral attitude toward the Axis powers displeased the State Department.[17]

As the war ended, the Mexican film industry seemed to have a bright future, but owing to a number of factors its situation was, in fact, precarious. Because U.S. aid was invested in the production sector only, it helped create an industry with greatly expanded capacity but one extremely dependent upon the favorable political and economic conditions created by the war for international distribution of its product. Mexico's wartime alliance with the United States, the drastic reduction in European imports to Latin America, and the willingness of the U.S. government to restrain Hollywood producers who opposed assistance to the Mexican film industry all contributed to create a conditional environment that hid the uneven development of Mexico's film sector. Following the war, Mexican producers lacked the financial ability to import innovative producer goods and technical expertise (which the OCIAA had provided during wartime) from the United States as well as the domestic and (especially) foreign distribution and exhibition networks necessary to exploit their productions fully. But perhaps equally important, an industry that had benefited from the positive relations between its government and the United States during World War II found that in the postwar period that close interstate relationship generally, and the aid advanced Mexico's film sector particularly, made it difficult for the regime to adopt radically protectionist measures. In other less transnationalized sectors, which had taken off during the war, the Mexican government resisted Washington's "free trade, no aid" line.[18] The Mexican film industry, however, had deepened its fundamental dependence on the United States, even as it had grown through collaboration. Hence, wartime transnationalization rendered postwar protection problematic; where Cardenista efforts at protection in the prewar period had failed due mainly to Mexican film's limited international distribution, protection failed following the war owing to the nature of the industry's recent foreign expansion. By the mid-1940s, Mexican cinema's problems could not be fixed through domestic regulation, since it was newly vulnerable to U.S. retaliation north of the Río Bravo as well as in Central and South America and the Caribbean.

~

Toward the end of World War II, U.S. government-coordinated assistance to the Mexican film industry ended. As in other areas of wartime economic and technical aid to Latin American nations, U.S. foreign policy toward Mexican cinema radically changed as victory in Europe approached.[19] The rhetoric of free trade displaced policies promoting development. This shift in U.S. policy, toward an industry whose wartime dependence on U.S. support cannot be overstated, had long-term ramifications for the development of Mexican cinema.[20]

Transformed by World War II, the State Department recognized more than ever the important role of motion pictures in furthering its agenda in the postwar world. However, the dynamics of that relationship shifted toward the end of the war; Hollywood's Motion Picture Producers and Distributors of America's agenda replaced that of the OCIAA's in determining Hollywood's official role in U.S.-Latin American relations. In 1944 the State Department sent a film questionnaire to diplomatic posts worldwide, which differed from earlier such wartime information-gathering in that it combined trade issues with broader ideological ones.[21] In making its case for diplomatic activism against nationalist media policies, Hollywood's Motion Picture Producers and Distributors of America (MPPDA) argued the congruence between its market objectives, the ideological goals of U.S. foreign policy, and the postwar U.S. economy's dependence on mass media to sustain exports. In October 1944, MPPDA President Will Hays sent Undersecretary of State Edward Stettinius a memorandum outlining the rationale for "Government Co-operation in Maintaining Foreign Markets for American Motion Pictures." The MPPDA memorandum explained that the motion picture "industry is unique in exports" because 40 percent of its product goes abroad: "That so large a portion of industry earnings must accrue abroad, renders the industry peculiarly susceptible to foreign governmental discrimination . . . inspired by interests competitive with United States pictures." It stated further that since the U.S. motion picture industry depended upon foreign revenue to cover production expenses, the quality of domestic mass culture would be determined by Hollywood's ability to penetrate foreign markets: "The approximate forty percent of motion picture revenue which is foreign, is the margin by which supremacy of United States' pictures is financed and maintained. Bereft of these revenues, product for home consumption might suffer proportionately."[22]

The memorandum went on to offer several interrelated arguments—which ranged from the domestic economy of the United States to its international political position—as to why undermining protectionist measures by other states was essential to U.S. foreign relations. Estimating that U.S. product controlled 80 percent of the world's screentime, the MPPDA argued that Hollywood's global power represented the natural order of things, based upon the universal appeal of the images, values, and sentiments represented in U.S. motion pictures: "These are the imperishable things of which pictures are made. And they are the same the world over. Geography leaves them untouched. They are the common ground of all men everywhere."[23] There was a special imperative to promote U.S. motion pictures in Latin America where U.S. foreign relations had been, according to the MPPDA, "immeasurably fostered by the showing of documentary and entertainment films." The memorandum emphasized that "it is ardently to be desired that the power of the film in all its forms should be preserved to the people of the United States, not surrendered to non-hemispheric productions."[24] And finally, the MPPDA made clear what it expected from U.S. foreign policy in opposing nationalist film practices: "Any degree of subsidy by foreign government of foreign industry for purposes of competing with the United States industry thus appears quite properly a matter for our government's active interest. The imposition of discriminatory taxes, restrictive orders, quotas and regulations in limitation of United States distribution, are matters clearly within the indicated sphere of our government's inquiry and action."[25] Although the MPPDA stressed the inherent superiority of Hollywood films, it was not willing to risk the development of foreign competition.

The convergence of Hollywood and U.S. foreign policy objectives served the general expansion of U.S. mass culture abroad, but it had particular significance for Latin America. The region's importance for Hollywood grew during World War II, as European and Asian markets were less accessible to North American product at the same time that the Mexican film industry expanded its domestic production and hemispheric exports (with U.S. support). Given the expanded wartime role of motion pictures as ideological weapons in the U.S. foreign policy arsenal, Hollywood sought to reestablish its position in Latin America by arguing that in the postwar world, U.S. commercial and cultural hegemony would converge. The Motion Picture Society for the Americas (MPSA), the Hollywood organization administered by top industry executives that coordinated the OCIAA's multifaceted film programs (including the modernization of the Mexican film industry), demonstrated this alteration. In formulating its postwar mission, the MPSA explained how Hollywood's mercantile objectives dovetailed with the government's political ones through the pursuit of expanded U.S. markets rather than sustaining Mexican film production: "An opportunity of historic proportions is now offered to our industry. The power of this great medium will be manifest not alone in money but in ideological influence over nations. Both the President of the United States and the State Department have publicly proclaimed the motion picture as the medium which can stabilize and insure two-way friendship. Needless to say, the Latin America area is a vital consideration for the industry on behalf of the people of the United States."

These industry leaders emphasized the unequally interdependent pattern of inter-American trade and investment to maintain the political economy of the United States by finding markets for consumer goods, raw materials for industrial production, and outlets for U.S. capital:

> The industrial development of the other American republics should exceed any other area of the world. . . . It has been estimated that in the decade following the war, Latin America will need $9,000,000,000 worth of heavy machinery. The United States [is] a market for Latin American raw materials in the post-war period due to the depletion of our own reserves.

This means more buying power in the Latin American countries, which builds a market for American export product. From the business standpoint, the Latin American market is the fastest expanding area in the world. Spot checks of motion picture progress in the various countries of Latin America are already beginning to reveal the enormous potential of this great area.[26]

This statement accurately articulates the basis of the State Department's postwar collaboration with Hollywood in Mexico. The social transformation of Latin American nations during World War II, marked by rapid urbanization combined with the wartime acceleration of Mexican film production, had expanded the demand for motion pictures throughout the hemisphere. As the producer of a major international commodity, Hollywood—organized in the MPPDA—historically had strong support from the State Department. The interests of the government complemented those of the studios. Washington's foreign policymakers saw Hollywood films as crucial to the ideological and cultural influence of the United States throughout the Western Hemisphere and to the broader reinforcement of internationalist economic patterns vital to the political economy of the United States. As Hollywood's pact with U.S. diplomacy returned to its prewar pattern, dominated by commercial concerns, it did so within a changed context that, owing to the war, added to the ideological mission of U.S. films in the world (which would expand during the Cold War.)

In justifying his request for a State Department assault on new Mexican attempts to regulate motion picture exhibition in 1944, Hays explained that he did so "merely out of a desire to further the development of the cooperative program in which we are both so interested."[27] The increasingly Hollywood-friendly attitude of U.S. foreign policy in the 1940s generated State Department sensitivity to the dilemma posed by Mexican film production for the U.S. industry. The U.S. embassy expert on the Mexican motion picture industry noted in 1944 the impact of the wartime growth in Mexican film production on that industry's distribution needs: "One of the results of this rapid development of the motion picture industry here has been the production of a larger number of films and a natural desire to find the Mexican outlets for the exhibition of these films." Ultimately, however, U.S. diplomats were confident that Hollywood's dominant position in Mexico was secure, owing to the dependence of Mexican producers on exports of films to the Spanish-speaking United States, Mexico's most profitable foreign market. If Mexico attempted to limit the distribution of U.S. films in order to develop its industry's domestic market, "it would eventually lead to retaliation in the United States against Mexican pictures. In view of this situation the Mexican Government might be willing to enter into some overall agreement for protecting the rights of American distributors in Mexico and the distribution of Mexican pictures in the United States."[28] Commercial containment of Mexican cinema through diplomatic insistence on free trade became the dominant feature of Hollywood and the U.S. government's joint approach toward Mexico.

Even before World War II ended, Mexican producers recognized their dependence on U.S. foreign policy and the pending threat of increasingly intense postwar Hollywood competition at home and abroad. In reviewing the situation, at the outset of 1945, an editorial in *El Cine Gráfico* argued that the Mexican industry was at a crossroads: to secure long-term growth and development it would have to resist the temptation of sacrificing quality for short-term profits. Instead of using Mexico's expanded plant to imitate Hollywood genres, the industry should aim for distinctively Mexican pictures, of high technical and artistic quality, that would carve out a special niche—like *Río Escondido*—not only in Mexico but also in foreign Spanish-speaking markets.[29]

This was a timely strategy, for the U.S. motion picture industry was planning to contain Mexican production even as the war continued.[30] No longer controlled by the need of the state-directed U.S. war complex to coordinate mass culture in the Western Hemisphere, Hollywood, working together with the State Department, began to reorganize itself in order to dominate Latin American movie screens. Its major competition for control of Spanish-speaking audiences was the Mexican industry. In 1944 the State Department official responsible for Hollywood articulated for his superiors the problems presented by the Mexican industry for U.S. distributors: "The leaders of the American film industry are increasingly disturbed over the inroads being made into their Latin American business by Mexican films and they attribute this almost entirely to [the O]CIAA's efforts in behalf of the Mexican industry."[31] And in appealing for diplomatic support, U.S. studios made clear to the State Department that since their actions had helped Mexico to take advantage of wartime market opportunities, they now expected their government to return to its traditional relationship with U.S. motion picture distributors operating in Latin America: facilitating the hegemony of U.S. motion pictures throughout the Western Hemisphere as a promoter of broader U.S. economic and political goals as well as providing a service to a major North American export industry.

In the immediate postwar period, when the Mexican industry was most vulnerable to U.S. government policies (especially regarding raw film supplies and Hollywood distribution services), the U.S.

industry and the State Department successfully preempted incipient attempts at protection. U.S. officials realized, however, that appreciation of wartime aid would not preserve Hollywood's hegemony in Mexico as wartime controls (especially of virgin film) ceased: "There is an extreme nationalistic movement in Mexico which you can be sure does not leave untouched the motion-picture industry, much as that industry owes for its development to us." As soon as the war ended, new protectionist projects surfaced to administer exhibition quotas through the establishment of a regulatory agency within the Secretaría de Gobernación. In response, Ambassador George Messersmith informed Eric Johnston, recent head of the United States Chamber of Commerce and incoming president of the (renamed MPPDA) Motion Picture Association of America (MPAA), that "the purpose of [these new tools] would be very largely to protect the Mexican moving picture industry by assuring through the machinery established the showing of Mexican pictures in preference to foreign." At the same time, the Departamento del Distrito Federal, the central government agency that administered Mexico City and its environs, announced new exhibition quotas designed to defend domestic production from the onslaught of postwar U.S. free-trade policies; it set aside 50 percent of local screentime for national production. In order to overcome such barriers, U.S. studios planned further transnationalization, building upon their wartime attempts to co-opt Mexican cinema through investment in foreign production. MGM Studios, for example, attempted to expand its access to Mexican exhibition by buying sixty-two Mexico City theaters.[32] This move was thwarted by nationalist motion picture legislation that limited foreign investment to minority status, enacted after RKO Studios' partnership in the construction of Estudios Churubusco in 1944.[33]

Markets and Demand

Like the U.S. film industry, Mexico's depended upon exports. With the postwar resumption of full-scale Hollywood production and the end of U.S. government assistance, Mexico required foreign markets not only in order to grow but also to survive. Mexican motion pictures were an unusual postwar Latin American export commodity, in that they were a manufactured good that had a vast intraregional market that outlasted the war.[34] They were unique also in terms of the traditional patterns of U.S.-Mexican economic interaction—that is, they flowed both ways in significant quantities across the Río Bravo. This two-way media flow reflected the cultural web that bound the historical development of the United States and Mexico, in this case the long-standing presence of U.S. movies in the Mexican market (preceding the development of Mexico's own sound film industry) and the large Latino population in the United States who demanded Mexican sound films since their advent in the early 1930s.

Beyond the importance of foreign markets for Mexico's domestic film industry, motion picture exports benefited other key international interests of the state. For one, they were a major source of foreign exchange, crucial for Mexico's balance of payments. Further, official eyes saw foreign exhibition of Mexican films crucial to promote trade, investment, tourism, and the nation's general cultural profile. For these reasons a Mexican Council of Foreign Commerce study argued for the "necessity of encouraging and coordinating, through the state or with its intervention, the activities of the film industry in Mexico, and of fixing the standards of quality which are necessary to the prestige and the economic standing of the country." The Mexican government viewed foreign film markets as integral to both postwar national development and international relations. The survival and growth of a major national industry would allow for the sovereign control of Mexican mass culture and the Mexican state's domestic and international project.[35] To this end, in 1947, the government consolidated the underdeveloped and diffuse private distribution sector in a new partially state-financed company, Películas Nacionales, S.A., aimed at provincial domestic audiences in the interior (including 16 mm. exhibition).

At the same time that government officials and capitalists looked inward to develop national audiences, they also looked outward to sustain recent international growth. Mexican producers viewed postwar Latin America as their own backyard. They had expanded their mass audiences throughout the region during World War II, and, in the early postwar period, they sought to streamline hemispheric distribution and increase Mexican cinema's share of Latin American screentime. Although the United States produced the single highest average gross for Mexican films, the combined national markets of the Western Hemisphere far exceeded it; and in Spanish-speaking countries, Mexican film imports appealed to national mass audiences, unlike their exports to the United States which, rarely subtitled, were limited to Spanish-speaking audiences served by regional exhibition circuits.[36]

In the long run, despite the dominance of U.S. motion pictures throughout the Western Hemisphere, Mexican films held obvious cultural advantages. In Latin America, such factors could counterbalance the economic and political advantages held by postwar Hollywood. Yet despite these attributes, Mexico faced serious direct and indirect problems generated by Hollywood and the U.S. government. Because Hollywood's films often accumulated profits or at least covered their costs in the U.S. market, Mexican officials complained that it was "possible for them to sell their pictures at a low price abroad or to sustain losses."[37] Particularly in Latin America (which held less political capital than, say, did Western Europe or the Far East during the early Cold War), Hollywood forcefully asserted its economic agenda with the State Department, demanding a postwar mass-media free market that would obstruct Mexican regulatory initiatives.[38] This was supported by the U.S. government's continued restrictive regulation of the international distribution of virgin film into the late 1940s. In 1947, for example, a Mexican government study reported that "the quota of unexposed film assigned by the United States government during the past war, continues to be insufficient for [our] already limited national film production needs."[39]

~

The question of popular demand for Mexican films is an important and complicated one involving regional, class, ethnic, and national factors. Nonetheless, the overall statistical and impressionistic evidence allows for drawing a comprehensive portrait that depicts the high popularity of Mexican films throughout the Spanish-speaking Western Hemisphere in the late 1940s: Mexican motion pictures were more popular than their major competition, Hollywood films.[40] While Golden Age films were not ideologically nationalist—that is, anti-imperialist—they did carve out a nationally oriented cinematic space that, in terms of audience reception, represented a popular alternative to Hollywood.

The Mexican film industry's most important market was, of course, its domestic audience. After World War II, reflecting its maturation, the industry's increasing number of higher-quality films were more popular than U.S. motion pictures throughout Mexico, though with regional and other variations. In 1947 the U.S. consulate in Monterrey stated that "distributors report that the income for good Mexican films is approximately 20 percent greater than that for U.S. films. The increase in production and improvements in Mexican films, especially those starring the leading Mexican stars, are beginning to make them more popular than United States films."[41] A year later, the U.S. embassy noted that "good Mexican films are preferred to any foreign films." Especially popular were "typically Mexican pictures. These films are the 'Westerns' of Mexico. Heavy melodrama, romance, and tear-jerkers."[42] In 1949 the embassy observed that "despite the predominant position of the United States in respect to the number of features shown, Mexicans [*sic*] absorbed a high percentage of the total number of exhibition hours." Even in Mexico City, where foreign films were more popular than in any other area of the country, national production controlled 42.44 percent of exhibition time in 1946, 41.2 percent in 1947, and 41.8 percent for the first half of 1948.[43] Mexico City box-office returns confirm this pattern. In the first half of 1949, for example, Mexican films earned 37.51 percent of net receipts (or 13,215,650 of a total of 35,234,733 pesos).[44]

Two icons of Mexican cinema, Pedro Infante and María Félix, in a scene from the film Tízoc, *directed by Ismael Rodríguez.*

Postwar trends among Mexican audiences were evident in other Latin American countries. In Cuba, arguably the Latin American nation most economically and culturally linked to the United States, the U.S. embassy reported: "Artistically and technically Mexican movies are not comparable with United States and European pictures. However, Mexican movies have been able to portray the national spirit, institutions, character and social organism of Mexico, which to a large degree are similar to those in Cuba." In fact, except for Hollywood productions that featured "fast-paced action," the kind of expensive spectacles beyond the production capacity of the rest of the world's film industries, Cuban "film distributors and theater owners say that Mexican movies are more popular [than Hollywood's] in Cuba [especially] outside of Habana and Santiago." The improved quality of postwar Mexican films made them successful not only in the provinces but also in large cities, where "more than a dozen distributors, including branches of United States studios, unanimously agree that Mexican films hold a unique, high place in the affections of the representative Cuban theatergoer." The popularity of Mexican films transcended the fact that they were in Spanish: not "having to read Spanish sub-titles of English-language movies, is an important but not the fundamental reason for the partiality shown Mexican films." The report further pointed out that "films produced in Argentina and Spain are in Spanish, yet their popularity outside of Habana is no greater than United States, Italian, and French films."[45] And Mexican officials proudly noted that, "although American pictures are duty free . . . Mexican films are preferred by the Cuban public."[46]

In the late 1940s, Spanish-speaking populations throughout the Americas chose high-quality Mexican productions over Hollywood's, as long as the supply satisfied the demand for entertainment. With few exceptions, in these markets Mexican films were second behind the United States in terms of the number of titles released. Mexico exported almost its entire production to each nation of the Western Hemisphere, sometimes exceeding 40 percent of the films shown in a given country and even surpassing Hollywood's distribution in certain Latin American markets, such as Venezuela. Moreover, despite the larger number of U.S. films distributed in Latin America, Mexican films played longer and on more screens than Hollywood fare. Generally, throughout Latin America the most popular Mexican films were comedies and musicals, which had cultural elements not present in Hollywood productions. (By contrast, the most popular Hollywood films were ones that represented distinctive U.S. genres such as gangster narratives, romances featuring North American images of beauty and sexuality, and high-budget spectaculars.) Mexican films were especially popular with working-class viewers in major cities and with provincial moviegoers region-wide. In part, this popularity reflected trends in literacy, since most U.S. films were subtitled and therefore difficult for even semiliterate audiences to follow. Yet it also represented a less internationalist (U.S.-centric) perspective than that held by the urban middle classes of capital cities. However, as Mexican films improved, they threatened to cut into Hollywood's control of middle-class audiences. The U.S. commercial attaché in Lima noted that "the advantage enjoyed by pictures with Spanish dialog [*sic*] . . . remains important, particularly in theaters catering to the less educated components of the population. An improvement in the quality of such pictures would immediately enhance their competitive position."[47]

In Chile, the U.S. embassy observed that Mexican "films offer competition to United States films because of their greater acceptance outside of the larger cities." Even in major urban centers, Hollywood "films are well received but in general do not enjoy any preference over other foreign-produced films."[48] The U.S. Bureau of Foreign and Domestic Commerce (BFDC) reported that "the recent improvement in the quality of Mexican films and the importation thereof on a larger scale has 'blown the lid' off of Nicaraguan box office receipts with individual pictures out-grossing even the best United States films." And the immediate outlook for Hollywood was bleak: "One theater chain," according to the U.S. commercial attaché in Managua, "has agreed to exhibit 109 Mexican pictures as compared with a tentative schedule of approximately 165 United States films" in 1947. A major cause for this regionwide surge was, according to U.S. observers, that "Mexican films more clearly depict the Latin American point of view."[49] In Venezuela, where the percentage of Mexican films shown in 1948 exceeded that of U.S. movies, trade representatives observed that "Mexican films are preferred to all other films and it is believed that they would enjoy an even greater share of the market if more films could be supplied."[50] In Peru, local distributors of U.S. films imported on average two or three prints "of the more popular films," while "distributors of Mexican motion pictures frequently import 10 or more prints for simultaneous release in several theaters."[51] In El Salvador, U.S. diplomats reported that not only had the popularity of Mexican films increased in recent years but also that they are "given preferential treatment by the distribution monopoly."[52] The increased and more advanced production of Mexican films during World War II had, U.S. diplomats argued, allowed for the postwar expansion of exports. The U.S. commercial attaché in Colombia concluded that "the enormous improvement in the technique of Mexican features" allowed for the Mexican film industry to take advantage of its linguistic and cultural advantages. It dwarfed the crippled postwar Argentine film industry's regional exports, which in Colombia were four times smaller than Mexico's.[53]

The evidence is clear that in the postwar 1940s the Mexican film industry had great potential to increase its influence in Latin America as the region's dominant cinema. Yet despite this popular demand, the market for Mexican product was limited by a concerted use of tactics collectively engaged in by major U.S. distributors, backed by the State Department. For example, they controlled independent theater owners through the business technique of "block booking." In order to obtain a company's best films, a studio required exhibitors to take an entire package of films, the bulk of which were mediocre but tied up the theater's screentime. In Peru, for instance, U.S. officials reported that despite inroads made by Mexican exports, the United States still held decisive advantages. In terms of demand, "such factors as outstanding direction and production techniques" as well as "steady and ample supplies" of films countered the growing popularity of Mexican productions. Even more important, however, to Hollywood's counteroffensive were the "special arrangements for the release of pictures in theaters owned or controlled by distributors [who] also favor United States productions."[54]

Toward overcoming such obstacles, the recently formed Comisión Nacional de Cinematografía publicly promoted commercial multilateralism in the pages of its weekly bulletin, *Cinevoz.* Echoing earlier anti-Hollywood campaigns, the periodical praised European and Latin American cinema and noticeably neglected mention of Hollywood's product.[55] Moreover, it published articles promoting the presence of Mexican films in Latin American and European markets. It particularly trumpeted the international recognition of postwar Mexican cinema in European film festivals, as a harbinger of potential First World commercial conquests. Privately the Comisión sought to expand international markets within Latin America through negotiated trade. For example, it sought to develop with Argentina—the very nation that prior to Mexico's World War II collaboration with the United States had dominated the region's movie screens—a special agreement establishing a reciprocal exhibition quota for each nation's films. However, the Secretaría de Relaciones Exteriores advised against pursuit of such an agreement since it would surely provoke new U.S. protests, "based upon the Most Favored Nation clause" in the existing trade agreement between the United States and Mexico, which demanded a proportionate quota for U.S. films and also called for retaliation against Mexican films in the U.S. market.[56]

Instead, Mexican diplomats constantly searched for more international screentime. For example, in order "to obtain a greater number of dates for Mexican films" in Central America, especially more access to El Salvador's state-run chain of movie theaters, Películas Mexicanas, S.A. (PELMEX), the Banco Nacional Cinematográfico's Latin American distribution arm (founded in 1945), recommended changing its regional partner, in 1950, from a Panama-based company to one directed by a better politically connected Salvadoran businessman.[57] Despite concerted government efforts at postwar promotion, Hollywood's international position and tactics, supported by the State Department, made it very difficult for Mexican producers to expand their exports. We turn to two brief cases which show how these forces played out internationally with regard to Mexican exports.

Postwar Spain

The controversy that developed between Mexico and the United States over postwar foreign film distribution in Spain exemplifies how Hollywood and the State Department contained Mexico's international distribution after World War II. By mid-1945, U.S. international trade policies were no longer shaped by anti-Fascist ideology; liberalism now simply referred to trade. Even before the war ended, the State Department took advantage of U.S. economic hegemony to expand U.S. markets and political power regardless of the rightist orientations of foreign states. The new international Satan was now on the left, and the main threat to U.S. media policy was economic not political.

As the war ended, Spain's film industry was completely dependent on U.S. policies. Like Mexico, Spain sought to develop a viable film industry through state regulation and international markets. According to U.S. Ambassador Norman Armour, the Madrid government held "the conviction that [it] should have a motion picture industry capable of producing films which can find ready markets in the countries of Latin America" as well as in the United States and European nations with which it "has historical, cultural and blood ties." Domestically, the Spanish government desired a national film industry that served "educational as well as entertainment" functions. Its officials estimated that with state support—including the imposition of film quotas and currency exchange controls on foreign distributors—Spain could produce 70 films in 1946, leaving screentime for about 150 foreign productions. Armour noted that "the American industry has complained against the measures which the Spanish government has taken to fortify its economic and exchange position or which have been used to protect and foster a domestic industry which Spain wishes to develop." He concluded that "the position of American films in Spain may become progressively worse unless some device is found to arrest the strong nationalistic trend," since "the Embassy's protests and exhortations have been unavailing."[58]

In opposing Spain's nationalist film policies, the State Department exploited the Spanish industry's desperate need for virgin film, a commodity in short supply in war-ravaged Europe. In April 1945, Armour reported: "It will be possible only to use raw stock as a bargaining power during the perhaps short period of scarcity and control and its value will be lost, therefore, unless used now. There is always the possibility that Spain may try to obtain raw stock relief from other supply countries."[59] The ambassador pointed out to Spanish officials that Hollywood's market objectives in Spain would have to be satisfied "before the United States can be expected to view sympathetically the problems which are resulting from shortage of raw stock."[60] As negotiations over the postwar Spanish market intensified, Assistant Secretary of State for Economic Affairs William Clayton in September 1945 instructed Armour: "In view of the present film negotiations under way at . . . Madrid, the Department believes that the American position . . . would be jeopardized by the release at this time of raw film shipments." He suggested that the Spanish government be advised that resolution of the "motion picture situation" would "find this Government receptive to suggestions for the resumption of raw stock shipments."[61]

The ambassador informed State Department media officials and MPPDA Foreign Director Carl Milliken that "it is suggested that 270 foreign films are required annually to service Spanish theatres adequately and that American films should constitute not less than two-thirds or 180 of this number." In addition to establishing this quota, the State Department sought other measures to guarantee that "American films [were] accorded equality of treatment in all respects with films of Spanish origin"—that is, that Spanish-language imports did not receive preferential treatment.[62] By late September, the U.S. embassy reported an agreement that achieved all of the U.S. industry's goals including the principal issue: "the number of films to be imported." Under the arrangement, Hollywood obtained two-thirds of Spain's 1946 foreign film quota, or 120 of 180 movies.[63]

As in other nations, Hollywood and the State Department worked hand-in-hand in Spain to negotiate an agreement that contradicted dominant U.S. rhetoric about free trade and open markets. Mexican producers, who considered Spain a natural market for their product and an important gateway to other European audiences, were outraged. Much like the United States, Mexico abandoned its anti-rightist foreign policies with the end of World War II. The government's anti-Franco position, crafted by the Cárdenas administration in the mid-1930s, went by the wayside as its anti-Fascist alliance with the United States metamorphosed into an anti-Communist pact, reflective of its ideological transformation during the war. And the Avila Camacho administration vigorously protested the advantageous position that Hollywood carved out in Spain, seeking commercial and cultural intercourse with the very nation whose political exiles (including Luis Buñuel) contributed to Mexican cultural production in the 1940s. Mexican diplomats accused the United States of taking advantage of its control of virgin film, and of Mexico's lapsed diplomatic relations with Spain, suspended since Francisco Franco's rise. The director of the Asociación de Productores y Distribuidores de Películas Mexicanas, Miguel A. Saña, complained to Foreign Minister Francisco Castillo Nájera that "during the period of the Spanish Civil War, and afterwards, owing to well-known motives, the exploitation of Mexican films suffered a very notable decline in the [Spanish] market." His organization requested that the Foreign Ministry demand that the United States "adjust its insupportable quota-share . . . in order to rectify this situation, that is profoundly discriminatory to foreign films in Spain."[64] Leading Mexican producers protested directly to U.S. officials that Hollywood's Spanish agreement left Mexico, Britain, France, Argentina, and Italy (the five principal non-U.S. film exporters to Spain) to "divide, arbitrarily, the balance of 60 full length pictures as remaining, after the agreement signed by the Spanish government and the representative of the Will H. Hays Committee. That would mean, if divided equally, that Mexico would be limited to the exportation of 12 full length pictures for the coming year."[65]

The U.S. embassy trade expert who monitored the Mexican industry recognized that Mexico's postwar dependence on Spanish-speaking U.S. markets, its single largest foreign audience, meant that its international bargaining power was small: "The market in the United States for Mexican pictures is many times greater than the Spanish market for Mexican films . . . [and it] will continue to be much more important than any Spanish market which could be developed." He further noted that Mexican producers recognized this dependence. Since the United States did not impose any restrictions on Mexican films, it was virtually impossible for Mexico to enact its own import quotas in retaliation for the Spanish situation, since it would likely bring similar U.S. measures that could destroy the Mexican industry.[66] Despite strenuous diplomatic efforts, Mexico was unable to alter the position of its ally and self-professed Good Neighbor, which had only recently assisted the Mexican film industry (when it had served U.S. foreign policy's wartime interests).[67]

The U.S. government maintained its restrictions on export of virgin film to Spain as an effective means to coerce favorable trade policies for Hollywood. In mid-1946 the State Department "determined that the embargo should be continued on motion picture raw stock in view of the fact that there was a possibility that Spain would remove certain restrictions on American motion pictures as a *quid pro quo* for removal of the embargo."[68] In the same year, Hollywood boasted that "the popularity of American pictures in Spain is unchallenged. Currently, 80 per cent of the pictures shown there are American . . . The Spanish exhibitor, who must work hard at selling even his native productions, finds selling American pictures easy."[69] When the Asociación de Productores y Distribuidores de Películas Mexicanas published "an effusive letter . . . to the Spanish Producers Organization," in *Ultimas Notícias*, the U.S. embassy judged it "a feeler with commercial aims . . . The letter of the Mexican producers is an indication of their desire to expand their export market. They would undoubtedly like Mexico to have a larger share of the Spanish quota," 65 percent of which the United States controlled.[70] Despite significant popular demand for Mexican films, Mexico in 1946 exported just 29 films to Spain and in 1947 only 22—about one-third and one-fourth, respectively, of its production in each of those years and less than one-fourth of the U.S. trade.[71] While Mexican cinema's European potential disappeared, its star, Doña María Félix, began to appear in Spanish films.

The United States and Regulation

The above episode was a significant precursor of postwar U.S.-Mexican film relations: U.S. betrayal of its free-trade creed undermined capitalist competition in the global culture market. This trend had devastating consequences for Mexico. Due to the combination of Hollywood's business practices and the diplomatic support of the United States, Mexican film exports lost momentum in the postwar world market as producers, under new commercial pressures, sacrificed quality, necessary for long-term growth, for short-term returns. In evaluating the condition of the national film industry's export potential at the outset of 1948, *El Cine Gráfico* lamented that "Mexican cinema had been in the position of possessing all the world's markets" but now found foreign distributors wary of the quality of many films. The inability to expand exports and organize itself domestically diminished quality and stalled development.[72]

By the late 1940s, Mexican officials worried not only about the difficulty in promoting exports but also how to protect the domestic market from U.S. domination. They lamented the fact that "there is no legislation in our country which limits the importation of foreign films and enables the Mexican industry to face the sharp competition which exists." Together, leading producers and organized labor urged special protection for domestic films as the Mexican government entered into (ultimately unsuccessful) negotiations in 1947 for a new comprehensive trade agreement with the United States to replace the expiring wartime agreement.[73] However, despite postwar proposals to require domestic exhibitors to reserve 50 percent of screentime for national product, no such measure was actually instituted. Instead, government film experts, consulting with leading producers. recommended a combination of state promotion (including moderate protection and much-needed credit) and the continued aggressive pursuit of foreign markets.[74]

Having failed to find significant new foreign markets or to erect meaningful import controls, the regime responded to the disintegrating tendencies in the film sector by increasing its organization and coordination of all facets of the industry. Beginning in 1947, the state undertook unprecedented measures aimed at developing its national film sector through bureaucratic innovations aimed to organize national production, distribution, and exhibition. The government sought to strengthen what was the weakest link in Mexican industry, distribution. As we have seen, in 1947 it helped to form Películas Nacionales, S.A., a nominally private company, which consolidated major domestic distributors. It aimed to create an efficient national distribution system with which to break national producers' dependence on Hollywood's Mexican networks and to reach the most provincial audiences, which U.S. distributors generally neglected. At the same time, the state reorganized the privately financed Banco Cinematográfico (established in 1942) as the Banco Nacional Cinematográfico. Recapitalized as a state-dominated body, it fulfilled earlier (stillborn) Cárdenas administration for official financing of commercial film production.[75]

At the end of the year, the government enacted legislation giving birth to the Comisión Nacional de Cinematografía, conceived as a presidential body to investigate the crisis facing postwar cinema.[76] Like Películas Nacionales and the Banco Nacional Cinematográfico, the Comisión aimed more to promote the private sector through coordination than protection. Motivated in part by the government's desire to quell continuing labor conflict between the Sindicato de Trabajadores de la Industria Cinematográfica (STIC) and its recently created rival, the Sindicato de Trabajadores de la Producción Cinematográfica (STPC), the Comisión reflected the Alemanismo mission to suppress any and all divisive social conflicts in order to preserve the emerging capitalist order, in the name of national development. The Comisión's tripartite composition combined state, capital, and labor representatives. The Secretaría de Gobernación, which oversaw the organization, appointed three members. The Comisión's nine other permanent representatives were named by the STPC and STIC, the Asociación de Productores de Películas Nacionales, Mexico City and provincial theater owners, independent national distributors, and distributors linked to the Banco Nacional Cinematográfico, which had its own delegate as well. In addition to shaping economic and cultural regulations regarding exhibition quotas, tariffs, and censorship policies, the new legislation also granted the Comisión authority to develop educational and propaganda films for the state's domestic and international culture project.[77] The Comisión, then, revived many of the state interventions conceived of in the Cárdenas administration's failed attempt to establish, in 1935, an Instituto Nacional Cinematográfico (before it was undone, to a large extent, by a Hollywood boycott).[78] And its directors included many of the central figures—such as Santiago Reachi, the president of Cantinflas's Posa Films production company, and Pablo Bush, the official representative of Mexican producers since the 1930s—who had facilitated motion picture collaboration with the United States during World War II. The Comisión's inauguration proved that industry bodies such as the Academía de Artes y Ciencias Cinematográficas (established in 1945), modeled after Hollywood's Academy of Motion Picture Arts and Sciences, could not sufficiently sustain wartime gains through simple publicity and promotion. The Comisión represented the need for film producers and the state to organize against Hollywood rather than simply to emulate the U.S. industry. Where collaboration had served development during the war, protecting that development in the postwar period meant pursuing policies of protection, albeit gingerly—that is, in ways that avoided U.S. retaliation.[79]

The Comisión's biweekly bulletin, *Cinevoz*, demonstrated the state's new commitment to promote national film production; it provided an official analogue for *El Cine Gráfico*, the industry's most important business publication since the inception of sound production in the early 1930s. The new publication concentrated not only on disseminating the state's activities (such as new legislation) but also in providing support for private production with analyses of international markets and updates about foreign film policies, especially those of European countries struggling with challenges similar to the ones faced by Mexico. In fact, *Cinevoz* promoted Europe much more prominently than the United States as both a motion picture market and source of imports. The artistic accomplishments of the best of Mexican cinema of the 1940s had, as noted above, received significant European recognition. Mexican producers recognized the international commercial possibilities of supporting a distinctive style of filmmaking that stood in contradistinction to conventional U.S. fare. *Cinevoz* trumpeted these affinities explicitly in its regular articles about European cinema and in its steady stream of updates on reciprocal trade possibilities with the Old World.

Underlining the inherent contradictions of the Mexican industry's development was the attention paid by *Cinevoz* to the positive European critical reception of *La Perla*, Figueroa and Fernández's interpretation of John Steinbeck's *The Pearl*. It publicized the film's success (it won a prize at the 1947s Venice film festival) as an exemplar of culturally nationalist production. Even more than its critical success, the movie's European recognition (it bombed in the United States) underlined for members of the Mexican government and film industry the cultural and economic possibilities for cinema, both as commodity and symbol, in improving their nation's European relations.[80] Understandably, *Cinevoz* paid no attention to the fact that, perhaps more than any other "Mexican" film, *La Perla* was a transnational production; Steinbeck's screenplay had been realized through RKO's partnership with FAMA and produced bilingually at the U.S. studio's Mexican facility, Estudios Churubusco.[81]

~

As indicated above, the Comisión's cultural and economic nationalism conformed to Alemanismo nonradical nationalist ideology, stressing development and political unity through economic growth and modernization rather than social change; in fomenting the film industry's development, it aimed at commercial expansion and artistic recognition of domestic production but did not encourage radical regulation of Hollywood. Bureaucratic innovation did not, however, end the dependence of Mexican producers on the U.S. market, given their inability to break the U.S. hold on most of the Spanish-speaking world's movie screens, including Mexico's. Therefore, the state soon attempted to utilize its new regulatory tools to once again attempt protection—through new taxes and quotas—to increase Mexico's share of its national market. Such measures provoked determined State Department opposition. Invoking the rhetoric of the Open Door policy, it insisted upon Mexican reciprocity for the accessibility of Spanish-speaking U.S. markets. Mexico, however, demonstrated its ability to resist complete U.S. mass-media domination.

During 1948 and 1949, the Mexican government began to address the limitations on film production imposed by the position of the United States in the Mexican motion-picture market with a variety of moderately protectionist measures. Among the most troublesome of the new regulations for Hollywood was the imposition of more taxes on the distribution of foreign films, which meant mainly U.S. productions. In fact, Mexico was not so much imposing new taxes as it was exempting domestic distributors from a long-standing 5 percent tax on gross film-exhibition receipts. This move supported the national industry in two ways: it reduced the relative profitability of the Mexican market for Hollywood, and it used new revenue to finance the Comisión Nacional de Cinematografía's promotional efforts. By taxing exhibition rather than imports, Mexico formally circumvented its 1942 reciprocal trade agreement with the United States. This new exemption—combined with a separate new 3 percent mercantile tax (that also exempted domestic product) and a drastic increase in censorship fees—panicked U.S. distributors, who warned the embassy that the "series of discriminatory burdens borne by our industry are rapidly making the distribution of American motion pictures in this country impossible."[82] Mexico City lawyer Enrique Zienert, the long-time representative of Hollywood's Film Board of Mexico, recommended "that only the strongest diplomatic pressure will bring the companies any relief."[83]

Hollywood's vigorous reaction to the new policies generated diplomatic support. The State Department protested the new regulations, arguing that they violated the spirit, if not the actual stipulations, of the 1942 Reciprocal Trade Agreement. The MPAA was pessimistic that the lapsed pact could be invoked to force revisions of the new and technically legal measures. It did believe, however, that political pressure and threats of retaliation would force Mexico to back down, keeping its movie screens open (except for token regulations) to U.S. films.[84] Mexico's new film policies were consistent with its emerging postwar industrial program that culminated in rejection of the General Agreement on Tariffs and Trade (GATT) in 1948, in favor of a system of tariffs and import restrictions to protect and expand import-substitution industrial gains made during the war.[85] Unlike most of Mexico's recent manufacturing boom, however, the film industry produced an industrial commodity that could not defend itself against foreign competition through simple protection, since it depended upon international as well as national distribution. The Mexican industry's foreign markets were central to its economic survival. Yet the industry's international markets actually limited the state's ability to intervene domestically versus Hollywood. The Comisión Nacional de Cinematografía's inability to overcome U.S. opposition to its new policies underlined this trend.

Responding to an unrelated recent Supreme Court decision, in 1949 the Internal Revenue Service (IRS) reevaluated its tax policies toward the two U.S. distributors of Mexican films operating in the United States, Azteca Films (established in 1932) and Clasa-Mohme (founded during the war). Although originally an independent matter, the IRS decision to tax (retroactive to 1936) the exhibition of Mexican motion pictures at the rate of 31 percent on rents and royalties became intertwined with State Department efforts to eliminate the new 5 percent foreign exhibition tax.[86] Leaders of the Mexican industry lobbied the ruling regime, pointing out that their films on average only covered 40 percent of their costs in the domestic market, relying on exports for the other 60 percent. By contrast, they argued, Hollywood was domestically self-sufficient and made huge profits in its foreign markets.[87] Moreover, long-standing postwar problems were becoming worse. As *Río Escondido*'s producer, Raúl de Anda, explained to President Alemán, Hollywood continued to exert pressure on the main Mexico City theaters to handle North American product exclusively: "Arrogant North American distributors demand that Mexican exhibitors contract for an entire year closing the Lido, Magerit, Roble, Chapultepec cinemas to Mexican films. Considering this injustice against the national industry, we beseech the highest authorities to intervene to protect Mexican interests."[88] As the conflict unfolded, *Cinevoz* declared on its front page that in order to reopen the North American market, "the government of Mexico would have to impose a strong tax on films that arrived from beyond the [Río] Bravo."[89]

For several months in 1949 and 1950, the two principal U.S. distributors of Mexican motion pictures refused to import Mexican films while the IRS and Mexican and U.S. diplomats considered the case.[90] In challenging the U.S. position, the Secretaría de Relaciones Exteriores invoked the same principles of reciprocal trade that the State Department asserted in opposing Mexican protection.[91] While the Mexican case stood on steadier ground, given the discriminatory nature of the U.S. action as compared to the (at least formally) nondiscriminatory Mexican measures,[92] the Secretaría's position revealed the central contradiction of the Mexican film industry's postwar development: nationalist measures were undermined by the industry's transnational structure. Two of the leading advocates of national film production personified this contradiction: Raúl de Anda, perhaps the industry's most vocal postwar advocate for protection; and his close friend, President Alemán, who sought to use state intervention to protect national filmmaking. Each had been core wartime collaborators with Hollywood and the U.S. government—the former as a producer of pro-United States propaganda, the latter as the engineer of U.S. motion-picture aid—in attempting to take advantage of favorable international relations to develop the wartime movie production.

Mexican producers understood that this contradiction limited their ability to confront Hollywood. Signaling this recognition, a letter from the Asociación de Productores y Distribuidores de Películas Mexicanas, signed by every major producer, urged their government to find an immediate compromise that would resolve the bilateral tax conflict. Despite their belief that the U.S. move was unjust, they declared: "We, the producers of Mexican films, cannot continue operating under such conditions. The loss of U.S. revenue has obliged us to cancel the production of various films, and the longer the situation continues will mean the loss of critical sources of money to the producers and investors, [and] will cause layoffs of workers, actors, and technical personnel of the Mexican studios."[93]

Mexican officials threatened retaliatory limits on U.S. film exhibition in Mexico. A leading diplomatic expert on the film industry defended such measures before U.S. embassy representatives. He argued that "American films in Mexico offer serious competition to Mexican films, and we cannot let our industry die."[94] Tellingly, it was Mexican producers, such as Santiago Reachi (whose Posa Films depended upon Columbia Pictures for its national and international distribution of Cantinflas's profitable farces), who in the end urged their government to sacrifice long-term principles for short-term survival.[95] Profits in the U.S. market, where ticket prices were higher than in Latin America, were roughly equal to the revenue derived by Mexican producers from their domestic audience. The Mexican industry could not afford to wait out the United States. It needed to return to the U.S. market and was willing to forsake the 5 percent tax in order to do so. It was the state, in fact, which encouraged resolve, especially after it had committed diplomatic capital to the negotiations.[96] But finally, direct pressure applied by prominent producers resulted in settlement. At a meeting between Reachi, the incoming head of Gobernación's Dirección General de Cinematográfica, Jesús Castillo López, and U.S. embassy trade expert William Nesselhof, Mexican officials offered to rescind the 5 percent income tax in return for suspension of the IRS decision,[97] which paved the way for resolution.[98]

Mexico opposed the U.S. taxes as a violation of the most-favored-nation understanding that hovered over bilateral trade relations. Unlike Mexico's new exhibition tax, which targeted all foreign films (although it mainly affected U.S. imports), the IRS ruling only targeted Mexico. Undersecretary of Foreign Relations Manuel Tello instructed Ambassador Rafael de la Colina to demand from the State Department the same exemptions that nations such as Great Britain received owing to bilateral agreements with the United States.[99] In his negotiations with Ambassador Walter Thurston, Tello distinguished between the discriminatory nature of the U.S. ruling versus the nondiscriminatory Mexican taxes, which formally applied to all foreign films. Nevertheless, Tello suggested a settlement of the IRS case as a basis for negotiating a motion picture agreement with the United States that linked open access to the U.S. market with similar nonregulation of Mexican movie screens.[100]

Despite the Mexican industry's overwhelming dependence on Latino U.S. audiences, the importance of the Mexican market to Hollywood was not lost on U.S. officials. The embassy recommended that the State Department work out a modus vivendi with the Mexican government, because "the loss of the Mexican market would deprive the United States motion picture industry of an estimated three to four million dollar[s]" annually. Recognizing their potential problems, U.S. producers encouraged the State Department to use the IRS to pressure Mexico into removing its new protectionist taxes. But rather than risk the loss of an important market—undercutting its worldwide drive for a mass-culture open door and possibly encouraging nationalist media policies in other nations—Hollywood supported the free flow of Mexican films (which were mainly consumed by Spanish-speaking audiences whom it did not compete for anyway) into the United States.[101] Moreover, due to the recent development of Mexico's film industry, U.S. producers feared that to boycott the Mexican market in 1949 (as they had effectively done in the prewar period) could, this time, dangerously stimulate production rather than stymie protection.[102]

To add pressure, Mexico increased its regulation of U.S. films during the taxation controversy by requiring import licenses for foreign reissues.[103] On one level, local U.S. diplomats interpreted this move as not simply part of the Mexican state's general effort to promote motion picture growth through "nondiscriminatory" bureaucratic obstacles to U.S. film imports, but rather as a tactic to harass U.S. interests into compromise. While denying that the delays were retaliatory, Jesús Castillo López, now head of the Dirección General de Cinematografía, told U.S. embassy officials that "because of the serious situation in which Mexican producers find themselves as the result of their temporary loss of the United States market," the entire question of distributing Hollywood reissues would be reconsidered.[104]

Nathan Golden, longtime chief of the U.S. Bureau of Foreign and Domestic Commerce's Motion Picture Unit, proved instrumental in resolving the IRS crisis. Understanding that Hollywood's long-term goals would be served by the return of Mexican product to the United States, he advised Zienert about how to handle their tax problems. In doing so, he demonstrated the U.S. industry's desire to maintain a status quo regarding Mexico. As long as Mexico had important U.S. audiences, it could not erect meaningful protectionist barriers to U.S. exports, preserving not only Hollywood's position in Mexico but also its hegemony throughout the Spanish-speaking world.[105]

For somewhat different reasons, U.S. diplomats in Mexico also urged accommodation. In protecting the interests of U.S. distributors, the embassy was more sensitive than the State Department to the political and ideological dynamics of the problem at hand. Ambassador Thurston warned against "antagonizing" the Mexican government, which considered the United States "morally responsible for heavy losses on the part of the Mexican motion picture industry" (owing to its forced withdrawal from U.S. markets).[106] Despite the State Department's hard line, the embassy encouraged a compromise that would serve Hollywood's long-term political and economic advantage in Mexico.[107] When Castillo López suggested a "provisional arrangement" to "forestall further retaliatory measures by Mexico," the embassy worked to implement a settlement.[108]

The embassy's acceptance of Mexican linkage of the two issues allowed the Mexican regime to save face. Eventually, Mexican motion pictures reentered the U.S. market without prohibitive taxes. The IRS issued a new ruling in June 1950 that paved the way for a permanent revision of the U.S. tax code in Mexico's favor[109] and for an indefinite suspension of the 5 percent exhibition tax on foreign distributors.[110] The Mexican government reviewed its measure and suspended implementation, although it continued to insist officially that, unlike the U.S. taxes, it was nondiscriminatory.[111] The embassy understood that the key issue for Mexico was to defend its film industry—the symbol of sovereign national mass culture—even if it meant more limited long-term growth. The State Department used the IRS controversy to eliminate protectionist measures. The dependence of Mexican producers on the U.S. market, however, made it difficult to combat U.S. domination of the Spanish-speaking world's movie screens. In finally urging capitulation, Mexican producers had come to terms with that dependence. Hollywood and the State Department had defeated another attempt to develop Mexican film through state intervention.

In this case, U.S. diplomacy offers another example of how the United States, despite its rhetoric of free trade, the Open Door, and antistatism, has intervened historically in pursuit of international hegemony. But the negotiations between Mexico and the United States also demonstrated the space that the former could find to defend basic interests, even if it could not fundamentally change the dependent position of its film industry. That dependence manifested itself not only externally but internally too. The segregation of production and exhibition and the relatively small and underdeveloped distribution systems in the Mexican industry added to Mexico's difficulty in developing effective protectionist policies. Exhibition was a huge sector that depended mainly upon U.S. product. In a market forged principally by U.S. product, the reduction of U.S. distribution, unless instituted gradually and in a controlled way (something that

Hollywood and the State Department always moved quickly to obstruct), would destroy the large privately owned and politically connected exhibition sector, leaving the market undersupplied, hurting workers, and disappointing audiences. Given the credible threat by U.S. companies to boycott Mexico if protectionist measures of any kind were enacted, there was no way conceivable that reduction in films would not be dramatic.

The dependence of exhibitors on U.S. product was deeper than that of producers on the U.S. market. Exhibitors made money by showing U.S. films and did not want to sacrifice those interests in the name of national production. In addition, the exhibition sector employed more workers than any other area of the film industry, and those workers were organized in the powerful STIC affiliated with the state-controlled Confederación de los Trabajadores de México (CTM). By the early Cold War, the STIC was no longer an advocate for radically nationalist film policies, as it had been at the end of World War II, and therefore did not obstruct efforts by producers and the government to reach a compromise with Hollywood and the State Department.[112] Despite serious labor conflict in the exhibition sector throughout the 1940s, there was a clear consensus when it came to the foreign interests of workers and private theater owners: both groups relied on the constant flow into Mexico of U.S. motion pictures.[113]

When serious limitations on U.S. film imports were threatened in 1949 during the IRS conflict, organized exhibitors made their interests clear to the regime. The president of the Asociación Nacional de Empresarios de Cines explained to President Alemán that national production "does not cover the needs of the [Mexican] market." Beyond problems of quantity—affecting capital and labor—there was also the question of the qualitative demands of Mexican audiences, the masses who had been introduced to the movies, and the ritual of moviegoing, principally by U.S. films. As Antonio de G. Osio pointed out, U.S. productions were "of great quality" and desired by the Mexican public. Moreover, Mexican producers required contact and even competition with "the forward advances of the [foreign] cinematographic industry" in order to progress.[114] U.S. distributors credited intervention by Mexican exhibitors in assessing their victories over state protection during the late 1940s. Hollywood's representatives believed that the Comisión Nacional de Cinematografía had been unable to challenge U.S. hegemony "largely because of opposition to them by exhibitors who have held membership on the Commission and as members have defended the interests of American producers and distributors."[115] Subsequent regulatory initiatives, such as the Ley de la Industria

Cinematográfica (1949) and the (Eduardo) Garduño Plan (1952), proved as ineffective as their immediate precursors owing to similar transnational dynamics.[116]

Final Thoughts

The early postwar years demonstrated that Mexico's position in the world culture system corresponded to its standing in the world economy. The advances and limits of postwar Mexican cinema underline its semiperipheral development. Lacking Hollywood's organization and power—derived from its size, backward and forward linkages, international organization, and long-standing influence in Mexico as well as the support of U.S. foreign policy—Mexican producers had trouble competing with U.S. companies not only abroad but also in their domestic market. Without heavy subsidization of the scale received from the United States during World War II, Mexican producers could not afford, for example, the start-up costs of importing new equipment and technologies. In 1953 when Internacional Cinematográfica, headed by Santiago Reachi, prepared to release a 3-D feature (Mexico's first), *El Valor de Vivir*, the company's director unsuccessfully appealed to the government to allow ticket prices higher than those stipulated by federal regulations for regular films, in order to compensate for the greater costs of production owing to the importation of special film, equipment, and experts as well as Hollywood processing of the Mexican-shot footage.[117] (Notably, *Tizoc* (1956), one of the last Golden Age films, the megaproduction starring María Félix and Pedro Infante, was a rare color production.)

The Mexican state chose to support its national film industry in a framework that did not directly challenge U.S. hegemony. The result was films of declining quality. Over time, despite notable exceptions, the U.S. and Mexican film industries settled into an international division of production for Spanish-speaking audiences: Mexico produced B-pictures, while Hollywood reconquered first-run screens surrendered during World War II. Although this division allowed Mexico's aggregate share of its screentime to grow, it grew at a much slower rate after the 1940s (see table on p. 129). Owing to a lack of worthy candidates, by the late 1950s the Academía de Artes y Ciencias Cinematográficas suspended the annual granting of Ariel Awards, which commemorated each year's best films and artists. María Félix went to Europe for parts in quality films; Pedro Armendáriz found a niche in Hollywood playing Native or Mexican Americans. The repatriation of Mexican talent from Hollywood to Mexico that had occurred during the Second World War, when the

Mexican industry was on the rise, reversed itself in the Cold War as that development unraveled.

Dependence on U.S. markets—enhanced U.S. diplomatic and economic power—was the major factor in obstructing Mexican attempts at protection. In the end, Mexican producers, less organized than their vertically integrated and internationally combined U.S. competitors, were unable to sacrifice short-term needs for long-term planning. Because of their dependence on foreign markets, they never fully supported the radical protection they called for; instead, they settled for expanded credit and promotion. For combined political and commercial motives, officials in the State Department aggressively obstructed even modest protection, in the name of free trade, as they violated self-proclaimed principles when it served their interests, as in Spain. Mexican exhibitors, whose strongest business links were with Hollywood distributors, aided U.S. efforts to undermine protection. But as much as economic shortcomings, Mexico lacked the political independence to develop a film industry that could take full advantage of the international demand for its product. Inevitably, producers turned to the state for help, but it was unable and unwilling to construct an effective system with which to regulate Mexican screens. Mexico learned that it was impossible for it to be a Cold War ally of the United States, part of the capitalist information order dominated by Washington, and at the same time build the internationally competitive film industry necessary in order to have a sovereign domestic one. However, despite its ties to the U.S. government, reflective of its own conservative postwar agenda, the Mexican state often came into conflict with the State Department and the MPAA in promoting its film industry's commercial interests in the late 1940s and early 1950s. Neither in the economic-political nor ideological-cultural sphere should U.S.-Mexico relations be any more construed as determined by instrumental links than they should be seen as formed out of simple dependence. Rather, commercial (and representational) limits were set by the collaborative political and economic structures that undergirded postwar U.S.-Mexico relations. In the Cold War that broader collaboration, first forged in World War II, contained not only challenges to U.S. (and PRI) hegemony but also to Hollywood's.

The Mexican film industry that seemed poised at the end of World War II to break the limitations of import-substitution industrialization, obtaining durable international markets, was in the end limited by the direct and indirect dependence of its three sectors on U.S. factors. The links between production, distribution, and exhibition sectors of the Mexican film industry and the United States were, in the final analysis, much stronger than their links to each other.

Paradoxically, so-called "nationalist" films of the Golden Age such as *Río Escondido*, were cultural products of an industrial situation to a large extent generated by Mexico's World War II alliance with the United States and then undone by the continuation of that alliance after the war. But that perhaps has been the paradox of the Mexican state since the 1940s: rhetorically nationalist but structurally aligned, both politically and economically, with its North American neighbor.

Notes

1. An earlier version of this essay appeared in Mexico as "La diplomacia de celuloide: Hollywood y la 'Edad de Oro' del cine mexicano," *Historia y Grafía* 4 (Spring 1995): 137–76; and in Spain as "Hollywood, U.S.-Mexican Relations, and the Devolution of the 'Golden Age' of Mexican Cinema," *Film Historia* 4.2 (June 1994): 103–35.

2. Santiago Reachi, *Un cine mexicano de interés mundial* (Mexico City: privately published report, 1955), 7.

3. Among his many international prizes, Figueroa won the 1948 award for Best Photography at the Karlovy Vary (Czechoslovakia) film festival for his work on *Río Escondido*.

4. Important "nationalist" interpretations of Figueroa's work are *El arte de Gabriel Figueroa: Artes de México* (Invierno, 1988); Charles Ramírez Berg, "The Cinematic Invention of Mexico: The Poetics and Politics of the Fernández-Figueroa Style," in *The Mexican Cinema Project*, ed. Chon A. Noriega and Steven Ricci (Los Angeles: UCLA Film and Television Archive, 1994), 13–24; Pedro Joaquín Coldwell, *Gabriel Figueroa: La mirada en el centro* (Mexico City: Miguel Angel Porrúa, 1993). For extensive reflections by Figueroa on his own work, see Alberto Isaac, *Conversaciones con Gabriel Figueroa* (Guadalajara: Universidad de Guadalajara, 1993). For two seminal statements about the centrality of Fernández (and Figueroa) to the cinematic construction of *lo mexicano*, see Julia Tuñón,"Between the Nation and Utopia: The Image of Mexico in the Films of Emilio 'Indio' Fernández," *Studies in Latin American Popular Culture* 12 (1993): 159–74; and Carlos Monsiváis, "Notas sobre la cultura mexicana en el siglo XX," in *Historia general de México*, vol. 2, 3d ed. (Mexico City: El Colegio de México, 1988), 434–59.

5. For how this ideological convergence manifested itself, see Seth Fein, "Transcultured Anticommunism: Cold War Hollywood in Postwar Mexico," in *Visible Nations: Latin American Cinema and Video*, ed. Chon Noriega (Minneapolis: University of Minnesota Press, 1999).

6. For a fuller discussion of interstate wartime propaganda, see Seth Fein, "La imagen de México: La segunda guerra mundial y la propaganda fílmica de Estados Unidos," in *México-Estados Unidos: Encuentros y desencuentros en el cine*, ed. Ignacio Duran, Ivan Trujillo, and Monica Verea (Mexico City: IMCINE/UNAM, 1996), 41–59.

7. The classic account of the organization of "nationalist" capital in the import-substitution manufacturing sector that emerged during the Second World War is still Sanford A. Mosk, *Industrial Revolution in Mexico* (Berkeley: University of California Press, 1954). For Mexico's wartime and early postwar international political economy, see the two works of Blanca Torres Ramírez, *Historia de la revolución*

mexicana, 1940–1952: México en la segunda guerra mundial (Mexico City: El Colegio de México, 1979), and *Historia de la revolución mexicana, 1940–1952: Hacia la utopía industrial* (Mexico City: El Colegio de México, 1979). See also Stephen R. Niblo, *War, Diplomacy, and Development: United States-Mexican Relations, 1938–1945* (Wilmington, DE: Scholarly Resources, 1995). On wartime mass media, see José Luis Ortiz Garza, *México en guerra: La historia secreta de los negocios entre empresarios mexicanos de la comunicación los nazis y E.U.A.* (Mexico City: Planeta, 1989). On the regime's postwar project, see Tzvi Medin, *El Sexenio Alemanista: Ideología y praxis política de Miguel Alemán* (Mexico City: Era, 1990).

8. I analyze these films, within the context of the Mexican industry's overall wartime relations with U.S. foreign policy, in "Transnationalization and Cultural Collaboration: 'Mexican' Cinema and the Second World War," *Studies in Latin American Popular Culture* 17 (1998): 105–28.

9. See Emilio Fernández to Miguel Alemán, 29 September 1947, Archivo General de la Nación, Mexico City (hereafter cited as AGN), Fondo Presidentes, Ramo Alemán, 523.3/15. Despite its reinforcement of official domestic political discourse, some prominent Mexicans, within and without the government, argued that the film should not be distributed internationally since its depiction of local corruption could be construed as denigrating to the nation's image; see AGN, Fondo Presidentes, Ramo Alemán, 523.3/24.

10. On the implementation of U.S. wartime aid to the Mexican film industry, including Alemán's role, see Fein, "Hollywood and United States-Mexico Relations in the Golden Age of Mexican Cinema" (Ph.D. diss., University of Texas at Austin, 1996), 299–333.

11. The influential Mexican company, España, México, Argentina (EMA), produced *noticieros*, or regular newsreels subsidized and approved by the Mexican government; see EMA to Rogerio de la Selva, AGN, Fondo Presidentes, Ramo Alemán, 523.3/4. Cold War propaganda films were part of an international regime of representation; see Seth Fein, "Everyday Forms of Transnational Collaboration: U.S. Film Propaganda in Cold War Mexico," in *Close Encounters of Empire: Writing the Cultural History of U.S.-Latin American Relations*, ed. Gilbert Joseph, Catherine LeGrand, and Ricardo Salvatore (Durham: Duke University Press, 1998), 400–50.

12. Important synthetic historical overviews of Golden Age Mexican cinema include Emilio García Riera's encyclopedia *Historia documental del cine mexicano*, 2d ed., 17 vols. (Guadalajara: Universidad de Guadalajara, 1992–1995); Jorge Ayala Blanco, *La aventura del cine mexicano en la época de oro y después* (Mexico City: Grijalbo, 1993); and Aurelio de los Reyes, *Un medio siglo de cine mexicano, 1896–1947* (Mexico City: Trillas, 1987). In English there is the important anthology, *Mexican Cinema*, ed. Paulo Antonio Paranguá, trans. Ana López (London: British Film Institute/IMCINE, 1995); and Carl J. Mora, *Mexican Cinema: Reflections of a Society, 1896–1988*, 2d ed. (Berkeley: University of California Press, 1988).

13. "A Study of the Exportation and Distribution Abroad of Mexican Motion Pictures," a copy of this report was "borrowed," copied, and translated by the U.S. embassy during trade negotiations with Mexico in 1947; enclosed with Merwin L. Bohan, Counselor for Economic Affairs, U.S. Embassy, to SD, 6 November 1947, 1–2, Central Files of the Department of State, Record Group 59 (hereafter cited as NARG 59), National Archives, Washington, DC, 812.4061-MP/11-647. There were probably closer to 2,000 exhibition spaces in Mexico when informal sites and those escaping official tabulations are factored in; see Federico Heuer, *La industria cinematográfica mexicana* (Mexico City: Federico Heuer, 1964), 58–69.

14. "Motion Picture Industry in Mexico, 1948," *World Trade in Commodities* (hereafter cited as *WTC*), Vol. VII, Part 4, No. 28 (Washington, DC: U.S. Bureau of Foreign and Domestic Commerce [hereafter cited as BFDC], September 1949), 2.

15. See "El Festival de Cannes," *Cinevoz* 57, 4 September 1949, 1; and "Los Premios del Festival de Venecia," *Cinevoz* 58, 11 September 1949, 1. An authoritative list of Mexican honors at international competitions and festivals is Ernesto Román and MariCarmen Figueroa Perea, *Premios y distinciones otorgados al cine mexicano: Festivales internacionales, 1938–1984,* No. 3 (Mexico City: Cineteca Nacional, November 1986).

16. For an extended definition of the place of Second (and Third) Cinema, see Teshome H. Gabriel, *Third Cinema in the Third World: The Aesthetics of Liberation* (Ann Arbor: University of Michigan Press, 1982).

17. For the mechanics of wartime film allocation, see Fein, "Hollywood and United States-Mexico Relations," 319–25.

18. See Niblo, *War, Diplomacy, and Development,* 165–248.

19. On Washington's postwar shift to free trade in Latin America, see Victor Bulmer-Thomas, *The Economic History of Latin America since Independence* (New York: Cambridge University Press, 1994), 257–65; and Rosemary Thorp, "The Latin American Economies in the 1940s," in *Latin America in the 1940s: War and Postwar Transitions,* ed. David Rock (Berkeley: University of California Press, 1992), 49–57.

20. For a descriptive analysis of United Artists' activities in Mexico in this period, see Gaizka de Usabel, *The High Noon of American Pictures in Latin America* (Ann Arbor: University of Michigan Press, 1982), 145–56. See also Jorge Schnitman, *Latin American Film Industries: Dependency and Development* (Norwood, NJ: Ablex Press, 1984), 21–26; and for a multiarchival comparative case, see Ian Jarvie, *Hollywood's Overseas Campaign: The North Atlantic Movie Trade, 1920–1950* (New York: Cambridge University Press, 1992).

21. State Department (hereafter cited as SD) Circular, "American Motion Pictures in the Postwar World," 22 February 1944, NARG 59, 800.4061/409A.

22. "Government Co-operation in Maintaining Foreign Markets for American Motion Pictures," Will H. Hays to Edward R. Stettinius, 12 October 1944, 1, 6, NARG 59, 800.4061-MP/10-1244.

23. Ibid., 3–5.

24. Ibid., 11–13.

25. Ibid., 10.

26. "Fourth Draft of History of Motion Picture Society of the Americas," 4 December 1944, 79–80, Records of the Office of the Coordinator of Inter-American Affairs, National Archives Record Group 229 (hereafter NARG 229), Entry 78, Box 961.

27. Hays to Stettinius, 15 June 1944, NARG 59, 812.4061-MP/6-1544.

28. "American Motion Pictures in the Post-War World," Guy W. Ray to SD, 11 April 1944, NARG 59, 812.4061-MP/319.

29. "De Enero a Diciembre," *El Cine Gráfico,* 1 January 1945, 18.

30. See Fein, "Hollywood and United States-Mexico Relations," 354–80.

31. Francis Colt de Wolf to Lawrence Duggan, 1 March 1944, NARG 59, 812.4061-MP/314. Promotional efforts by España, México, Argentina (EMA) on behalf of its wartime films throughout Latin America caused great anxiety for the State Department and Hollywood; see George Messersmith, U.S. Embassy, Mexico City, to SD, 18 April 1944, NARG 59, 812.4061-MP/318. On EMA's wartime activities and the response of the U.S. government, see Fein, "Hollywood and United States-Mexico Relations," 475–85.

32. Messersmith to Eric Johnston, United States Chamber of Commerce, 11 January 1946; Messersmith to Johnston, 10 January 1945, U.S. Embassy and Consular Records, National Archives Record Group 84, Mexico City Embassy General Records, 840.6-MP-Metro Goldwyn Mayer Co.

33. See Fein, "Hollywood and United States-Mexico Relations," 370–71.

34. On the postwar decline of intraregional trade, see Bulmer-Thomas, *Economic History*, 297–308.

35. "A Study of the Exportation and Distribution Abroad of Mexican Motion Pictures," 8–9, NARG 59, 812.4061-MP/11-647; see also Heuer, *La industria cinematográfica mexicana*, 4–5.

36. On average, a Mexican film grossed U.S.$76,000 in foreign exhibition in the 1940s, with the U.S. market contributing the most (U.S.$15,000, almost twice the value of the next most lucrative market) but representing only about 20 percent of the total foreign gross receipts; these statistics come from "A Study of the Exportation and Distribution Abroad of Mexican Motion Pictures," 7, NARG 59, 812.4061-MP/11-647.

37. This was the motion picture equivalent to "dumping," the practice of underselling foreign producers in their home markets by selling consumer goods below cost as a way to preempt competition.

38. "A Study of the Exportation and Distribution Abroad of Mexican Motion Pictures," 21–22, NARG 59, 812.4061- MP/11-647.

39. Ibid., 27.

40. Recent scholarship shows how foreign audiences and international politics shaped the representation of various nationalities, including Mexico's, in Hollywood films; see Ruth Vasey, *The World According to Hollywood, 1918–1939* (Madison: University of Wisconsin Press, 1997).

41. "Motion Pictures in Monterrey Consular District of Mexico," *WTC*, Vol. V, Part 3, No. 23 (BFDC, October 1947), 1.

42. "Motion Picture Industry in Mexico and Costa Rica," *WTC: Motion Pictures and Equipment*, Vol. VI, Part 4, No. 18 (BFDC, June 1948), 2.

43. "Motion Picture Industry in Mexico, 1948," *WTC*, Vol. VII, Part 4, No. 28 (BFDC, September 1949), 2.

44. "Ingresos netos de los cines del Distrito Federal en el primer semestre de 1949," *Cinevoz* 2, No. 61, 9 October 1949, 1.

45. "Digest of International Development: Motion Pictures," *WTC*, Vol. VII, Part 4, No. 35 (BFDC, November 1949), 3.

46. "A Study of the Exportation and Distribution Abroad of Mexican Motion Pictures," 21, NARG 59, 812.4061-MP/11-647.

47. "Digest of International Developments," *WTC*, Vol. VII, Part 4, No. 9 (BFDC, February 1949), 3.

48. "Motion Picture Industry in Chile," *WTC*, Vol. VII, Part 4, No. 22 (BFDC, July 1949), 2.

49. "Motion Picture Industry and Equipment in Nicaragua," *Industrial Reference Service: Motion Pictures and Equipment*, Vol. V, Part 3, No. 14 (BFDC, June 1947), 1–2.

50. "Motion Picture Industry in Venezuela," *WTC*, Vol. VI, Part 4, No. 26 (BFDC, November 1948), 2.

51. "Motion Picture Industry in Peru," *WTC*, Vol. VII, Part 4, No. 5 (BFDC, January 1949), 2.

52. "Motion Picture Industry in El Salvador," *WTC: Motion Pictures and Equipment*, Vol. VI, Part 4, No. 11 (BFDC, March 1948), 2.

53. "Motion Picture Market in Colombia," *Industrial Reference Service*, Vol. V, Part 3, No. 2 (BFDC, January 1947), 2.

54. "Digest of International Developments," *WTC*, Vol. VII, Part 4, No. 9 (BFDC, February 1949), 3.

55. In the mid-1930s, when the Cardenista state challenged Hollywood's hegemony, Mexican movie interests encouraged expanded business with European pro-

ducers; see Fein, "Hollywood and United States-Mexico Relations," 93–97.

56. Enrique Bravo (Comisión de Intercambio Comercial y Créditos Bilaterales) to Antonio Castro Leal, President of the Comisión Nacional de Cinematografía, 9 September 1949, Secretaría de Relaciones Exteriores Archivo Concentración, Mexico City (hereafter cited as SREAC), OM-150-13. For U.S. concern over Mexico's attempts to create a Latin American mass media common market, see NARG 59, 812.452/3-1050.

57. Juan Bandera Molina (Director), Películas Mexicanas, S.A., to Rogerio de la Selva (Secretario Particular to President Alemán), 28 February 1950; Serra Rojas (Banco Nacional Cinematográfico, S.A.) to de la Selva, 23 February 1950, AGN, Fondo Presidentes, Ramo Alemán, 523.3/72.

58. Norman Armour to SD, "American Motion Picture Industry in Spain," 12 April 1945, NARG 59, 852.4061-MP/4-1245.

59. Armour to SD, 2 May 1945, NARG 59, 852.4061-MP/5-245.

60. Armour to SD, 13 June 1945, NARG 59, 852.4061-MP/6-1345.

61. William L. Clayton to Armour, 7 September 1945, NARG 59, 852.4061-MP/9-1245.

62. Armour to William Colt de Wolf (SD) and Carl Milliken (MPPDA), 19 September 1945, NARG 59, 852.4061-MP/9-1945.

63. Norman Armour (U.S. Embassy, Madrid) to Colt de Wolf and Milliken, 22 September 1945, NARG 59, 852.4061-MP/9-2245.

64. Miguel A. Saña (Director), Asociación de Productores y Distribuidores de Películas Mexicanas) to Francisco Castillo Nájera, 29 November 1945, Secretaría de Relaciones Exteriores Archivo Histórico, Mexico City (hereafter cited as SREAH), III-2495-5.

65. "Letter of Protest from the Association of Mexican Film Producers and Distributors Concerning Allocation of Spanish Film Quota," 1–2, quoted in Guy Ray to SD, 11 December 1945, NARG 59, 812.4061-MP/12-1145.

66. Guy Ray to SD, 11 December 1945, NARG 59, 812.4061-MP/12-1145.

67. Francisco Castillo Nájera to Mexican Embassy, Washington, DC, 22 December 1945; Castillo Nájera to Miguel A. Saña, 22 December 1945; Saña to Secretaría de Relaciones Exteriores (hereafter cited as SRE), 9 January 1946; Rafael de la Colina, Mexican Embassy, Washington, DC, to SRE, 23 January 1946, SREAH, III-2495-5.

68. "Export Control Policy with Respect to Spain," State Department Memorandum of Conversation, 1 May 1946, 1, NARG 59, 652.119/5-146, emphasis in original.

69. "U.S. Product Is Leader in Spain, Director Says," Motion Picture Herald, 19 January 1946, 28.

70. "Mexican Film Producers Address Effusive Letter to Spanish Producers," Frederick R. Mangold (Economic Analyst), 1946, NARG 84, 840.6-MP.

71. "Motion Picture Industry in Spain, 1948," *WTC*, Vol. VII, Part 4, No. 17 (BFDC, June 1949), 2. These trends persisted; see "U.S. Pictures Lead in Spain," *Motion Picture Herald*, 19 February 1949, 36.

72. "Año Nuevo, Vida Nueva," *El Cine Gráfico*, 4 January 1948, 2.

73. See Adolfo Fernández Bustamante (Sindicato de la Producción Cinematográfica) to Miguel Alemán, 22 April 1947; Asociación de Productores y Distribuidores de Películas Mexicanas to Alemán, 24 April 1947; Juan Pérez Grovas (Manager), Cámara Nacional Cinematográfica, to Miguel Alemán, 27 April 1947, AGN, Fondo Presidentes, Ramo Alemán, 523.3/11.

74. "A Study of the Exportation and Distribution Abroad of Mexican Motion Pictures," 7, 26–27, NARG 59, 812.4061-MP/11-647.

75. See Fein, "Hollywood and United States-Mexico Relations," 86–102.

76. See Antonio Castro Leal (president of the Comisión Nacional de Cinematografía) to Alemán, 29 December 1948, AGN, Fondo Presidentes, Ramo Alemán, 523.3/49.

77. The text of the Ley que Crea la Comisión Nacional de Cinematografía was published in the government's *Diario Oficial*, 31 December 1947.

78. See Fein, "Hollywood and United States-Mexico Relations," 102–27.

79. These measures resemble the pattern observed by Peter Evans, where the regulatory power of Third World states grows as they confront transnational capital; see "Transnational Linkages and the Economic Role of the State: An Analysis of Developing and Industrialized Nations in the Post-World War II Period," in *Bringing the State Back In*, ed. Peter Evans, Dietrich Rueschemeyer, and Theda Skocpol (New York: Cambridge University Press, 1985), 192–226. For an analysis of the interrelationship between the state and the development of the film sector in other Latin American nations during the 1940s, see Schnitman, *Latin American Film Industries*, 27–47; and Randal Johnson, *The Film Industry in Brazil: Culture and the State* (Pittsburgh: University of Pittsburgh Press, 1987), 41–63.

80. See " 'La Perla' en Bélgica," *Cinevoz* 2, No. 33, 13 March 1949, 1–2. Throughout the year an article in this vein appeared in virtually every issue.

81. See Fein, "Hollywood and United States-Mexico Relations," 409–17. The irony of this film's international production is also noted by Alberto Ruy Sánchez in *Mitología de un cine en crisi* (Mexico City: La Red de Jonás, 1981), 78.

82. "Difficulties of American Motion Picture Industry in Mexico," Merwin L. Bohan to SD, 27 December 1948, NARG 59, 812.4061-MP/12-2748. When first enacted in 1948, three of the U.S. distributors had withheld payment of the 3 percent tax until it was revised at the start of 1949 to include domestic distributors.

83. Quoted in letter from John McCarthy (Manager of the MPAA's International Division) to Merril C. Gay (SD), 11 April 1949, NARG 59, 812.4061-MP/4-1149.

84. In different areas of Mexico, local laws reserved minimum amounts of screentime for domestic product but not enough to be threatening to U.S. interests.

85. See Niblo, *War, Diplomacy, and Development*, 210.

86. Ambassador Rafael de la Colina to SRE, 7 November 1949, SREAC, III-1654-9.

87. Miguel A. Saña (Asociación de Productores y Distribuidores Nacionales) to SRE, 4 November 1949, SREAC, III-1654-9.

88. Raúl de Anda (President of the Asociación de Productores y Distribuidores de Películas Mexicanas) to Miguel Alemán, 18 November 1949, AGN, Fondo Presidentes, Ramo Alemán, 564.2/398.

89. "En Estados Unidos las Películas Mexicanas Pagarán el 30 por Ciento de Impuesto," *Cinevoz*, No. 66–67, 20 November 1949, 1.

90. See Secretaría General del Consejo Superior Ejecutivo de Comercio Exterior to de la Colina, SRE, 5 November 1949, SREAC, III-1654-9.

91. Memorandum by Manuel Tello, Subsecretario Encargado del Despacho, 5 November 1949, SREAC, III-1654-9; and SRE to Washington Embassy, 15 November 1949, SREAC, III-1654-9.

92. See Secretaría General del Consejo Superior Ejecutivo de Comercio Exterior to de la Colina, 6 December 1949, SREAC, III-1654-9.

93. Asociación de Productores y Distribuidores de Películas Mexicanas to Manuel Tello, SRE, 9 November 1949, SREAC, III-1654-9.

94. William Nesselhof to SD, 10 March 1950, NARG 59, 812.452/3-1050.

95. See Raúl de Anda (President), Asociación de Productores y Distribuidores de Películas Mexicanas, to Miguel Alemán, 29 October 1949; and Miguel A. Saña to Alemán, 9 February 1950, AGN, Fondo Presidentes, Ramo Alemán, 564.2/398.

96. "Reaction of Mexican Motion Picture Producers to Proposed United States Tax on Mexican Films," Nesselhof to SD, 6 February 1950, NARG 59, 812.452/2-650.

97. "Transmission of Memorandum of Conversation," Nesselhof to SD, 3 February 1950, NARG 59, 812.452/2-350

98. "Impuestos norteamericanos que gravan a las películas mexicanas," SRE Memorandum, 15 February 1950, SREAC, III-1654-9.

99. Tello to de la Colina, 14 March 1950, SREAC, III-1654-9.

100. Tello to Thurston, 13 March 1950, ibid.

101. Nesselhof to SD, 24 March 1950, NARG 59, 812.452/3-2450.

102. See "Discriminatory Taxation of United States Film Distributors in Mexico," Lew B. Clark to SD, 3 November 1949, 4, NARG 59, 812.4061-MP/11-349.

103. A reissue, as defined by the Dirección General de Cinematografía, was a film that had played in Mexico more than thirty months earlier.

104. Nesselhof to SD, 14 April 1950, NARG 59, 812.452/4-1450.

105. "Tax Problem in Connection with Distribution of Mexican Motion Pictures in the United States," State Department Memorandum of Conversation, 15 November 1949 (between Rafael Nieto and Nicolás Graham Gurría of the Mexican Embassy; Ruben Calderón, Azteca Films, Inc.; Richard Dunlap, Clasa-Mohme, Inc.; Nathan Golden, Chief, BFDC Motion Picture Unit; Isaiah Frank, Division of Commercial Policy, State Department), NARG 59, 812.4061-MP/11-1549.

106. Thurston to SD, 19 May 1950, NARG 59, 812.452/5-1950.

107. "Impuestos norteamericanos que gravan a las películas mexicanas," SRE Memorandum, 15 February 1950, summarizing Ambassador de la Colina's communication to the Foreign Ministry on the tax situation, SREAC, III-1654-9; Assistant Secretary of State Dean Acheson to U.S. Embassy, 25 April 1950, NARG 59, 812.452/3-1450.

108. Thurston to SD, 6 June 1950, NARG 59, 812.452/2-250.

109. Acheson to U.S. Embassy, 19 June 1950, NARG 59, 812.452/6-1950.

110. Nesselhof to SD, 14 July 1950, NARG 59, 812.452/7-145.

111. Angel González de la Vega (Undersecretary of Taxes and Revenue) to Manuel Tello, 18 November 1950; SRE to U.S. Embassy, 27 November 1950, SREAC, III-1654-9; Nesselhof to SD, 30 August 1950, NARG 59, 812.452/8-3050; Abbey Schoen (Chief of Commodities Branch, SD) to U.S. Embassy, 14 December 1950, NARG 59, 812.452/12-1450.

112. See Fein, "Hollywood and United States-Mexico Relations," 380–409.

113. Merwin L. Bohan to SD, 13 September 1948, NARG 59, 812.4061-MP/9-1348.

114. Antonio de G. Osio to Miguel Alemán, 9 November 1949, AGN, Fondo Presidentes, Ramo Alemán, 523.3/57.

115. "Discriminatory Taxation of United States Film Distributors in Mexico," Lew B. Clark to SD, 3 November 1949, NARG 59, 812.4061-MP/11-349.

116. The fate of these projects is analyzed in Fein, "Hollywood and United States-Mexican Relations," 600–23.

117. Santiago Reachi to Adolfo Ruiz Cortines, 18 December 1953; Gustavo Treviño F. (Departamento del Distrito Federal) to Ruiz Cortines, 5 January 1954; Fernando García Bringas (Manager of Teatro Metropolitano, Mexico City), undated, AGN, Fondo Presidentes, Ramo Ruiz Cortines, 545.2/12.

8

The Decline of the Golden Age and the Making of the Crisis

Eduardo de la Vega Alfaro

Against all expectations, during the early years of the post-World War II period, the Mexican film industry experienced a brief era of structural crisis characterized by a sudden decline in its volume of production. In 1946 seventy-one feature films were produced (eleven less than in 1945), while the following year yielded only fifty-seven. Thcse figures were a result, and perhaps logically so, of the following factors that should be emphasized: first, and perhaps most important, the resurgence of Hollywood film production, which now had as a goal the complete recovery of its Latin American market; second, the almost immediate withdrawal of the financial and technological support that producers from the United States had extended to the Mexican film industry during the war years; and finally, but no less important, the decline in investment rates, which resulted in less financial investment per film. In other words, the producers, taken aback by Hollywood's formidable success, were fearful of risking their capital, a factor which brought about a pronounced decline in the thematic and aesthetic quality of Mexican films.

There are, however, a few films produced in 1946 which are definitely worth mentioning: *El Ahijado de la Muerte*, a good rural drama directed by Norman Foster, a filmmaker from the United States who was residing in Mexico at the time; *Voces de Primavera*, by Jaime Salvador, the debut of actor Adalberto Martínez "Resortes,"who later would become one of the Mexican film industry's most popular comics and also one of its most important box-office successes; *La Otra*, an excellent *film noir* melodrama by Roberto Gavaldón, starring the popular diva Dolores del Río; *Sucedió en Jalisco o Los Cristeros*, by Raúl de Anda, where for the first time the controversial topic of the Cristero Rebellion (1926–1929), a confrontation of the postrevolutionary government with the Catholic Church and its followers, is examined within a public medium such as film; *Yo Maté a Rosita Alavírez*, also directed by de Anda, a cowboy melodrama (*ranchero*) that had the unusual box-office success of remaining for thirteen straight weeks in the same theater where it had premiered; *El Moderno Barbazul*, also directed by Jaime Salvador, a failed comedy starring the great Buster Keaton; *Los Tres García* and *Vuelven los García*, a double film project directed by Ismael Rodríguez that enabled one of its actors, Pedro Infante, to reach stardom; and *Gran Casino*, the film with which Luis Buñuel initiated the Mexican period of his filmography—a filmography as disquieting in its innumerable production difficulties as the brilliance reflected in its artistic legacy. All of these movies, plus several more, constituted isolated attempts that endeavored above all to maintain or open up artistic and economic opportunities for the Mexican film industry but, for the abovementioned reasons, began to lose the enormous Latin American markets it had gained owing to the tremendous success of *Allá en el Rancho Grande* and its sequels.

Nevertheless, in 1947 (without doubt the worst year of the postwar period for film production), in order to confront its obvious crisis, Mexican cinema found a formula: the production of low-budget films that began to place the plot in an urban setting, preferably in working-class neighborhoods. During the early part of this period, these films sought to satisfy the public demand of the growing population of the cities (particularly the capital), whose increasing demographics were an immediate effect of the accelerated process of industrialization that had begun some years earlier. Two filmmakers, Ismael Rodríguez and Alejandro Galindo, who were influenced by Italy's neorealist movement and the *film noir* drama series of Hollywood—trends in filmmaking considered to be avant-garde at the time—set about to discover a new style. Ismael Rodríguez made *Nosotros los Pobres* and *Ustedes los Ricos*, resulting in another twofold box-office success starring Pedro Infante, while Galindo directed two films starring the excellent actor, David Silva: *¡Esquina. . . Bajan!* and *Hay Lugar Para . . . Dos*. These films contrast in their respective plots and plot development: Galindo's films are situated in the world of bus and trolley drivers, giving the characters sociological and even anthropological interpretations with the use of colloquial speech and an authentic working-class context. At the same time, the films of Rodríguez seek to portray, with bruising drama that at times becomes outright sensationalist and mystical, the oppressive daily life of the residents of low-income housing in urban areas characterized by misery, violence, overcrowding, and promiscuity. The considerable box-office success of these films (especially those with the Rodríguez-Infante collaboration) took Mexican film production on a commercial route dedicated to fulfilling the demand of the urban working populace, for whom movies had become the main source of entertainment during hours of leisure. At the same time, however, this new strategy resulted in the disfavor of the middle-class sector, who, endowed with greater purchasing power, began to prefer Hollywood films to the detriment of those of national origin.

This genre of films with urban themes stimulated production; and during the period from 1948 until 1952, an era that coincided with the rapid growth characterizing the presidential years of Miguel Alemán Valdés, the average annual number of feature films produced reached 102, creating a phenomenon observed as a prolongation of the Golden Age. Some of the more representative films of this time attempted to pay homage to the economically disadvantaged social sectors and utilized titles that tended to be associated with religious references (*La Santa del Barrio, Angeles del Arrabal, Los Pobres Van al Cielo, Un Rincón Cerca del Cielo*); with identifiable urban spaces (*Barrio Bajo, La Marquesa del Barrio, Casa de Vecindad, Café de Chinos, La Tienda de la Esquina, Sangre en el Barrio, Salón de Belleza, El Ruiseñor del Barrio*); or with many types of low-income but "decent and honorable" professions (*El Ropavejero, El Billetero, El Papelerito, Nosotras las Taquígrafas, Nosotras las Sirvientas, Secretaria Particular, Comisario en Turno, El Gendarme de la Esquina*). The making of these types of films, the majority of which were based on conventional wisdom that was both simplistic and moralistic, coincided (and not by chance) with the appearance of brothel-*cabaretera* melodramas, a genre that in its way attempted to reflect on screen the emergence of a nightlife as dissolute as it was intense, but that at the same time summed up some of the defining aspects of the political term of Alemán: corruption in all spheres of politics, accelerated demographic explosion in the urban areas, and a rise in unemployment, violence, and prostitution.

The background and elements for the brothel-*cabaretera* genre can be traced to the films of the 1930s (particularly in *Santa, La Mujer del Puerto*, and *La Mancha de Sangre*), to the erotic dramas of cheap popular literature, and to the compositions of Agustín Lara, a composer of extremely popular songs, that in most cases idealized the female type dominant in the brothels and cabarets that were frequented by men of all social classes. The making of films such as *Pervertida* (José Díaz Morales, 1945), the screenplay of which was liberally inspired by Lara's song of the same name, and the box-office success of *Humo en los Ojos* (1946), made by Alberto Gout, starring David Silva and Mercedes Barba and also based on a Lara melody, gave the impetus to a rise in a considerable number of movies that carried implicitly in their titles the social stigma of the protagonists: *La Sin Ventura* (Tito Davison, 1947), *La Bien Pagada* (Gout, 1947), *Cortesana* (Gout, 1947), *La Venus de Fuego* (Jaime Salvador, 1948), *Una Mujer con Pasado* (Rafael J. Sevilla, 1948), *Pecadora* (José Díaz Morales, 1947), *Señora Tentación* (Díaz Morales, 1947), *La Venenosa* (Miguel Morayta, 1949), *El Pecado de Laura* (René Cardona, 1948), *La Bandida* (Agustín P. Delgado, 1948), *Traicionera* (Ernesto Cortázar, 1950), *Hipócrita* (Morayta, 1949), *Vagabunda* (Morayta, 1950), *Callejera* (Cortázar, 1949), *Una Mujer sin Destino* (Salvador, 1950), *Arrabalera* (Joaquín Pardavé, 1950), *Ladronzuela* (Delgado, 1949), *Perdida* (Fernando A. Rivero, 1950), *Aventurera* (Gout, 1949), *Coqueta* (Rivero, 1949), *Mala Hembra* (Miguel M. Delgado, 1950), *Burlada* (Rivero, 1950), *Pasionaria* (Pardavé, 1951), *La Mujer Desnuda* (Fernando Méndez, 1951), *Apasionada* (Alfredo B. Crevenna, 1952), *Ambiciosa* (Cortázar, 1952), and *Sandra* (*La Mujer de Fuego*) (Juan Orol, 1952).

As Emilio García Riera correctly points out, many films of this genre narrated with slight variations the same story: a provincial girl, or one of humble origins, whose circumstances lead her to find work in a city cabaret, where a pimp takes advantage of her naiveté. Often the girl becomes simultaneously a prostitute and a famous "artist," thanks to her singing abilities, or even more often, to her ability to dance the rumba. This twofold hypocritical message, typical of the melodrama, gives the heroine a ruinous destiny while it glorifies the cabaret, a reflection of the true conventions of the times. Within this milieu, putting many musical numbers in these films filled the holes in the plots, especially during the difficult last third part of the movie. In addition to Mercedes Barba, the stars of the brothel-*cabaretera* films included María Antonieta Pons, Emilia Guiú, Susana Guízar, Gloria Marín, Rosa Carmina, Leticia Palma, Marga López, Guillermina Grin, Rosita Quintana, Brenda Conde, Miroslava, Lilia Prado, Elsa Aguirre, Ninón Sevilla, Amalia Aquilar, Rosita Fornés, and Yolanda Montes "Tongolele." Some of the actresses mentioned (Pons, Carmina, Sevilla, Fornés, and Aquilar) came from Cuba and were able to shine, thanks to their talent for performing musical numbers inspired by Caribbean rhythms (*danzón*, *clave*, conga, rumba, mambo, *bembé*, *bahiao*, etc.)— dances that served as a means for expressing an eroticism that often reached unusual dimensions for the times.

Owing to her exceptional beauty and her previous roles in films (particularly her performances in *Doña Bárbara*, *La Mujer sin Alma*, and *Vértigo y Amok*, filmed by Fernando de Fuentes or Antonio Momplet during the biennial 1943–44), it was left to María Félix to portray several variations of the "high-class harlot," a stereotype that she played in *La Devoradora* (Fernando de Fuentes, 1946), *La Mujer de Todos* (Julio Bracho, 1946), and *Doña Diabla* (Tito Davison, 1948), all of which preceded a first series of films that established the diva in European productions of the postwar era (*Mare Nostrum, Una Mujer Cualquiera, La Noche del Sábado, La Corona Negra, Mesalina, Hechizo Trágico,* and *La Pasión Desnuda*), made between 1948–1952 by directors such as Rafael Gil, Luis Saslavsky, Carmine Gallone, Mario Sequi, and Luis César Amadori.

From the overwhelming list of brothel-*cabaretera* melodramas there is always room to praise a trilogy directed by Alberto Gout and starring Ninón Sevilla. In *Aventurera, Sensualidad* (1950), and *No Niego Mi Pasado* (1951), films produced by the Calderón brothers and written by Alvaro Custodio, a Spanish immigrant and film critic of that era, Gout knew how to use the conventions of the genre to develop profoundly "subversive" films. In fact, in the first of these movies, clearly the best of the three, there is evidence of an attempt to cut through myths apparently inspired by surrealist proclamations against the tenets of bourgeois art: the heroine played by Sevilla belongs to the family of evil characters in whom André Breton and his followers delighted. At the height of the "moral revolt" (according to García Riera), Gout's film makes explicit the fact that the prostitute, who earlier had been portrayed as seeking revenge and being perverse, is not punished but, on the contrary, deserves a future alongside the man who loves her in spite of her sinful past. *Aventurera* is also the most biting critic of the hypocritical discourse of Mexican film of the era (and even subsequent eras) and a revealing document on the social corruption prevalent during the Alemán administration.

Simultaneously, along with the brothel-*cabaretera* films, came the tradition which, openly inspired by the Hollywood *film noir*, tried adapting to the conditions of urban Mexico the passions and doomed adventures of gangsters pursued by justice or fatalism. With local backgrounds in films such as *¿Quien Mató a Eva?*, *Luponini (El Terror de Chicago)*, *Marihuana (El Monstruo Verde)* (all three directed by José Bohr from 1934 to 1936) and *Los Misterios del Hampa* (Juan Orol, 1944), the "gangster melodrama" proposed a gallery of evil characters who in the end become victims of their ambitions for an easy life. From the simple perspective of *El Reino de los Gángsters* (Orol, 1947) would follow *Carta Brava* (Agustín P. Delgado, 1948), *Ventarrón* (Chano Urueta, 1949), *Cuatro contra el Mundo* (Alejandro Galindo, 1949), *Cabaret Shanghai* (Orol, 1949), *El Desalmado* (Urueta, 1950), *El Suavecito* (Fernando Méndez, 1950), *Quinto Patio* (Rafael J. Sevilla, 1950), *Paco el Elegante* (Adolfo Fernández, 1951), and *Manos de Seda* (Urueta, 1950), examples of more pretentious films. Nevertheless, only in *El Suavecito* can we speak of aspirations that would transcend the rigid conventions of the subgenera, thanks to the narrative talents of its director, who years later gained fame by making Westerns or horror films. The character created by Méndez offers dimensions much richer and more complex than the melodramatic ambience in which his co-characters move. The final sequence of the Méndez film, where the hero is massacred in a bus station, is comparable in quality to the intensity and drama of the ending in Robert Wise's masterpiece, *The Set-Up* (1949).

Another successful genre of the era, also derived from the urban film, was the comedy. It is worth mentioning that after his respective lead roles in *Barrio Bajo* or *Confidencias de un Ruletero* (Alejandro Galindo, 1949) and the musical comedy *Al Son del Mambo* (Chano Urueta, 1950), Adalberto Martínez "Resortes" began to adapt to a series of urban prototypes that, with the least pretext, allowed him to exploit and develop his artistic potential to the maximum. In *Dicen que Soy Comunista* (Alejando Galindo, 1951), *Baile Mi Rey* (Roberto Rodríguez, 1951), *El Besibolista Fenómeno* (Fernando Cortés, 1951), or *El Luchador Fenómeno* (Cortés, 1952), Resortes was able to display most of his dance repertoire linked to a type of comedy that distanced him from the styles of Cantinflas or Tin Tan.

During this period also proliferated the family melodrama, a genre that attempted to reflect on the morals of the ambitions of the rapidly growing urban middle class. Having as its most notable precedent the example of *La Familia Dressel* (1935), directed by the great Fernando de Fuentes, and shielded by the box-office formula of *Cuando los Hijos Se Van* (1941), made by Juan Bustillo Oro (a film portraying a middle-class family who begins to anxiously live out its inevitable parting of the ways), after 1948 we see films such as *El Cuarto Mandamiento*, by Rolando Aquilar; *La Familia Pérez*, by Gilberto Martínez Solares; *Cuando los Padres Se Quedan Solos*, by Bustillo Oro; and *El Dolor de los Hijos*, by Miguel Zacarías. The genre continued for several more years and reached its apotheosis with films such as *Azahares para Tu Boda* (1950), by Julián Soler, brother of Fernando Soler, who along with Sara García was the archetype of the "institutional marriage" of Mexican film. Moving astutely within the camp of this genre, Alejando Galindo was able to direct, also in 1948, *Una Familia de Tantas*, without doubt the most representative example of the talents of this filmmaker and at the same time his most beloved film. As a diligent observer of contemporary social realities, Galindo was able to both narrate and question, from an internal perspective, the authoritarian logic of family structure. Many years passed before this masterpiece by Galindo was followed by sequels as significant in importance.

Toward the end of the decade of the 1940s, the rural comedy (*ranchera*), deteriorated drastically. After the commercial success of *Los Tres García, Vuelven los García, Si Me Han de Matar Mañana* (Miguel Zacarías, 1946), *La Barca de Oro* and *Soy Charro de Rancho Grande* (both filmed in 1947 by Joaquín Pardavé), and *Cartas Marcadas* (René Cardona, 1947), all starring Pedro Infante, and after the failure of films such as *El Gallero* (Emilio Gómez Muriel, 1948), in which the decline of Tito Guizar becomes evident, the producers and directors looked desperately for alternatives that permitted some evolution, no matter how minute, away from the conventions of a series weighed down by the simplistic character of its elements. Between 1948 and 1950 this genre attempted to advance itself through various channels: the route of remakes, the most representative of which is the second version, in color, of *Allá en el Rancho Grande*, made in 1948 by Fernando de Fuentes and starring Jorge Negrete; and the route of co-productions (*Jalisco Canta en Sevilla*, 1948, also by Fuentes) in order to take advantage of the far-reaching popularity of those film idols established years earlier. The most significant advance, initiated in 1950 with *El Gavilán Pollero* (starring Infante and Antonio Badú and marking the directorial début of Rogelio A. González), took place thanks to the consistent formula of putting together two or more actors well known in the genre. The brief but successful cycle continued with *Los Tres Alegres Compadres* (Julián Soler, 1951) and reached its height in 1952 with *Los Hijos de María Morales* by Fuentes, who again reunites the team of Infante and Badú; *Tal para Cual*, by Rogelio A. González, with Jorge Negrete and Luis Aguilar, and, above all, *Dos Tipos de Ciudado*, by Ismael Rodríguez, starring Negrete and Infante, thus giving the film the character of being mythical and at the same time apotheosized. From this point on, the characters, symbols, and typical situations of the "rural comedy" would tend to mix with traits of other genres, an effect that would lead to its total decline.

The conditions that prevailed during the postwar years left their mark in a peculiar way on the respective careers of the most outstanding directors of the era. The case of Emilio Fernández, the great lyrical-nationalist filmmaker, exemplifies, perhaps better than any other, these conditions. After making *Enamorada* (1946), *Río Escondido* (1948), and *Maclovia* (1948), all of them starring María Félix, "El Indio" Fernández began to film from 1948 onward a series characterized by very low budgets in comparison to the years of the industrial boom. Films such as *Salón México* (1948), *Pueblerina* (1948), *La Malquerida* (1949), *Duelo en las Montañas* (1949), *Un Día de Vida* (1950), *Víctimas del Pecado* (1950), *Islas Marías* (1950), *Siempre Tuya* (1950), *La Bienamada* (1951), *Acapulco* (1951), *El*

Rodolfo Acosta and Marga López in Salón México, *directed by Emilio "El Indio" Fernández.*

Mar y Tú (1951), and *Cuando Levanta la Niebla* (1952) relied on pro-duction formulas that attempted to save costs at the expense of devel-oping a creative project that would have been more reflexive and elaborated. Even in the case of *Pueblerina* (that over time rose to the rank of an authentic director's masterpiece) or *La Malquerida*, with its favorable financial support, the truth is that the films of Fernández suffered a significant decline in quality and pretensions. The well-earned fame of El Indio rapidly faded, and it was not long before this process of decadence brought down with it the prestige of the art of Mexican cinema, which in a few years, with some honest exceptions, became only a nostalgic reference.

In contrast to the notorious downfall of Fernandez's career, the case of Roberto Gavaldón took exception in a different way. After the artistic and commercial success of *La Otra*, Gavaldón was able to as-semble a good team of collaborators who, with the exception of writer José Revueltas, cameraman Alex Phillips, and actor Arturo de Córdova, had participated alongside Fernández, sharing in his artistic successes. Aside from those already mentioned, the group included Gabriel Figueroa and the actors Pedro Armendáriz, Dolores del Río, María Félix, and Carlos López Moctezuma. This new joining of tal-ents resulted in a good many films that began to establish Gavaldón's prestige, even beyond the borders: *A la Sombra del Puente* (1946), *La Diosa Arrodillada* (1947), *La Casa Chica* (1949), *Deseada* (1950), *Rosauro Castro* (1950), *En la Palma de Tu Mano* (1950), *La Noche Avanza* (1951), and *El Rebozo de Soledad* (1952). With *Deseada, Rosauro Castro,* and *El Rebozo de Soledad,* Gavaldón, acclaimed as the creator of quality films, was able to prolong at a high level the nationalist aesthetic on which the fame of the Fernández-Figueroa duo had been sustained; from then on during this period he was considered as a worthy successor to the author of *Flor Silvestre.* At any rate, the Gavaldonian style was much better suited to urban

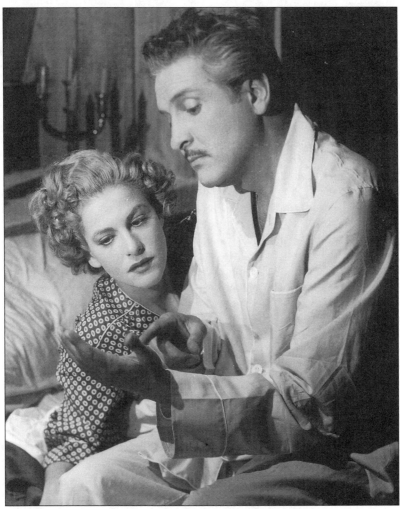

Arturo de Córdova and Carmen Montego in the film En la Palma de Tu Mano, *directed by Roberto Gavaldón.*

themes, as confirmed by such examples as *A la Sombra del Puente* (an interesting adaptation of a play by the U.S. writer Maxwell Anderson); *En la Palma de Tu Mano* (an excellent urban melodrama full of irony and necrophilia); and *La Noche Avanza*, without doubt one of the most faithful portrayals of the corrupt universe of the underworld, with influences from the *film noir* series at its best.

As for the films of Julio Bracho, also characterized by their stylistic refinements, they succumbed to industry demands. Throughout Alemán's presidential term, and with the only exception being the film *Rosenda* (1948), a serious and passionate drama with a provincial setting at the end of the 1930s, the career of Bracho alternated between the most offensive examples of glorifying dictator Porfirio Díaz's Belle Epoque (*Don Simón de Lira*, 1946), to moralistic tales made to illuminate the stereotype of María Félix (*La Mujer de Todos*, 1946), to "nationalistic" biographies of poverty-stricken saints (*San Felipe de Jesús*, 1949), to insignificant mundane comedies (*El Ladrón*, 1947), to poor adaptations of nineteenth-century Mexican literature (*La Posesión*, 1949), and, especially, to all types of melodramas that communicated the themes of the series of soap operas made to cater to the moralistic tastes of the middle class: from *Inmaculada* to *Mujeres que Trabajan*, including *Historia de un Corazón*, *Paraíso Robado*, *La Usente*, *Rostros Olvidados*, and *La Cobarde*.

After the widely discussed commercial failure of *Gran Casino* and an interlude of three years, Luis Buñuel was able to make *El Gran Calavera* (1949), a film that allowed him to become an established member of the Mexican film industry. Thanks to the support of Oscar Danzinger, a businessman who had emigrated from Europe to Mexico due to the World War, the Spanish filmmaker made *Los Olvidados* (1950), the masterpiece that allowed him to regain some of the prestige he had earned at the end of the 1920s with the two surrealist films, *Un Perro Andaluz* and *La Edad de Oro*. Along with many other attributes, *Los Olvidados* resulted in being the most overwhelming response to the phenomenon of mystification, which sustained the plots and styles of the immense majority of films that subscribed to the genre concerned with urban life. Situated in the sordid ambience of *lumpenproletariat* neighborhoods in Mexico City, Buñuel's work even today remains valid as a film that denounces the profound mechanisms of juvenile delinquency (and delinquency in general) without diminishing its undeniable artistic value.

In spite of the fact that *Los Olvidados* won an important award at the Cannes Film Festival, the prevailing circumstances in Mexican cinema of that era were the main obstacle to permitting Buñuel to maintain a level worthy of his genius. Nevertheless, along with a number of *alimenticia* films (those made to put food on the table) not exempt from moments that revealed his talent and capacity to draw upon irony (such was the case in *Susana*, 1950; *La Hija del Engaño*, 1951; *Una Mujer sin Amor*, 1951; *Subida al Cielo*, 1951, and *Robinson Crusoe*, 1952), Buñuel was able to express his distinct worldview through two films whose merits have increased over time: *El Bruto* (1952), an intense urban melodrama that recalls *Los Olvidados*; and *El* (1952), a film that takes on the obsessions of a paranoid figure, majestically played by Arturo de Córdova, and ends by deeply criticizing the bourgeois ethic as well as being one of the most explicitly sadistic films in cinema history.

It was left to Miguel Alemán's government to take steps in order to provide support for the continuing development of the film industry. Thus, in 1947 the Banco Cinematográfico, established five years earlier, changed its name to the Banco Nacional Cinematográfico, constituting a credit institution of primarily state capital and given the assignment of protecting and promoting the production sector, which in that year was experiencing a severe crisis. In the same year the distributor Películas Nacionales, S.A., was established with mixed capital; its purpose was to release national films within the internal market, joining with the company Películas Mexicanas, whose objective since 1945 was to distribute Mexican films in Latin America, Europe, and the southern United States. In 1949 the Ley de la Industria Cinematográfica was passed whereby legal foundations were established to allow state intervention in the film medium. One of the articles of this law pointed out explicitly the creation of the Dirección General de Cinematografía under the auspices of the Secretaría de Gobernación, an organization whose principal assignment would be that of censorship (euphemistically called "supervision") and preservation of national films through the creation of official film archives (Cineteca Nacional) which, due to bureaucratic problems, did not formally begin to operate for another twenty-six years.

Upon the decree of the Ley de la Industria Cinematográfica, attention was called to the fact that in some of its articles the development of monopolies was prohibited in all sectors of the film medium. This measure, however, was outdated, because in 1949 a monopoly owned by the U.S. citizen William Jenkins and his "associates" (Mexican nationals who were paid for the use of their names in business interests to comply with Mexican laws concerning business ownership)—Manuel Espinoza Yglesias, Manuel Alarcón, and the heirs of Maximino Avila Camacho, brother of the former president—controlled around 80 percent of the movie theaters in the country. This monopoly had been growing during the six-year presidential term of Manuel Avila Camacho and by the end of the 1940s had reached proportions theretofore unknown in Mexico. From a hierarchical position of uncontrolled power, the group headed by Jenkins started to implement some sinister political measures designed to impose on the entrepreneurs of the film production sector the type of movies that were most advantageous to their interests. It was in this way that, during the last year of the Alemán regime, film production was subject to dictated commercial interests; in fact, several of the most powerful producers (Gregorio Wallerstein, Raúl de Anda) ended up by becoming partners with the fictitious associates of Jenkins in order to supply theater owners with the kinds of films destined not so much for the ever-widening internal market, but exclusively for the mass populace. Thus, the very foundations of Mexican cinema began to experience its worst moments in spite of the fact that its annual averages of production volume were sustained, or even increased.

~

The long period in the history of Mexican cinema during which it suffered a structural crisis of quality coincided with the presidential terms of Adolfo Ruiz Cortines (December 1952–December 1958) and of Adolfo López Mateos (December 1958–December 1964). At the same time, both governmental regimes were labeled as the initial period of the era of "stabilizing development," an economical and political strategy that was applied after a large devaluation of the peso against the U.S. dollar. The positive results of this strategy would permit Mexico to experience for nearly two decades an unusual era of relative prosperity and social stability.

The social and political situation generated from the gains of "stabilizing development" was, in general terms, a favorable context in which Mexican cinema could increase its volume of production, though at the expense of a marked decline in quality. The crisis of quality generated by the commercial strategy dictated by Jenkins's monopoly was aggravated, as in the rest of the world, by the competition introduced with the arrival of television. The new audiovisual medium, a sort of synthesis of both film and radio, began transmission in Mexico in July 1950. Consumers' purchase of television sets proceeded at a very slow rate, but nevertheless Mexican film producers thought that their interests were threatened, which translated into even lower production costs per film. An alarming policy of "closed doors" avoided to the extreme the incorporation of new generations of filmmakers, using as an argument the pretext of the imminent crisis and seniority rights. The film unions, particularly the sector of directors, denied at all costs the entrance into their ranks of young filmmakers. As a result, Mexican cinema began to suffer from out-

Stars Roberto Cañedo, Columbia Domínguez, and Fernando Fernández in the patriotic film of the Mexican Revolution Un Día de Vida, *directed by Emilio "El Indio" Fernández.*

dated aesthetics and subject material, which at the same time rendered impossible the recovery of markets lost after the postwar period. The picture became complete with the deaths of some of the most popular actors: Jorge Negrete in 1953, Joaquín Pardavé in 1955, and Pedro Infante in 1956.

These economic circumstances permitted, at least during the remaining years of the decade of the 1950s, the volume of film production, on the average, to be maintained at above 90 films per year, reaching the record number of 118 produced in 1953—the highest volume produced by a film industry in the Spanish-speaking world. However, as mentioned above, the majority of these films were made with increasingly lower budgets for audiences whose inability to buy television sets obliged them to continue to flock to the movie theaters for entertainment during their hours of leisure.

Given the increasing decline in the quality of Mexican films, the recently inaugurated government of Ruiz Cortines tried to implement several measures. In 1953 the president appointed Eduardo Garduño

as the head of the Banco Nacional Cinematográfico, who implemented a policy that was controversial. It had as its main idea
strengthening the alliance between film entrepreneurs and those distributors dependent on the bank (especially Películas Nacionales,
S.A.), all with the objective of counteracting the power of the theater
owners' monopoly. However, the Garduño Plan, as it was called, not
only demonstrated its inefficiency but also submitted itself to several
corrupt moves and mistakes that made it a complete failure in its aspirations to stimulate the production of good-quality films, propitiat-
ing instead the emergence, not of new directors and technicians, but
of a new climate for film stars. Garduño seemed not to be aware that
to confront the united group associated with Jenkins implied much
more than implementing good intentions or simple strategies to un-
dercut the power of the monopoly. And although at the end of the
decade of the 1950s the state finally was able to intervene in the sector of exhibitors, literally annulling Jenkins's monopoly with the creation of a state monopoly (Compañia Operadora de Teatros, S.A.),
the crisis situation did not change a great deal.

As the thematic-aesthetic crisis of Mexican cinema became more
acute, the important film producers, each time more subject to the
politics dictated by successive exhibitors' monopolies, began to finance films made in color and in the Cinemascope format, with the
goal of attracting a new urban middle class who were no longer able
to digest so easily the stories proposed by anachronistic and moralistic genres such as the brothel-*cabaretera* melodrama (the decline of
which coincided with the end of the six-year political term of
Alemán), the rural comedy (*ranchera*), films about family, or films
with a historical-biographical theme, to cite the best known. These
new efforts had disappointing results; the members of this social sector were rapidly becoming the main consumers to acquire television
sets and, in addition, becoming potential consumers of other forms of
entertainment. Another cost-cutting strategy consisted in producing
film in series starting in 1957 with Estudios América. These series
permitted a larger participation of workers affiliated with the Sindicato de Trabajadores de la Producción Cinematográfica, or STPC,
whose members, because of a ruling issued several years earlier,
could not work in feature films. These features, which as a whole
subscribed to several genres that were popular at that time, usually
were divided into three films of thirty minutes each and were premiered as a series lasting for a total of one-and-one-half hours at one
screening.

Satisfied with their privileges and without demonstrating any real
desire to overcome the crisis, the rest of the film entrepreneurs, with
few exceptions, exploited as much as possible the possibilities that

the new situation offered them. Some of them were able to produce films that could be considered within "new" or even "risky" genres. Such was the case of the brief but commercially successful series of films employing "artistic nudity" financed between 1955 and 1956 by the Calderón brothers, which included *La Fuerza del Deseo*, *El Seductor*, and *La Ilegítima*, a trilogy directed by Chano Urueta; *La Virtud Desnuda*, *Esposas Infieles*, and *Juventud Desenfrenada*, all three directed by José Díaz Morales; and *La Diana Cazadora*, directed by Tito Davison. However, it was not long before pressure from conservative groups resulted in censorship and put an end to the supposed audacity of showing on film a group of female bodies (Ana Luisa Peluffo, Amanda del llano, Columbia Domínguez, Kitty de Hoyos, Aída Araceli, and the extras who accompanied them), almost always static, with their breasts bared or total nudity suggested under transparent clothing.

Other genres characterized by low costs and simplistic themes had better luck. The favorable box-office response to several films made in 1952, all starring wrestlers (*La Bestia Magnífica*, by Chano Urueta; *Huracán Ramírez*, by Joselito Rodríguez; *El Enmascarado de Plata*, by René Cardona, and the already mentioned *El Luchador Fenómeno*), supported from 1954 onward the ever more recurrent production of this type of film. After the respected trilogies of *La Sombra Vengadora* (Rafael Baledón, 1954) and *Los Tigres del Ring* (Chano Urueta, 1957) followed a legendary series that adhered to the tastes of a large percentage of moviegoers: between 1958 and 1964 more than thirty films set in the world of wrestling were made, many of which starred El Santo, who had reached enormous popularity thanks to his triumph in wrestling arenas throughout the republic. From the repertoire of films produced to display the accomplishments of this wrestler, the following stand out: *Santo contra el Cerebro del Mal* (Joselito Rodríguez, 1958), *Santo contra los Hombres Infernales* (Rodríguez, 1958), *Santo contra los Zombies* (Benito Alazraki, 1961), *Santo contra el Cerebro Diabólico* (Federico Curiel, 1961), *Santo contra el Rey del Crimen* (Curiel, 1961), *Santo en el Hotel de la Muerte* (Curiel, 1961), *Santo contra las Mujeres Vampiros* (Alfonso Corona Blake, 1962), *Santo en el Museo de Cera* (Corona Blake, 1963), *Santo vs. El Estrangulador* (René Cardona, 1963), *Santo contra el Espectro* (Cardona, 1963), and *Atacan las brujas* (José Díaz Morales, 1964). *Santo contra las Mujeres Vampiros* became practically a cult film thanks to writers from some of the European magazines who specialized in horror films. This fact, and other qualities worth noting when compared to other films of the same genre, made this movie a Mexican cinema classic of the early 1960s.

Other famous wrestlers of the era (Lobo Negro, Cacama, Black Shadow, Cavernario Galindo, Karloff Lagarde, René Guajardo "Copetes", Blue Demond, Sugi Sito, Dorrel Dixon, Enrique Yanes, Murciélago Velásquez, et al.) also took part in the declining era of Mexican cinema but were never able to reach the mystic dimensions of El Santo. On the other hand, the feminine variant of the genre was found in a trilogy directed by René Cardona (*Las Luchadoras vs. El Médico Asesino*, *Las Luchadoras contra la Monia*, and *Las Lobas del Ring*, 1962–1964), where actress Lorena Velázquez was able to reach the rank of heroine in a realm almost exclusively dominated by the professional gladiators.

As the film titles indicate, almost from the beginning the cinema of wrestling was mixed with characters and conventions of other genres such as horror, science fiction, and parody. This phenomenon of a hybrid genre also was one of the primary characteristics of the "chili Western" or "Mexican Western," which were derived from the films set within the sphere of the Mexican Revolution—for example, the very popular series entitled *Calaveras del Terror*, directed by Fernando Méndez in 1943 that included twelve episodes set in the typical ambience of Westerns. With evident homage to old Hollywood films, the first vengeful heroes of the "chili Western" (*El Lobo Solitario*, *El Aguila Negra*, *El Diablo*, *El Látigo Negro*, *El Jinete Solitario*, *El Zorro Escarlata*) covered their faces with all types of masks; later, these tributes could be made without this anonymity, such as in the film series that starred *El Rayo Justiciero*, *El Puma*, *El Hijo del Charro Negro*, or *Juan Sin Miedo*. Other examples, such as *Estampida* (Raúl de Anda, 1958) or *Tierra de Violencia* and *Fuera de la Ley* (Raúl de Anda, Jr., 1965), were more serious attempts to approximate the genre's characteristic elements, but minimum results were achieved.

The best examples of this era, without doubt, are indebted to the skilled craftsmanship of Fernando Méndez, precursor to the "chili Western," who between 1954 and 1959 directed a number of films for several production companies that transcended the prevailing mediocrity of the times: *Los Aventureros*, *¡Vaya Tipos!*, *Tres Bribones*, *Los Tres Villalobos*, *La Venganza de los Villalobos*, *Fugitivos* (*Pueblo de Proscritos*), *Los Diablos del Terror*, *El Grito de la Muerte*, *Los Hermanos Diablo*, *El Renegado Blanco*, and *Venganza Apache*. In spite of sharing with colleagues the same budget limitations, Méndez was able to give all of these films the correct rhythm; and, in some cases, his work was comparable to the commendable Hollywood craftsmen who cultivated the "Grade B" Western. The other notable accomplishment was achieved by Ismael Rodríguez, who in 1961 filmed *Los Hermanos de Hierro*, a psychological drama with the atmosphere of a Western, which penetrates the myth surrounding the maternal figure and asks its audience to reflect on the mechanisms of violence.

Méndez's skills for good narrative also brought him recognition through his fantasy and horror films, another of the most popular and commercially successful genres of the crisis period. After making an excellent hybrid of wrestling and horror (*Ladrón de Cadáveres*, 1956), Méndez was hired by producer and actor Abel Salazar to direct *El Vampiro* (1957), which remained for several weeks in the theater where it premiered, thus confirming its surprising box-office success. Obviously inspired by Anglo-Saxon models (especially the films of "The Hammer" directed by Terrence Fisher), *El Vampiro* is set in an old Mexican hacienda (an obvious replica of a castle of the Middle Ages) with the theme made famous by Bram Stoker in his celebrated book, *Dracula*. The cinematography of Rosalío Solano along with the splendid scenography of Gunter Gerszo and the magnificent stage presence of actor Germán Robles gave *El Vampiro* an ideal ambience that stirred its audience.

The box-office triumph of Méndez's film triggered the serial production of many films that attempt to subscribe to the elements of the fantastic and bizarre. The same crew of *El Vampiro* immediately produced a sequel (*El Ataúd del Vampiro*, 1957), and a year later Méndez again made another commendable contribution to the genre with his *Misterios de Ultratumba*, made for Alameda Films.

Ramón Obón in the title role in El Vampiro, *directed by Fernando Méndez.*

Between 1957 and 1964 this type of film, including parodies, pro-
liferated until thematic ideas were exhausted. The pillaging of clas-
sical sources was evident: a group of directors (Rafael Portillo,
Alfonso Corona Blake, Rafael Baledón, Federico Curiel, Julián
Soler, Benito Alazraki, Chano Urueta, Ramón Obón, Miguel M.
Delgado, Alfredo B. Crevenna, Rogelio A. González, René
Cardona, Fernando Fernández, and José Díaz Morales) specialized
in lavishly employing titles such as *Misterios de la Magia Negra,
El Castillo de los Monstruos, La Momia Azteca, El Robot Humano,
El Regreso del Monstruo, El Fistol del Diablo, La Casa del Terror,
La Maldición de Nostradamus, La Llorona, Muñecos Infernales,
Orlak, El Infierno de Frankenstein, El Mundo de los Vampiros, El
Espejo de la Bruja, La Marca del Muerto, Espiritismo, Cien Gritos
de Terror*, and *El Hacha Diabólica*. However, the precarious econ-
omy together with a shortage of talent unfortunately produced re-
sults that were in most cases deficient, or even close to being
caricatures. During its declining phase, Mexican cinema character-
ized as fantastic or bizarre was nourished by Hollywood or
Japanese science fiction, invariably resulting in a film's first scene
denouncing its lack of quality and simplistic theme: *Los Platillos
Voladores, La Nave de los Monstruos, Gigantes Planetarios, El
Planeta de las Mujeres Invasoras, El Conquistador de la Luna*, or
La Isla de los Dinosaurios.

Coinciding with the initiative and development of horror films,
other producers and directors discovered new generic paths in an attempt to reach the growing audience that included children and adolescents. In this case, the obvious model was the cinematographic
production implemented by Walt Disney some years earlier. Themes
derived from classics of children's literature or Anglo-Saxon legends
adapted to the Mexican medium were the guidelines for such films as
Pulgarcito (René Cardona, 1957), *Santa Claus* (Cardona, 1959),
Caperucita Roja (Roberto Rodríguez, 1959) and its sequels (*Caperucita y Sus Tres Amigos, Caperucita y Pulgarcito contra los
Monstruos*, and *Los Espadachines de la Reina*, 1960–1961), *El Gato
con Botas* (Rodríguez, 1960), and *El Espadachín* (Arturo Martínez,
1963) and its sequels (*Dos Caballeros de Espada* and *La Duquesa
Diabólica*, 1963). Inadequate production plus a lack of imagination
on the part of the filmmakers deprived the movies of a tone more
parodic than fantastic, such a tone generally being the dignified
counterpart to the morals upon which the fantasies were based.

In reference to production volume, another of the important genres developed by the Mexican film industry during this era was the
comedy that revolved around the figures of Cantinflas, Tin Tan, and
Resortes. To them were added other comics from popular variety

shows, radio, or television: Antonio Espino "Clavillazo," Eulalio González "Piporro," Manuel Valdés "Loco," and the team of Marco Antonio Campos "Viruta" and Gaspar Henaine "Capulina." Cantinflas appeared in a series of films, all of which were directed by Miguel M. Delgado, in which his character ended up in a world plagued by conventions that were too simplistic or Manichaean. *Caballero a la Medida, Abajo el Talón, El Bolero de Raquel, Sube y Baja, El Analfabeto, El Extra, Entrega Inmediata,* and *El Padrecito* revealed a total loss of the comedy with popular roots that had carried him to fame. Not even attempts to conquer the English-speaking market with leading roles in films financed by Hollywood producers (*Around the World in Eighty Days,* 1956, by Michael Anderson; *Pepe,* 1960, by George Sydney) permitted Cantinflas to lose the marked tendency of a stereotype. On the other hand, in the case of Tin Tan, one can speak of a decline through satiation, proven by the fact that out of fifty-four films only a few, owing to scarce moments of brilliance, are worth remembering: *El Mariachi Desconocido* (Gilberto Martínez Solares, 1953), *Lo Que le Pasó a Sansón* (Martínez Solares, 1953), *Las Aventuras de Pito Pérez* (Juan Bustillo Oro, 1956), *El Cofre del Pirata* (Fernando Méndez, 1958), and *El Violetero* (Martínez Solares, 1960). Resortes was the least affected of the comic actors of the era: under the direction of Alejandro Galindo this popular dancer adapted to the interesting urban world proposed in a series of films produced between 1956 and 1958: *Hora y Media de Balazos, Policías y Ladrones, Te Vi en TV, Manos Arriba, Echenme al Gato* and *¡Ni Hablar del Peluquín!*

With his formal debut in *En Genial Detective Peter Pérez,* a film made by Agustín P. Delgado in 1952, Clavillazo developed a career that reached its height of popularity during the years of the presidency of Ruiz Cortines. In this period the comic starred in *Sindicato de Telemirones* (René Cardona, 1953), *Una Movida Chueca* (Rogelio A. González, 1955), *Pura vida* (Gilberto Martínez Solares, 1955), *Nunca Me Hagan Eso* (Rafael Baledón, 1956), *Piernas de Oro* (Alejandro Galindo, 1957), *El sordo* (Cardona, 1958), and *El Joven del Carrito* (Cardona, 1958)—films that revealed a hypothetical grace based on hand gestures (the principal characteristic of Clavillazo) and dialogue without great satiric relief. As the archetype of the grace of the verbal gesturing of the people from the north of Mexico, El Piporro reached full notoriety in *Calibre .44* (Julián Soler, 1959), and from then on his comic figure dominated a series of films that resulted in surprising commercial successes throughout the six-year presidential term of López Mateos; among them it is worth mentioning *El Padre Pistolas* (Soler, 1960), *Ruletero a Toda Marcha* (Rafael Baledón, 1962), *El Terror de la Frontera* (Zacarías Gómez

Urquiza, 1962), *El Rey del Tomate* (Miguel M. Delgado, 1962), *El Bracero del Año* (Rafael Baledón, 1963), *Torero por un Día* (Gilberto Martínez Solares, 1964), *El Tragabalas* (Martínez Solares, 1964), and *Alías el Rata* (Rogelio A. González, 1964).

As for El Loco, the brother of Germán Valdés "Tin Tan," he was promoted to a leading role in *El Supermacho* (Alejando Galindo, 1958), which was followed by *¿Con Quién Andan Nuestros Locos?* (Benito Alazraki, 1960), films that marked both his debut and his finale; the medium did not let this comedian use his best talent, which was his spontaneous roguishness. On the other hand, Viruta and Capulina, emulators of Laurel and Hardy, managed to let their unrefined comedy be heard, particularly among the young audience who was accustomed to seeing them on television programs. After their film debut in *Se los Chupó la Bruja* (Jaime Salvador, 1957), the duo starred in several comedies that were box-office successes (*Angelitos del Trapecio, Dos Criados Malcriados, El Dolor de Pagar la Renta*, and *Dos Locos en Escena*, all directed by Agustín P. Delgado, 1958–59); *Limosneros con Garrote* and *Pegando con Tubo*, both by Jaime Salvador, 1960) and ended up falling into a routine that lasted for several more years.

Derived from the old family melodrama, around 1955 a new genre broke onto the scene that at first attempted to exploit contemporary music (Rock 'n' Roll, the Twist, Go Go) coming from the United States. In a somewhat systematic way, films were produced such as *Los Chiflados del Rock 'n' Roll* (José Díaz Morales, 1956), *La Locura del Rock 'n' Roll* (Fernando Méndez, 1956), *Al Compás del Rock 'n' Roll* (Díaz Morales, 1956), *A Ritmo de Twist* (Benito Alazraki, 1962), *Twist, Locura de Juventud* (Miguel M. Delgado, 1962), *Juventud sin Ley (Rebeldes a Go Go)* (Gilberto Martínez Solares, 1965), and *Los Perversos (A Go Go)* (Martínez Solares, 1965), in which groups of young people made dancing their best and sometimes only means of expression. Simultaneously, films began to appear that, along with this music, set forth in a moralistic tone the generational conflict occurring during this time in the heart of middle-class families. It is not accidental that an entire trend among genres, represented in films such as *!Y Mañana Serán Mujeres!* (Alejandro Galindo, 1954), *¿Con Quién Andan Nuestras Hijas?* (Emilio Gómez Muriel, 1955), *El Caso de Una Adolescente* (Gómez Muriel, 1957), *Señoritas* (Fernando Méndez, 1958), *Quinceañera* (Alfredo B. Crevenna, 1958), *Chicas Casaderas* (Crevenna, 1959), *Ellas También Son Rebeldes* (Galindo, 1959), and *Teresa* (Crevenna, 1960), was a catalog of warnings of the dangers and threats confronted by adolescents in the modern world. The other view began with the supposed glorification of the overflowing happiness of young middle-class students (*¡Viva la Juventud!* by Fernando Cortés, 1955; *Paso a la Juventud*, by Gilberto Martínez Solares, 1957) but ended by criticizing, always in a paternalistic tone, the breakdown of values manifested in certain attitudes and conduct of these same youths. Examples of this paternalism exercised through the screen continued to be abundant and symptomatic: *La Rebelión de los Adolescentes, Juventud Desenfrenada, La Edad de la Tentación* (Galindo, 1958), *Juventud Rebelde* (Julián Soler, 1961), *La Edad de Violencia* (Soler, 1963), and *El Pecador* (Rafael Baledón, 1964). Many of these films and some tragicomedies such as *El Cielo y la Tierra* (Alfonso Corona Blake, 1962), *Mi Vida es una Canción* (Miguel M. Delgado, 1963), *Dile Que la Quiero* (Fernando Cortés, 1963), *Los Hijos Que Yo Soñé* (Roberto Gavaldón, 1964), *La Juventud Se Impone* (Soler, 1964), or *Canta Mi Corazón* (Gómez Muriel, 1964) were the vehicles for the film promotion of a group of "pop star" idols (César Costa, Enrique Guzmán, Angélica María, Julissa, Alberto Vásquez, Manolo Muñoz, Oscar Madrigal, Johnny Laboriel, Roberto Jordán) who had been successful on radio and television programs. The outstanding film of this genre was made in 1960 by Luis Alcoriza, former actor, scriptwriter, and frequent collaborator of Luis Buñuel. In *Los Jovenes*, situations that are much more realistic are portrayed by Alcoriza, even showing on screen some of the profound motivations behind the behavior of members of the new generation, but the film's principal merit remains its rejection of moralism and of a simplistic perspective.

The most ambitious film productions of the era were those concerned with the Mexican Revolution that, with one or two exceptions, continued to be routinely cultivated through film from an openly official perspective. The new cycle with this theme started with *Tierra de Hombres* (Ismael Rodríguez, 1956) and continued with a trilogy that Rodríguez himself directed where he glorifies the figure of the celebrated revolutionary Francisco Villa, played by Pedro Armendáriz: *Así Era Pancho Villa* (1957), *Pancho Villa y La Valentina* (1957), and *Cuando ¡Viva Villa! Es la Muerte* (1958). Thanks to another film by Rodríguez, *La Cucaracha* (1958), María Félix became the new symbol of the revolutionary soldier, which was exploited to the point of satiation in several films portraying the starlet during this time: *Juana Gallo* (Miguel Zacarías, 1960), *La Bandida* (Roberto Rodríguez, 1962), and *La Valentina* (Rogelio A. González, 1965). Much less ostentatious in the use of their leading roles were the rest of the films that dared to take on this ever polemic theme: *Cielito Lindo* (Miguel M. Delgado, 1956), *Carabina .30-30* (Delgado, 1956), *Pueblo en Armas* (Miguel Contreras Torres, 1958), *¡Viva la Soldadera!* (Contreras Torres, 1958), *El Correo del*

Norte (Zacarías Gómez Urquiza, 1960), *La Máscara de la Muerte* (Gómez Urquiza, 1960), *El Centauro del Norte* (Ramón Pereda, 1960), *Sol en Llamas* (Alfredo B. Crevenna, 1961), *Atrás de las Nubes* (Gilberto Gazcón, 1961), *Los Hermanos Muertes* (Rafael Baledón, 1964), *Gabino Barrera* (René Cardona, 1962), and a few more. Even in films such as *María Pistolas* and *El Corrido de María Pistolas* (René Cardona, 1962) or in those such as *Los Cuatro Juanes* (1964) and *Juan Colorado* (1965), both by Miguel Zacarías, the Mexican Revolution was simply a decorative element of parodies or "chili Westerns" set in the arid desert regions of northern Mexico.

The crisis continued to affect, in one way or another, the respective careers of the best known directors. Emilio Fernández tried to restore his prestige, but not one of the eleven films that he made in the period from 1953 until 1962 reached the dimensions in scope and quality of his best era. Only one, *Una Cita de Amor* (1956), a brilliant and passionate melodrama set in rural Mexico before the Revolution, was on the verge of distinction. The rest of the films of Fernández, from *La Red* to *Paloma Herida*, including *Reportaje*, *El Rapto* (Jorge Negrete's last film), *La Rosa Blanca* (filmed in Cuba), *La Rebelión de los Colgados*, *Nosotros Dos* (filmed in Spain), *La Tierra de Fuego se Apaga* (made in Argentina), *El impostor*, and *Pueblito*, only demonstrated to Mexicans and foreigners alike that the other, more vigorous style of Mexican film had been put at the service of melodramas without depth or rigor. This stylistic reiteration was attacked by even the least disparaging critics. In order to survive, El Indio had to accept all kinds of acting roles, including some in which he appeared dressed in black to accentuate the tragic dimension of the character.

In spite of the fact that he had to make several films adhering to popular genres, Roberto Gavaldón was able to maintain his career and became, aside from Buñuel, the only exponent of Mexican film whose work was respected abroad. The films most representative of this stage in Gavaldón's career were *El Niño y la Niebla*; *La Escondida*, the saga of the bandit Heraclio Bernal (*Aquí Está Heraclio Bernal*, *La Venganza de Heraclio Bernal*, and *La Ley de la Sierra*); *Macario*, which won an impressive number of awards in international festivals; *La Rosa Blanca*, *Días de Otoño*, and *El Gallo de Oro*. It is worth mentioning two events that involved this unique filmmaker whose trajectory has been the focus of reevaluation in recent years. In 1961, Gavaldón was part of a commission whose goal was to formulate a series of changes to update the anachronistic Ley de la Industria Cinematográfica Mexicana. A year later, *La Rosa Blanca*, based on the novel of the same name by B. Traven, was the victim of censorship owing to its anti-imperialist statements; the film premiered ten years later when it had lost most of its effectiveness.

La Sombra del Caudillo (1960), which was without doubt the best and most relevant of the little over twenty films directed by Julio Bracho during this time, also suffered censorship: in this case its exhibition was prohibited for thirty years, thus becoming the "bad" film par excellence of Mexican cinema. An impeccable screen version of the story of the same name by Martín Luis Guzmán, Bracho's film, a project that this director had embraced many years before, had the merit of revealing the genesis of the Mexican political system, characterized by fierce authoritarianism and a profoundly antidemocratic structure. Compared to the achievements of *La Sombra del Caudillo*, Bracho's remaining films made before or afterward (*María la Voz, Canasta de Cuentos Mexicanos, México Lindo y Querido, Una Canción para Recordar, Corazón de Niño, Historia de un Canalla, Guadalajara en Verano*) were wholly negligible.

Aside from the already mentioned incursions of Alejandro Galindo into genres such as comedy or youth melodrama, it is worth looking at two cases in which this filmmaker was able to develop his output more in accordance with his personal concerns. With *Espaldas Mojadas* (1953), whose exhibition was prohibited for three years immediately following its release because it denounced the living conditions of immigrant Mexican workers, Galindo established himself once more as an excellent storyteller for the disenfranchised. He achieved the same with *Los Fernández de Peralvillo* (1953), which questions opportunism and corruption in the cities. From then on, the skilled craftsmanship of Galindo suffered a relentless process of deterioration from which only some moments of his comedy films with Resortes are saved.

The career of Ismael Rodríguez, another of the great exponents of Mexican cinema, followed a bumpy but more interesting road than that of many of his colleagues, including Galindo. In this stage of the career of the director of *Nosotros los Pobres*, several of his new incursions into the camp of the urban tragicomedy stand out (*Maldita Ciudad, Los Paquetes de Paquita, Cupido Pierde a Paquita*, and *El Hombre de Papel*) in which he shows his intuition for taking advantage of funny or unusual situations. And, though failed attempts, worth mentioning are another two films directed by Rodríguez that aspired in their time to dignify Mexican film with an indigenous theme: *Tizoc* (1956) with Pedro Infante and María Félix; and *Animas Trujano* (1961), for which, at the height of international pretensions, the celebrated Japanese actor, Toshiro Mifune, was hired.

Another interesting case is that of Rogelio A. González, who, owing to a number of films made in this period, deserves a place alongside Rodríguez, with whom he worked as an actor and from whom he learned the secrets of directing. During the period from 1954 to 1956, González was able to direct the last box-office hits of Pedro Infante (*El Mil Amores, Escuela de Vagabundos, La Vida No Vale Nada, El Inocente,* and *Escuela de Rateros*). In the majority of these films it is easy to detect an excellent rhythm and the impeccable direction of the actors. Both merits served him well in *El Esqueleto de la Señora Morales* (1959), a surprising example of black humor, the good results of which, as well as in the case of *La Vida No Vale Nada,* had a lot to do with the screenplay of Luis Alcoriza.

After his debut as director of *Los Jóvenes,* Alcoriza was able to direct, in series form, a trilogy that immediately placed him as one of the best directors whom the declining Mexican film industry could depend on in the early 1960s. *Tlayucan* (1961), a veiled criticism of provincial mentality, *Tiburoneros* (1962), an emotional elegy to the free spirit, and *Tarahumara* (1964), a brave denouncement of the exploitative conditions suffered by the Tarahumara Indians who live in the highlands of the state of Chihuahua, constitute unsurpassable models of film made against the current trend of exhausted conventions prevailing in the era. The lens of Alcoriza, combined with the influence of Buñuel and the Spanish tradition of satire, goes further than the simple conformist image or official rhetoric. Thanks to this aspect, these films acquired the rank of classics at a moment when nothing favored these types of accomplishments. However, it is necessary to mention that Alcoriza could not completely escape failure: his other two films from around the same time (*Amor y Sexo,* with María Félix, *El Gángster,* with Arturo de Córdova) can only be remembered either as frustrated endeavors or as the price that the director had to pay to a medium in the process of falling apart.

Definitely established in Mexico, Luis Buñuel continued with his vocation of filmmaking with yet another new cycle of movies, including two that were made in France for producers of that country (*Eso Se Llama la Aurora,* 1955; *El Diario de una Recamarera,* 1964), two Mexican-French coproductions (*La Muerte en Este Jardín,* 1956; *Los Ambiciosos,* 1959), a Mexican-U.S. coproduction (*La Joven,* 1960), and a Mexican-Spanish coproduction (*Viridiana,* 1961), which decidedly placed him on the international scene. Of the strictly Mexican films directed by Buñuel during this time, those worthy of mention include *La Ilusión Viaja en Tranvía* (1953), *Ensayo de un Crimen* (1955), *Nazarín* (1958), *El Ángel Exterminador* (1962), and *Simón del Desierto* (1965); after the last mentioned, the great filmmaker did not work again in Mexico. During this time, characterized by several triumphs in important international festivals, Buñuel regained the enormous prestige that he had earned years ago in Europe, the continent on which, while still living in Mexico, he carried out the last stage of his fascinating artistic career. The Buñuelian trilogy of *Viridiana*, *El Ángel Exterminador*, and *Simón del Desierto* is associated with two important figures of the Mexican film milieu: producer Gustavo Alatriste and actress Silvia Pinal, who had leading roles. Years later, Buñuel would declare that Alatriste had been the investor who had given him the most freedom for creative expression.

María Félix in La Diosa Arrodillada, *directed by Roberto Gavaldón.*

Simón del Desierto was financed by Manuel Barbachano Ponce, who without doubt was the most outstanding personality in a trend of films produced on the sidelines of the industry, mainly because of the closed-door policy established by the film union STPC, which blocked access to the industrial sector. In spite of having antecedents that can be traced to the 1940s, this trend, called "independent Mexican film," had its real origin in the activities carried out by Barbachano Ponce through his company, Teleproducciones S.A., established in 1952 and sponsor of weekly short films known as Tele Revista and Cine Verdad (the last one a tribute to the newsreel "Kino-Pravda" of Dziga Vertov) as well as other short films such as *El Hombre de la Isla* (1952), *Tierra de Chicle* (1953), and *Historia de un Río*, a trilogy made by the immigrant German, Walter Reuter. Thanks to the work of Barbachano Ponce and his group (the documentarians Carlos Velo, Nacho López, and Reuter, and the intellectuals Fernando Gamboa, Elena Urrutia, Fernando Espejo, Carlos Fuentes, Gabriel García Márquez, Gastón García Cantú, Alvaro Matute, and Jomí García Ascot), it was possible for Mexican cinema gradually to have some alternative forms of financing that at the same time permitted other thematic statements and aesthetics. The first result of the efforts of Teleproducciones was *Raíces* (Benito Alazraki, 1953), a film version of several stories by Francisco Rojas González. The film, with anthropological pretensions, won the Critics' International FIPRESCI Award at the Cannes Film Festival in 1953 and was recognized with the Cantaclaro Award by the the Círculo de Cronistas Cinematográficos de Venezuela. These accomplishments demonstrated the great possibilities of independent films. *¡Torero!* (1956), an excellent documentary drama made by Carlos Velo and inspired by the experiences of bullfighter Luis Procuna, was another example of Barbachano Ponce's work that achieved recognition abroad, thus greatly encouraging the production of these kinds of films, which were cheaper than those made by the industry.

Between 1958 and 1962 some eight independent feature films were produced, among which it is worth mentioning *El Brazo Fuerte* (1958), an interesting political farce about a filmmaker who grows through his experience with the team at Teleproducciones; *Cantar de los Cantares* (1959), an experimental film by the Spanish poet Manuel Altolaguirre; *Yanco* (1960), a failed indigenous melodrama directed by Servando González; *En el Balcón Vacío* (1961), by Jomí García Ascot, an intimate chronicle of a whole generation affected by the Spanish Civil War and its consequent exile; and *Los Mediocres* (1962), the second film of Servando González in which this director attempts to question the mentality of the urban middle class. Of the short films and medium-length features that stand out are those of

Adolfo Garnica (also a participant in the experiences of Barbachano Ponce), producer and director of *Ellos También Tienen Ilusiones* (1956), *¡Viva la Tierra!* (1958), *Sueño de Plata* (1960), *Río Arriba* (1961), *Xekik* (1964), and *México es . . .* (1965), all of which won awards in festivals and international exhibitions; and, in addition, three films representative of new trends: the anthropological documentary *Carnaval Chamula* (1959), of José Báez Esponda; *El Despojo* (1960), of Antonio Reynoso and Rafael Corkidi, a film inspired by an improvised story by Juan Rulfo in which, as in *El Brazo Fuerte*, the prevailing landowning system in the countryside is denounced; and *El es Dios* (1965), an interesting ethnographic testimony filmed by Alfonso Muñoz.

As part of the zeal for innovation in Mexican cinema, in 1961 the Grupo Nuevo Cine was formed, which included fans, critics, independent filmmakers, and aspiring filmmakers who, influenced by the theories of camera and directors' styles praised by the writers of the French magazine *Cahiers du Cinéma*, wrote a manifesto stating the urgent necessity of restructuring the industry. In the same way, the members of the group (Jomí García Ascot, José de la Colina, Salvador Elizondo, Gabriel Ramírez, Emilio García Riera, Carlos Monsiváis, José Luis González de León, Eduardo Lizalde, Salomón Laiater, Manuel Michel, Rafael Corkidi, Julio Pliego, Luis Vicens, Manuel González Casanova, Heriberto Lanfranchi, Tomás Pérez Turrent, Nancy Cárdenas, Armando Bartra, José Báez Esponda, José María Sbert, Fernando Macotela, Juan Manuel Torres, Jorge Yala Blanco, Lopoldo Chagoya, et al.) made *En el Balcón Vacío* their artistic banner and began to publish the ephemeral magazine *Nuevo Cine*, in which they carried out a demolishing and systematic criticism against films produced in the heart of the industry, by then affected by a deeper crisis. Due to increased sales of television sets, television had replaced the movies as the preferred entertainment for a large sector of the population.

Another aspect worth noting is that in the Universidad Nacional Autónoma de México (UNAM) between the end of the 1950s and the beginning of the 1960s, an important film club prospered, headed by Manuel González Casanova, which was the basis for the establishment in 1963 of the Centro Universitario de Estudios Cinematográficos, or CUEC, the first school created for the formal study of filmmaking in the country. It was not long before the students of the first generations graduating from the CUEC began to be noticed, together with diverse independent filmmakers, as representatives and exponents of what would finally become known as the "new Mexican cinema."

III
The Contemporary Era

The downfall of the famed Golden Age brought forth the makings of a deep-rooted crisis for Mexican cinema beginning in the 1960s. There were various attempts to revive the declining film industry, with the most important initiative coming from the filmmakers themselves in conjunction with other sectors of the industry. A brief moment of reversal occurred when the state program, *películas de aliento*, was conceived to produce interesting and artistic films such as *La Rosa Blanca*, *Macario*, and *La Sombra del Caudillo*. The trend did not sustain itself and the overall decline continued throughout the 1960s, finally reaching alarming proportions.

A second attempt to revive the industry and attract some much-needed talent was the initiation of two celebrated national film festivals that exhibited only première films of debuting directors. The festivals of 1965 and 1967 did indeed meet and exceed their stated purpose of debuting new generations of filmmakers and bringing them into the industry. In spite of the general decline of the industry, the festivals showed that there was ample creativity just waiting for its chance to demonstrate its energy and modernist discourse.

However, the tumultuous nature of the 1960s in Mexico had a profound and lasting effect on all walks of life, including cinema. The political climate that led to the student and opposition movement of 1968 and the tragic events of the confrontation and government repression of the night on October 2 changed the country forever. The dominant political order faced its most serious challenge against the existing one-party authoritarian system. Activists and supporters of the movement waged a violent struggle in an attempt to bring about necessary reform. The response of the state was armed repression and the unleashing of army units against the civilian population. The emerging generation of artists and filmmakers brought to their craft and art their political and individual perspectives of the generation of 1968.

The change of political leadership in the 1970s signaled a definitive shift for the cinema of Mexico. Responding to the valid concern of the disappearance of its national film industry, the newly elected president, Luis Echeverría, intervened to the point of a near nationalization of the film industry. An essential strategy of Echeverría's policies was to be more inclusive and to seek and promote fresh new talent. The first generation of filmmakers who replaced the Golden Age generation emerged with an impressive revisionist narrative. The films of this new generation broke all rules and conventions in terms of themes, archetypes, and issues addressed. Filmmakers were encouraged to deal with social issues and even Mexico's sacred historical past. Other changes in representation quickly began to appear on the screen; particularly discernable were the representation of gender and sexuality. Moreover, the status and participation of women behind the camera also expanded significantly. In fact, the generation of 1968 incorporated new talents in every phase of the filmmaking process. Gifted actors, cinematographers, musicians, scriptwriters, and postproduction experts made solid contributions to contemporary filmmaking.

This brief flowering of Mexican cinema in an eight-year period (1970–1978) was not enough to prevent the industry's continued decline in the face of institutional crises. Three production formulas would be followed by the industry after 1978: state-supported productions, private-sector films, and independent cinema. Each formula responded to diverse interests, had different narrative discourses and themes, and addressed different audiences. Independent and state-supported films tended to be artistic, more carefully crafted, and employed better talent, while private-sector films were generic formulas produced with commercial success as the overriding goal. Many of the movies in the second category were degrading, sexist, and ultra-violent; they have accelerated and deepened the ongoing crisis of Mexican cinema.

Two generations of filmmakers debuted in the contemporary era: the generation of the crisis, and the generation of the 1990s. These talented people have sustained the cinema of Mexico against all odds. The contemporary period has seen an unprecedented release of independent feature films. In less than twenty years, a record number of new directors completed and exhibited an impressive output of narrative films of excellent quality. In addition, documentaries, shorts, and student experimental films excelled and obtained international recognition and received prestigious awards. A direct influence on this cinematic renaissance has been the creative maturation and institutional growth of the two leading film schools: the Centro Universitario de Estudios Cinematográficos of the Universidad Nacional Autónomo de Mexico, and the state-supported Centro de Capacitación Cinematográfica. While Mexican cinema made box-office history with the international returns of its most successful film to date, *Como Agua para Chocolate*, the industry continues to face ever-growing obstacles that threaten its very existence. That the cinema of Mexico survives is due to the film community's creativity, tenacity, and will to endure.

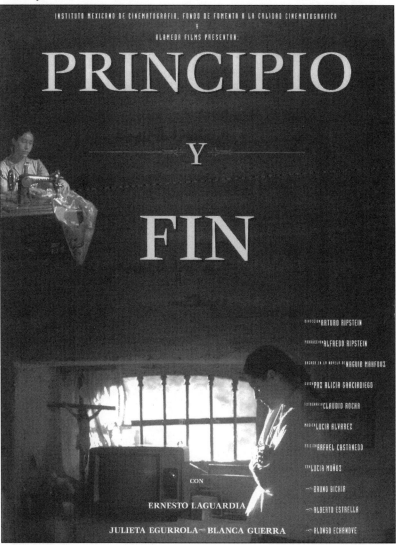

Movie poster of Principio y Fin.

The final essays in this anthology explore the last thirty years of Mexican cinema and reflect on its future. David Maciel traces and analyzes the complex and always changing relationship between the government, the private sector, and the cinema during the past three decades. Mexican communications scholar Norma Iglesias examines border cinema and its audience, those whose lives are situated in a geographic and cultural space that is neither Mexico nor the United States but rather a new postmodern space created and continuously transformed by the people who populate it.

David Maciel and Joanne Hershfield document the increased participation of women in Mexican cinema and analyze the characteristics of the contemporary *cine de mujer*. Looking at a number of recent films directed by women, the essay comments on the ways in which women directors have reflected on history, national identity, and gender roles. Finally, Ann Marie Stock analyzes the discourse of national authenticity in the context of transnational production and reception. She examines the way in which two recent Mexican films interrogate the complexity of a contemporary culture that crisscrosses languages and borders and, at the same time, forces cultural observers to rethink the role of critical praxis in shaping this culture.

9

Cinema and the State in Contemporary Mexico, 1970–1999

David R. Maciel

The relationship between the state and culture in Mexico is both historical and complex. From the nineteenth century to the present, the state has involved itself in the promotion, diffusion, and even the shaping of national cultural manifestations.[1] In the specific case of the cinema, the state has had an intimate and all-encompassing influence. There is no single aspect of films or the film industry that escapes its involvement. In production, the state in the contemporary period has acted as either sponsor, coproducer, or even sole producer of numerous recent films.[2] In exhibition and distribution, it has played a major role by establishing distribution companies for national and international markets. In certain years it has been a major partner and stockholder in the ownership and management of movie theaters. The Cineteca Nacional in Mexico City, the main exhibitor of foreign and artistic films, is government owned and operated. In archival terms, the Cineteca Nacional is the main repository of contemporary films and of source material on Mexican cinema. By law, every producer who exhibits a commercial film in Mexico is required to donate one print to the Cineteca Nacional.[3]

The fact remains that the state has been instrumental in the production of many quality films. Either as the sole producer or as a partner, it has made the resources available or the conditions possible for the completion of certain classic films such as *Redes*, *El Rayo del Sur*, *Vámonos con Pancho Villa*, *Canoa*, *La Pasión Según Berenice*, *El Imperío de la Fortuna*, *Cadena Perpetua*, and *Como Agua para Chocolate*.[4] As with other aspects of culture, the state has subsidized film production for art's sake. In contemporary times it also has been one of the few producers of artistic commercial films.[5] In fact, it is widely acknowledged that without state support the great majority of Mexican artistic and quality films probably would not have been produced or exhibited. It should be noted, however, that state-financed features make up only a small percentage of the total of the country's film production. Over 80 percent of the films exhibited in contemporary Mexico are produced by private producers. This contemporary generation of producers is unlike previous ones—individuals who displayed a rare combination of business sense with a genuine desire for making popular and artistic films. The current private-sector producers unfortunately do not follow this tradition. With the escalation in the cost of film production and the loss of revenue because of the disappearance of international and national film markets and audiences, recent private producers became interested solely in sure moneymakers. Their formula for success was for inexpensive, tested sequels.6 Thus, in contemporary times, the private producers have not been known for artistic, experimental, or quality commercial cinema. In fact, in the last three decades, for the most part only independent and state-produced cinema have made avant-garde or artistic films.7

It is, however, in the contents or themes of national films where the state has manifested its most consistent preoccupation and direct influence. It devised a rigorous system of "artistic supervision," which is actually the censorship of movie content. Censorship, or this so-called artistic supervision by the state, is practiced from the project stage to the exhibition of a completed film.8 First, the screenplay is reviewed by the "supervisors," who might suggest changes to "improve the artistic worth." If such suggestions are followed or the screenplay is approved as is, the state can then send a supervisor to the site to observe the filming and to preview rushes. Once a film is completed, before it can be shown in Mexico it must have the seal of authorization by the Director General de Cinematografía of the Secretaría de Gobernación.9 Approval is granted only after a careful screening of each film by a board of supervisors, and only after they are satisfied that the topic is not politically or socially unacceptable to state directives. After that, the state along with the producers determines the opening date and directs the exhibition to the theater of its choice. If the film is permissible but still controversial, it might be shown in an obscure run-down, undesirable theater in the capital or sent outside Mexico City for only a brief screening period and then removed and shelved permanently (*enlatada*, as this process is known).10

While on one level the state has indeed censored or shown little favor in having certain themes or subject matter brought to the screen, on the other hand, it has clearly attempted to use certain films to create or foster a particular type of patriotism or nationalism. The favorite state cinematic genre has always been the historical or biographical film and those that closely follow "official historical views" of either figures or events.[11] These productions are consistent with the officially endorsed interpretations of the past that appear in educational texts, other official media programs, and in political discourse. Generally, the ideological constructs of such films are interpreting the past or a prominent historical figure as precursors to the modern Mexican state. Examples are numerous, including such films as *Zapata*, *El Padre Morelos*, *La Virgen que Forjó una Patria*, *En Busca de un Muro*, *Río Escondido*, *Mexicanos al Grito de Guerra*, *El Cementerio de las Aguilas*, and *Juárez y Maximiliano*.[12]

The other major area of state influence has been through the design of cinematic policies. In such a process, the personalistic agendas of the government officials placed in charge of the cinema and its institutions have defined the government support to filmmaking. The actions of these administrators as well as the lack of a coherent state cultural policy that would transcend six-year (*sexenio*) presidential politics have impacted significantly upon the cinema.[13] Because of the nature of their political appointments these officials not only set the tone and direction for state cinema policies but also personally decide questions of production, distribution, publicity, and censorship. These high-level administrators are in a position either to promote certain careers or projects or stymie others.[14] Thus, in order to fully study or analyze the origins, process, and current status of the cinema in Mexico, it is essential to provide a critical interpretation of the role and impact of the state's policies and the impact of its agenda. Such a study also provides a method and a field of study for the shaping of other Mexican cultural manifestations such as literature, art, and music that have also had strong state influence.

In the case of cinema, certain questions are essential for such an analysis and provide the central conceptual basis for this essay. Why has the state been so interested in all phases of the cinema? What are the different levels and spheres of state influence in cinema and the film industry? What is the legacy of the experience of having such a powerful role of the state in cinema? And what are the possible alternatives to state involvement?

The Origins and Development of Contemporary State Intervention in Cinema, 1970–1976

Although the involvement and influence of the Mexican state in cinema dates as far back as the early twentieth century,[15] it is in the period after 1970 when the levels of state intervention became so all-pervasive that it extended into all spheres of cinema production and into the entire Mexican film industry. During this recent period, cinema has received even presidential attention and policymaking. In two of the last five political administrations, the president's own family members have been the dominant administrators in charge of the film industry.

The immediate antecedents that prompted the accelerated involvement of the state were due to the grave political crisis of the late 1960s as well as to a second crisis, that of an acute decline of Mexican cinema in the same period. As the government of President Gustavo Díaz Ordaz (1964–1970) moved to the right and as the disparities and limitations of the developmental policies of the state became more apparent, opposition began to be voiced by various sectors of society.[16] As the dissident forces gained momentum, repressive tactics by the law enforcement agencies became the official response. University students came forward as the principal opposition pressure group against the ruling political order. The student movement developed into a significant social and political force that would include intellectuals, artists, middle-class sectors, and workers. They demanded social justice, freedom of expression, a stop to police and army repression, the release of political prisoners, more prudent expenditures for the upcoming Olympic Games, and real autonomy of the universities. Hundreds of thousands of Mexicans joined and supported these goals and actions.[17] Rather than negotiate, President Díaz Ordaz opted to end the hostilities, which were threatening the Olympics, and to restore tranquility at all costs. What occurred next has gone down in the annals of Mexican history as one of the most infamous chapters since the Revolution of 1910. On October 2, 1968, one of the largest demonstrations ever held gathered in Tlatelolco in protest. As thousands of people listened to speakers, army units began to surround the square. Suddenly and without warning, soldiers and tanks opened fire indiscriminately killing and wounding hundreds of civilians. Although the state crushed its opposition, the political cost was definitive.[18]

At the same time the cinema was facing its own severe crisis. By the end of the 1950s, it had entered a period of general decline. National films had become static and repetitive and lost in appeal to Hollywood. Audiences turned to North American and European cinema for their primary entertainment. There was no substantial effort to curb the expansion of American film distribution in Mexico. The stars of the Golden Age, Pedro Infante and Jorge Negrete, died in that decade while others faded. Production of movies fell to an all-time low. Mexican cinema had become complacent and seemed to be without direction or purpose.[19] As one noted producer stated, "Our beloved Mexican motion picture industry had become artistically inane, without any real writers, without a critical viewpoint, and without even the saving grace of portraying reality."[20]

It was under these grave internal conditions that the regime of Díaz Ordaz came to an end, and the administration of Luis Echeverría Alvarez began. President Echeverría, upon taking power in 1970, faced a formidable task: to restore confidence in the state after the political opposition movement and confrontation events of 1968; to bring together the fragmented political and social sectors; and to integrate or co-opt the intellectual opposition to the state by such measures as the appearance of lifting censorship and the curtailing of repression. To appear sincere, Echeverría eased restraints on the media, freed certain political prisoners, and fostered nationalism through political rhetoric and the arts.[21]

The cinema was to be central in Echeverría's domestic nationalistic policy. In no other presidential regime did the movie industry in general and certain filmmakers in particular receive more interest and state financial support than during the years of his regime (1970–1976). Four essential factors dictated this attitude: (1) the movie industry had reached an economic crisis that was counterproductive to both the state and the private sector—if cinema was going to survive as a national industry and art in Mexico, it was imperative to resolve its serious economic situation; (2) central to President Echeverría's "democratic aperture" (*apertura democrática*) was the effort to encourage those intellectuals and artists who had been a powerful opposition group against the government to now work within the existing system; (3) films could be used to promote official cultural nationalism, reflect critical issues, and give a new direction to the Mexican state; (4) President Echeverría's brother, Rodolfo, was a professional actor and had been an Actors' Guild director for many years, a fact of seminal importance.[22]

The restructuring of the film industry began with the naming of Rodolfo Echeverría as head of the Banco Cinematográfico. He was to use all of his experience and abilities to revitalize the movie industry and effectively move it in the direction of the policy of *apertura democrática*. Soon thereafter, the state began to exert added influence and participate more directly in all aspects of the industry. Three official production companies with extensive financial resources were established: Corporación Nacional de Cinematografía (CONACINE), Corporación Nacional Cinematográfica de Trabajadores y Estado I (CONACITE I), and Corporación Nacional Cinematográfica de Trabajadores y Estado II (CONACITE II). In essence, all three companies functioned as producers and co-producers of films.[23]

Concurrently with the founding of the three state companies, President Echeverría in a celebrated speech castigated the private-sector producers for the content and ideology of their films. In addition, he practically defied and discouraged the private-enterprise productions and warned that the future of film production in Mexico would now be the responsibility of the state. He went on to add that only with such measures would the cinema improve dramatically, restore its national and international prestige, and reclaim its audiences.[24]

Following the creation of the three companies, other major innovations in the cinema industry took place. Enormous economic resources were made available for the renovation of the studios, modern equipment was purchased, additional postproduction laboratories were constructed, advertising and promotion of films was improved both internally and externally, and increases in the salaries of the Actors' Union workers were negotiated.[25]

Another significant change for the better was in the overall distribution and screening of Mexican movies. During the decades of the 1950s and 1960s, when audiences had turned away from Mexican cinema to North American and foreign films, the showing of domestic movies had been restricted to second-class theaters (*cines de segunda*) and were clearly a minority of the overall showings.[26] Over 80 percent of screen time was alloted to North American cinema in 1970. This policy dramatically changed during the Echeverría years. First class theaters (*cines de primera*) were pressured to screen national films.[27] By 1974 this policy had reversed earlier trends, and over 50 percent of the exhibitions in Mexico City and elsewhere were now of Mexican productions.[28]

In a short period of time, the new policies and the other reforms were being felt. With the resources available, momentum gathering, and the proper cultural and political ambiance in place, the makings of a second Golden Age seemed possible. A 1960s generation of young creative filmmakers was making its mark nationally and internationally. Directors Jaime Humberto Hermosillo, Jorge Fons, Arturo Ripstein, Marcela Fernández Violante, Felipe Casals, Sergio Olhovich, Gonzalo Martínez, Juan Manuel Torres, Alberto Bojórquez, Alberto Isaac, and others received ample support and opportunities to film extensively throughout the sexenio.[29] By the early 1970s the state project in cinema seemed to be achieving its ambitious goals.

Realizing that in order to sustain this cinematic flowering it was essential to invigorate the education and training of new talent in all phases of filmmaking, the state established the Centro de Capacitación Cinematográfica (CCC). In 1974 its curriculum included courses in directing, cinematography, screenwriting, and postproduction as well as in other aspects of filmmaking. From the onset, its teaching philosophy was based upon theory with actual experi-

ence. All students actively participated in the filming process of productions under way.[30] Today the CCC is recognized as one of the
outstanding film schools in the world.

As a symbol of the break with previous policies by the government
officials in charge of cinema, directors now were encouraged to address social and political themes. Socially relevant productions, which
indeed focused upon contemporary as well as historical critical issues,
were filmed. Among the most representative of this trend are *Canoa,
Actas de Marusia, La Casta Divina, El Apando, Las Poquianchis, La
Casa del Sur, El Principio*, and *Cascabel*. These productions were revisionist thematically as well as structurally and artistically. Their view
of the past and the present showed a more complex society with its
deep problems as well as its promise.[31]

However, even though the president and other officials spoke of
an openness and political democratization in expression and art, filmmakers were fully conscious that years of strict control and censorship were not going to be entirely eradicated in one presidential term
or by one or two high-level politicians. Even with certain signs of
change, filmmakers were somewhat skeptical and were cautious in
not wanting to appear too bold or daring in their screen adaptations.
This situation resulted in the detrimental process of self-censorship
by members of the film community. Wishing to avoid conflicts,
delays, or outright censorship, filmmakers remained wary and were
reluctant to be outright critical of the dominant order in their themes.
Directors, producers, and screenwriters had realized that certain issues, themes, traditions, or political personalities were not open to revisionist cinematic interpretations. It had been evident that three
particular issues in commercial cinema would not be tolerated by
government officials. First, there was the religious question, especially if a national religious symbol was involved, such as the Virgin
of Guadalupe. Second, the military clearly would not permit films
that depicted the dark side of their history. And third, of course, no
critical filmic statement on the chief executive or other high-level
party official was possible.[32] In this period, as in others in the past,
there exist numerous examples of completed films that were much
less interesting and creative because of the self-censorship of their
filmmakers.[33]

Two contemporary examples, *Nuevo Mundo* and *Viaje al
Paraíso*, clearly show how a film, because of self-censorship, became merely a poor imitation of what had the makings of interesting
and original themes. Each began with an excellent, award-winning
screenplay praised for its novel perspectives, but the end result was
far distant from the original idea.[34] It is clear that a combination of
indirect or direct official pressure and self-censorship through

extensive script changes undermined the factors that had made the original scripts award winners. *Nuevo Mundo* followed certain current historiographical writings that claimed that the apparition of the Virgin of Guadalupe was really an ingenious Spanish plot to subjugate and control the indigenous population by providing a native religious patron who espoused Catholicism and demonstrated obedience

Nuevo Mundo, *directed by Gabriel Retes*

to Spanish colonialism. The original screenplay traced the origins and implementation of the fabrication of the idea into accepted religious teachings.[35] The director, Gabriel Retes, in an obvious act of self-censorship, dramatically changed the ideological constructs of the screenplay. By attempting to allude or suggest in such a watered-down version, the filmic result was unsuccessful either as historical reconstruction, myth, or even as good artistic craft. The screenwriter was so outraged with the changes and the end result that he demanded the omission of his name from the final credits.[36]

Viaje al Paraíso in its original form was a superb screenplay that dealt with corruption and the struggle for power within the most powerful union in Mexico, the national petroleum industry. Government officials bowing to pressure from the petroleum syndicate demanded extensive changes in the screenplay to focus on ecological and social issues. The writer-director, Ignacio Retes, thought that he had to agree to the directives and thus compromised the project. In spite of a stellar cast, this confusing and uninteresting film resulted in a regrettable production for all those involved in its making.[37]

In spite of these carryover institutional limitations, the 1970s gave way to important productions and new cinematic directions. One other singular characteristic of the Echeverría period was the cinema of the *auteur*. Many of the directors were able to produce very personal films. Women, complex human relationships, social satire, and literary themes predominate in state-produced cinema of this generation. Certain excellent films in this period include *La Pasión Según Berenice*, *Naufragio*, *Lo Mejor de Teresa*, *Tivoli*, *Matiné*, *El Apando*, *Los Dias del Amor*, *Mecánica Nacional*, *El Rincón de las Virgenes*, *El Castillo de la Pureza*, *Cascabel*, *La Otra Virginidad*, *Auandar Anapu*, and *Los Albañiles*.[38]

At the same time that new trends and themes were fostered in Mexican cinema, filmmakers were likewise encouraged and extensively supported to produce patriotic films that would follow the nationalistic policies of the Luis Echeverría government. Biographies of artists Ramon López Velarde and José Clemente Orozco were brought to the screen in *Vals sin Fin* and *En Busca de un Muro*. In 1972, to commemorate the one-hundredth anniversary of Benito Juárez's death, the most ambitious film of that historical period was produced, *Aquellos Años*.[39] The effort was uninspiring and flat. All the drama, heroic events, and towering figures in the formation of the Mexican nation in those years were lost in this film, a traditional and lifeless history lesson.

President Echeverría throughout his six-year term implemented an aggressive foreign policy based upon a leadership role for Mexico in Latin American and Third World affairs. To further promote this

Publicity photo of the film La Pasión Según Berenice, *directed by Jaime Humberto Hermosillo.*

agenda, state cinema productions encompassed various social and historical Latin American themes in such films as *Actas de Marusia*, *Mina*, *Viento de Libertad*, and *Maten al León*. For the most part these films on Latin American themes were the least successful of the state productions during the Echeverría years. Their overemphasis on ideological message at the expense of art and cinema craft sealed their fate. Only *Actas de Marusia* received critical acclaim and positive box-office returns.[40]

However, in spite of their privileged conditions, the filmmakers of the generation of 1968 were not altogether able to live up to their potential fully or rise to expectations. The extensive economic and other governmental supports that they received did not necessarily translate into artistic creativity or worth. Many of their films—produced under optimum conditions, generous budgets, ample shooting time, and an open process of postproduction—clearly revealed their shortcomings. The most notable example is *Longitud de Guerra*. Director Gonzalo Martínez wanted to film the epic struggle of the townspeople of Tomochic, Chihuahua, against the forces of then-dictator Porfirio Díaz. The heroic episode of rural people fighting to the last man for their land and traditions had the potential to be a screen classic. However, the director, in spite of having an almost unlimited production budget, showed no filmic structure and was content with endless shooting and constant script changes. It was rumored that the version of the movie that was released was only half of the material filmed. This example shows that the repeated criticism of waste and abuses by filmmakers during this period was a valid one.[41]

The Echeverría cinema project, which showed much promise, had laid the basis for the renovation and flowering of films and the film industry and certainly had accentuated the positive potential of state intervention that ended with the close of the *sexenio*. Rodolfo Echeverría in his last official speech stated emphatically that his policies and measures were irreversible and that the momentum would continue into the next administration.[42] Nothing would be further from reality. His policies were completely reversed. Since nationalization of the film industry had been only partially accomplished, this reversal was not a difficult task. Moreover, the cinema project clearly had been a personal one for the president and his brother. At the close of the regime the cinematic renaissance met the traditional fate of all end-of-presidential-administration programs: pass on to history, be overturned, or just be forgotten.[43]

Official Cinematic Policies, 1976–1988

The next *sexenio* would be one of the most dramatic and the most tragic in the contemporary history of Mexico. José López Portillo assumed the presidency under difficult economic conditions. The economic policies of the outgoing administration had not materialized and had run into serious problems caused mostly by a deep rift between the president and the private sector. The end result of this conflict as well as adverse international economic factors resulted in inflation, capital flight, a downturn in the national economy, and a devaluation of the peso, which had remained stable for over two decades.[44] The adverse economic scene quickly changed to the other extreme because of the public disclosure of the "discovery" of vast oil reserves in southern Mexico. Oil output was increased significantly and brought in astronomical amounts of revenue. Thus, oil would be the panacea that would effect Mexico's transformation from a country on the verge of development to one of new riches.

The policies of the regime were not restricted to economic or political matters. Since President López Portillo came from an academic and intellectual tradition, there were high expectations for his administration in all areas, particularly in culture.[45]

In the case of cinema, not only would the expectation not be so, but the *sexenio* overall would also be one of the darkest chapters in its entire history. President López Portillo continued the tradition of nepotism by naming family members to the directorship of the state cinema. He called upon his sister, Margarita López Portillo, as director not only of cinema but of radio and television as well. In his authoritarian style, he upgraded her position and at the same time created a new bureaucratic apparatus for tighter media control: the Dirección de Radio, Televisión y Cinematografía. The title of the agency reflected the media priorities of the López Portillo administration—in last place was cinema.[46] Margarita López Portillo thus became supreme director of all mass media in Mexico.[47] The end result of these policies would prove to be disastrous for Mexican cinema and, contrary to the previous *sexenio*, would clearly demonstrate all of the possible ills and abuses of state intervention in culture.

The regime, however, began innocently enough, and for a short time there even seemed to be certain continuities with the recent past. Experienced cinema officials such as Hiram García Borja, Fernando Macotela, and Jorge Durán Chávez retained important administrative positions within the state film industry and initially were able to carry out several important projects.[48] Certain outstanding contemporary films were indeed completed in the first two years of Margarita López Portillo's administration: *Cadena Perpetua*, *La Guerra Santa*, *Los Indolentes*, *El Lugar sin Límites*, *Llovizna*, *En la Trampa*, *Amor Libre*, and *Retrato de una Mujer Casada*. Taken as a whole, the state productions of 1977 and 1978 are the high point of contemporary Mexican commercial cinema. In no recent time frame did such varied and innovative films appear. Indeed, most of the directors of these films would never achieve such excellence again. Feminism, alternative life-styles, historical revisionism, and political corruption were the principal themes for these movies.[49] These productions, however, were already in process when Margarita López Portillo took control and before she began to impose her capricious and ill-informed decisions on cinema. Once she extended her sphere of influence, she completely changed state policies toward such productions.[50]

As persistent critic of the themes of films produced earlier, Margarita López Portillo repeatedly spoke out against reflecting political or social issues in cinema. The official policy ranged from her vague comments, such as "the need for family-oriented films," to coproductions with other countries.[51] Her justification for coproductions was that no real national talent existed within the Mexican cinema industry. She sought out foreign directors in the United States, Europe, and Japan and attempted to interest them in coproductions. The great majority of those whom she contacted either flatly refused or showed no interest in such projects.[52]

The two expensive coproductions that did result from this effort were *Antonieta*, by respected Spanish director Carlos Saura, based on the life and times of the Mexican journalist, Antonieta Rivas Mercado, a political activist in the 1920's who committed suicide in Paris; and the two-part *Campañas Rojas*, by Russian veteran director Sergei Bonderchuk, which focused on the participation of the American journalist and radical, John Reed, in the Mexican and Russian Revolutions. It would be a difficult task to evaluate which of the two movies is more flawed. Although the intentions of the film-

Gabriela Roel pouring a drink in a scene from Amor a la Vuelta de la Esquina, *directed by Alberto Cortés, in an unconventional representation of the lead character and of Mexico's dark side.*

makers were good and both had ample source material available, the completed productions were perhaps the least remembered films in the careers of these two directors. Both screenplays, written principally by non-Mexicans, lacked an important understanding of the nation's historical events and key personalities. The characters and dialogue in *Antonieta* and *Campañas Rojas* are confusing, flat, and static. Both films were total disasters at the box office and were mocked by the critics as well as by general audiences.[53] Their failure can be attributed to the inept film advisers of Margarita López Portillo and to her own shortcomings as the director of state cinema policies.[54]

At the same time that Margarita López Portillo sought out co-productions, her web of influence and her personal style of governance were being felt in other areas of the film industry. To make sure that her directives were clearly implemented, Ramon Charles, her closest adviser on cinema matters, formally pressed charges of graft and massive fraud against certain state cinema officials. Influential officials such as Jorge Hernández Campos, Fernando Macotela, Bosco Areche Cuevas, Carlos Velo, Jorge Durán Chávez, Aaron Sánchez, Luis Fernández García, Ana Rosa Campillo, Miguel Angel Jaimes, and Benjamín Jolloy were arbitrarily arrested and even jailed. It was alleged that two of these administrators were even tortured by their captors, although the charges were never proven and ultimately the officials were released.[55] However, their jobs had already been handed over to other hand-picked replacements. These actions were carried out without any due process of law, because the officials were never arraigned or tried. Their guilt or innocence was never decided in court. The charges became more dubious as time elapsed, and it became obvious that the allegations were falsely contrived for political reasons. And the fact that these actions were carried out without question reveals the nature of executive power in Mexico.[56]

Margarita López Portillo then began to dismantle the state's lending institution for film production, the Banco Cinematográfico. Early in her administration she withdrew all support for the two official production companies, CONACITE I and CONACITE II, thus eliminating almost all state-sponsored film production. These policies resulted in the near impossibility of securing production resources for filmmakers who were interested in making quality artistic movies.[57] The generation of 1968 had been almost entirely financed by the state for their productions. Now, when this option faded, most turned to commercial television for their livelihood. Since then, many have been on the payroll of Televisa, Mexico's largest private television and media conglomerate, usually directing soap operas. Some have never directed another motion picture.[58]

With the state diminishing its support for production and excluding an entire generation of directors, the private sector once again returned to the forefront of national film production, exhibition, and distribution. Having no competition to speak of, the private producers embarked on a sustained project. At the same time that Margarita López Portillo spoke of family-oriented films, the private productions were the complete opposite. Three cycles—U.S-Mexican border issues, cheap risqué comedies, and action films—dominated the scene. These films focused on extreme violence, nudity, and degrading characters.[59] The fact that the state gained revenue from the distribution and exhibition of these films offset their offensive nature. If there was ever a basis for censorship on the grounds of "artistic supervision," it would be with these films. Yet the fact that these productions had no problems with the board of supervisors makes it clear that only films that contain material critical of the dominant political order would be censored outright. It mattered little to censors whether a film was sexist, racist, or had any redeeming artistic or social value.[60]

Shortly before the close of the López Portillo *sexenio*, the Cineteca Nacional caught fire. Because of their age and composition, film negatives are highly flammable and need to be stored in special protective cases and under controlled conditions; upkeep and constant restoration are essential not only for their preservation but for safety purposes as well. The precarious state of the film storage procedures and conditions at the Cineteca were repeatedly brought to the attention of Margarita López Portillo and her staff. They completely disregarded the warnings and took no preventive measures. Given the dangerous situation, it was no wonder that a spark set off a major blaze. Before the fire was extinguished, over five thousand prints and other irreplaceable material were lost.[61] It was a cruel legacy that the López Portillo regime left not only to the cinema industry but also to Mexico itself. By this time the country was swept by one of its most serious economic and social crises of the twentieth century.[62]

After the tragic period of Margarita López Portillo, members of the film community speculated that the situation could only improve under the incoming administration of Miguel De la Madrid (1982–1988). Changes did begin to occur, and initially there was optimism within the industry. The Instituto Mexicano de Cinematografía (IMCINE), which repeatedly had been called for, was finally created. Its main function was to oversee cinema policy including production, exhibition, and distribution,[63] and its first director was the respected veteran filmmaker, Alberto Isaac. It was believed that because the officials in charge of cinema affairs were now members of the film community, the overall situation would certainly improve. It was not to be so. Even the best of intentions could not triumph over the corruption and vested interests that had become institutionalized in Mexican cinema.

Although Isaac attempted to stimulate productions that would raise the quality and creativity of Mexican cinema, he received poor overall financial support from the central political administration. In spite of being a personal friend of the president and having obtained his promises for substantial resources and authority, Isaac faced an impasse in attempting to confront the state-run exhibitors and other hostile, high-ranking politicians. Time after time he was stymied in trying to implement essential reforms.[64] Isaac also discovered that serving as decision-maker on questions of productions that concerned his contemporaries was a difficult assignment. It seemed that he could please few individuals or sectors in deciding what film projects to support. In addition, Isaac made poor judgment calls regarding financial support for three costly state productions: *Orinoco*, *Astucia*, and *Robachicos*. These state-produced films did not break new ground and were major disappointments. In fact, they are three of the worst contemporary Mexican movies ever made.[65]

The directors who were receiving state support were part of the generation of Alberto Isaac, yet their films no longer reflected the freshness of style and themes that they had in the 1970s. The damage of the Margarita López Portillo years had been profound and lasting. Moreover, new talent was not initially supported by the state cinema institutions.[66] In 1984, Isaac resigned, to be replaced by Enrique Soto Izquierdo, a lesser-rank PRI (Partido Revolucionario Institucional) member whose only familiarity with cinema was a short-lived marriage to a little-known actress. As a politician, Soto Izquierdo had ambitions of becoming the next governor of his native state of Chihuahua. For him, being assigned the post of director of IMCINE was like being politically exiled. He therefore gave little priority or care to the cinema industry. His policies and administrative actions plunged the state cinema to an all-time low, even topping some of the worst moments of Margarita López Portillo's regimes. Enrique Soto Izquierdo's tenure as head of IMCINE was characterized by corruption, authoritarianism, a total lack of direction, and sheer favoritism.[67] He used almost all of the state-allocated film production resources for one ill-fated project, *El Ultimo Tunel*, directed by fellow Chihuahuan Servando González.[68]

The film became one of the most expensive and poorly thought-out contemporary projects. Planned as a sequel to the earlier successful *Viento Negro* of director González, *El Ultimo Tunel* did not come even close to the acting, writing, or directorial level of the original. The result was a slow, boring, and flawed production. The huge costs of the project did not save or enhance the film. *El Ultimo Tunel* was an absolute box-office disaster and vividly displayed the bleak condition of state cinematic policies.[69]

Toward the end of the *sexenio*, Soto Izquierdo and his associates were accused of violating copyright laws by supplying original film negatives of state-produced cinema to North American Spanish-language video companies for mass sales distribution without proper authorization. It should be noted that most of these videos were not distributed or sold in Mexico. The original filmmakers did not receive one cent of the profits from the sale or distribution of their movies. These charges were substantiated by ample documented proof and brought to the attention of cabinet-level officials, yet they chose to dismiss the claims since for the dominant order only disloyalty, not corruption, would result in punishment. The filmmakers who provided the evidence and met with officials from the Secretaría de Gobernación were informed that although the allegations were serious, the delicate nature of the issue and the turbulent political ambiance prevented a resolution for the time being.

The Soto Izquierdo administration also marked an unfortunate tradition for IMCINE. The directors named followed the two extremes: an excellent choice consistently replaced by a poor one, who would undo much of the gains and progress of his predecessor. Enrique Soto Izquierdo and his staff in no way helped or improved the condition of state cinema initiatives but, in fact, aggravated and deepened the industry crisis.[70]

The worsening of the general economic crisis in Mexico had serious repercussions. Inflation ran close to a 100-percent yearly increase from 1982 to 1986, while film production costs reflected a parallel increase. With the capricious and personalistic policies of Soto Izquierdo, state film production was greatly reduced.[71] Independent films, financed with great sacrifice, continued to be made, and there were important efforts produced by cooperatives, universities, and other centers. By now, the private sector dominated film production, distribution, and exhibition in Mexico and abroad.[72] This process was accomplished at the cost of film quality and artistic value. The private-sector producers seemed interested solely in the profit aspect of filmmaking with little regard for creativity, aesthetics, or even professional standards. Thus, it is difficult to find many artistic, cultural, or social values in these contemporary films.[73]

There were, however, two important accomplishments of state cinematic initiatives in this *sexenio*. The first was the 1985 experimental film festival, Concurso de Cine Experimental. As a result of the festival an emerging generation of filmmakers were able to display their talent and promise.[74] The first- and second-place winners—Alberto Cortés's *Amor a la Vuelta de la Esquina* and Diego López's *Crónica de Familia*—are important and innovative and clearly demonstrated the trends of the next generation of Mexican filmmakers. Nevertheless, as with earlier film festivals, the main organizers and promoters were the filmmakers themselves and the cinema unions, not the state or its administrators.[75]

A second initiative was undertaken by IMCINE in a quest to promote Mexican cinema both in national and international markets. A yearly festival of Mexican films in the city of Guadalajara was

inaugurated. Working in cosponsorship with the Centro de Investigación y Estudios Cinematográficos at the Universidad de
Guadalajara, a festival was organized to premier narratives, shorts,
and documentaries that would be exhibited in the coming year.
Invitations were extended to both Mexican distributors as well as foreign ones and also to the press and film scholars of note. The Muestra
del Cine Mexicano was most successful and more than met its expectations. The tradition has continued, becoming the single most
awaited event of Mexican cinema. Although securing other sponsors,
IMCINE is still the principal organizer and founder of the festival.

The Apogee of State Cinematic Policies, 1988–1994

Upon coming to power in 1988, the administration of President
Salinas faced a difficult task in attempting to regain political control,
diminish the gains of the opposition, and bring legitimacy to various
agencies and areas that had deteriorated both in efficiency and purpose. One such entity was the cinema and its various bureaucratic ap-
paratuses.[76] A major problem of the state and its film interests was
IMCINE. As stated earlier, IMCINE, in total disarray, was completely ineffective in meeting filmmakers' needs in establishing any
clear policies. President Salinas named Ignacio Durán, an experienced member of the film and political community, to restore order
and provide much-needed direction. He was, in fact, the first experienced administrator to direct IMCINE. The mandate set forth by
Durán was clear: to lessen the role of the state in the production of
national films, give new impetus to coproductions, promote national
and foreign exhibition of Mexican films, and help launch emerging
new talent in the industry.[77]

In the Salinas administration the relationship between the cinema
and the state was further complicated by the creation of yet another
state agency, the Consejo Nacional para la Cultura y las Artes. While
its necessity or even exact functions remained unclear, IMCINE came
under its authority.[78] The director of the Consejo Nacional, Víctor
Flores Olea, though without a set policy for all of the arts, pushed hard
for further, if not complete, control of government-related cinema
activities and agencies. He attempted unsuccessfully to have the
Consejo Nacional put in full control of any and all cinema-related
activities.[79] The Dirección Mexicana de Cine-matografía continued for
the time being under the wing of the Dirección General de Radio,
Televisión y Cinematografía of the Secretaría de Gober-nación.[80]
Judging from the winners and the losers in the struggle for control
under Salinas it was obvious that Gobernación was in no mood to

relinquish control of cinema to the arts. As far as Gober-nación was concerned, cinema was mass media. As such, its potential for influence upon society was great and therefore should be carefully monitored, censored when necessary, and always made available for the use of the state and for the dominant political party.[81]

Another consistent policy of the Carlos Salinas administration was the privatization of state-run companies. Azteca Films, the major state distributor in the United States, was the first cinema institution to be affected. Badly mismanaged, inept, and riddled with incompetent political appointments, Azteca Films could no longer compete with the recently created distribution companies set up by the new czars of private-sector production. Thus, Azteca Films became a burden and an unjustifiable subsidiary for the state. The decision was made to end all operations and close its doors permanently.[82]

In a similar move, the state decided to cease the activities of CONACINE, its principal remaining film production company. CONACINE had also been much more of a liability than an asset. With few exceptions, the recent films produced by CONACINE in the last decade had been expensive box-office failures, badly flawed and of little interest to national or international audiences. More than creative or artistic worth, the majority of films produced by CONACINE reflected favoritism and patronage to certain directors, stars, and film crews over others. Decisions as to which films were to receive production support by CONACINE officials were not always based upon merit but on personal reasons. It was no surprise that, faced with this reality, the state began the process of reducing its role as a film producer. The last vestige of outright state support for movie production was the seed money provided by the Fondo de Fomento a la Calidad Cinematografica administered by IMCINE. Films such as *Goita, El Secreto de Romelia, Lola, Pueblo de Madera, Danzón, Cabeza de Vaca, Mi Querido Tom Mix, Nocturno a Rosarío, Serpientes y Escaleras, El Jinete de la Divina Providencia, Solo con Tu Pareja, Los Años de Greta, Modelo Antiguo, Angel de Fuego, Miroslava, Gertrudis,* and *Padre Kino* were all coproductions with the state providing only a partial share of the costs.[83]

Besides reducing its role as producer, the state also closed its interest in distribution by putting up for sale COTSA (Compañía Operadora de Teatros), the principal state-run distribution and exhibition theater chain. The sale of COTSA theaters further responded to the policy initiative of privatization of state-owned companies. The stated justifications were that the private sector would be more efficient in management and the sale would produce important revenue. While in theory this argument had validity, in the case of cinema the sale of COTSA not only did not produce any gains for the film industry but also actually eliminated the few theaters that exhibited Mexican films. Moreover, the profits from the sale of COTSA, like the great majority of other state-owned companies, benefited only the elites and not the sectors intended. The film industry did not receive any proceeds from the sale.[84] In a related move, the state further reduced its cinema holdings by selling the second-largest film studio, Estudios América, to the private sector.[85] A related change was a move to somewhat decentralize the state's influence in production to the regional governments. Mexican states such as Veracruz, Hidalgo, and Tlaxcala had already offered substantial support for recent film productions,[86] and this trend will continue. The films *Danzón* and *Pueblo de Madera* are two examples of this initiative.[87]

The other detrimental policy initiative enacted under the leadership of Ignacio Durán was the revisions made to the Ley Cinematográfica. This law, among its most important provisions, decreed the screen time that should be devoted to Mexican cinema by the theaters. The final revisions consistent with the spirit of the North American Free Trade Agreement (NAFTA), which included mass media and entertainment, did nothing to secure or expand protection for the exhibition or distribution of Mexican films.[88] It was clear that the Salinas policies, as was the case with cinema, did nothing to enact any safeguards to protect the national culture. In actuality, these policies were designed to facilitate the expansion of U.S. investments and monopolies throughout the Mexican economy and society.[89]

In the Salinas *sexenio* even censorship felt the winds of change and the diminished power of the dominant political order. Whereas the public outcry and outrage expressed by the film and intellectual community against the political censorship of mostly Mexican films in the past went totally unheeded, pressure and media campaigns resulted in dramatic changes. The 1990 politically charged *Rojo Amanecer*, based on the actual events of October 1968, after initially being censored was given official authorization for commercial exhibition and had its première in October 1990. *Rojo Amanecer* is a powerful, well-written, -acted, and -directed film that squarely focuses on the social movement of 1968. The entire action of the movie takes place within the confines of an apartment in Tlatelolco, the area where the tragic events occurred. The narrative develops through the lives of the members of a middle-class family and their involvement in the 1968 movement. *Rojo Amanecer* is the first commercial full-length film to be produced and exhibited on this subject.[90]

On an elementary level, *Rojo Amanecer* can certainly be viewed as a daring and critical cinematic interpretation of one of the most seminal events in the contemporary history of Mexico. However, a more in-depth reading reveals that the film is not entirely the heralded breakthrough or the complete demise of state political censorship in cinema. After much private and public confrontation over the initial censorship of *Rojo Amanecer*, the state did allow its exhibition, but with several scenes cut. In the original version, the ending showed two fully armed soldiers marching in the street while a little boy, the sole survivor of the family who was massacred, looks on. The released print eliminated this scene and closed with the boy walking down the stairs of the apartment building with death all around him. The cut of the final scene and the deletion of dramatic dialogue from two other scenes indeed alters the tone and message of *Rojo Amanecer*.[91]

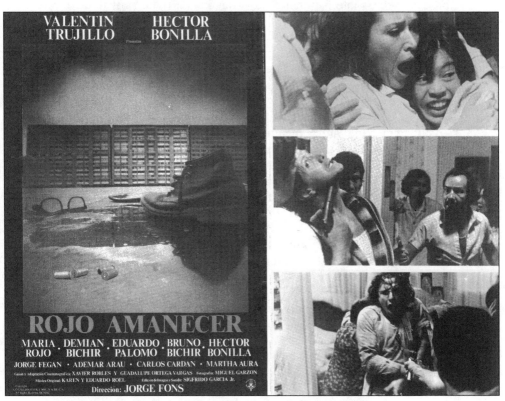

Rojo Amanecer *was the first film to address the social movement of 1968.*

In addition, two scenes that contain key dialogue and a recounting of the brutal events of the night of Tlatelolco and, in particular, the direct participation of the army were eliminated. Javier Robles, the screenwriter, stated in a published interview that the filmmakers had no choice in accepting these three cuts. It became a matter of either abiding by such restraints or not having the film released.

Going to great lengths to minimize the role of the military is consistent throughout the movie. The principal villains in the censored version of *Rojo Amanecer* are the secret police and not the army. In reality, as is well documented, it was indeed the military forces that were unleashed on the demonstrators, and it was the army that was responsible for the acts of repression and the killings of hundreds of participants. In the released film, the army is largely portrayed as orderly and peacekeeping. By denouncing and focusing on atrocities carried out by the secret police, the film is fully in keeping with the current political climate and suits the state's purposes. Since the secret police organizations have come under intense criticism by national as well as international groups for human rights violations, it could be argued that by allowing the exhibition of *Rojo Amanecer*, the state not only appears to be moving toward political democratization but also is sensitive to the national concern for human rights.[92] Thus, the state seems to be on the verge of controlling a problematic rogue agency, the secret police, that seems to operate in defiance of even executive directives.[93]

There are other problems with *Rojo Amanecer*. The violence carried out against the family members appears sensationalist and exaggerated. In addition, the dialogue of the sons and other supporters explaining their cause and motives is not altogether convincing. Nonetheless, *Rojo Amanecer* is an landmark film both socially and artistically. There are exceptional performances, particularly that of María Rojo. Jorge Fons, once considered one of the most talented directors of the generation of 1960, demonstrates his claim to this assertion. Important also is the fact that the production has been a major box-office success.[94] And now that the door has been opened, no doubt other films that offer perspectives of 1968 will follow. Moreover, one curious note is that *Rojo Amanecer* in its original form is distributed nationally and internationally in video format. According to Carlos Monsiváis, the distinction is that the state considers video an individual activity, whereas a film shown commercially in a theater is collective and thus more potentially dangerous as a catalyst for social or political action.[95]

Intriga contra México is another film which for two years had not received authorization for commercial showing. As part of this current process of political openness, it was finally exhibited in Mexico City during the Muestra Internacional in November and December 1990. The movie, based on a highly praised contemporary political novel by Juan Miguel de Mora, deals with a contrived plot by the United States against the outgoing Mexican president to force him to choose a designated successor—one favorable toward U.S. interests, especially in foreign policy. Extreme diplomatic pressure, personal threats, and even the possibility of a military coup form part of the intrigue against Mexico and its president. Ultimately, he is able to defeat the plot and save the sovereignty and self-determination of Mexico. However, *Intriga contra México*, which had the makings of an interesting political thriller, resulted in a poorly executed production. The acting, script, photography, and direction are poor. The few interesting moments and good intentions are lost because of improbable characterizations and a weak narrative.

Censorship was even lifted for the classic *La Sombra del Caudillo*.[96] This film, which had been censored for over thirty years, was finally released for a commercial showing in various theaters in Mexico City in 1990. The then director of Radio, Televisión y Cinematografía, Javier Nájera Torres, was the principal government official who made the decision to exhibit it.[97] The 1960 production, directed by celebrated director Julio Bracho, is one of the most insightful accounts not only of historical events of the post-Revolution of 1910 period but also of the workings and nature of Mexican politics. Faithful to the novel by author Martín Luis Guzmán, *La Sombra del Caudillo* narrates the politics and characteristics of presidential succession in Mexico. Its political message and situations are applicable to the present day. In fact, many analysts have observed that *La Sombra del Caudillo* is more revealing of present political struggles than of historical ones. Artistically, *La Sombra del Caudillo* is outstanding at all levels—script, direction, performances, and photography.

Because the events narrated in the film involve military generals, presidential use and misuse of the army, and political assassinations against opposition forces carried out by the military, the high command objected strongly to a reminder on the silver screen of these historical deeds. Fearful of reprisals and not wishing to offend such a powerful force, officials censored *La Sombra del Caudillo* until 1990.[98] Again, as a gesture of freedom of artistic expression and a demonstration of civil authority over the military, the decision was made by the state to release and widely exhibit *La Sombra del Caudillo*.[99] As was the case with *Rojo Amanecer*, *La Sombra del Caudillo* has been well received by audiences and the film community and has been a major financial success. By exhibiting such controversial artistic productions, the Mexican state gained not only political legitimacy but also began to rescue a lost audience. The lifting of censorship in the case of these three films brought concrete and important benefits both nationally as well as internationally to the state, and both politically and culturally it was a critical step in the right direction.

One consistent policy of IMCINE implemented by director Durán was to strongly support the films of the generation of the

1990s—that is, those directors who debuted in the decade of the 1990s. Before the *sexenio* ended, thirty-two directors completed their first work and exhibited it commercially. Seldom in the history of Mexican cinema have so many new directors emerged on the scene in one brief period of time.[100] Even more singular was the fact that a record number of women filmmakers, supported by IMCINE, made not only their first feature but also finished their second and, in some cases, their third narrative film.

In a relatively short period, an impressive body of artistic work began to impress audiences and critics alike in Mexico and elsewhere. Films such as *La Mujer de Benjamín, Danzón, Angel de Fuego, En Medio de la Nada, Lola, Hasta Morir, El Secreto de Romelia, Novia Que Te Vea, Un Año Perdido, Los Pasos de Ana, En el Aire*, and *Dos Crímenes* clearly reflected novel discursive narratives and structures. All received high praise from critics and international awards, and all were successful at the box office. These most recent of directors along with newly emerging talent in acting, screenwriting, and cinematography were instrumental in bringing about an impressive flowering of Mexican cinema. The impetus and positive ambiance that IMCINE had generated also stimulated the previous generations of filmmakers to return to their craft and produce notable films such as *Como Agua para Chocolate, Rojo Amanecer, Miroslava, Golpe de Suerte, Nocturno a Rosarío*, and *El Callejón de los Milagros*.

As a whole, the administration of Ignacio Durán marked the high point of the role and influence of IMCINE. It laid the foundation, created the necessary production formulas, and supported new talent while at the same time encouraging proven filmmakers and working on the distribution and exhibition of Mexican films, all in a six-year period. A major cinematic renaissance was taking place and had already moved Mexican cinema to the forefront of all Spanish-language national cinemas. Durán exemplified the positive role that thoughtful, intelligent, honest, and creative state policies could play in the growth and development of Mexican cinema.

The Recent Era, 1994–1997

President Ernesto Zedillo's administration continued the tradition of a pattern that has characterized the fortunes of IMCINE and overall governmental cinema policies. Dismissing excellent candidates, President Zedillo named Ambassador Jorge Alberto Lozoya to serve as director of IMCINE. The newly named director's expertise was in the area of foreign relations and certainly not in cinema. Worse than

A FILM BY ALFONSO ARAU

Like Water for Chocolate

Como Agua para Chocolate (Like Water for Chocolate) *garnered
unprecedented success in U.S. and European markets.*

his own appointment were the people whom Lozoya chose to serve
in key policymaking divisions. In the three years of their tenure, film
production and distribution declined to an all-time low. The only visible and constant activity of IMCINE during this period was the frequent visits of the director and several of his aides to most of the

international film festivals throughout the world at the expense of the taxpayers.[101] It was the misfortune of Mexican cinema that its one-hundredth-year anniversary would fall during this particular administration. Even this momentous event was handled poorly by the officials of IMCINE.

The notable successes of the previous administration were completely stymied by a combination of the inept, unwise, and capricious policies of IMCINE. Another calamity that had reverse repercussions for the cinema was yet another deep economic crisis that plunged Mexico once again into an economic downturn. Experts point to an even more acute fall of the economy than in the crisis of the recent past. Once again, the peso was devalued, more loans had to be secured from the international banking community, and severe austerity measures were implemented. Funding for cultural programs, including cinema, were drastically reduced. Although these events and circumstances were indeed serious and detrimental to the progress of Mexican cinema, the policies of the recently appointed administrators of IMCINE were even more harmful.[102] The director of international and cultural programs, Salvador Flores, personally was responsible for innumerable disasters and for undermining almost every positive project presented to IMCINE. Few individuals have done so much harm in such a short period to the cinema of Mexico as this one official.

IMCINE's inertia and negative policies began to generate widespread criticism and even outrage from all sectors of the film industry, the press, other governmental agencies, and even from international film circles. Such unanimous concerns and later condemnation of the policies and practices of IMCINE started to appear consistently in the press and were exposed on a daily basis from all quarters of the film community. In no other period did a three-year lapse result in not one quality film being produced and exhibited by IMCINE. At the start of the fourth year its first coproduction, *El Anzuelo*, written and directed by Ernesto Rimoch, finally premiered. This lighthearted situation comedy is a social satire of middle-class traditions and mores that are accentuated in the ritual of a wedding. The one other film cosponsored by IMCINE at this time was *Cilantro y Perejil*, directed by Rafael Montero. Audiences related to this well-written and -acted romantic comedy, which describes the modern crisis of relationships and the family, thus making the film one of the most successful box-office hits of recent years.[103] The film, which set attendance records for the 1990s, examines the condition of upper middle-class couples living in present-day Mexico City. Their lives are complicated ones, influenced by diverse factors, generations, income, and the country's economic crisis, which has its repercussions on the couple's relationship.

Attempting to avert a major crisis in the state film industry as well as to curtail consistent criticism domestically and from abroad, Lozoya in mid-1996 was replaced by the respected film director and administrator, Diego López Rivera.[104] At least in this one instance, the state realized its error and corrected it instead of letting the situation worsen as the *sexenio* unfolded. As was expected, the fortunes of IMCINE improved considerably under the able directorship of Diego López, who had gained a solid reputation as head of the Estudios Churubusco and as the director of respected shorts and two artistically sound narrative films, *Crónica de Familia* and *Goita*. In his short tenure, certain positive changes occurred: a solid staff in charge of the various divisions of IMCINE was hired, an aggressive campaign to secure additional resources for production was launched, and decisions of production were made quickly and filming began on important projects. Features now in progress include the work of established directors such as Maryse Sistach, Jaime Humberto Hermosillo, and Arturo Ripstein as well as emerging ones who will debut with their first full-length narrative films.[105]

Additionally, Diego López was a seasoned administrator and director with excellent contacts in the international film community, thereby aiding him in securing agreements with foreign producers. He and his collaborators managed to restore some of the lost prestige and presence of IMCINE internationally and throughout Mexico. During Diego Lopez's fifteen months as director, ten narrative films were coproduced and exhibited, and seed money was made available to begin production on three others. A new center for documentation of and information on Mexican cinema was established for the use of scholars and the general public. Also, nine short films entirely produced by IMCINE were completed by emerging young filmmakers. All were exhibited in Mexico and internationally. Besides production, IMCINE sponsored various exhibitions in remembrance of such icons as Germán Váldez "Tin Tan," Silvia Pinal, Jorge Negrete, and Luis Buñuel.[106]

One major recent success that filmmakers accomplished against established state cinema policies was that the Cineteca Nacional and its operations no longer serve under the Secretaría de Gobernación but now are an integral part of the Consejo Nacional para la Cultura y las Artes. Thus, the Cineteca Nacional leaves the web of national security to be under the auspices of cultural programs exclusively. Decades of struggle on this important issue in official cinema policy finally yielded the desired outcome.

The new restructuring plan for the Cineteca Nacional also included a change of leadership. The able and highly respected director and academic, Alejandro Pelayo, was named as general director.

As a filmmaker, he brought a wealth of proven experience and outstanding credentials to the Cineteca Nacional. Upon assuming the
directorship, Pelayo drew up an exciting and ambitious agenda.
Among his new initiatives was the creation of a national chain of
theaters affiliated with the Cineteca throughout the country that
would exhibit quality cinema, particularly Mexican features. In addition, the Cineteca's equipment would be modernized to current
standards. Other innovative projects included a teaching and research program and the granting of graduate degrees in film studies.
Finally, further collaborative efforts with Mexican and international
institutions would be sought for better distribution and exhibition of
Mexican cinema.

After conferring, however, both officials found themselves faced
with one salient reality: inadequate resources for any of their proposals. It was obvious that without securing additional funding, no
changes—much less new ambitious initiatives or directions—were
possible. The financial situation seemed critical, with little hope for
optimism. Once again the film community and its leadership appealed
to the state for the very survival of the national film industry. And,
once more, the state, assuming its responsibility in preserving and fos-
tering national culture, came to the rescue. President Zedillo personally responded by hosting a luncheon with one hundred of the most
distinguished members of the film community. As spokesman for the
group, film director Arturo Ripstein stated to the president, in the
opening remarks of the meeting, that "cinema is the face and the spirit
of a people; cinema is, without doubt, the art form of our age." He
added, "A country without cinema, Mr. President, is a sad country."

Reacting with concrete actions, President Zedillo announced the
granting of an additional 10 million pesos to the budget of the
Cineteca Nacional and IMCINE:

> The government wants to, and should, support the enormous cinemato-
> graphic talent in Mexico so that filmmakers will be able to obtain the fi-
> nancial backing their creativity requires. As a long-range incentive, I have
> given instructions to the Secretary of Education and to the President of
> CONACULTA (the National Council for Culture and the Arts) that, in
> consultation with the Secretary of the Treasury, and in a period of no more
> than three months, they will prepare, and we will be able to count on, a
> fund for the production of quality films . . . . I want to state that as an im-
> mediate action that serves as a prelude to our long-term efforts, we have
> allocated ten million pesos to the Mexican Film Institute to begin to articu-
> late some film production projects.[107]

To better facilitate the administration and distribution of the funds a
new agency was created by presidential decree, the Fondo para la
Producción Cinematográfica de Calidad.

This presidential initiative of support for the film industry did not end there. Using the occasion of awarding the Premio Nacional de Bellas Artes to Arturo Ripstein in December 1997, President Zedillo, in a surprising move, announced the granting of an additional 100 million pesos to the Fondo para la Producción Cinematográfica de Calidad to be allocated for the production of Mexican films: "Quiero informales que esta mañana he instruido al Secretario de Hacienda para que, gracias al buen estado en que nos dan las finanzas publicas, incremente en otros 100 millones de pesos dicho capital inicial. . . . Dichos apoyos consistran en la adecuada combinacion de capital de riesgo,

President Ernesto Zedillo with Arturo Ripstein.

credito de fomento y otorgamiento de garantias conforme a criterios de calidad, competividad y rentabilidad de cada proyecto." In the same ceremony, Ripstein, in his acceptance speech, alluded to the intimate and—according to him—indispensable relationship between the cinema and the state: "debemos de recordar que el cine es la única de las artes que requiere una infraestructura nacional. Por ello, el cine nacional que trasciende los intereses de lucro immediato, ese cine que es arte, no podria subsistir sin el apoyo y la protección del Estado."

On the next day another dramatic decision by the state on cinema policies was made by Presidential decree. Diego López was to be replaced as director of IMCINE by official Eduardo Amerena Lagunes. Although for months there had been rumors that there was friction between Diego López and the director of CONACULTA, his immediate superior, the appointment still was received with surprise and dismay by the film community (CONACULTA, the National Council for Culture and the Arts, is a major government agency that coordinates, promotes, and funds cultural and artistic programs, including cinema.) One of their own who had performed in an able manner was now being replaced by a bureaucrat and party official. After all, Diego López Rivera and his staff had provided the conditions and impetus for positive directions for Mexican cinema. Although certain criticisms had been levied at his indecisiveness at times or at his overly ambitious policies, none of these reasons really warranted such an abrupt change in the middle of a successful administration. Instead this presidential decision reveals the capricious and personalistic nature of Mexican politics. Authoritarianism and presidential intervention predominate even in the realm of cinema and culture.[108]

These encounters between President Zedillo and filmmakers and recent state cinematic initiatives dramatically exemplify the intimate relationship between the cinema and the state in Mexico. The recent actions also highlight the complex contradictions of the social construction of this relationship. Artistic freedom demands autonomy from the state to be free of coercion or undue influence, yet, without state assistance, artistic cinema might be without seed money to secure additional resources. There is still no substitute for state funding in certain of the arts, including cinema. Thus, political power and culture continue to exist side by side in present-day Mexico.

The summer elections of 1997 brought about dramatic changes for Mexican politics and potentially for its national cinema. The opposition parties, especially the PRD (Partido de la Revolución Democrática), swept all the Federal District elections, including the mayorship of Mexico City and all of its candidates to Congress, including famed superstar María Rojo. Thus, she now becomes the third filmmaker in Congress and in national politics. The momentum of the victory of mayoral candidate Cuauhtémoc Cárdenas and the deep dissatisfaction with the dominant political order caused, for the first time in its history, the PRI to lose its majority in Congress.[109]

Shortly after María Rojo's victory, a letter signed by over two hundred of the most celebrated members of the film community pleaded with her to carry out a vigorous political struggle to save and revitalize the film industry and its various institutions. The letter included concrete suggestions on measures that would enhance filmmaking in Mexico. Their demands were quickly addressed in an interview with Congresswoman María Rojo published in the weekly political magazine, *Proceso*. She responded that through her memberships in the congressional committees on culture and media, she would make the campaign to "save" Mexican cinema her absolute priority.[110] A few months later, María Rojo was named chair of the cultural affairs committee of the Chamber of Deputies. As a first step in revising the current legislation on cinema, the Ley Federal de Cinematografía, the chair convened public hearings with members of the film community in order to have the members of Congress learn firsthand the issues surrounding the urgent need to revise the law. Hearings were held for a two-day period on

November 24–25, 1997, when over thirty position papers were presented by filmmakers.

María Rojo crusaded for over a year on this effort. Slowly but effectively she was able to secure bipartisan support for changes in legislation that governed cinema, and all this was accomplished in spite of a massive and expensive campaign by the exhibitors and theater owners. These sectors launched one of the most concentrated single efforts at undermining a prospective legislative initiative. As Congress was about to end its session for 1998, the Ley Cinematográfica came up for discussion and vote. It was approved unanimously by the members of the Chamber of Deputies and sent to the Senate for final approval. With certain modifications, the Senate ratified the legislation, thus making it the law of the land.

The most important provisions of the Ley Cinematográfica are:

- A 10 percent exhibition time for Mexican cinema
- Better stimulus and conditions for the production of Mexican films in Mexico and abroad
- A substantial fund entitled FIDECINE established for the production of Mexican films with monies from the government and the private sector
- The statement that Mexican cinema is a valuable national artistic and educational manifestation and as such should be supported and partially financed by the federal government. The Ley makes it clear that cinema, like other arts, should be a major responsibility of the state.
- The dubbing of films to remain as is, mostly limited to television and video. The Ley states that a film and its negative is a cultural and artistic work, and as such should be exhibited and maintained in its original form.

Although these points are not revolutionary, nonetheless they will aid Mexican cinema and provide it with much-needed additional resources as well as certain guarantees and protection against Hollywood. Congresswoman María Rojo and her supporters are to be congratulated on this successful endeavor against powerful interests.

Conclusion

The Mexican state's continued involvement in the cinema faces an uncertain future. Its ninety-or-so-year history might be either coming to an end or, at best, will be dramatically changed. Given certain ill-fated state-produced films of the last decades, the grave economic conditions facing the country, the escalated costs of commercial cinema today, and the loss of national and international audiences and markets for Mexican cinema, it seems only correct that the state as a major producer and exhibitor should be a thing of the past. If this were to occur, the benefits might certainly outweigh the limitations. For example, certain filmmakers will no longer look exclusively to the state for their main support for production. To no longer have the time loss and aggravation of the infamous *antesala* (the anteroom of a bureaucrat's office) while waiting for approval in itself would be a marked improvement. The loss of state revenue might make filmmakers become more creative in raising funds and be more supportive of each other, instead of pitting one against the other as has been the case until now. Financing of a proposed film by members of a cooperative or through coproductions with other countries would be determined by the quality of the project and not by personal favoritism or cronyism.

Still, the search for and securing of funding sources for such an expensive and risky endeavor as filmmaking will take time, luck, and the coming together of optimum national and international conditions. And, for the present, there is no substitute for state support of certain cinematic projects, which include narrative films, the Muestra del Cine Mexicano, the Centro de Capacitación Cinematográfica, and the production of artistic shorts and documentaries. One also must acknowledge that as a direct consequence of state support, the very best of most contemporary Mexican films were coproduced and exhibited in the nation and throughout the world.

In certain moments and in select instances the state and cinema have collaborated in a positive and creative manner. IMCINE has finally begun to realize its potential. In the *sexenio* of the Salinas administration, it had its best years. Director Ignacio Durán demonstrated sound and imaginative leadership. He and his advisers were instrumental in providing the material and political conditions that resulted in a boom of exciting and novel productions. Although there was a certain optimism and a definitive resurgence of artistic films, the first half of the Zedillo administration was disastrous for cinema. The remaining years under Diego López already have shown much potential, and it is hoped that he will be able to reverse earlier setbacks and move IMCINE and cinema forward. Then, of course, there is the question of who will follow in the next administration. For sustained progress to persist there has to be continuity in efforts and in those policies that have demonstrated promise and positive results.

More difficult to predict, however, is the role of the Secretaría de Gobernación as ultimate censor. Cinema can be viewed as a central part of the question of the further democratization of the PRI. For

Gobernación to drop entirely or drastically change its cinema policies, the state would have to move toward a real condition of openness and true freedom of expression. When the Mexican state
tolerates criticism and revisionism and acknowledges its shortcomings, negative deeds, and less-than-perfect presidents and other high-
level officials, then censorship will be entirely lifted. As difficult as it
may be to imagine that situation, events of the recent past have
seemed improbable, yet they have occurred. Thus, if all of the above
would happen, then the state in its relations with the cinema on questions of artistic freedom would enter the dawn of a new age.

Notes

1. Although there exist general histories of Mexican cinema, none offers an extensive discussion of the role of the state. Each contains important isolated incidents and examples but not in-depth analyses.

2. Gustavo García, "El cine de gobierno. La Muerte de un burocrata," *Intolerancia* 7 (November–December 1990): 15–22.

3. Interview with Arturo Ripstein, Mexico City, June 14, 1986.

4. See the first two chapters of the well-researched and well-written book by Paola Costa, *La apertura cinematográfica* (Pueblo, 1988).

5. Interview with Carlos Monsiváis, Mexico City, August 10, 1985.

6. José Felipe Coria is one of the few scholars who has studied the recent private-sector productions. See his interpretive article, "Un cine popular mexicano. El progreso de un libertino," *Intolerancia* 7 (November–December 1990): 53–65.

7. Interview with Ivan Trujillo, Mexico City, May 28, 1989.

8. Interview with Marío Hernández, Mexico City, July 10, 1987.

9. Aurelio de los Reyes devotes an entire chapter to the Porfirío Diaz period and the beginnings of Mexican cinema in his excellent study, *Los origenes del cine en México (1896–1900)* (México, 1973), 130–49.

10. Moises Vinas, *Historia del cine mexicano* (México, 1987), 32–34.

11. Gabriel Ramírez, *Cronica del cine mudo mexicano* (México, 1987), 87.

12. De los Reyes, *Los origenes*, 126–38.

13. Carlos Monsiváis, "Notas sobre la cultura mexicana en la decada de los setentas," in Jean Franco et al., *Cultura y dependencia* (México, 1976), 197–229.

14. Interview with Tomas Pérez Turrent, Mexico City, July 14, 1987.

15. Aurelio de los Reyes, *Medio siglo de cine mexicano (1896–1947)* (México, 1987), 78–81.

16. Sergio Zarmeno, *México: Una democracia utópica* (México, 1978), is an excellent recent authoritative analysis of the tragic events and legacy of the student movement of 1968.

17. Carlos Monsiváis in his powerful and insightful book, *Dias de Guardar* (México, 1971), analyzes these events and actions in detail.

18. Miguel Basanez offers a solid interpretation in his study, *La lucha por la hegemonia en México, 1968–1976* (México, 1981).

19. Armando Lazo, "Diez años de cine mexicano: Un primer acercamiento," in *Hojas de cine* (México, 1988), 2:92–93.

20. Cited in José de la Colina, "Situación de los nuevos cineastas," *Revista de la Universidad* 10 (June 1972): 8.

21. Carlos Monsiváis, "La dependencia y la cultura mexicana de los setentas," *Cambio* 4:1 (August–September 1976): 47–48.

22. Alma Rossbach and Leticia Canel, "Política cinematográfica del sexenio de Luis Echeverría, 1970–1976," in *Hojas de cine* (México, 1988), 2:89–92.

23. Ibid., 93–96

24. Francisco Sánchez, *Cronica antisolemne del cine mexicano* (México, 1989), 99–101.

25. Costa, *La apertura*, 72–75.

26. Ibid., 83–85.

27. Interview with Fernando Macotela, Mexico City, November 19, 1985.

28. Interview with Carlos Savage, Mexico City, August 10, 1986.

29. Interview with Alejandro Pelayo, Mexico City, June 12, 1989.

30. "Film Schools in Mexico," *Cinema México* 2:1 (December 1997): 5.

31. Jorge Ayala Blanco, in his controversial two-volume work *La búsqueda del cine mexicano* (México, 1974), offers an insightful and critical review of these films.

32. Interview with Arturo Ripstein, Mexico City, July 7, 1989.

33. Interview with Marcela Fernández Violante, Mexico City, June 23, 1990.

34. Interview with José Luis Gallegos, Mexico City, July 16, 1990.

35. Screenplay, *Nuevo Mundo*, CONACINE (Mexico, 1974).

36. Interview with Pedro Miret, Mexico City, June 22, 1986

37. *Excelsior* (May 19, 1977): 18.

38. One of the more in-depth analyses of the films of the Echeverría period is provided by David Ramon in his well-written article, "Un sexenio de cine en México," *Comunicación* 21 (March 1977): 24–33.

39. Interview with Luis González, San José de Gracia, June 18, 1979.

40. Interview with Jorge Ayala Blanco, Mexico City, August 12, 1982.

41. Ayala Blanco offers valuable insights and an interpretation of the production aspects of the films of the Echeverría period in *La búsqueda*.

42. *Cine informe general* (México, 1976), 455–57.

43. Interview with Eduardo de la Vega, Guadalajara, July 12, 1986.

44. Daniel Levy and Gabriel Székely, *Mexico: Paradoxes of Stability and Change* (Boulder, CO, 1987), 162–65.

45. Interview with Hector Aguilar Camin, Mexico City, July 18, 1990.

46. Alma Rossbach and Leticia Canel, "Política cinematográfica del sexenio de José López-Portillo, 1976–1982," *Hojas de cine* (México, 1988), 2:177–80.

47. Interview with Emilio García Riera, Guadalajara, June 18, 1990.

48. Interview with Fernando Macotela, Mexico City, July 12, 1987.

49. Rossbach and Canel, "Política cinematográfica . . . José López-Portillo," 2:181–84.

50. *Uno Mas Uno* (November 26, 1978): 14.

51. *Esto* (November 28, 1978): 21.

52. Interview with Tomas Pérez Turrent, Mexico City, June 24, 1987.

53. Interview with Andres de Luna, Mexico City, August 4, 1979.

54. *Uno Mas Uno*, in a series of articles in November 1978, reported these apprehensions and other state cinematic policies. No scholar to date has discussed this period or these themes in detail.

55. Interview with Marcela Fernández Violante, Mexico City, June 23, 1979.

56. Daniel Cosio Villegas offers a classic study of presidential power and style in *El estilo personal de gobernar* (México, 1987), 274–75.

57. Vinas, *Historia*, 282–86.

58. Interview with Jorge Fons, Mexico City, June 3, 1978.

59. Jorge Ayala Blanco, *La condición del cine mexicano (1973–1985)* (México, 1986), 19–171.

60. Interview with Carlos Monsiváis, Mexico City, July 17, 1979.

61. Vinas, *Historia*, 276.

62. Pablo González Casanova and Hector Aguilar Camin's two-volume edited work, *México ante la crisis* (México, 1985), discusses the various aspects and effects of the recent crisis.

63. Interview with Alberto Isaac, Mexico City, August 18, 1984.

64. Ibid.

65. Interview with Ernesto Roman, Mexico City, July 12, 1990.

66. García, "El cine de gobierno," 31.

67. Interview with Alejandro Pelayo, Mexico City, June 14, 1989.

68. Sánchez, *Cronica antisolemne*, 156–57.

69. Interview with Nelson Carro, Mexico City, June 28, 1990.

70. Interview with Sergio Olhovich, Mexico City, July 7, 1990.

71. Interview with Alejandro Pelayo, Mexico City, June 24, 1991.

72. Interview with José Felipe Coria, Mexico City, August 10, 1991.

73. *Excelsior* (June 28, 1984): 18.

74. Hector Rivera, "El Concurso de Cine Experimental," *Proceso* 498 (April 1986): 52–55.

75. Alberto Cortes Calderón, "La generación de los 80, los cineastas en México," in *Cine, T.V. y Video en América Latina* (México, 1989), 65–73.

76. An important, perceptive, and favorable analysis of the first years of Carlos Salinas de Gortari's regime is Hector Aguilar Camin's *Despues del milagro* (México, 1990).

77. Interview with Tomas Pérez Turrent, Mexico City, June 24, 1991.

78. Interview with Carlos Monsiváis, Mexico City, June 18, 1991.

79. Interview with Gustavo García, Mexico City, June 21, 1991.

80. *La Jornada*, September 12, 1983.

81. Interview with Eduardo de la Vega, Guadalajara, July 19, 1989.

82. Interview with Michael Donnelly, Los Angeles, June 23, 1988.

83. Interview with Dana Rotberg, Mexico City, July 14, 1992.

84. *Excelsior* (March 18, 1991): 19.

85. Gustavo García and José Felipe Coria, *Nuevo Cine Mexicano* (México, 1977), 72–73.

86. *El Universal*, April 21, 1992.

87. Interview with Juan de la Riva, Stanford, May 26, 1991.

88. Interview with Marcela Fernández Violante, Mexico City, June 12, 1993.

89. On this theme see the study by Sidney Weintraub, *A Marriage of Convenience* (New York, 1990).

90. Interview with María Rojo, Mexico City, July 20, 1994.

91. *La Jornada*, April 26, 1991.

92. Interview with Patricia Dávalos, Mexico City, July 29, 1991.

93. The film journal *Dicine* published various notes and reviews of *Rojo Amanecer* in the months after its showing in June 1991 that examine this aspect and others of the film.

94. *Revista de la Camara de la Industria Cinematográfica* (November 1991): 34–35.

95. Interview with Carlos Monsiváis, Mexico City, August 4, 1992.

96. *La Jornada*, June 19, 1990.

97. Interview with Alejandro Pelayo, Mexico City, August 2, 1992.

98. Issue No. 4 of the journal *Intolerancia* has three excellent articles that narrate the dark history of censorship of *La Sombra del Caudillo*.

99. Interview with Diana Bracho, Mexico City, July 12, 1986.

100. Gustavo García, "El cine de gobierno," 28–30.

101. Interview with José Felipe Coria, Mexico City, July 5, 1996.
102. Interview with Julian Pastor, Mexico City, July 5, 1996.
103. *Cinema Mexico* 2 (December 1997): 4.
104. *Reforma*, October 12, 1996.
105. Interview with Marina Stavenhagen, Mexico City, December 18, 1997.
106. *La Jornada*, December 12, 1997.
107. *Reforma*, September 21, 1997.
108. *Reforma*, December 18, 1997.
109. *Proceso* (July 13, 1997): 4–6.
110. *Proceso* (September 28, 1997): 64–65.

10

Reconstructing the Border
Mexican Border Cinema and
Its Relationship to Its Audience[1]

Norma Iglesias

Right there in Mexico, Mexican cinema is ending. We think that in the future Mexican films are not going to exist anymore. We will have to exhibit American films. . . . In Mexico, they might feel they are not losing Mexico because, after all, they are there, in their country. But for those of us who are not there, for whom cinema is one of the ways of connecting with our country, our culture, our roots, what are we going to do? For us it is like losing part of ourselves

—Juan J. Torres, Bay Theater owner,
San Diego, 1989

"Border cinema" is an important cinematographic genre not only because of the vast number of films it encompasses (more than three hundred between 1936 and 1992) but also because of its substantial audience—an audience who has a strong emotional link with the genre—along the U.S.-Mexican border and in the central part of Mexico. It has changed with time and in its definition. During the initial phase of the genre, between 1940 and 1957, the border was not visible on the screen; it only appeared in dialogue or in the context of the tragedies faced by a film's protagonists when they return from the border (for example, in *Primero Soy Mexicano* [1950] and *Acá las Tortas* [1951]). With the development and boom of Mexican Westerns in the 1960s, the border began to appear as a set, as the small and dirty town that served as a haven for thieves on the run from justice (*El Terror de la Frontera* [1962] and *Pistoleros de la Frontera* [1964]). Until then, border cinema consisted of films talking about the border, or those that used it as an interesting narrative space for the development of a plot. In other words, the border was not a physical boundary but rather a construction erected through dialogue or in the film studios.

In the 1970s, and particularly in the 1980s, the definition of border cinema became more complex. This category now included not only films that referred to the border but also to any film that was produced there. In the 1980s some of the most important producers—family businesses for the most part such as Aguilar, Galindo, and Agrasánchez—used their properties in Brownsville and Laredo, Texas, and Tijuana, Mexico, to shoot their films. The defining characteristic of these new movies was that the border was not only a narrative reference but also the site of production for a large number of melodramas about immigration as well as films of action and adventure related to drug dealing.

The producers' use of their own properties for these films resulted in a decrease in production expenses, which were reduced further by shooting a series of films at the same time. For example, production companies used the same crew of actors to make two or three different films at once. By shooting on their properties on the American side of the border, the producers also saved money by not having to pay either the Mexican or American cinematographic workers' union rates. Thus, the border became the site of production as well as the site of any kind of horror or action film that did not necessarily make any explicit reference to the border region or people (*La Niña de los Hoyitos* [1983] and *Cementerio de Terror* [1984]). While the narratives of these films could have been situated anywhere, they may be considered as part of the genre because they were shot on the border.

The most recent kind of border cinema is characterized by a crisis of cultural identity in which the characters confront an encounter of two national cultures. These narratives could happen in Tijuana or Los Angeles as well as in Chicago or any other city in Mexico or the United States. In this new kind of film, the border functions as a symbol or cultural barrier rather than as a geopolitical line. Considering all of the above, border cinema may therefore be defined in a broad fashion. A border film must include at least one of the following characteristics:

1. its plot, or a significant part of it, develops on the U.S. Mexican border;
2. it refers to a character who lives on the border;
3. it deals with the problems of being Mexican in the United States;
4. it is produced on the border; or
5. a significant part of the plot deals with the problems of confrontation between Mexican and American culture.

This definition is as complex as the meaning of the term "border." Sometimes it refers to an encounter, a crossing, a mixture, a confrontation, or a limit. Thus, the label "border cinema" alludes to types of characters, a production form, a specific geographic space, a question of limits, and a confrontation between "us" in relation to the "other." These classifications are constantly shifting and reorganizing.

In addition to the complexity of the definition of border cinema, it is important to consider two issues. First, the majority of producers became interested in this genre because of its profitability and not because of a more profound interest in filmmaking or in the border as a social problem. As a result, the genre in general is distinguished by being a cinema of poor technical and narrative quality. Moreover, the profitability and the growth of border cinema was linked to the discovery of a broad market, primarily in the United States but also in the Mexican cities and towns of origin of migrant workers. Some of the important families of producers and directors, such as Galindo and Agrasánchez, realized that border issues were central to thousands of Mexicans and Latin Americans who were part of the immigration phenomenon. One needs to consider that, in Mexico, we are all potential migrants. The idea of crossing to "the other side" is a hope that has been converted into a myth for a large number of Mexicans. Thus, from the audience's point of view, border cinema was a way of learning about the border and about the process of becoming an undocumented migrant for those who had the ambition of some day working in the United States. Additionally, the genre served as a mirror and as a link with their land and culture for those who were already working in this country.

The second important consideration is linked to the fact that this cinema, in spite of its low quality, is widely accepted by its public. It is therefore important to acknowledge the genre as a phenomenon of popular culture on the Mexican-U.S. border and in other places in Mexico. Border cinema is an example of the postmodern and mass-mediated definition of popular culture. It is not popular because it is produced by the people (*el pueblo*) or by a resourceful business person; rather, it is popular because its major audience is the people.

The Audiences

One of the ways to discover the profile of the audience of border cinema is through the film "programmers" of the Compañía Operadora de Teatros (COTSA). These programmers are an important part of the Mexican film industry and have rarely been studied.[2] We need to consider these people from Mexico City and the criteria they have developed in their lengthy career of deciding which film should be projected in each of the theaters of the region that a programmer manages. That decision is made after considering the characteristics of each film in relation to the characteristics or profile of the audience who attends each movie theater. The characteristics and location of a theater are usually indicative of a specific type of audience in terms of socioeconomic stratum, age, level of education, and preference of themes and cinematographic genres.

According to the programmers' perceptions, Mexican audiences of border cinema and Mexican cinema in general are different from those who go to see American and other foreign films. In general, there is a marked preference for Mexican cinema and, in particular, border cinema on the part of audiences of lower socioeconomic and educational levels, while people of higher levels prefer American and other foreign cinema. Thus, behind the decision to watch or not to watch border cinema lies a question of social status and a certain mark of social class.

At the same time that we conducted interviews with programmers, we administered a poll in all theaters in San Diego, California, and Tijuana that exhibited border cinema.[3] This poll was designed to allow us to define the profile of the audiences. In the sample, we observed that audiences of border cinema, on both sides of the frontier, are predominantly male (83%). It is also a young audience: of the total number of people surveyed, it was found that 83% are within the age range of 16 to 35 years (28% between 16 to 20, 28% between 21 to 25, 15% between 26 to 30, and 12% between 31 to 35 years). In nearly half of the cases, audience members attend without a partner (43.6%), nearly one-third in groups of two (29.3%), and 27.1% in groups of two or more. Some 22.3% rarely go to the movies, while 23% go at least once per month and 48% attend two or more times per month (of which 51% go more than once per week). These statistics permit us to confirm that, in general, it is an assiduous audience.

Of the total surveyed, 83% are of migrant origin from Mexican states that are not on the border. If we separate the audience in Tijuana from that of San Diego, we find that in Tijuana 16.6% were born in that city, while 54.7% have been there less than five years; 10.5% have been there five to nine years, 13.5% have between ten and nineteen years of residency, and only 4.7% have lived in Tijuana for twenty years or more. These facts contrast with the general characteristics of the population of Tijuana, in which one-half was born in the city while of those who were not born there, 76.23% have lived in Tijuana for more than five years.[4] These figures seem to indicate that there is a greater preference for border cinema among the population of migrant origin who have lived in the city for only a few years and who are thus more linked to the phenomenon of undocumented migration.

From the sample in San Diego, it was found that only 1.8% were born in the United States; 10.5% of the immigrants had lived in that city less than a year and one-half, 32.5% had lived there between two and four years and 24.5% between five and six years; 18% disclosed that they had lived there between seven and nine years, while only 14.5% had been there more than ten but less than fifteen years. We did not find any one who had lived in San Diego for more than fifteen years. Three-fourths of those surveyed from both sides of the border have not been able to visit their place of origin. Indeed, more than half of those interviewed in San Diego declared themselves to be undocumented laborers working in trade jobs (such as bricklaying and carpentry) and services within the same urban area. It is very probable, according to the data generated by the surveys (type of work and time of residéncy declared in that country), that many more are undocumented—more than 90%—but for obvious reasons did not declare it.

We were also dealing with audiences on both sides of the border who have had little schooling. Some 9.2% of the total audience surveyed turned out to be illiterate, and 67.2% do not have an education higher than secondary level, which makes it difficult for them to attend movies with subtitlcs. If we again separate the audience data of Tijuana from that of San Diego, we find that the percentage of illiterates of those surveyed in San Diego is 13.3%, while the total of those surveyed in Tijuana is 4.75%. Another 19.9% of the audience from San Diego had not finished elementary school and 21.55% had completed their elementary education, while of the audience from Tijuana, 12.2% had not finished elementary school and 20% had completed their elementary education. The percentage of the audience who had a high-school education was very similar in Tijuana and San Diego: out of the total of each of these groups, 30.5% completed a secondary education and 14.6% had postsecondary studies. Again, the difference was clear in that 5.5% of the public in Tijuana had completed university studies versus less than 1% of the audience in San Diego.

It is worth emphasizing that in Tijuana the percentage of the illiterate population is slightly smaller (4.2%) than the illiterate population in the audience of Mexican cinema in the same city (4.7%), and notably smaller than the percentage found in the audience of Mexican cinema in San Diego (13.3%). This figure is also significant in relation to the fact that 50% of the undocumented population in 1989 had a level of six to nine years of schooling, and no more than 10% had between ten to twelve years of school. In other words, according to this indicator, in terms of levels schooling the undocumented population is actually found to be above the national average.

This information confirms the perception of the programmers in the sense that a preference and taste for border cinema is concentrated in the population with lower educational levels.

Of the total number surveyed, 38.6% in both cities declared that they liked border cinema because it reflects reality and because they identify with the characters. This answer demonstrates how important it is for the films to talk about problems and characters that are central to their audience. In this way, spectators feel represented on the screen and also "live" the film more intensely. In addition, 31.2% like border cinema because it has "a lot of action," which seems to be linked to the desire for amusement and entertainment and perhaps for "escape." Another 30.2% responded that they like these movies for other reasons; for example, these films are the only place where they are able to see actors who are Mexican.

From the results of the sample and the interviews with the exhibitors, we are able to observe that in both cities the audiences of border cinema (and of Mexican cinema, according to the views of the exhibitors) do not speak English. This finding is confirmed by the sparse attendance of the audience in the United States at movie theaters where American films are exhibited. It seems therefore to be a matter of an audience who sees only Mexican cinema not merely out of interest, conviction, or pleasure but also because it does not have an alternative. It is also important to point out that because the audience in the United States is composed primarily of an undocumented population, attendance at movie theaters may be considered risky. These people could be exposing themselves to being apprehended by agents of the Immigration and Naturalization Service (*la migra*). This observation is important for two reasons: on one hand, it indicates that this population's needs for free space and time and recreational activities is so great that in spite of the risks involved, they still choose to attend the movies; and on the other hand, the need is also great to share with a group of people who find themselves in the same situation as migrants, as foreigners, and as undocumented people. According to the study, it follows that there seems in general to be a connection between the migration of undocumented workers to the United States and the liking for Mexican cinema, where border cinema has occupied a special place.

This audience also sees in cinema a source of contact with its culture. According to the interviews conducted in the United States, a major segment of the audience does not read newspapers. It is a population who listen to Mexican and American radio stations that broadcast musical programs in Spanish for two to three hours per day, and who have television in their homes on which they watch Mexican and Spanish-language American channels (Channels 12 and

33 in Tijuana, 34 and 52 in Los Angeles) for two to three hours daily. A great number of nightly programs air Mexican films, many of which are of the border cinema genre. For a major portion of those interviewed, cinema is one of the few public spectacles to which they have access. Thus, border cinema in the theaters and on television occupies a central place in their leisure activities and is also considered as a way to maintain contact with their culture.

The Enjoyment of Border Cinema

When we ask "Why do people go to the movies to see border cinema?" we find various reasons related to taste, but we have to acknowledge that "cinematographic pleasure" does not depend solely on audience choice. Pierre Sorlin asserts that it also depends on various questions such as the possibilities or alternatives that this audience might have to attend other cultural activities—the fewer the cultural options, the greater the need for that activity to which they do have access.[5] This leads us to think that, in the case of the audience of border cinema, the preference for cinema is only slightly related to a decision to individually or socially select from other options. It is instead often a matter of being the only option available for creative and cultural activity.

Film preference is also related to the degree to which cinema is acknowledged as a legitimate medium of communication. We must remember that the ability to read subtitles is an important prerequisite in the selection of a film for this audience, as is migratory status for the selection of one movie theater over another. In other words, audiences that cannot read subtitles and do not know how to speak English have no film option other than to see films in their own language. Additionally, the availability of public transportation as well as the freedom to move from one place to another without the problem of having to demonstrate legal status are decisive factors in the impetus to see border cinema.

The audience of this cinema is identified by certain positions of social status. Merchants seldom attend, and businessmen and college students never do. In the United States it is rare to see Mexican Americans; this phenomenon marks the distance between those who had arrived in the United States earlier from those who came later. Those who have legal papers and those who do not are also distinguished by a certain status.

Cinematic preference is also determined by the very production and distribution entities that decide what films are going to be exhibited. Thus, it would be logical to ask if this audience watches what it

likes or what it has as its only option. According to our sample, one
of the differences between the public of border cinema in San Diego
and the public in Tijuana is that 65% of those surveyed in San Diego
knew when they arrived at the theater which movie they were going
to see. Thus, their knowledge of the film's title would have motivated
their decision to go to the cinema. On the other hand, only 20% of
those interviewed in Tijuana knew what they were going to see. In
Tijuana, there is a public who regularly attends the same movie theater regardless of what is playing.

Although the data demonstrate that in San Diego 65% of the audience went to the cinema looking for a certain movie, the fact that
there is only one theater that projects Mexican films compels us to
assume that the options or possibilities of selective activity are inop-
erative. In this context, the decision is just about going or not going
to the movie theater and not about the selection of one among various films. On average, if we observe the number of times per month
those surveyed will decide to go to the movies, we know that it is an
assiduous public who, in general, attends all the films that are
shown in the movie theaters. In the case of San Diego, it also seems
that attendance at the theater constitutes a social act in which people
can come together and be with others who, in both real and cinematographic life, lead lives similar to their own. The exhibition of a
Mexican film in a movie theater such as the Bay Theater in San
Diego is thus transformed into a social ceremony that helps an audience to feel less alone in the face of its foreign and undocumented
status. It is a question of a group of people working long and hard
days who must decide whether to (1) risk going out into the streets,
(2) often make a long journey, and (3) pay between five and six dollars in exchange for two hours of entertainment and escape from
everyday concerns.

On the other hand, we have to consider that taste in modern society has also been linked to advertising. How much truth to this is
there in the case of border cinema? The advertising directed to the
public in Tijuana does not seem to exercise an important influence.
First, we must remember that 80% of those surveyed at the movie
theaters in Tijuana did not know at the time of their arrival which
movie they were going to see. Second, in Tijuana, as in other cities of
the Mexican Republic, the only publicity for movies is in the press
and, in a few cases, on the radio. However, as we also saw, the audience for border cinema does not usually read the newspapers.
Therefore, we can say that they do not have access to those ads,
which in any case are small and illegible, with poor pictures and in-
complete information. Neither does there exist in the local newspapers nor journals any reference to movie theaters (with only one

Movie poster for Santo en la Frontera del Terror

exception, some articles that appear in the weekly publication, *Zeta*). There is no promotion of these films on local television channels, although there is some publicity on two U.S. radio stations (one in San Diego and the other in Los Angeles) that are heard in some parts of the city of Tijuana. Publicity seems to have greater importance for the audience of border cinema in the United States. It appears not only on those two radio stations but also on two Los Angeles television channels that can be seen in San Diego. These theaters also have a telephone number that can be dialed where, at any hour, a recording will inform callers about the movie titles, casts, and screening schedules.

Another important element that explains the preference for border cinema is what Sorlin has named the "accumulative phenomenon." Border cinema has insisted on reappropriating characters, themes, situations, stereotypes, and actors. Instead of boring the spectator, this tactic seems to produce a phenomenon of "habit" and includes the pleasure of repetition. Thus, the repetition of the formula topics of migration and drugs is not seen by the audience as boring or negative. On the contrary, it has repeatedly enjoyed reliving those adventures and sufferings that a great many of them remember having experienced during their crossing into the United States.

Movie Scenes

The three movie theaters studied in Tijuana are very old and rarely have been remodeled. They have beat-up seats, screens in very bad condition, poor speakers, and damaged films full of scratches, and the restrooms are in a deplorable state. The movie itself seems to be the least important focus for audience members' attention: many read the newspaper or a comic book when the lighting permits it. The theater never reaches one-fourth of its capacity, as the spectators are constantly going in and out. On many occasions, one's concentration on the movie is broken because of chatter, whistling, and jokes in loud voices. The audience applauds when something thrilling happens and is either touched or laughs during a sad moment: some sing along with the four or five songs that religiously appear in all Mexican movies. There is nervous laughter when the hero-migrant is trapped by *la migra*, in the same way that someone from the audience has been caught. When the actor playing the migrant dies, the audience laughs. Submission to the plot and forgetfulness, integration, and isolation all take place in less than 140 minutes.

In San Diego, the scene is different. The Bay Theater is about to open. The owner and manager prepare for the first showing of the day at 6:15 P.M. People start to arrive one by one. "Premiering today! *Tres Veces Mojado*," the publicity states. A Salvadorian woman reviews the poster hanging in the lobby: "Filmed in El Salvador, Guatemala, Mexico, and the United States." "What a thrill, three times illegal like me?" she asks. *La migra* relinquishes his turn. Everyone knows that the custom of not making round-ups in this movie theater will be respected.

The ticket booth opens, a sparse line of men and women, alone or in pairs, waits to go in and see the adventures of people just like them—people who, with courage and nostalgia, decide to leave their homeland for the country of dollars and opportunities. *La migra* returns to take a stroll. Nobody is ruffled, the booth keeps on selling tickets, people buy popcorn. The theater is clean and is filled to half of its capacity.

The movie begins. "Mother, I leave you the only thing I have. I'm going with my cousin to the north . . . Give me your blessing!" The audience surrenders to the plot amid quiet chatter that relates events in the film to their own experience. Then panoramic scenes of San Salvador and Guatemala City, recognizable places, call for sighs and comments. The characters arrive in Mexico, leave for Veracruz, live their misfortunes and love affairs. "Without you, I could never live," the protagonist sings; and then she says "Why don't we form a trio of a rose and two thorns?" We hear laughter and some jokes among the audience. Now scenes from congested Mexico City (more sighs and comments), third-class buses, shoving, and then the characters arrive in Nogales. To the third complete song, the audience sings in unison.

After many hardships, the protagonists meet with *el pollero*, the guide who will lead them to the United States. "Jumped goat, paid goat, it's four hundred dollars for each one. Can you handle it?" They walk three days through the desert, their suffering enormous. The face of the hero is full of pain, like those of many in the audience. "We are going to die, Juan!" People move in their seats, and some laugh nervously. "Think of your family, we have to get there." The drama and the laughter continue. "Silvia doesn't suffer any more." We hear sobbing from the audience and tears fall discreetly. The adventures of the rest of the protagonists continue. They finally succeed in reaching North American territory. "Juan, Juan, there's a road . . . we made it!" They barely complete their harrowing journey when *la migra* appears and arrests them. After that, in letters in a style from the 1950s, appears on the screen "The End." The audience shouts, "¡Va pa'tras!" (Go back!). Unquestionably moved, they leave their seats and exit the theater.

It has been said that spectators are more responsive to what they know and pay attention to tiny details when it is a matter of familiar territory. Thus, we could theorize that border audiences are acute critics of border cinema. However, on the contrary, they are convinced not because the films show reality just as it is, like a documentary might, but because the films do not show reality as it is. Border cinema simply takes elements from reality to give life to fictional situations and characters. As one spectator put it, "I live reality and I see it in my house and outside of my house. I come to the movies for amusement and to see things that are not true: that's why it's cinema, isn't it?"[6]

In the case of border cinema the attraction seems to fall on the affective order ("I like it, it's amusing") and not on the cognitive order, which is more related to the question of credibility. If it were a question of credibility, then the cases of spectators who go to the movies without knowing what they are going to see would be rare. Border cinema and its audiences have not characterized themselves by conscious selection and criticisms of the film. Instead, according to the same spectator, "I want to see movies in Spanish, with jokes I can understand, with people who resemble me, with fantasies that I can identify with."[7]

Border cinema is not appreciated or disparaged because of its authenticity but because of its action and adventure—and because of the possibility that the theme, the plot, the actors, and other elements may be identified with a particular character, group, or community. Director Rubén Galindo, son of the famous Golden Age director, Alejandro Galindo, argues that

> in border cinema it is a question of characters who live in those geographical areas, surrounded by the characteristic conflicts of that region, but set in the formula of the cinema, which is: There are always three acts. First, introduce your character; next, throw him in the river and the problems begin; and then, just when he's going to plummet over the waterfall, you rescue him. That is the dramatic structure of world cinema. Place all those things in a situation of the border and there's your movie.[8]

The fact that the film is a narrative makes the public interested. This narrative includes the spectator and involves him in such a way that he loses himself in the screen. In border cinema there are two moments for this kind of reaction—the spectator takes the role of the protagonist, and re-creates the character and the plot; and when he knows that he is merely a spectator in the theater, surrounded by people like him who are sharing in the event of going to the movies. In the first moment, the border narrative presents two strengths, good and evil, faced by characters of two nationalities, the Americans and the Mexicans; the audience always sides with the Mexicans even when its favorite actor may be playing the role of the American.

The possibility of illusion, reality, amusement, and spectacle that represent cinema has contributed to the creation of a culture specifically cinematographic. The movie theater is the place where we "enter to find faces, schemes, attitudes, and places that touch, attract, irritate, and seduce us"[9] but may also show and teach us norms of conduct that we can or cannot imitate. However, as we see in border cinema, the way of viewing the movie is not a traditional one. At times, members of the audience give in to the plot and live the image of some character, but a few minutes later they may become aware of a friend sitting next to or behind them. In this case, the movie theater is not only a dark and private place in which they yield to fantasy but also a public place in which they share a common situation—the longing for their homeland and, in some cases, their status as "illegals."

Conclusion

The movie audiences in the cities of Tijuana and San Diego go searching for mexican cinema in general but are especially interested in border cinema. This preference is linked to the migratory experience. In general, for a majority of the audience in both cities but especially in the United States, cinema represents the only public spectacle to which they have access and thus one of the few channels of contact with their cultural roots. Independently from its producers and exhibitors, border cinema is a cultural product to which the audience has given social and educational roles. This is how the exhibitor from San Diego expressed it:

> In the United States and maybe also in Mexico, Mexican cinema is maintained thanks to the humble Mexicans and to those who have had to abandon their family and their homeland to live better and not to imitate the "gringos," but for pure necessity. They are proud to be Mexicans, and to me they deserve a lot of respect. It's for them that I decided that on Tuesdays the movie theater will be used for different activities and not only to show movies. On Tuesdays we hold a contest for amateur singers, and you should see how beautiful Mexico feels here. With this we promote something that is very Mexican, which is music, specifically Mexican songs. The movie theater gets full and people of all ages compete. We're searching that our roots are not forgotten and that Mexicans feel pride in being, and this public is doing it through cinema and music. Cinema is the only amusement that is within reach of our Mexican families. We should all do something to maintain it. The public deserves it, let us have respect. Our clientele is my race, it's good, noble, and one to whom I owe all respect. Those who do not respect their race have no forgiveness from God.[10]

There is no doubt about the importance of these messages to the lives of the audiences. For this reason it is even more necessary to seek a way that conciliates the making of commercial cinema with a worthy representation of the border. We know that the representation of reality is compatible with an entertaining cinema, as the history of chicano, Brazilian, and European cinema shows us. Indeed, the film industry, entertainment, and art are all compatible. It is necessary to criticize the erosion of the Mexican film industry. We must argue for the need for research and for a commitment to authentic cinematic representations that take into account not only the reality of the images but also the reality of the history and experiences of the audience to whom the films are addressed. The fact that in 275 films about the border, the participation of people from the border was missing, is very significant, especially when we know that they are the ones who constitute the principal audience of this genre.

Movies are not merely individual and vain expressions of a film director. Instead, the cinema "constitutes one of the instruments which a society makes use of to put itself on stage to display itself."[11] We know that the audience of border films, especially in the United States, expects a lot from them, that they value and have a feeling for their border culture—a feeling that has been ignored by the producers. By acknowledging the important cultural role of these films in the border population, a more realistic and critical projection of the border will be presented.

Notes

1. This article is part of a wider research project entitled "The Vision of the Border Through Mexican Cinema." The project was divided into four parts: production, analysis of the message (the movies), the audience, and the process of reception. In this document, only the last two are discussed.

2. They are those workers whose job is to select the movies that are going to be exhibited in theaters in predetermined sections of the country. In the selection, they take into account socioeconomic characteristics of the audience who attends each theater that they control.

3. The polls were determined by taking into account two questions: the city referred to (Tijuana and San Diego) and the type of film (Mexican border and Mexican non-border cinema). The poll contained twenty-three semiopen variables.

4. El Colegio de la Frontera Norte, *Encuesta socioeconómica anual de la Frontera* (Tijuana, 1987).

5. Pierre Sorlin, *Sociología del cine* (México: Fondo de Cultura Económica, 1985),

6. Interview with Mrs. Muñoz, Bay Theater, National City, California, June 1989.

7. Ibid.

8. Interview with Rubén Galindo, México, D.F., October 6, 1988.

9. Gabriel Careaga, *Estrellas de cine* (Mexico: Oceano, 1984), 9.

10. Juan J. Torres, *Owners and Exhibitors of the Bay Theater* (San Diego, 1989).

11. Sorlin, *Sociología del cine,* 252.

Bibliography

Ayala Blanco, Jorge. *La aventura del cine mexicano*. 4th ed., México: Posada, 1985.

———. *La búsqueda del cine mexicano*. 2d ed. México: Posada, 1986.

———. *La condición del cine mexicano*. México: Posada, 1986.

Bertetto, Paolo. *Cine, fábrica y vanguardia*. Barcelona, Spain: Gusta Gili, 1977.

Bettetini, Gianfranco. *Cine: Lengua y escritura*. México: Fondo de Cultura Económica, 1975.

Bustillo Oro, Juan. *Vida cinematográfica*. México: Cineteca Nacional, 1984.

Careaga, Gabriel. *Erotismo, violencia y política en el cine*. México: Joaquín Mortiz, 1981.

―――. *Estrellas de cine. Los mitos del siglo XX*. México: Océano, 1984.

Costa, Antonio. *Saber ver el cine*. Barcelona, Spain: Paidós, 1988.

Creel, Charles, Mercedes and Guillermo Orozco G. *Educación para recepción. Hacia una lectura crítica de los medios*. México: Trillas, 1990.

Estudios Churubusco. *La fábrica de suenos. Estudios Churubusco, 1945–1985*. México: Instituto Mexicano de Cinematografía, 1985.

Fregoso, Rosa Linda. *Bronze Screen: Chicana and Chicano Film Culture*. Minneapolis: University of Minnesota Press. 1995.

Galindo, Alejandro. *¿Qué es el cine?* México: Nuestro Tiempo, 1975.

―――. *Verdad y mentira del cine mexicano*. México: Katun, 1981.

García Canclini, Nestor. "Escenas sin territorio: Cultura de los migrantes e identidades en transición," in *Decadencia y auge de las identidades. Cultura nacional, identidad cultural y modernización*, pp. 119–31. Tijuana: El Colegio de la Frontera Norte, Programa Cultural de las Fronteras, 1992.

García Riera, Emilio. *Historia documental del cine mexicano*. 10 vols. México: ERA, 1978.

―――. *Historia del cine mexicano*. México: Secretaría de Educación Pública (Foro 2000), 1985.

Greer, Germaine. "La magia entrañable. Entrevista con Federico Fellini," *La Jornada* 3 (México) (July 2, 1989): 16.

Gutiérrez Alea, Tomás. *Dialéctica del espectador*. México: Federación Editorial Mexicana, 1983.

Iglesias Prieto, Norma. *Entre yerba, polvo y plomo. Lo fronterizo visto por el cine mexicano*. Tijuana: El Colegio de la Frontera Norte, 1991.

―――. *La visión de la frontera a través del cine mexicano*. Tijuana: Centro de Estudios Fronterizos del Norte de México, 1985.

Keller, Gary, et al. *Chicano Cinema: Research, Reviews and Resources*. Binghamton, NY: Bilingual Review Press, 1985.

Películas Nacionales. *Catálogo de distribución cinematográfica, 1982*. México: Películas Nacionales, 1983.

―――. "Películas Mexicanas," 1983, 1984, 1985, 1986, 1987 (mimeo).

Posada, Pablo Humberto. *Apreciación de cine*. Reprint. México: Alhambra Mexicana-Universidad Iberoamericana, Plantel Golfo Centro, 1984.

Solórzano, Javier. "El nuevo cine en México, entrevista a Emilio García Riera" *Comunicación y Cultura* 5 (México) (March 1978): 7–18.

Sorlin, Pierre, *Sociología del cine. La apertura para la historia del mañana*. 1st ed. México: Fondo de Cultura Económica, 1985.

Trevino, Jesús. "Presencia del cine mexicano," in *A través de la frontera.* México: Centro de Estudios Económicos y Sociales del Tercer Mundo— Instituto de Investigaciones Estéticas de la UNAM, 1983.

Wolf, Mauro. *La investigación de la comunicación de masas. Crítica y perspectivas.* 1st ed. Barcelona, Spain: Paidós, 1987.

11

Women and Gender Representation in the Contemporary Cinema of Mexico

David R. Maciel and Joanne Hershfield

In the last decade the cinema of Mexico has been undergoing a remarkable resurgence. Current generations of filmmakers have introduced fresh new themes, novel artistic discourses, and innovative approaches to the production process, and, most important, have begun to attract sizable national and international audiences. This present artistic ambiance has also prompted veteran directors to return to their craft. Recent films have not only received acclaim and impressive box-office returns in Mexico but also have earned prestigious international awards at such film festivals as Berlin, Cannes, Havana, Moscow, San Sebastian, Toronto, and Venice. In fact, between 1991 and 1992, Mexican films received forty-five major awards at international festivals,[1] thus verifying that Mexican cinema today is unquestionably the leading artistic cinema in Latin America.[2]

One factor that accounts for this flowering is the increased participation of women in a multitude of key aspects of filmmaking, primarily as directors. A second factor is the emphasis upon women's stories in recent productions. Although women historically have been an integral part of Mexican cinema, their presence was almost exclusively in the field of acting.[3] Legendary stars of the Golden Age (1940–1954) such as María Félix and Dolores del Río, among others, certainly left a rich tradition and even reached *diva* status.[4] Yet, principally because of machismo and institutionalized sexism, women were excluded from other spheres of filmmaking, a situation that remained static until the 1970s.[5] In the late 1970s and early 1980s this situation began to change. Progressively, as women graduated from film schools and earned practical experience, they moved up the ladder and into the forefront of Mexican cinema. By the mid-1980s women had become a visible and influential force within the film industry. The end result has been that, for the first time in the history of the cinema of Mexico, women are participating in almost all aspects of filmmaking.6

Three major reasons contribute to this dramatic turnabout. First, the changing status of women in cinema mirrors the country as a whole. Various scholars have postulated that one of the most profound societal changes in contemporary Mexico has been the evolving role of women and the rise of feminism.7 Because of the recurring economic crisis, women have had to enter the labor force in record numbers. In addition, they enrolled in universities in impressive percentages in the 1960s and 1970s. Thus, by the 1980s women occupied certain positions and spaces traditionally held only by men.8

Second, during this same period, the two film schools—the Centro Universitario de Estudios Cinematográficos (CUEC) of the Universidad Nacional Autónoma de México and the Centro de Capacitación Cinematográfica (CCC)—had been maturing and consolidating their study programs.9 Various filmmakers from before and after the crisis of 1968 taught and contributed their expertise to the incoming students in the 1980s and 1990s.10 Besides recruiting excellent faculty, the film schools received solid financial support from university administrators and from the state. The contemporary generations of graduates in film studies included a record number of women students who specialized not only in film direction but also in other spheres of filmmaking. As a former student who is now a prominent director recalled, "In the 1970s, there were few women students in the CUEC. By the 1980s, there were already eighty female students there. Meanwhile in the CCC, at the end of the 1980s, the majority of the students were women."11

And third, the demise of the once-powerful unions in the film industry by the late 1970s was also an important factor that contributed to the opening of the industry to women. In previous decades the union leadership had the power to control who was admitted into syndicate ranks and thus allowed to work within the film industry. The top officials of the unions were male, and they tended to be traditional in their attitudes toward women. By design, their policies excluded women from participation. For example, there existed a written clause in the union's charter that banned women from serving as assistant film directors. This condition was detrimental in many ways, especially since the task of serving as assistant director is critical in the learning process of any prospective director.12 María Novaro elaborates on this issue by pointing out that "the film unions were a legacy of the Golden Age . . . they were antiquated and weighed heavily on the industry. . . . I think that there were very pernicious processes in many of the powerful unions. Evidently they had a strong command over the industry and, because of that, it is my understanding that they were one of the most *machista* institutions imaginable . . . with their constraints, they impeded the incorporation of new generations of filmmakers and stifled Mexican cinema."13

CLASA FILMS, presenta Una Producción de FRANCISCO y PABLO BARBACHANO
LETICIA PERDIGON
SOCORRO BONILLA **ANOCHE SOÑE CONTIGO**
MOISES IVAN MORA
PATRICIA AGUIRRE · MARTIN ALTOMARO · JOSE ALONSO   Dirección MARYSE SISTACH

Maryse Sistach directs Anoche Soñe Contigo.

For the first time ever in the Mexican film industry, women are visible behind the camera as directors, producers, and screenwriters as well as in technical positions. This phenomenon distinguishes Mexican cinema from almost any other national cinema today. A record number of women directors have debuted with feature films within the last ten years. At no other time has there been such a significant number of women directors; in fact, there had been only a few major ones prior to this recent period.14 Unique in the history of Mexico's cinema is the fact that over one-third of the directors of the generation of the 1990s are women, including María Novaro, Busi Cortés, Dana Rotberg, Sabina Berman, Guita Schyfter, Maryse Sistach, and María Elena Velasco, all of whom have already completed at least two narrative feature films. In addition to the emergence of these new directors, two veterans—Matilde Landeta and

Marcela Fernández Violante—each made a narrative film during this decade, while Alejandra Moya, Valentina Leduc Navarro, and Silvana Zuanetti completed important shorts and documentaries.[15]

Many women directors, such as Maryse Sistach, write their own screenplays; others team up with a female coscreenwriter, as in the case of Busi Cortés and her sister Carmen Cortés, María Novaro and her sister Beatríz Novaro, and Guita Schyfter with Rosa Nissan. An increasing number of women writers have developed their own scripts that have been brought to the screen by other directors. Susana Cato, María del Pozo, Dominique Dufatel, Laura Esquivel, Alicia García, Paz Alicia Garciadiego, Consuelo Garrido, Guadalupe Ortega Vargas, Cecilia Pérez Grovas, and Lidia Torres Fernández have each had at least one of their scripts produced.[16] Women also have made great strides in the production area and are now handling a good deal of the executive production of contemporary films. The most notable of these producers are Dulce Kuri (*Danzón*, 1992), Bertha Navarro (*Cabeza de Vaca*, 1989), Alma Rossbach (*Miroslava*, 1993), Georgina Terán (*Serpientes y Escaleras*, 1981), and Catalina Zepeda Aranda (*Gertrudis*, 1992).

As in every social movement, the success of women in the contemporary cinema of Mexico had its immediate precursors. An im-

Publicity photo for the film Gertrudis, *directed by Ernesto Medina and starring Ofelia Medina.*

portant first step was the founding of the Colectivo Cine-Mujer in the late 1970s. As one recent scholar notes, "The Colectivo denounced the oppression of women in capitalist society. It addressed themes previously forbidden . . . . It attacked the dominant attitude that censured female pleasure; it did not accept the expropriation of the female body by the law or the Church. Likewise, it opposed the attitude that all women who were raped are at fault or at least suspect."[17] The group was made up principally of students from film studies but also from other disciplines—anthropology, psychology, and sociology. Among the most active members were its founders, Rosa Martha Fernández and Beatríz Mira, and such women as Amalia Attolini, Pilar Calvo, Ellen Camus, Sonia Fritz, Sibelle Hayen, Ana Victoria Jiménez, María del Carmen de Lara, Mónica Mae, Angeles Necoechea, María Novaro, Laura Rosetti, María Eugenia Tamés, and Guadalupe Sánchez. The Colectivo Cine-Mujer was an integral part of the rise of independent feature cinema in Mexico, a movement defined by its films, which were produced outside the confines of the major film studios. Moreover, the Colectivo, an essential chapter in the development of the documentary genre, saw itself as part of a greater moment of feminism in international cinema.[18]

This pioneer organization of women filmmakers was premised upon activism as well as upon the construction of a feminist cinematic discourse that addressed women's issues on the screen. As Margarita Millán Moncayo has stated:

> The films of the Colectivo had the undeniable virtue of treating issues that were not discussed prior to those years, such as abortion and sexual abuse, and highlighting others that emerged as the beginnings of a collective consciousness, such as the consideration of domestic labor, the condition of woman as object, the relation of women with sexuality, and the position of women in oppressed classes. In addition, it was a cinema that aspired to distribution outside the commercial circuit—in schools, factories, and hospitals.[19]

The legacy and significance of the Colectivo Cine-Mujer was twofold: to introduce and raise the consciousness of feminism and women's issues in cinema; and to pressure for greater opportunities for women in the film industry. Moreover, for the members of the Colectivo, the experience of participation in a collective cinematic project was seminal. As Millán Moncayo's study has noted:

> The women in cinema sought another way of telling stories, more personal, more removed from politics, looking at the political from the focus of the personal . . . . They adopted a point of view that recognized feminism as an effect of personal experience. Ideological mandates vanish in

favor of authentic exploration marked by the necessity of introspection. They are women who interrogate themselves, who act as themselves, who reveal themselves. And through this process, history as well as the image gains strength and reality. It is the subject who has the voice.[20]

The Colectivo Cine-Mujer produced a number of important and pioneering documentaries on women's issues, such as *Cosas de Mujeres* (1975), a short that dealt with abortion, and *Rompiendo el Silencio* (1979), a hard-hitting documentary on rape and violence toward women, directed by Rosa Martha Fernández; *¿Y Si Eres Mujer?* (1979), a clever animated short by Guadalupe Sánchez on the consumer barrage directed at women; *Vida de Angel* (1981), a documentary by Angeles Necoechea on domestic work; *No Es por Gusto* (1981), a pioneer documentary by María Eugenia Tamés and María del Carmen de Lara that focuses on prostitution in Mexico City; and *Es Primera* (1981), a short by Beatríz Mira on a celebrated feminist Congress held in Mexico. By the 1980s the work of the Colectivo Cine-Mujer declined and the group ultimately disbanded. Material and ideological conditions in Mexico were dramatically different and changing at a fast pace while the cinematic production format and technology also had moved in different directions. Yet the contributions of the Colectivo were instrumental to the rise of feminism in cinema and to the future participation of women in the commercial film industry.

It would be almost a decade later that the next major stage for women in Mexican cinema would emerge. Whereas the previous generation concentrated on the documentary and 16mm. format, the succeeding group of women filmmakers would contribute narrative features produced, for the most part, within the parameters of the industry. Their films were co-produced by the state or produced with money from the private sector.

Women directors have completed more than sixteen full-length narrative films in less than a decade. In less than ten years, they have directed more productions in Mexico than in the last one hundred years of the country's film history. In general, these directors of the 1980s and 1990s share the following characteristics:

1. Conceptually, the cinema of women's lives in the recent era can be categorized as *auteur* cinema, where the director's own personal narrative style and thematic elements stand out. In most *auteur* films, the director is intimately involved in most of the critical elements of the movies— directing, screenwriting, editing, and final cut.
2. Collectively, these women directors characterize their films as *cine de mujer*, or woman's cinema. These films offer "a

feminist viewpoint that intervenes not only in the themes of the films but also in the construction of the image, the spatial-temporal priorities, the feelings and relations."[21]

3. Unlike previous directors who studied filmmaking in Eastern or Western Europe, the Soviet Union, or the United States, the women of this generation studied and received their entire film training in Mexico.[22]

4. The influence of the documentary filmmaking tradition is evident in their productions. Many of these directors have made important documentaries, and several still make both narrative and documentary films. Additionally, documentary styles and techniques are evident in the fiction films of Busi Cortés and Marisa Sistach, among others.

5. These woman directors, as a whole, are part of a filmic generation that is perhaps the youngest ever.

6. Unlike previous directors, members of this generation have established more control over most aspects of their productions. The material conditions of the country and the current cinematic policies have forced these young directors to become more creative in terms of financing and production techniques and involved in all aspects of filmmaking, including fund-raising, production, exhibition, publicity, and even distribution.[23]

Women and Women's Issues in Contemporary Films

Many films by women directors feature female protagonists in stories that are specifically concerned with women's lives. These films contest the ways in which the classical Mexican cinema has portrayed women either as virtuous and suffering mothers, seduced and abandoned young girls, or outright *mala mujeres* (bad women). Important and complex roles finally have been written for women, who are portrayed in a variety of settings and represent all age groups, social classes, and professions. Recent women characters are diverse, multidimensional, and reflective of the complexity of contemporary society.[24] Women directors have appropriated and transformed traditional cinematic conventions in order to tell stories about and for women that pay attention to the changing nature of social relations in Mexico's history and within current social conditions.[25]

Although these directors focus on women's stories, there are major differences in their aesthetic approaches, themes addressed, and narrative discourses. For example, Busi Cortés seeks to construct

Director Dana Rotberg on the set of Angel de Fuego.

an intimate cinema with touches of magical realism within an innovative reading of family relationships. María Novaro defines her cinema as a *cine de autor* that reflects her individual dreams and reality while addressing gender consciousness. Maryse Sistach attempts to combine a *cine de mujer* with a commercial one without losing emphasis on a solid narrative that incorporates a woman's perspective into the popular filmic discourse.

The effects of the profound economic, political, and social crisis of twentieth-century Mexico upon members and sectors of society—particularly women—is one central theme in contemporary cinema, and many of the recent female characters are portrayed in a struggle against this crisis. Another recurrent theme is that of unconventional relationships. The messages are similar in features such as *Danzón, Lola* (1989), *Los Pasos de Ana* (1988–89), and *Serpientes y Escaleras*—relationships for both women and men can and do serve different needs, but these relationships are less stable than at any time in the past, and few last forever. No longer is the image projected of fixed gender roles, conventional heterosexual couples, or traditional family structures. In fact, the disintegration of the family and its values is strikingly visible in recent films. Alternative life-styles, sexuality expressed outside of marriage, a concern with individual survival, and the loss of optimism for the future seem to be the norm for these new women characters.

Publicity photo of the film Serpientes y Escaleras, *directed by Busi Cortés and starring Arcelia Ramírez and Lumi Cavazos.*

Lola, *Los Pasos de Ana*, and *Danzón* deal with single mothers and their search for self-discovery and survival within their own modern reality. Both María Novaro's *Lola* and Marisa Sistach's *Los Pasos de Ana* vividly recount a woman's attempt to reconcile the pursuit of career, motherhood, and intimate relationships. The two films portray the harsh realities of urban life as faced by single women who are the heads of their households in the Mexico of today.

Danzón, María Novaro's second work, is a modern-day version of the classical cabaretera, or dance-hall film. Those earlier movies featured good women who were forced by economic necessity into selling their bodies. In *Danzón*, dancing is celebrated for the pleasure it brings to women rather than the shame. Novaro's film convincingly traces the odyssey of Julia (María Rojo) in her search for meaning to her life and independence from her everyday routine as a single mother and telephone operator. Her passion is dancing, and it is in the dance halls of Mexico City's suburbs where she spends her evenings. When Carmelo, her dancing partner, disappears, Julia travels to Vera Cruz in search of him. While Carmelo is nowhere to be found, Julia discovers herself with the help of a transvestite named Suzi, a young mother who works as a prostitute to support her fatherless children, and an older woman who runs a hotel and who has gone through many men.

Film poster of Danzón, *directed by María Novaro.*

Unlike earlier Mexican cinematic representations of women, femininity in this film is not defined in opposition to masculinity. In fact, men do not figure at all in *Danzón* except in conventional feminized roles. And women are not the passive objects of the man's gaze. Each of the women whom we encounter—from Julia's teenage daughter to the prostitute, Rojo, to Suzi—is portrayed as a person whose self-reliance is not dependent on the whims of men, as in the classical narratives, but on her own strengths and on the support of other women. For Julia and her daughter, it is the help provided by the female telephone operators whom they work with; for the prostitute, Rojo, it is the mother figure—the woman who runs the hotel where she lives and who takes care of her infant son while she works; for Suzi, it is her transvestite friends who confirm the identity that she has chosen for herself. And throughout the narrative, it is Julia who occupies the traditional masculine position of the pursuer, seducer, desirer, and possessor of the gaze.

Danzón shares with other recent women's films a focus on women's daily lives. *Lola*, *Los Pasos de Ana*, and *Danzón* document, narrativize, and represent the distinctive unconscious and social realities of women's experiences. Meaningful change does not usually occur in the wider arena of social or political relations for women, especially for lower-class women who typically lack access to political and social power, but in the narrower and more personal realm of everyday life. Thus, these films emphasize the spaces in which women's lives take place (bathrooms, kitchens, places of work, children's rooms and playgrounds) and the relations that define their lives (divorced husbands, faithless lovers, their young children and teenagers moving into independence and adulthood).[26]

A number of contemporary films by women question Mexico's traditional notion of national identity. *Novia Que Te Vea* (1993), Guita Schyfter's first work, confronts problems of ethnicity, feminism, identity, and national culture. It is a coming-of-age story told in flashback through an extended conversation between two Jewish women, Rifke and Oshi, whose families emigrated to Mexico and who grew up in Mexico City in the turbulent 1950s and 1960s. Like many classical films, this one confronts the postrevolutionary myth of *la gran familia mexicana*. While this film focuses on the ways in which Jews were socially and culturally set apart from the Catholic majority, it also highlights the differences between Jewish groups in Mexico—differences based on cultural heritage and religious and cultural practices. The central question posed by Schyfter's film seems to be whether or not the notion of difference needs to be retained or discarded in Mexico's continuing search for an "authentic" national identity.

Rifke's family, Ashkenazi Jews from Poland, fled when Hitler came to power in the 1930s. Oshi's grandparents, Sephardic Jews from Turkey, went to Mexico in the late 1920s.[27] Both the Eastern European Ashkenazis and the Southern European Sephardim ghettoized themselves in that part of Mexico City known as Lagunilla. While the two girls grew up in very different familial and social environments, Oshi and Rifke both felt excluded from the narrowly defined parameters of Mexican identity because of their Jewishness.

Novia Que Te Vea questions national identity within the boundaries of melodrama. Like the traditional melodramas of the Golden Age, Rifke and Oshi's ambivalence about their identities is represented through their relationships with men. Rifke falls in love with a young Mexican, Saavedra, a committed Marxist who is the son of a prominent and well-to-do liberal politician. The romance is opposed by her parents, who expect her to marry a Jew. Oshi, also risking the wrath of her parents, rejects an arranged marriage to a young doctor who refuses to acknowledge her desire to be a painter, an identity apart from that of a traditional Sephardic wife and mother.

Unlike traditional melodramas, however, this film ends on a hopeful note: Oshi and Rifke have both taken their lives and their futures into their own hands. While both women have retained their Jewishness, each has also realized that her identity as a Mexican is not compromised by this choice. Rifka marries Saavedra and names her son Pedro instead of Abraham, while Oshi marries Ari, an old Jewish friend. Unlike the doctor whom Oshi's parents chose for her, Ari rejects the restrictive religious and cultural traditions that Oshi's family brought over from the "old country." He and Oshi have forged another kind of Jewishness, one that embraces their sense of identities as Mexicans.

Biographies of celebrated feminine figures are also a clear trend of the cinema of the 1990s. Film and television star Ofelia Medina, who had already masterfully portrayed the legendary painter Frida Kahlo, played two important historical and cultural figures of Mexico's past. Director Ernesto Medina brought to the screen *Gertrudis Bocanegra*, the story of a woman who took part in the War of Independence in 1812. And Golden Age veteran director Matilde Landeta returned to the screen after a thirty-year absence with *Nocturno a Rosarío*, while re-creates the cultural and social ambiance of Mexico City in the nineteenth century through the relationship of two of the best-known literary figures of that era, poet Manuel Acuña and celebrated intellectual *diva* Rosario de la Peña, played by Medina.

Features such as *El Secreto de Romelia* (1988) and *Serpientes y Escaleras*, both directed by Busi Cortés, also reframe history through the lens of a woman's life. In *El Secreto de Romelia*, based on a short novel, *El Viuda Roman*, by Mexican writer Rosario Castellanos, three generations of women's personal lives are interwoven with political and social history. Unlike Castellanos's novel, which takes place in the 1930s, the film uses flashbacks to move back and forth between the 1930s and the present. Cortés's film is narrated through the perspectives of an elderly woman named Romelia, her daughter Dolores, and Dolores's daughters. The flashbacks enable the viewer to connect historical social discourses about sexuality to contemporary discourses.[28] The dialogue is structured through conversations about sexuality and sexual relations between Romelia and her daughter, between Dolores and her daughters, and between Romelia and her granddaughters.

Following the death of her former husband, Dr. Román, Romelia returns to her rural childhood home with her daughter and granddaughters to settle the estate. The film proceeds to unravel Romelia's humiliating "secret"—Román had married her out of revenge and then dismissed her on the day after their wedding, never knowing that she bore his daughter nine months later. This secret is revealed through the interplay between Romelia's vocalized memories and Román's letters, which are discovered by the granddaughters.

Through repeated linkings of personal history with social history, *El Secreto de Romelia* reminds us that ideological oppression occurs across and within the social and individual spheres of gender relations as well as those of class and race. Romelia's family vehemently opposed President Lázaro Cárdenas's reformist policies in the 1930s.[29] When her granddaughter informs her that Cárdenas "was the best President Mexico ever had, he was for the people," Romelia smiles cynically. "Ah, but which people?" she asks. "After he gave the land to the Indians, everything fell apart." In the 1930s in Mexico, the politics of repression was forced upon the bodies of women as well as upon Indians. Romelia, a member of a privileged white upper-class family, could not see the relation of oppression she shared with the Indians. Similarly, Dr. Román, who was a socialist committed to land and social reforms, exploited his position as a white male in a rigid patriarchal society in order to avenge his injured male ego by destroying Romelia's life.

Like *Novia Que Te Vea*, Cortés's *Serpientes y Escaleras* uses the friendship of two young women, Rebecca and Valentina, as the driving narrative force. The film, whose title is borrowed from a children's board game of "chance and destiny," is based on a novel by Angeles Mastreta, *Arráncame la Vida*. Through the melodrama of familial relations, *Serpientes y Escaleras* examines the link between Mexican postrevolutionary politics and patriarchy, between *machismo* and state paternalism, in a story that traces the intertwining lives of Rebecca and Valentina from their childhood in the 1940s to the brink of womanhood in the 1950s.

Unlike the narratives of classical Mexican cinema that focused on romantic relationships, the friendship between the two women lies at the center of this familial narrative. Their relations with men— lovers and fathers—circle around this central attachment. Female sexual desire is acknowledged and celebrated, as is the relation be- tween mothers and daughters. However, it is the bond between Rebecca and Valentina, sanctified in blood as children, that gives the women strength and their lives meaning.

While most films by women directors examine the lives of middle- and upper-class women, others, such as Dana Rotberg's *Angel de Fuego* (1992), look at women on the fringes of society. *Angel de Fuego* is an unconventional story about a thirteen-year-old girl, Alma, a fire-eater in the circus, who must fend for herself after being evicted by the circus boss because she is pregnant. This film is obviously allegorical in style, theme, and aesthetics. Alma and a num- ber of other female characters represent the eternal suffering of women forced to play the dual role of mother and whore. Visually and narratively these women portray different aspects of Catholicism's Virgin Mother, Mary. Alma in *Angel de Fuego* is no virgin and has committed incest, one of the most carnal sins in Catholic theology. Yet, like the Virgin Mary, she is carrying her "father's child"; and, ac- cording to her circus family, "she will give birth to a monster" or a figure not quite human. Rather than have an abortion, Alma goes to Mexico City and tries to make a living as one of the many fire-eaters performing on the busy corners of the city's streets. When fits of coughing end this brief career, Alma joins a band of traveling pup- peteers, headed by another Mary figure, who preach a strange mixture of Catholic and Indian theology. The audiences of these performers are the poorest of the poor, whose lives are so peripheral to the func- tioning of the state that politics has no meaning for them. The leader of the band, an older woman with two sons, is a prophet for these peo- ple, who have no stake in Mexico's past or future. All she can do is write their names down in her Book of Life and bless them.

The puppeteers' show re-creates the Biblical story of God's command to Abraham to sacrifice his only son. The film inverts this story, however, and forces both Alma and the prophet to sacrifice their sons to God—Alma through a miscarriage caused by the prophet, and the prophet's son through suicide. He refuses to be the Jesus-like celibate his mother wants him to be. Unlike the other films discussed above, Rotberg's offers no hope for its female audi- ence. While Alma ravages those who destroyed her happiness and her hope, this destruction comes at the cost of her life. In the final scene, the *angel de fuego* dies in the flames of fire that sustained her in life.

Conclusion

Even with the impressive gains outlined above, the status of women in the Mexican film industry is mixed. There still exist certain areas of filmmaking that remain resistant to real change; for example, cinematography is the principal area that is still totally represented by men. The guild of cinematographers has been less than open or encouraging toward women as directors of photography, and a number of sexist perceptions persist within the guild. Two of the most common are that cameras are too heavy for women to carry or move adequately[30] and that women are better suited for artistic endeavors than for technical ones.

Another field in the industry where change has not come about for women is in administrative appointments of film units. Men currently hold all senior administrative positions of cinema entities at IMCINE, the two leading film schools, the Cineteca Nacional, the Filmoteca of the Universidad Nacional Autónoma de México, and the Centro de Investigación y Estudios Cinematográficos at the Universidad de Guadalajara. This situation mirrors national trends. The upper echelons of power in Mexico are still dominated by men.

The significant gains by women within the film industry are tenuous and are intimately tied to the fortunes of the country and its national cinema. Mexico is in the midst of a deep economic downturn and a grave crisis of the dominant political order, which has affected every aspect of the nation's life. All projects and initiatives in the arts have been reduced, and filmmakers will be hardpressed to secure funding in the near future. The devaluation of the peso and the accompanying inflation have compounded the adversity. And an acute lack of space for exhibition of Mexican cinema remains.

On the other hand, the much-proven talent and creative energy of aspiring and established women filmmakers will act as a catalyst to overcome difficulties.[31] These women will not let this latest crisis be an absolute deterrent to the development of the cinema of women's lives. Women filmmakers are used to laboring in a climate of adversity and struggle.[32] The *mujeres insumisas*[33] of the cinema are aggressive, self-reliant, and tenacious, and they will continue to grow and mature while persevering with their contribution toward a unique new vision in the cinematic discourse of contemporary Mexico.

Films such as *Lola, Danzón, Angel de Fuego, Novia Que Te Vea, El Secreto de Romelia,* and *Serpientes y Escaleras* are narratives about women's search for identities that are not defined by social boundaries of gender or by economic function but by individual desire. The character of Ana in Sistach's film, *Los Pasos de Ana,* sums it up best in the concluding scene: "Each one of us copes and manages to survive in her individual way, and mine is through the eyes of the lens."

Notes

1. Héctor Rivera, "Con el resurgimiento de nuestro cine, México volverá a sonar en los premios de Cannes," *Proceso* (May 18, 1992): 48–51.
2. David R. Maciel, "The Cinematic Renascence of Contemporary Mexico," *Spectator* 13:1 (Fall 1992).
3. Emilio García Riera, *Historia del cine mexicano* (México: Secretaría de Educación Pública, 1985), 134.
4. Interview with Gustavo García, Mexico City, July 19, 1995.
5. Interview with Marcela Fernández Violante, Mexico City, July 3, 1994.
6. Interview with Leticia Huijara, Mexico City, June 19, 1995.
7. Interview with Carlos Monsiváis, Mexico City, July 28, 1995.
8. Interview with Alejandro Pelayo, Mexico City, July 30, 1995.
9. Gustavo García, "Retrato del cineasta adolescente," *Intolerancia* 4 (1985): 2–10.
10. Interview with Eduardo de La Vega, Mexico City, June 28, 1994.
11. Margarita Millán Moncayo, "Género y representación en tres directoras de cine en México." (Master's thesis, Department of Sociology, UNAM, May 1995), 58.
12. Interview with Dana Rotberg, Stanford, California, April 19, 1990.
13. Millán, "Género y representación," 135.
14. Interview with Marisa Sistach, Mexico City, May 31, 1994.
15. Susana López Aranda et al., "Cine mexicano actual," *Dicine* (August–September 1992): 66–70.
16. Interview with Busi Cortés, Mexico City, May 30, 1993.
17. Millán, *Género y representación,* 45.
18. Jorge Ayala Blanco, *La condición del cine mexicano* (México: Editorial Posada, 1986), 447–48.
19. Millán, *Género y representación,* 45.
20. Ibid., 49.
21. Ibid., 43.
22. Interview with Eva López Sánchez, Mexico City, July 6, 1994.
23. López Aranda et al., "Cine mexicano actual," 64–73.
24. Interview with Cortés.
25. See Carlos Monsiváis, "El fin de la diosa arrodillada," *NEXOS* (February 1992): 79–82; and Joanne Hershfield, "Women's Pictures: Identity and Representation in Recent Mexican Cinema," *Canadian Journal of Film Studies* 6, no.1 (Spring 1997): 61–77.
26. In her analysis of Chantal Akerman's *Jeanne Dielman, Quai du Commerce, 1080, Bruxelles* (1975), for example, Teresa de Lauretis writes that the film is feminist not because of its formal experimentation or technical superiority or because it does not rely on the shot-reverse-shot system of classical cinema, but because it is

"women's actions, gestures, body, and look that define the space of our vision." See "Rethinking Women's Cinema: Aesthetics and Feminist Theory" in *Multiple Voices in Feminist Film Criticism*, ed. Diane Carson, Linda Dittmar, and Janice R. Welsch (Minneapolis: University of Minnesota Press, 1994), 144.

27. Jews divide themselves into two major historical families: the Ashkenazi, whose ancestors came from the region now known as Eastern Europe and who spoke European languages such as German, Ukrainian, Romanian, and Russian; and the Sephardim, who trace their ancestry to Spain and North Africa and who spoke Ladino, a language very similar to Castilian Spanish.

28. See Maureen Turim's *Flashbacks in Film: Memory and History* (New York: Routledge, 1989) for a discussion of the temporal function of film flashbacks.

29. Much of Castellanos's work is somewhat autobiographical. She grew up in the state of Chiapas, the daughter of a wealthy landowner who opposed Cárdenas. When her parents died, she dispersed her inheritance, both land and money, among the Indians who had lived on the family's property for generations.

30. Interview with Alejandra Islas, Mexico City, June 21, 1994.

31. Interview with Gabriela Roel, Mexico City, November 19, 1995.

32. Interview with Lumi Cavazos, Albuquerque, New Mexico, May 1, 1994.

33. A reference to the title of the 1995 film directed by Alberto Isaacs, *Mujeres Insumisas*, which may be translated as "unsubmissive women."

12

Authentically Mexican?
Mi Querido Tom Mix and *Cronos* Reframe
Critical Questions

*Ann Marie Stock**

The notion of an authentic culture as an autonomous and internally coherent universe is no longer sustainable except perhaps as a "useful fiction"or a revealing distortion.

—*Renato Rosaldo*

In Frida Kahlo's 1932 "Self-Portrait on the Borderline between Mexico and the United States," the painter has centered herself on the canvas. Her image simultaneously conjoins and separates the two worlds: the left half of the composition with a crumbling pyramid, prehistoric figurines, and a maguey cactus represents Mexico; the right, with Ford factory smokestacks, the starred and striped flag, and skyscrapers, evokes the United States. From this position "on the borderline," Kahlo has acknowledged the power of expressive culture to draw the lines; and, in portraying the artist as gazing off the canvas, she has alluded to the complicity of artist, text, and critic in that process.

Situated between the two territories, the self-portrait prophesies the artist's trajectory some sixty years later. Kahlo "speaks to the '90s," according to the *New York Times*, for, as "a Hispanic woman, bisexual, an invalid, and an artist [she has] all the qualifications for a cult figure; even Madonna is a fan."[1] She indeed has upstaged Madonna. Publications such as *Artnews* and *The Oxford Art Journal* have covered the Kahlo cult, and international fashion magazines, including *Elle* and *Vogue*, have featured the Frida Kahlo aesthetic.[2] The northern celebration of this southern artist would seem to consolidate her position on the borderline.

*I am grateful to Teresa Longo and Joanne Hershfield for their valuable comments during the preparation of this essay. Research for this project was supported by the College of William and Mary in the form of a Faculty Summer Research Grant and travel grants from the Charles Center for Interdisciplinary Studies.

Recent events in Hollywood, however, indicate an unwillingness to recognize Kahlo as a cultural migrant who moves between geopolitical territories and aesthetic spaces. When Luis Valdez selected Laura San Giacomo to play the lead in *Frida and Diego*, a film about Kahlo's relationship with Mexican muralist Diego Rivera, Latino actors and actresses in Los Angeles protested vehemently. They accused the Chicano playwright-director of "selling out," claiming that in casting an Italian-American rather than a Latina for this role, he was replicating Hollywood practices of marginalizing actors and actresses with accents. Valdez defended his decision. In a press release issued from the Teatro Campesino office in San Juan Bautista, he argued that he chose San Giacomo not because of her ethnicity but because of her marketable talent and resemblance to the Mexican painter. He then drew attention to Frida Kahlo's own complex heritage: she was "a child of America," conceived from the union of her "German-Jewish immigrant father and her Spanish-Indian (Mexican) mother." Valdez challenged the protesters' criterion of ethnic purity by asking, "Who is to say what determines the Latino identity if we start counting drops of blood?"[3] That Valdez—longtime activist and founding father of Chicano theater—was recently accused of selling out and denying his Hispanic heritage illustrates the resilience of authenticity claims. And that *Frida and Diego* was abandoned in the wake of such controversy indicates that such claims are not benign. This incident reveals what I term an "authenticity paradox"—that is, despite the migrancy of cultural practitioners and consumers, and despite the prevalence of textual hybridity, a critical insistence on authenticity prevails.

The tug-of-war between a critical discourse invested in authenticity, on the one hand, and a transnational cultural praxis, on the other, will be examined here. Two recent films illuminate this striking paradox: critics frame *Mi Querido Tom Mix* (Carlos García Agraz, 1992) and *Cronos* (Guillermo del Toro, 1992) in singular national terms despite their markedly international trajectories of production and circulation and their textual hybridity. Both films combine conventions from various genres, incorporate elements from Mexico's and Hollywood's cinema traditions, and blend Spanish and English. *Mi Querido Tom Mix* and *Cronos* indeed locate themselves on Frida Kahlo's borderline, and from that position they provide strategies for embracing rather than erasing contemporary culture. In drawing upon and reshaping Mexican and U.S. film traditions, these movies urge us to look beyond the confines of strict geopolitical parameters; and in directing their gaze toward the viewer/critic, they illuminate our complicity in cultural production. By reflecting on our framing of expressive culture, we will be less intent on delineating the "Mexican" features of films and policing the borders of "Mexican cinema," and better equipped to analyze the points of convergence between Mexico's rich tradition and other cinemas heretofore constructed in geopolitical terms. It is only by removing our authenticity blinders and meeting the gaze of films like these that we will be poised to make sense of cinema in a global era.

Claiming Authenticity: Cinema, Criticism, Identity

> Identity is not transparent; it is not unproblematic; it is no guarantee of authenticity.
>
> —*Stuart Hall*

"What remains of national identities in a time of globalization and interculturalism, of multinational coproduction and the Chain of the Americas, of free trade agreements and regional integration?" asks cultural critic Néstor García Canclini. "What remains when information, artists, and capital constantly cross borders?"[4] These questions, posed from within the context of post-NAFTA Mexico, resonate throughout Latin America where cinema has become increasingly transnational. Reduced budgets, devalued currencies, and increased production costs compel directors to seek collaborative financing. Even before reaching this stage in the filmmaking process, would-be directors often perfect their craft with international mentors in faraway places. The distribution of Latin American films, like the production and training, has also become increasingly transnational, and important venues for these films exist outside of the region. In the United States, for example, festivals such as those of Chicago, Los Angeles, New York, the Twin Cities, and Sundance showcase recent films, thereby enhancing the works' marketability abroad and back home; distributors such as Miramax transform Latin American films into international blockbusters and subsequently distribute them widely; and centers such as Video del Sur, the International Media Resource Exchange, and Cine-Acción promote Latino films and videos and facilitate their dissemination. Current production and distribution practices, then, are decidedly transnational.

The film texts themselves evidence this shift away from the strict geopolitical concerns that characterized the cinema movements of the 1960s, 1970s, and 1980s. Whereas adherents to revolutionary filmmaking—proponents of Cuban cinema, New Latin American Cinema, and Third Cinema, for example—lauded local places, faces, and histories and rejected Hollywood-style narratives and techniques, filmmakers working in the present decade strive to "universalize" their product. Severe economic crises and the corresponding reduction in state support have left filmmakers scrambling to recover most if not all of their production costs. In order to do so, their films must be carefully constructed so as to please viewers outside of the region. Some works, such as those of the late María Luisa Bemberg, increase their market potential by showcasing international talent and developing border-crossing narratives: *Miss Mary* (1986) casts Julie Christie as the British governess working in Argentina; *Yo la Peor de Todas* (1990) gives top billing to Spain's Asumpta de la Serna in the role of Sor Juana; and *De Eso No Se Habla* (1993) stars Italy's Marcello Mastroianni as the mysterious visitor. Other films feature migrancy and deterritorialization at the narrative level, themes of immediate concern to a variety of viewers: *Madagascar* (Fernando Pérez, 1994) and *El Viaje* (Fernando Solanas, 1992) constitute two examples. Still others locate themselves within a "cinemascape"; both *El Elefante y la Bicicleta* (Juan Carlos Tabio, 1995) and *El Amante de las Películas Mudas* (Pablo Torre, 1994) highlight the cinema rather than identifiable landscapes. The coding of these texts for international rather than local audiences reflects the larger tendency in the region.

Yet, despite the move away from a markedly geopolitical cinema in Latin America, critical discourse continues to privilege cultural authenticity. Let us consider *Mi Querido Tom Mix* and *Cronos*, two films that share transnational histories of production and projection. A combination of Mexican and international currencies supported the respective projects: *Mi Querido Tom Mix* was produced by Mexico's Amaranta with support from the Cuba-based Fundación del Nuevo Cine Latinoamericano; *Cronos* was financed by Mexico's Iguana Productions and Los Angeles-based Ventana Films. Internationally renowned acting talent enhances the appeal of each work: the popular Argentine actor, Federico Luppi, stars in both films—opposite Ana Ofelia Murguia in *Mi Querido Tom Mix*, and alongside Claudio Brook and Ron Perlman in *Cronos*.[5] Prominent professionals have been credited with offering guidance and support in all stages of the projects: Gabriel García Marquez directed the workshop in which Consuelo Garrido scripted *Mi Querido Tom Mix*; Del Toro consulted with Jaime Humberto Hermosillo in writing his screenplay and making the film.[6] Their respective production histories, then, clearly locate these films outside of strict national categories.

So, too, do the projection trajectories; these films have traveled widely. *Mi Querido Tom Mix* was featured at the International Festival of New Latin American Cinema in Havana, where Murguia was named Best Actress; at the Cartagena International Film Festival, where it was awarded the prize for Best Cinematography; and as part of the Mexican Film Series in Los Angeles. *Cronos* earned the top nine Ariel de Oro Awards (Mexico's Oscar equivalent), received the Critics Week Prize at the 1993 Cannes Film Festival, and was selected as Mexico's official entry for the Oscars in Hollywood. Del Toro's film was shown at festivals in Guadalajara, London, Los Angeles, New York, Toronto, and Sundance. Both screenplays earned prestigious Ariel prizes and have been published by Ediciones El Milagro in Mexico City.[7] The two films are distributed in Mexico as well as in the United States: the International Media Resource Exchange carries *Mi Querido Tom Mix*, and October

Actress Ana Ofelia Murguia and director Carlos García Agraz discuss Mi Querido Tom Mix *at a press conference held during the International Festival of New Latin American Cinema in Havana, December 1992. Photo by Ann Marie Stock.*

Films markets *Cronos*. The production and projection trajectories of these two films are not at all exceptional; rather, they correspond with the markedly extranational making and viewing of films in post-NAFTA Mexico as well as in the entire region.[8]

Critics, however, insist upon imbuing these films with a national identity, categorizing *Mi Querido Tom Mix* and *Cronos* as first and foremost Mexican films. The remarks of Miguel Barnet typify the reception of *Mi Querido Tom Mix*: the film "exudes an absolute

Mexicanness"; it is "authentically Mexican."[9] Critics employ the
same adjective with *Cronos*: "Guillermo del Toro Brings a Mexican
Perspective to Horror Films" reads the headline for Adriana S.
Pardo's article in the *Los Angeles Times*;[10] Anthony De Palma finds
in *Cronos* the "very Mexicanness of connecting decay and salva-
tion—crossing horror with hope";[11] Janet Maslin considers the film
"a very stylish and sophisticated Mexican variation on some age-old
themes";[12] and David Overbey states that Del Toro "gets to the heart
of the eternal myth in Mexican style."[13] In spite of the collaboration
of individuals carrying different passports, the combination of distinct production currencies, and the careful marketing to diverse audiences, the "genealogical rhetoric of blood, property, and frontiers"
prevails with *Mi Querido Tom Mix* and *Cronos*.[14] Even in cases like
these, where the production and circulation are decidedly international, the critical task consists of accumulating sufficient evidence to
prove authenticity.

To return to García Canclini's question, it seems that what remains when filmmakers and films constantly cross borders is, in
fact, a fervent yearning for authentic culture. Yet the notion of authentic culture is tenable only as "a useful fiction" or a "revealing
distortion," as Renato Rosaldo reminds us, for "rapidly increasing
global interdependence has made it more and more clear that neither 'we' nor 'they' are as neatly bounded and homogeneous as
once seemed to be the case." Our present-day world, he observes, is
"marked by borrowing and lending across porous national and cultural boundaries that are saturated with inequality, power, and domination."[15] To take as the critical task the enumeration of "Mexican"
techniques, and to police the borders of "Mexican cinema," is (1) to
ignore the points of convergence between the nation's century-long
tradition and others; and (2) to deny the politics inherent in cultural
analysis.

If we no longer ask what makes a film authentic, so as to affix our
singular geopolitical label, how do we reformulate the question? The
ideas of Robert Stam and Ella Shohat in *Unthinking Eurocentrism* are
instructive: they express their interest not in "identity as something
one 'has,' " but in "identification as something one 'does,' " thereby
emphasizing the process rather than the product.[16] Our questions,
then, will have to do with how the film engages with multiple national
and formal identities rather than what makes it authentic. This attention to the "how" rather than the "what" echoes the sentiments of
García Canclini. In addressing the role of culture in geopolitical con-
figuration, he notes: "The key problem seems not to be the risk that
globalization erase [nations and ethnicities] but rather to understand
how ethnic, regional, and national identities reconstitute themselves

through processes of intercultural hybridization" [my emphasis].[17] These formulations reroute the critical activity: instead of highlighting those elements presumed to render a film authentic, they compel us to examine the perceived impurities—sites where one tradition meets another. Thus, *Mi Querido Tom Mix* and *Cronos* guide us in reframing our critical questions.

Mi Querido Tom Mix: Updating the Western

> The Old West is not a certain place in a certain time, it's a state of mind. It's whatever you want it to be.
>
> —*Tom Mix*

Mi Querido Tom Mix locates itself between tradition and modernization. Set in 1930s Mexico—when rural dwellers began migrating to the city, when agriculture began to give way to industry, and when "silent" moving pictures became "talkies"—the film underscores the clash between past and future. Joaquina (Ana Ofelia Murguia) is most comfortable either in the patio with her animals or in the movie house viewing the latest silent picture. Her niece Antonia (Mercedes Olea), in contrast, disdains village life in Ocotito and yearns instead for the city; she frequently threatens to get rid of Joaquina's animals and implores her husband, Evaristo (Manuel Ojeda), to make his patients pay not with pigs and cows but with money, "like they do in the city." Joaquina's grandnephew Felipe (Damian García Vasquez) mediates these two extremes. A stranger comes to town one day, the gallant Domingo (Federico Luppi), and he satisfies Joaquina's desire for bygone days "cuando los hombres fueron hombres de verdad" [when men were truly men].

In *Mi Querido Tom Mix*, Joaquina's daily world becomes increasingly linked with the Hollywood adventures of her hero, Tom Mix.[18] She slips into the movie theater to see the latest Tom Mix serial every chance she gets. Between screenings, Joaquina writes letters to "her darling" Tom, and she gazes at the cowboy smiling back at her from her scrapbook pages. Her vivid imagination permits her to "hear" beating hooves and "see" Tom ride through the town from time to time. Eventually, she takes part in a Tom Mix-style adventure of her own: she is kidnapped by reckless bandits and then saved by her silver-haired hero. After Domingo rescues Joaquina, she compares him to her screen idol, saying, "Usted es muy valiente. Solo un amigo que tengo podría haber hecho lo que usted hizo. ¿Fue en *El ciclón* o en *Fama y fortuna*?" [You are very brave. Only one friend could have done what you did. Was it in *Cyclone* or in *Fame and Fortune?*] It becomes increasingly difficult for Joaquina (and the viewer) to separate Tom Mix and Domingo, and their respective adventures.[19]

When asked where he comes from, Domingo replies simply, "Vengo de lejos, del norte" [I come from far away, from the north]. And indeed, this border-crossing Tom Mix comes from the north with all the trappings of the Hollywood "Cadillac cowboy" tradition. *Mi Querido Tom Mix* actually subsumes the northern film star and his work; the resultant hybrid obliterates origins and destinations, occupying instead multiple territories and traditions. In blending Mexican and Hollywood film conventions, *Mi Querido Tom Mix* reveals to viewers on both sides of the Río Grande the links between the two traditions.

Mi Querido Tom Mix reproduces the techniques of early motion pictures familiar to audiences across the Americas and beyond.[20] The opening sequence proffers images of a wedding accompanied by the requisite music. The bride and groom appear together at the top of an elegant stairway and smile at the guests waiting below. Suddenly, mounted intruders disrupt the scene. They gallop between laden tables and up the central staircase, firing their guns in the air. When one bandit manages to grab the bride and hoist her up onto his horse, their mission is accomplished and they all ride away. Predictably, a single white horse with its rider gallops into the frame and pursues the band of kidnappers. After a few shots and a toss of the rope, the bad guys lie on the ground. The good guy now turns his attention to the runaway horse carrying the satin-clad bride. He rides up alongside the horse, executes a skillful midair transfer, and pulls back on the reins. The horse stops. As the wind-blown pair dismount, they turn toward one another. He lifts her veil. This entire sequence—filtered in sepia tones, shot with an unstable camera, framed off-center, and accompanied by a piano-pounding chase score—is reminiscent of early moving pictures from both sides of the border.

Just before the expected kiss, a woman's nagging voice interrupts the musical score: "Tia Joaquina, ¿Qué hace alli?" [Aunt Joaquina, what are you doing over there?]. Cut to the image of a day-dreaming Joaquina. She is framed by the window through which she stares; her niece stands centered in the doorway. Multiple frames—created by the windows, curtains, doors, and pictures on the wall—coupled with the chiaroscuro lighting re-create the atmosphere of Mexico's classic melodramas. This montage interrupts the narrative, revealing that we've been experiencing the images and sounds of Joaquina's imagination rather than those of the actual film. With this reframing, silent moving pictures merge with talkies.

The flavor of the Mexican-style melodrama blends with that of the Hollywood-style Western.[21] *Mi Querido Tom Mix* pits good guys against bad in proper Western fashion. It deviates significantly from the traditional formula, however, in distorting or discarding tried-and-true techniques. The hero and heroine are not virile and voluptuous, but aging misfits: Joaquina makes a nuisance of herself at home, forgetting to feed her animals and slipping out after having been told to remain indoors; Domingo has seen his better cowboy days, managing only to tangle himself up in his lasso. The bad guys are not feathered Indians or grubby bandits but city slickers dressed in suits. These marauders race into town not on horseback but behind the wheel of a shiny gray automobile. What ensues is a shooting and looting sequence whose staged quality and lengthy duration draws attention to the convention as such.[22] They then make off with jewelry, bank notes, and paintings as well as with Joaquina.

The hero arrives just in time, of course; he gets rid of the bandits and rescues the woman. In this melodrama-inflected Western, the hero teams up with the heroine. Domingo and Joaquina will spend their remaining days together, but rather than riding off into the sunset on galloping horses, they stroll off toward the sunrise while leading a cow. In blending conventions associated with two traditions, *Mi Querido Tom Mix* interrupts narratives that consider as mutually exclusive Mexican cinema and Hollywood cinema, and that construct a "we" as separate from a "they." García Agraz's film illustrates "cultural reconversion," the process of "cultural exchange" through which, according to García Canclini, "we are making the most of what we have and are trying to say something more or different." This cross-fertilization of "high" and "popular" art across territories, he emphasizes, sets into motion new cultural flows that cannot be reduced to mere cases of "imperialist domination."[23]

Mi Querido Tom Mix reshapes Western techniques through exaggeration and replacement, thereby flaunting the transparency of its own construction. Viewers see through the conventions and, in doing so, engage in a dialogic relationship with the text. It becomes impossible to watch this genre film passively. This dialogic relationship between the text and the viewer/critic is especially poignant in the sequence in which Domingo, as the incarnation of Tom Mix, practices and polishes his cowboy persona. He throws his rope, attempts to mount his horse on the run, and then works on his lingo. He looks at the camera and asks in English, "Are you talking to me? Are you talking to me?" Here Domingo's quoting of a Western cliché effectively locates *Tom Mix* within a larger cinematic tradition; the utterance appeals to—and attests to—a transnational discursive community acutely aware of Western genre conventions. The rupture created by the English utterance familiar to film fans, the gaze directed at the viewer, and Domingo's pointed finger seem to be daring us to reiterate our authenticity rhetoric. The film talks back to critics who are content to merely reiterate distorting fictions. Only by engaging in the dialogue will we make sense of the mix.

Cronos: Taming the Terror

> What confronts the Western scholar is the discomforting fact that the natives are no longer staying in their frames.
>
> —Rey Chow

Cronos, like *Mi Querido Tom Mix*, defies containment within extant critical categories that privilege formal purity and national authenticity. "People are going to say [that *Cronos* is] a Mexican, Catholic, vampire movie with mariachis," predicted Guillermo del Toro, "but it's not. I think of it more as a sick but really very tender love story." Indeed, the film flaunts its familiarity with both the Mexican and Hollywood traditions, combines English and Spanish dialogue, and draws upon genres as diverse as wrestling films and melodramas, horror movies and comedies. For Del Toro, "*Cronos* is a 'B' picture premise shot in the style of an 'A' picture. Mixing these things together gives me a strange taste that I like."[24] It is the vampire flavor, however, that predominates in *Cronos*.[25]

The revisionist vampire tale begins with a brief prologue. In 1536 a Spanish watchmaker, fleeing the Inquisition, arrived in Veracruz. He carried with him his fantastic invention, the *cronos* device capable of regenerating life; this explains his life span of some four hundred years. When he was killed in an explosion in 1937, the watchmaker left behind the life-prolonging *cronos* mechanism, a diary explaining how it worked, and a mysterious aura. "What they found there," an off-screen male voice narrates ominously as a camera surveys crushed bodies amid the crumbled structure, "was never fully revealed to the public." The diary makes its way into the hands of the dying Dieter de la Guardia (Claudio Brook), who becomes obsessed with finding the miraculous invention in order to halt his own rapid deterioration. Confined and immobile, he enlists the assistance of his burly nephew, Angel de la Guardia (Ron Perlman), who agrees to look for the *cronos*. Although Angel seeks, it is Jesús Gris (Federico Luppi) who finds; he pries the bug-like device from inside the statue of an angel in his Mexico City antique shop. Jesús learns how to use the *cronos* to manipulate time but pays the price: he develops, among other vampire traits, an insatiable thirst for blood. A parallel narrative traces the growing love between the fifty-seven-year-old shop proprietor and his young granddaughter, Aurora (Tamara Shanath).

In Cronos, *Aurora (Tamara Shanath) watches her grandfather (Federico Luppi) unwrap the golden* cronos *mechanism in his Mexico City antique shop. Photo courtesy of IMCINE.*

Cronos is indeed reminiscent of vampire tales. Jesús occupies two distinct worlds. By day, he is a responsible family man—conversing at breakfast with his wife, Mercedes (Margarita Isabel), playing hopscotch with his granddaughter, and waiting on customers in his shop. By night, however, he winds the sharp prongs of the *cronos* into his skin and then prowls for blood. Initially finding that a raw steak satisfies his craving, he later demands only human blood. Like other vampires, Jesús has the power to avoid death for the most part, and to resurrect himself if necessary. When Angel locks him in a car and pushes it off a cliff to burst into flames, Jesús emerges—scarred but alive. When the cremator slides his coffin-contained body into the fiery oven, Jesús lifts the lid and slips out unnoticed. True to the formula, this vampire need only fear death by dagger in the heart.

Yet *Cronos* is not just another vampire tale. Rather than merely incorporating often-used conventions, the film distorts and reshapes them. This is evident in the construction of the set and the characters, the employment of Spanish and English, and the self-conscious attention to cinema as a mode of representation. Jesús divides his time between domestic places and futuristic spaces—the former include the antique shop, a dance studio, the family dining room, and the young girl's bedroom; the latter include a cremation parlor, a freight elevator, the de la Guardia family warehouse, and the metal-walled room in which the obsessive Dieter displays his collection of plastic-wrapped angels alongside his excised tumors. Warm gold and orange tones characterize the familiar domestic places, while blue and gray filters mediate the strange impersonal spaces. The delineation of all these spaces is further achieved through framing, with medium and close-up shots used in the former, and long shots predominating in the latter. Thus, this juxtaposition of recognizable places and deterritorialized spaces sets the stage.

Del Toro's characters blur boundaries, too, eluding categorization in strictly heroic or demonic terms. His vampire, aptly named Jesús, embodies good in spite of his socially unacceptable urges. The bad guy, too, has his redeeming qualities. Angel plays a gentle game of hide-and-seek with young Aurora and offers her a piece of chewing gum, and he elicits our sympathy as the badgered victim of his cruel uncle. *Cronos* twists the conventions in yet another way: in the film, the villain is Anglo and speaks English with an occasional gringo-accented word in Spanish; the hero is Latino and speaks Spanish. The dialogue develops in Spanish and English without any paraphrasing or translation. In an early scene, Angel de la Guardia strolls into the antique shop, calling out "Good day." Shop proprietor Jesús Gris returns the greeting with "Buen día. ¿Busca alguna cosa en particular?" [Are you looking for anything in particular?]. The gum-chewing Angel wanders around the shop, spots the angel he is after, checks the tag, and mutters, "Pricey." "Es una pieza muy cara" [It's a very valuable piece], counters Jesús. "Yeah, sure, they all are," complains Angel. He then pulls out his wallet and hands over several bills, remarking, "but no es mi dinero [but it isn't my money]—keep the change." The protagonists communicate effectively this way. Their dialogue parallels conversations taking place in communities throughout the Americas and reminds us that Spanish and English do not exist as separate languages for the millions who rely on a blend of both to express themselves.

Cronos's dual-language approach effectively addresses a wide audience—speakers of Spanish, of English, and of both Spanish and English—across the continent.[26] Del Toro has commented on the mixture of the two languages in the film, saying: "I know how lazy American audiences are to read subtitles, and this blending makes

Cronos almost an unsubtitled movie."[27] Whereas most "foreign" films require English-speaking U.S. viewers to read subtitles, this film offers a respite by interrupting the Spanish utterances with English ones. An all-Spanish version of *Cronos* exists as well. Interestingly, this single-language version, in which the film-maker's voice replaces that of Perlman on the soundtrack, was made primarily for the Latino market in the United States; it is Del Toro's preferred dual-language version that is shown in Mexico.[28] In its unique employment of Spanish and English, *Cronos* straddles a linguistic borderline and, with it, a geopolitical one. The film prevents us from correlating linguistic systems with national territories in a one-to-one correspondence. Instead, *Cronos* reminds us that "official" languages may have little to do with actual communication: Spanish is spoken not only in Mexico but also in the United States and elsewhere; and English is spoken not only in the United States, but in Mexico and beyond. In reproducing polyphonic dialogues rather than constructing singular linguistic traditions, the film acknowledges the porosity of borders, the migrancy of populations, and the hybridity of expressive culture.

Jesús Gris (Federico Luppi) scrutinizes the cronos *device and the blood that it has drawn from his hand. Photo courtesy of IMCINE.*

This film draws our attention to yet another borderline—that perceived to separate the text from the viewer/critic. It does so by repeatedly emphasizing the film's own location within a larger cinematic tradition. The framed image of Mexico's masked star, El Santo, is but one of many "quotes" that invite us to recognize and respond to familiar film references.[29] And, in fact, we do. *Cronos* is consistently described in terms of its relationship to other genre films. It "nods to cult items" such as *Phantasm*;[30] contains "over-the-top Grand Guignol scenes," portrays vampires "in the vein of *The Hunger*," and "quotes" *Videodrome, The Fly,* and *Naked Lunch*.[31] Further, it "recalls another film about obsession," *The Hairdresser's Husband*;[32] uses make-up reminiscent of *Scanners*;[33] and resembles "in sentiment creepy wonders" such as *The Black Cat* and Francis Ford Coppola's *Dracula*.[34] The film brought to the fore memories of *King Kong* and James Whale's *Frankenstein* for Trevor Johnston, who credits Del Toro with "wear[ing] his influences like Dracula wears his cape: with poise, style, and elegance."[35] In employing the transnational language of cinema, *Cronos* communicates effectively with genre fans across geopolitical boundaries.

Cronos further invokes cinema by underlining its own status as representation. The film calls attention to identity as multiple, mutable, and, above all, constructed. Jesús's death-resurrection cycle has left him with a face held together by scars, stitches, and staples; he fears that even his own wife will not recognize him behind his monster-like visage. Desperate to replace this ghoulish face with a pleasant countenance, he solicits the advice of the diary-holding Dieter. The man instructs him to "peel it off." "¿De qué habla?" [What are you talking about?] asks the confused Jesús. "Peel it off," comes the reply. And he does. Here we see the simulated flesh (carefully crafted by the make-up artists of Necropia) removed layer by layer; the vampire gives way to the grandfather, who then gives way to the actor himself. As we observe these layers peeled away, and with them the corresponding personalities, we are reminded once again that cinematic identity is a careful construction.

The continuing popularity of genre films, coupled with the success of Del Toro's first feature, has not gone unnoticed in Hollywood. James Cameron saw *Cronos* and immediately invited Del Toro to draft the script for his next project, *Spanky*. Del Toro accepted the offer, saying that he would put his "filthy mind" and "corny heart" into creating a blend "somewhere between *It's a Wonderful Life* and the Book of Job."[36] Del Toro is also working on two of his own horror screenplays, "Meat Market: A Love Story" and "The Devil's Backbone" as well as on a project that explores the theme of the Day of the Dead, in collaboration with Dana Rotberg

(*Angel de Fuego*) and Alfonso Cuarón (*El Amor en los Tiempos de la Histeria*). The thirty-five-year-old filmmaker intends to continue drawing upon genre films from both the Mexican and Hollywood traditions in his work. Genre films, he maintains, "are extremely valuable because they have concrete rules; you either respect these or break them, but they help you reach a wider audience."[37] He disapproves of the "stupid pose" adopted by many young filmmakers who claim that they "don't watch Mexican films and can't talk about [Fernando] Méndez, or Chano Urueta, or Fernando de Fuentes, or Emilio Fernández." And unlike other Mexican filmmakers who have relocated to Southern California, Del Toro stresses that in spite of his interest in making movies in Los Angeles, he continues to consider Mexico his home: "I will always be a 'round-trip ticket' filmmaker."[38]

Meeting the Gaze: Critical Praxis Reframed

> Identity, as a narrative we constantly reconstruct with others, is also a co-production.
>
> *—Nestór Garcia Canclini*

As information and capital criss-cross continents in this post-NAFTA era, it becomes increasingly apparent that authentic national films exist only as our "distorting fictions." To discern the authentic is to jettison the complexity of contemporary culture and to perpetuate cultural colonization. Henry Louis Gates, Jr., observes that "some people dream of the world as a cultural museum, in which mixing is eschewed as contamination." When "intercultural contact is allowed" at all, "the flow must be one-way from them, the Exotic Other, to us, the corrupted metropole."[39] One-way-flow narratives obfuscate cultural convergence and, in this case, perpetuate the notion of a southern culture entirely separate from a northern one.

The case of *Serpientes y Escaleras* (1981) demonstrates the limitations of such one-way-flow narratives. Busi Cortés discussed the Mexico City première of her film with participants at the 1994 Cine-Lit International Conference in Oregon. Upon hearing that *Serpientes y Escaleras* opened alongside *Batman* (Tim Burton, 1989) in a multiscreen cineplex, the audience of scholars and critics groaned sympathetically. How was this *pobre-cito* Mexican film supposed to compete with the Hollywood giant, they wondered? Cortés surprised her listeners by noting that as soon as *Batman* sold out each evening, moviegoers purchased tickets for *Serpientes y Escaleras*. Film fans in the capital who might otherwise have overlooked a Mexican-made feature saw and approved of the film. As

Dieter de la Guardia (Claudio Brook) shows off his display of excised tumors to Jesús Gris (Federico Luppi). Photo courtesy of IMCINE.

word of their enthusiastic reception spread, ticket receipts soared and favorable reviews multiplied. Busi Cortés, then, credits *Batman* with the extraordinary box-office takes and the critical success of *Serpientes y Escaleras.*[40]

While Cortés may have been entertaining her audience and modestly downplaying the success of her film, her observations are useful in drawing our attention once again to the framing of the critical question. To ask whether Cortés and her film are "authentically" Mexican is to elide any engagement with issues of transnational production, reception, and texts. To separate S*erpientes y Escaleras* from *Batman* and other border-crossing blockbusters is to locate Cortés outside of the international channels within which directors and films and audiences move. And to cast the film and its creator as Exotic Others is to consolidate the centrality of the critic's position. Gates encourages us instead to "learn to live without the age-old deleterious dream of purity—whether purity of bloodlines or cultural inheritance—and learn to find comfort, solace, and even fulfillment in the rough magic of the mix, however imperfect and mutable." He concludes by asserting that "the truth is, there are no one-way flows."[41]

Indeed, there are no one-way flows—not between south and north, nor between text and critic. By setting a body of "native" works apart from "our" critical praxis, we construct objects of inquiry presumed to be at once internally homogeneous and different from "us." Rather than examining those points where the text meets the critic, where cultural expression engages with critical discourse, we stubbornly approach our objects of inquiry as if they were completely separate from our praxis.

The quest for authenticity and its concomitant focus on difference yield what Renato Rosaldo considers "a peculiar ratio: as the 'other' becomes more culturally visible, the 'self' becomes correspondingly less so." If we are to rejuvenate our critical praxis, then we must acknowledge our role in shaping expressive culture. We need to render ourselves more visible in the process by considering questions such as the ones Rosaldo directed at anthropologists: "How do 'they' see 'us'? Who are 'we' looking at 'them'?"[42] Questions such as these illuminate the complex relationship between expressive culture and critical inquiry; they enable us to acknowledge the dialogue in which we are engaged or the gaze in which we are implicated. The dialogue or gaze is not a naïve one, nor is it accusatory.[43] Rather, it is one of provocation: "Are you talking to me?" It encourages us to locate texts within their transnational contexts of production and reception. It reminds us that we do not merely react to culture but actively participate in shaping it. And it suggests that films that refuse to satisfy our desire for authentic national culture, such as *Mi Querido Tom Mix* and *Cronos*, serve as points of departure for reframing our critical questions. Rather than imposing our paradigms upon works of expressive culture, we can allow them to instruct us. García Canclini reminds us, after all, that identity, as a narrative we constantly reconstruct with others, is a coproduction.[44]

Notes

1. See Hayden Herrera, "Why Frida Speaks to the '90s," *New York Times*, October 28, 1990.

2. See Judd Tully, "The Kahlo Cult," *Artnews* (April 1994): 126–33; and Oriana Baddeley, " 'Her Dress Hangs Here': De-frocking the Kahlo Cult," *The Oxford Art Journal* 14:1 (1991): 10–17.

3. Luis Valdez, "A Statement on Artistic Freedom," *Teatro Campesino News* (1992).

4. Nestór García Canclini, "Will There Be Latin American Cinema in the Year 2000: Visual Culture in a Postnational Era," in *Framing Latin American Cinema: Contemporary Critical Perspectives*, ed. Ann Marie Stock (Minneapolis: University of Minnesota Press, 1997).

5. Federico Luppi, during an acting career spanning more than four decades, has starred in such award-winning films as *Un Lugar en el Mundo* (1992), *Las Tumbas* (1991), *No Habra ni Penas ni Olvido* (1983), and *Tiempo de Revancha* (1981). Veteran actress Ana Ofelia Murguia played leading roles in such recent hits as *Los Motivos de Luz* (1985) and *Naufragio* (1977). Claudio Brook acted in several films directed by Luis Buñuel; his recent works include *Miroslava* (1993), *Romero* (1989), and *Frida: Naturaleza Viva* (1984). The versatile Ron Perlman has played in some two dozen films and television productions since his acting debut in the early 1980s; recent titles include *Beauty and the Beast, The Island of Dr. Moreau* (1996), *The Adventures of Captain Zoom in Outer Space* (1995), and *The Name of the Rose* (1986).

6. The Nobel Prize-winning Colombian author, Gabriel García Marquez, has supported the development and dissemination of films in Latin America for more than a decade. He founded the New Latin American Cinema Foundation, located just outside Havana; he has designed and directed collaborative projects such as the *Amores Dificiles* series; and he guides screenwriters in frequent workshops. Jaime Humberto Hermosillo is a popular and prolific Mexican filmmaker best known for his comic wit and irreverence toward sexual mores, as evidenced in such films as *Doña Herlinda y Su Hijo* (1985) and *La Tarea* (1990).

7. Other titles in the cinema series besides *Mi Querido Tom Mix* and *La Invención del Cronos* include *Solo con Tu Pareja* (Carlos Cuarón), *La Mujer de Benjamín* (Carlos Carrera and Ignacio Ortiz), *Angel de Fuego* (Omar A. Rodrigo and Dana Rotberg), *En el Aire* (Juan Carlos de Llaca), *Cabeza de Vaca* (Guillermo Sheridan), and *Danzón* (María Novaro and Beatriz Novaro).

8. Even internationally renowned filmmakers such as the late Tomás Gutiérrez Alea must seek support beyond their local industries. *Fresa y Chocolate* (1993), for example, was coproduced with Mexico; *Guantamera* (1995) was financed in part with Spanish currency.

9. Barnet has credited *Mi Querido Tom Mix* with bringing about the resurgence of Mexican cinema, saying that "this film marks the poetics of new cinema in Latin America, and a new direction in Mexican cinema." Carlos García Agraz downplayed the film's importance, attributing the "resurgence" to the collaboration of talented filmmakers, increased support for filmmaking through Fomento de Cine (FOCINE) and coproduction efforts, and greater interest on the part of the public in Mexican films. He concluded by saying, "We have to take advantage of this moment." See Miguel Barnet, Press conference with Carlos García Agraz, Ana Ofelia Murguia, and Mercedes Olea, at the International Festival of New Latin American Cinema, Havana, December 1992.

10. Adriana S. Pardo, "True to His Frightful Visions: Guillermo Del Toro Brings a Mexican Perspective to Horror Films," *Los Angeles Times*, April 19, 1994.

11. Anthony De Palma, "From a Mexican Grave Comes *Cronos*," *New York Times*, May 20, 1994.

12. Janet Maslin, "Undead Again: A Suave Vampire," *Hollywood Reporter*, March 24, 1994.

13. David Overbey, "Latin American Panorama," in *Catalog of Toronto Festival of Films* (1993).

14. This is the phrase of Paul Carter in *Living in a New Country: History, Travelling and Language* (London: Faber and Faber, 1992), 7–8.

15. Renato Rosaldo, *Culture and Truth: The Remaking of Social Analysis* (Boston: Beacon Press, 1989), 217.

16. Robert Stam and Ella Shohat, *Unthinking Eurocentrism: Multiculturalism and the Media* (London and New York: Routledge, 1994), 346.

17. García Canclini, "Will There Be Latin American Cinema in the Year 2000?"

18. Tom Mix began his career in motion pictures in 1910 with a single-reeler entitled *Ranch Life in the Great Southwest*. Soon thereafter he joined with Selig Productions, starring first in *Back to the Primitive* and then in several other one- and two-reelers over the next few years. He signed with William Fox Studios (now 20th-Century Fox) in 1917 and soon—touted as "the first of the rhinestone-and-neon cowboy-heroes" and a "Hollywood, show-biz Cowboy"—became their biggest star. With the advent of sound in 1927, the popularity of the nearly fifty-year-old Mix waned. The wrangling cowboy turned to the circus for a few years, continuing to please his fans with live performances before rounding out his acting career with a couple of films for Universal in the early 1930s. Mix died in 1940. See James Horwitz, *They Went Thataway* (New York: E. P. Dutton, 1976), 64.

19. This ambiguity challenged even the filmmaker. In the screenplay, Domingo tells Joaquina that he played Tom in all the range-riding movies. The two gallant riders merge into a single individual. The appearance of the legendary Tom Mix in Ocotito enables Joaquina to live her dream. In the film version, however, the identity of Domingo remains elusive. García Agraz explained that during the filming, Luppi and Murguia deviated from the script, and their improvised dialogue was far more genuine than the scripted lines, so he retained this sequence for the final version. See Carlos García Agraz, Press conference with García Agraz, Ana Ofelia Murguia, and Mercedes Olea, International Festival of New Latin American Cinema, Havana, December 1992.

20. García Agraz has, in fact, noted his interest in creating for the viewer the effect of watching a 1930s or 1940s film that would seem like a 1990s one. See Luciano Castillo, "Nuestro Querido Tom Mix," in *Con la locura de los sentidos: Entrevistas a cineastas latinoamericanos* (Buenos Aires: Colección Artesiete, 1994).

21. García Agraz has acknowledged the influence of Hollywood genre films in this work. "My great love of cinema began with the North American cinema of the 1940s, especially the Western, with John Ford, with Walsh. We first viewed Westerns of the 1940s and later the films of Tom Mix; I felt that in some way we had to approximate this ingenious aesthetic." See Castillo, "Nuestro Querido Tom Mix," 107.

22. The employment of a gray getaway car and the repeated breaking-entering-looting sequences are reminiscent of Enrique Rosas's eminently popular *El automóvil gris* (1919) from Mexico's silent era.

23. Nestór García Canclini, "Cultural Reconversion," in *On Edge: The Crisis of Contemporary Latin American Culture*, ed. George Yúdice, Jean Franco, and Juan Flores (Minneapolis: University of Minnesota Press, 1992), 31, 38.

24. Trevor Johnston, "Day of the Dead," in *Time Out* (London, n.d.), 1.

25. Experienced producer Berta Navarro (*Reed: Mexico Insurgente, Camila, Victoria de un Pueblo en Armas,* and *Nicaragua, Los que Harán la Libertad*) insisted from the outset that the film be "an international coproduction with an eye toward a high profile outside Mexico." Del Toro determined that a genre formula would help achieve this goal. See Pardo, "True to His Frightful Visions," F8.

26. Del Toro's dual-language vampire tale has an interesting precursor in the 1931 *Dracula*. Bram Stoker's novel and the play by Hamilton Deane and John Balderston were adapted for the screen and then filmed simultaneously in Spanish and English. George Melford directed the Spanish-speaking cast (Carlos Vallarias,

Lupita Tovar, Pablo Alvarez Rubio), and Todd Browning directed the English-language actors (Bela Lugosi); both projects were filmed on the same expressionistic sets. This parallel production strategy was employed frequently in the early 1930s as the advent of the "talkies" suddenly necessitated language-specific moving pictures.

27. Richard Harrington, "A Monster Hit That's Not Out to Scare You," *Washington Post*, May 22, 1994.

28. Doris Toumarkine, "October Strikes Deal for *Cronos*," *Hollywood Reporter*, July 13, 1993.

29. With his performance in *Santo contra los Zombies*, El Santo introduced a new genre, the *lucha libre*, or wrestling film. During the 1960s and 1970s the masked wrestler was one of the most popular figures in Mexican cinema; any film billing the cult hero as its leading man enjoyed impressive box-office takes. In 1984, while appearing on the television program "Lucha libre: Circo, Maroma, Teatro y Deporte," El Santo shocked his fans by removing his mask. Thus ended the forty-year mystery surrounding his identity; the audience learned that Rodolfo Guzmán Huerta (1917–1984) was El Santo—both on screen and in the ring.

30. Tom Crow, "*Cronos* Crawling: Writer-Director Guillermo del Toro Delivers a Deliciously Unique Gothic Gorefest," *Los Angeles Village View*, April 22, 1994.

31. Kenneth Turan, "*Cronos* Alive with Charms Eternal," *Los Angeles Times*, April 22, 1994.

32. John Kraniauskas, Review of *Cronos* in *Sight and Sound* (October 1994).

33. Crow, "*Cronos* Crawling."

34. Manohla Dargis, "Tinkering with Terror: Freak Shows, Mechanical and Sublime," in *Los Angeles Weekly*, April 22, 1994.

35. Johnston, "Day of the Dead," 1.

36. Ibid., 1.

37. Guillermo del Toro, "A Return to Genre Films," *Artes de México* 10 (Winter 1990): 93.

38. De Palma, "From a Mexican Grave Comes *Cronos*."

39. Henry Louis Gates, Jr., "Planet Rap: Notes on the Globalization of Culture," in *Field Work: Sites in Literary and Cultural Studies*, ed. Marjorie Garber, Rebecca L. Walkowitz, and Paul B. Franklin (London and New York: Routledge, 1996), 65.

40. Busi Cortés, "Presente y futuro del cine hispano," at Cine-Lit II: International Conference on Hispanic Literatures and Cinematographies, Portland, Oregon, February 1994.

41. Gates, "Planet Rap," 65.

42. Rosaldo, *Culture and Truth*, 207.

43. In her study of postcolonial culture and criticism, Rey Chow examines the gaze and its potential for collapsing dichotomies: "This gaze, which is neither a threat nor a retaliation, makes the colonizer 'conscious' of himself, leading to his need to turn this gaze around and look at himself, henceforth 'reflected' in the native-object. It is the self-reflection of the colonizer that produces the colonizer as subject (potent gaze, source of meaning and action) and the native as his image, with all the pejorative meanings of 'lack' attached to the word 'image.' " See Chow, *Writing Diaspora: Tactics of Intervention in Contemporary Cultural Studies* (Bloomington: Indiana University Press, 1993), 51.

44. García Canclini, "Will There Be Latin American Cinema in the Year 2000?"

Epilogue

The current and future state of the cinema of Mexico is unclear at best. On the positive side there is ample evidence of outstanding talent in almost all areas of filmmaking: direction, photography, acting, production, musical scoring, and postproduction facilities. Thematically and aesthetically, contemporary Mexican productions reveal a rich variety of themes, conceptual modes, narrative discourses, stylistic elements, gender considerations, and innovative modes of production. The two leading film schools, the Centro de Capacitación Cinematográfica and the Centro Universitario de Estudios Cinematográficas, have improved remarkably to the point where they are now recognized as among the most outstanding and innovative in the world. And recent films are receiving unprecedented critical recognition and box-office acclaim: *Como Agua para Chocolate* (Alfonso Arau, 1994) was the highest-grossing foreign language film of all time in the United States and elsewhere.

Besides narrative cinema, Mexican filmmakers are also excelling in other cinematic genres such as the documentary, the narrative short, student films, and independent experimental cinema. Last year's grand prize for best short at the prestigious Cannes Film Festival was Luis Carlos Carrera's *El Heroe*, while Luis Urrutia's *De Tripas Corazón* (1997) was among the Oscar nominees for best short. And these filmmakers have transcended national boundaries and are now working successfully in other countries, particularly the United States and Spain and in Latin America. There is currently an impressive group of Mexican directors, actors, photographers, and producers who are residing and working full-time in Los Angeles and are contributing significantly to Hollywood cinema.

These and other accomplishments are even more remarkable given the context of the grave Mexican crisis. Since the late 1970s the nation has been riddled with deep economic downturns, political instability, social and class conflict, and erratic cultural policies that have profoundly impacted the entire social and cultural fabric of contemporary Mexico. Through sheer determination and tenacity, filmmakers have been able to complete a number of outstanding films. In the 1990s over forty directors debuted with full-length feature films. Moreover, an impressive number of these emerging filmmakers were women. In fact, in perhaps no other national cinema is the increasing role and presence of women in all aspects of filmmaking so dominant as in the case of Mexico. And women now make up over half of the recent and current students in film and communication schools throughout the country, thus ensuring that this trend will continue.

Not only did new talent appear on the Mexican screen, but previous generations of filmmakers also returned to their craft and completed successful and creative productions. In fact, there currently exist at least three generations who are producing notable work: the generation of 1968, the generation of the crisis, and the generation of the 1990s. Altogether, these filmmakers have made some of the most acclaimed films of the Spanish-speaking world.

While these accomplishments might suggest an optimistic future for Mexican cinema, there are serious issues and deep problems that the industry faces. At the very forefront of the crisis is the question of exhibition and distribution. The major theater circuits are now owned by multinational corporations linked to Hollywood that, for the most part, only exhibit North American films. This is the case throughout the country, and it is becoming more pervasive. There are now few spaces open for the exhibition and distribution of Mexican cinema other than the art circuit, Cineteca Nacional, and other cultural centers, universities, and cine clubs. If Mexican cinema is to survive, then the state, the industry, and the filmmakers themselves will have to reverse this process and create significant spaces for their films.

A related need is to engage with Mexican and foreign audiences and persuade them to seek and support Mexican cinema. With the demise of the Golden Age and the overall decline of Mexican cinema in the late 1950s and 1960s, audiences in Mexico turned away from their own cinema toward Hollywood and Europe. However, whenever interesting and well-made Mexican films premiered, audiences have responded well. Films such as *La Pasión Según Berenice*, *Canoa*, and *El Lugar sin Limites* of the 1970s and *Como Agua para Chocolate*, *Dos Crímenes*, *El Callejón de los Milagros*, *Rojo Amanecer*, and the recent productions *Cilantro y Perejil* and *Por Si no Te Vuelvo a Ver* have all been popular in Mexico, and many have also been box-office draws abroad. Nonetheless, a more aggressive publicity campaign at all levels will have to be implemented by the film industry in order to retain and expand upon these successes.

A major problem faced by filmmakers is the lack of resources for financial backing. The Mexican Film Institute (IMCINE) now only

Movie poster of the film Cilantro y Perejil, *directed by Rafael Montero and starring Arcelia Ramírez and Demian Bichir as a married couple of the 1990s.*

contributes a small percentage of the overall financial package needed to complete a film. Thus, filmmakers need to secure 80 percent of the entire projected cost before they even approach IMCINE with a proposal. At the same time, each year the cost to produce a film increases significantly. And given the high risk of return, prospective producers are reluctant to invest large sums on risky endeavors.

Second, the success of the industry is still, to a large extent, dependent on the cultural politics of the current administration and its appointed state officials. When responsible and committed individuals are placed in charge of Mexican cinema policies, the industry prospers creatively and economically. Such is the case at the moment. There is, however, no expectation that this condition will continue since officials are named by each successive presidential administration, which only lasts six years. As several of the essays in this volume have shown, the trend has been a cyclical one that ranges from excellent appointments to absolutely disastrous ones.

Finally, there is the problem of local competition. The closing of movie houses and the increase in the purchase of television sets and videocassette players have meant that people no longer go to the movies as often as they once did. While the growth of low-budget videos made for direct release to the home market may have given some filmmakers wider opportunities for seeing their work brought to an audience, it also has had a negative impact on the profits of the industry at large. Most of the videos available in Mexico are imported from Hollywood, while Mexican cinema available on videocassette is generally limited to films produced during the Golden Age and to low-budget formula pictures.

There is one additional and divergent trend. The extraordinary success of *Como Agua para Chocolate* brought Mexican filmmakers to the attention of Hollywood. The director, Alfonso Arau, was sought out to direct American commercial films. His initial production was *A Walk in the Clouds*, and Arau is currently working on his second Hollywood feature, *Zapata*. Another director, Alfonso Cuarón of *Solo con Tu Pareja* fame, also scored well in his directorial debut with *The Little Princess*. Although not a big box-office success, it nonetheless was well received by select audiences and the critics. The most recent Mexican director with the most impressive first Hollywood film is Guillermo del Toro with the well-crafted horror movie, *Mimic*. Luis Mandoki also has directed three major Hollywood productions.

Besides directors, certain Mexican actresses—Salma Hayek, Lumi Cavazos, Elpidia Carrillo, and Zaide Silvia Gutiérrez—have starred or costarred in important Hollywood and independent productions. In addition, select Mexican cinematographers of the generation of the 1990s are working consistently in Hollywood. Thus, Mexican filmmakers are exerting a significant presence and influence in American cinema, again underlining the fact of the impressive talent that exists within the contemporary Mexican film community. This trend of artistic immigration should continue and invigorate cinema beyond the borders.

The future of Mexico's cinema, however, is not totally dependent on the policies and practices of its government and its filmmakers. The industry has become a global concern not entirely linked to individual nations. Capital, production, distribution, and even legislation operate at an international level and are dominated by the relationships of multinational corporations with each other and with individual nations. Films are financed by Japanese money, produced by

French entities, and distributed to international audiences by U.S. companies partly owned by the Japanese. Markets for these films are also international in their demographics. Therefore, to be successful, films must appeal to a wide range of cultural and social preferences.

According to Nestór García Canclini, in order for Mexico's national cinema to survive, the state must reconsider its status "as a locus of public interest, as arbiter or guarantor of the collective need for information, recreation, and innovation" in the face of questions of commercial profit.* If we look back at the complex history of Mexican cinema and at the essays in this volume, it is clear that state intervention and protectionist policies are what bolstered the industry during times of economic and social crisis. While it was never a question that these policies necessarily translated into higher production quotas or increased profits, they did sustain a cinema devoted to various elaborations of Mexican histories and identities.

Most important, it will be necessary for filmmakers to develop new conceptions of cinema in terms of content, mode, and exhibition venues. Given the contemporary technologies and economics of production, distribution, and exhibition, films that explore new forms of national and other identities can be made and distributed with minimal investments through video, satellite, and computer technologies. Lower investments mean that producers, directors, investors, and distributors can aim for narrower, more local audiences and thus do not have to compete in global markets. Of course, traditional conventions of cinematic narrative and aesthetic practices will also need to be modified.

Those who wish to continue to produce big-budget projects for wider audiences will need to explore alternative forms of financing and distribution. Given the escalating nature of production costs, it is apparent that the state will never be able to provide much monetary support for filmmakers. Producers will need to pursue (to a greater extent than they already have) private investment and coproduction backing beyond the borders of Mexico. And they must be willing to respond to and negotiate the demands of these outside sources who in turn must answer to their global shareholders and audiences. But how can Mexican cinema reach a transnational audience and still be specifically "Mexican"? The aesthetic future of individual national cinemas seems as grim as the economic future. Where are the global niches for small industries?

The notion of a "Mexican nation," or any nation, has a different currency today than it did fifty or even twenty years ago. Not only

---

*Nestór García Canclini, *Hybrid Cultures: Strategies for Entering and Leaving Modernity*, trans. Christopher L. Chiappari and Silvia L. López (Minneapolis: University of Minnesota Press, 1995), 268.

labor, money, and products cross national borders, but cultural symbols and practices also move freely around the world and are adapted, transformed, and handed new meanings in different contexts. Given these economic and symbolic migrations, might the possibility, or even the idea, of a specifically Mexican cinema be obsolete? In order to disprove this possibility, Mexican writers, directors, producers, and actors will need to create in the global audience a desire for their work by transforming the nation's cinema into a transnational one that draws on, but is not dependent on, the rich history of Mexican cultural, narrative, and popular practices—a cinema that is responsive to the postmodern conditions of transnational cultural products and practices.

About the Contributors

SETH FEIN is an assistant professor of history at Georgia State University. He has held a research appointment at the Instituto José María Luis Mora in Mexico City. His areas of specialization are American diplomatic history and U.S.-Mexican relations on the history of Mexico. Professor Fein has published widely in the United States, Mexico, and Europe on related aspects of the Golden Age of Mexican cinema, and is currently completing a book-length study of the relationship and influence of Hollywood upon Mexican cinema in the 1940s and 1950s.

GUSTAVO A. GARCÍA is a leading film and cultural critic as well as professor of film studies at the Universidad Autónoma Metropolitana and founder and coeditor of the film journal, *Intolerancia*. He has published extensively on diverse periods and themes of Mexican cinema in such studies as *La decada perdida*, *El cine mudo mexicano*, *Epoca de oro del cine mexicano*, *El nuevo cine mexicano*, *Pedro Infante*, and *Pedro Armendáriz*.

RAFAEL HERNÁNDEZ RODRÍGUEZ is an ABD instructor in the Department of Spanish and Portuguese at New York University. He is currently finishing his dissertation, which deals with Mexican and Brazilian poetry and culture, including film. Mr. Hernández Rodríguez has published articles on Latin American literature and film in American journals such as *Mester*, *Revista Hispánica Moderna*, *Hispanic Journal*, and *Latin American Literary Review*.

NORMA IGLESIAS is the director of media projects and research professor at El Colegio de la Frontera in Tijuana. She has carried out extensive studies of media, communications, cinema, and gender of the U.S.-Mexican border. Professor Iglesias is the author of *La flo mas bella de la maquiladora*, *Medios de comunicación en la fronter norte*, and *Entre yerba, polvo y plomo. Lo fronterizo visto por el cin mexicano.*

CARLOS MONSIVÁIS is acknowledged as Mexico's leading cul tural essayist, principal journalist, and dean of cultural studies. He i a regular contributor to *La Jornada*, *Proceso*, and *La Opinión* Among his prolific literary output, *Días de guardar*, *Amor perdido Los rituales del caos*, *Mexican Postcards*, and *A traves del Espej* stand out.

FEDERICO DÁVALOS OROZCO is professor of communication and cinema at the Universidad Nacional Autónoma de México. He i considered one of the leading scholars of the silent period o Mexican cinema. His publications include *Filmográfico general de cine mexicano*, *Albores del cine mexicano*, and *Carlos Villatoro Pasajes en la vida de un hombre de cine.*

ANN MARIE STOCK teaches in the Department of Moder Languages and Literatures at the College of William and Mary. Sh is the editor of *Framing Latin American Cinema: Contemporar Critical Perspectives* and has published widely on Latin America cinema in both English and Spanish.

PATRICIA TORRES DE SAN MARTÍN is research professor at th Centro de Investigación y Estudios Cinematográficos at th Universidad de Guadalajara. She has published extensively o women filmmakers of Mexico and Latin America. Recently she co authored the first major study of *Adela Sequeyro*, a pioneer woma director of Mexican cinema.

EDUARDO DE LA VEGA ALFARO is director of research of th Centro de Investigación y Estudios Cinematográficos at th Universidad de Guadalajara. A prolific film critic and historian, h has to his credit monographic studies of directors *Alberto Gout*, *Jua Orol*, *Raúl de Anda*, *Gabriel Soria*, *Arcady Boytler*, *José Bohr*, an *Fernando Méndez*. His latest book, *Del muro a la pantalla. S. M Eisenstein y el arte pictórico mexicano*, was the recipient of th Premio Nacional de Critica de Artes Plásticas.

Index

Mexican Film Index

Latin American Silhouettes
Studies in History and Culture

William H. Beezley and
Judith Ewell
Editors

Volumes Published

Silvia Marina Arrom and Servando Ortoll, eds., *Riots in the Cities: Popular Politics and the Urban Poor in Latin America, 1765–1910* (1996). Cloth ISBN 0-8420-2580-4   Paper ISBN 0-8420-2581-2

Roderic Ai Camp, ed., *Polling for Democracy: Public Opinion and Political Liberalization in Mexico* (1996). ISBN 0-8420-2583-9

Brian Loveman and Thomas M Davies, Jr., eds., *The Politics of Antipolitics: The Military in Latin America*, 3d ed., revised and updated (1996). Cloth ISBN 0-8420-2609-6   Paper ISBN 0-8420-2611-8

Joseph S. Tulchin, Andrés Serbín, and Rafael Hernández, eds., *Cuba and the Caribbean: Regional Issues and Trends in the Post-Cold War Era* (1997). ISBN 0-8420-2652-5

Thomas W. Walker, ed., *Nicaragua without Illusions: Regime Transition and Structural Adjustment in the 1990s* (1997). Cloth ISBN 0-8420-2578-2   Paper ISBN 0-8420-2579-0

Dianne Walta Hart, *Undocumented in L.A.: An Immigrant's Story* (1997). Cloth ISBN 0-8420-2648-7   Paper ISBN 0-8420-2649-5

Jaime E. Rodríguez O. and Kathryn Vincent, eds., *Myths, Misdeeds, and Misunderstandings: The Roots of Conflict in U.S.-Mexican Relations* (1997). ISBN 0-8420-2662-2

Jaime E. Rodríguez O. and Kathryn Vincent, eds., *Common Border, Uncommon Paths: Race, Culture, and National Identity in U.S.-Mexican Relations* (1997). ISBN 0-8420-2673-8

William H. Beezley and Judith Ewell, eds., *The Human Tradition in Modern Latin America* (1997). Cloth ISBN 0-8420-2612-6   Paper ISBN 0-8420-2613-4

Donald F. Stevens, ed., *Based on a True Story: Latin American History at the Movies* (1997). Cloth ISBN 0-8420-2582-0   Paper ISBN 0-8420-2781-5

Jaime E. Rodríguez O., ed., *The Origins of Mexican National Politics, 1808–1847* (1997). Paper ISBN 0-8420-2723-8

Che Guevara, *Guerrilla Warfare*, with revised and updated introduction and case studies by Brian Loveman and Thomas M. Davies, Jr., 3d ed. (1997). Cloth ISBN 0-8420-2677-0   Paper ISBN 0-8420-2678-9

Adrian A. Bantjes, *As If Jesus Walked on Earth: Cardenismo, Sonora, and the Mexican Revolution* (1998). ISBN 0-8420-2653-3

Henry A. Dietz and Gil Shidlo, eds., *Urban Elections in Democratic Latin America* (1998). Cloth ISBN 0-8420-2627-4   Paper ISBN 0-8420-2628-2

A. Kim Clark, *The Redemptive Work: Railway and Nation in Ecuador, 1895–1930* (1998). ISBN 0-8420-2674-6

Joseph S. Tulchin, ed., with Allison M. Garland, *Argentina: The Challenges of Modernization* (1998). ISBN 0-8420-2721-1

Louis A. Pérez, Jr., ed., *Impressions of Cuba in the Nineteenth Century: The Travel Diary of Joseph J. Dimock* (1998). Cloth ISBN 0-8420-2657-6   Paper ISBN 0-8420-2658-4

June E. Hahner, ed., *Women through Women's Eyes: Latin American Women in Nineteenth-Century Travel Accounts* (1998). Cloth ISBN 0-8420-2633-9   Paper ISBN 0-8420-2634-7

James P. Brennan, ed., *Peronism and Argentina* (1998). ISBN 0-8420-2706-8

John Mason Hart, ed., *Border Crossings: Mexican and Mexican-American Workers* (1998). Cloth ISBN 0-8420-2716-5   Paper ISBN 0-8420-2717-3

Brian Loveman, *For* la Patria: *Politics and the Armed Forces in Latin America* (1999). Cloth ISBN 0-8420-2772-6 Paper ISBN 0-8420-2773-4

Guy P. C. Thomson, with David G. LaFrance, *Patriotism, Politics, and Popular Liberalism in Nineteenth-Century Mexico: Juan Francisco Lucas and the Puebla Sierra* (1999). ISBN 0-8420-2683-5

Robert Woodmansee Herr, in collaboration with Richard Herr, *An American Family in the Mexican Revolution* (1999). ISBN 0-8420-2724-6

Juan Pedro Viqueira Albán, trans. Sonya Lipsett-Rivera and Sergio Rivera Ayala, *Propriety and Permissiveness in Bourbon Mexico* (1999). Cloth ISBN 0-8420-2466-2 Paper ISBN 0-8420-2467-0

Stephen R. Niblo, *Mexico in the 1940s: Modernity, Politics, and Corruption* (1999). ISBN 0-8420-2794-7

David E. Lorey, *The U.S.-Mexican Border in the Twentieth Century* (1999).

Cloth ISBN 0-8420-2755-6 Paper ISBN 0-8420-2756-4

Joanne Hershfield and David R. Maciel, eds., *Mexico's Cinema: A Century of Films and Filmmakers* (2000). Cloth ISBN 0-8420-2681-9 Paper ISBN 0-8420-2682-7

Peter V. N. Henderson, *In the Absence of Don Porfirio: Francisco León de la Barra and the Mexican Revolution* (2000). ISBN 0-8420-2774-2

Mark T. Gilderhus, *The Second Century: U.S.-Latin American Relations since 1889* (2000). Cloth ISBN 0-8420-2413-1 Paper ISBN 0-8420-2414-X

Catherine Moses, *Real Life in Castro's Cuba* (2000). Cloth ISBN 0-8420-2836-6 Paper ISBN 0-8420-2837-4

K. Lynn Stoner, ed./comp., with Luis Hipólito Serrano Pérez, *Cuban and Cuban-American Women: An Annotated Bibliography* (2000). ISBN 0-8420-2643-6

Thomas D. Schoonover, *The French in Central America: Culture and Commerce, 1820–1930* (2000). ISBN 0-8420-2792-0